EARLY IRISH MONASTICISM

EARLY IRISH MONASTICISM

AN UNDERSTANDING OF ITS CULTURAL ROOTS

Catherine Thom

t&t clark

Published by T&T Clark
A Continuum imprint
The Tower Building, 11 York Road, London SE1 7NX
80 Maiden Lane, Suite 704, New York, NY 10038

www.tandtclark.com

All rights reserved. No part of this publication may be reproduced or transmitted in any form or by any means, electronic or mechanical, including photocopying, recording or any information storage or retrieval system, without permission in writing from the publishers.

Catherine Thom has asserted her right under the Copyright, Designs and Patents Act, 1988, to be identified as Author of this work.
Copyright © Catherine Thom, 2006

First published 2006
Reprinted 2006
Paperback edition 2007

Every effort has been made to trace and acknowledge copyright holders of all the images included in this book. We apologise for any errors or omissions that may remain, and would ask those concerned to contact the publishers, who will ensure that full acknowledgement is made in future.

British Library Cataloguing-in-Publication Data
A catalogue record for this book is available from the British Library

Typeset by Free Range Book Production & Design Ltd
Printed on acid-free paper in Great Britain by Biddles Ltd, King's Lynn, Norfolk

ISBN 978-0-567-03071-9 (hardback)
       978-0-567-03275-1 (paperback)

Dedicated to Mary Monica and Arthur Robert,
who shared their faith with me,
and to Bishop David, whose compassionate and
creative ministry in Australia reveals one deeply
in touch with his own Celtic roots.

Contents

List of Illustrations	ix
Abbreviations	xi
Preface	xiii
Acknowledgements	xv
Introduction	xix
The Genesis of this Study	xix
Context	xxi
Meaning of *Celtic* Church	xxv
Methodology	xxvii

1 TOWARDS AN UNDERSTANDING OF THE MAJOR ASPECTS OF IRISH MONASTICISM IN THE SIXTH TO THE EIGHTH CENTURY

Introduction	1
Celtic Consciousness and Culture	7
The Irish Notion of History	18
The Celtic Church and its Relationship with Irish Monasticism	21
Theology	24
Asceticism	27
Radicality	29
Conclusion	32

2 THE ASCETICAL THEOLOGY AND PRAXIS OF THE EARLY IRISH PENITENTIALS

Introduction	36
Negative and Positive Assessment of Penitentials	37
Origins of Penitentials	39
Relationship with Ancient Laws	42
Purpose of the Penitentials	44
Penitential of Vinnian	49
Penitential of Columbanus	54
Penitential of Cummean	60
Canones Hibernenses	67
Commutations	68
Asceticism as *geilt*	72
Conclusion	73

3 Irish Monastic Rules of the Sixth to the Eighth Century

Introduction	77
Membership of Irish Monasteries	81
Ascetical Theology and Praxis in the Irish Monastic Rules in General	84
Rule of Ailbe	86
Rule of Ciarán	94
Rule of Comgall	97
Rule of ColumCille	100
Rule of Columbanus	109
Rule of Carthage	117
Conclusion	119

4 ColumCille – Founder of Iona

Introduction	125
Ancestry and Personal Characteristics of ColumCille	126
Sanctity	129
The Influence of ColumCille	133
The 'Voice' of ColumCille: Book One	137
Image of the Soldier of Christ	140
ColumCille Speaks through his Miracles	141
ColumCille Speaks in Revelations	144
Conclusion	148

5 Columbanus – Quintessential Irish *Peregrinus*

Introduction	151
Ancestry and Personal Characteristics of Columbanus	152
Sanctity and Pilgrimage	155
The Influence of Columbanus – Monastic Foundations on the Continent	158
The 'Voice' of Columbanus in General	161
The 'Voice' of Faith Heard on the Roadway	164
A Warning 'Voice': Sermons IX and X	167
Image of the Soldier of Christ	167
The 'Voice' and the 'Fountain of Life': Sermon XIII	168
Conclusion	170

6 Conclusions

	173
Appendices	181
Bibliography	195
Primary Sources	195
Secondary Sources	197
Journals, Papers, Theses	211
Index	219

List of Illustrations

Appendix I
B Ogham Script   183
D Detail of Monograph Initial, Book of Kells   185
E Table of Abbots of Iona   186

Appendix III
G Photograph of the island of Hinba   191
H Photograph of Skellig Michael   191

Appendix IV
A View from both sides of the stone in Elgin Cathedral grounds   192
B 'Monument' in Westport, Ireland   193

Appendix V
Map showing the journeys of Columbanus on the continent and
the many places called after him   194

Abbreviations

AS	*Augustinian Studies*
ACJ	*Australian Celtic Journal*
AFM	*Annals of the Four Masters*
AI	*Annals of Innisfallen*
AT	*Annals of Tigernach*
AU	*Annals of Ulster*
CMCS	*Cambrian Medieval Celtic Studies*
CHR	*Catholic Historical Review*
CS	*Cistercian Studies*
CIH	*Corpus Iuris Hibernici*
DR	*Downside Review*
EHR	*English Historical Review*
EMH	*Early Medieval History*
HTR	*Harvard Theological Review*
HI	*History Ireland*
ITC	*International Theological Commission*
IHR	*Irish Historical Records*
IHS	*Irish Historical Studies*
IER	*Irish Ecclesiastical Records*
IER	*Irish Ecclesiastical Review*
JEH	*Journal of Ecclesiastical History*
JMS	*Journal of Monastic Studies*
JRSAI	*Journal of the Royal Society of Antiquaries of Ireland*
JTS	*Journal of Theological Studies*
MO	*Martyrology of Oengnus*
MR	*Maynooth Review*
MS	*Monastic Studies*
NTS	*New Testament Studies*
PP	*Priests and People*
Pro R.I.A.	*Proceedings of Royal Irish Academy*
RC	*Revue Celtique*
SCHS	*Scottish Church Historical Society*
SH	*Studia Hibernica*
SCH	*Studies in Church History*
TF	*The Furrow*
TM	*The Month*

Preface

This work is an exploration of the ascetical theology and *praxis* of sixth- to eighth-century Irish monasticism viewed as a radical response to the Christian *evangelium*.[1] It also aims to analyse the extent to which the distinctive response of the monastic Irish in the period arose from their Celtic cultural context. Culture influences all aspects of life and given that this work is addressing the critical period of the emergence of a people from primitive forms of religious belief and practice to Christianity it is important to evaluate the influence of culture. The work is an exploration in the sense that, though much has been written about monasticism and specifically the Irish monastic movement up to and beyond the tenth century, the discussion of ascetical theology and *praxis* has the potential to open up new pathways to better understanding and appreciation of this phenomenon within the wider Irish Church.

The scope of the work ranges briefly over the cultural context of Irish society in the pre- and post-Christian era: its social organization, sagas, Brehon laws and druidism. The primary sources utilized include the penitentials, the monastic rules, the *Vitae* and writings of ColumCille and Columbanus. These formative works regarding two of the most influential early Irish monastic founders are seen as encapsulating, and broadly illustrating, the ascetical emphasis and *praxis* of this time. The work draws on the ancient notions and practices of asceticism and the principle of *contraries* emphasized by Cassian. One facet of the radicality of Irish monasticism, manifested specifically in the penitentials, lies partly in the fact that, whereas asceticism is usually perceived as a personal response to the call to change one's lifestyle, the Irish *praxis* was, on the whole, undertaken in the context of a community.

Chapter 1 looks briefly at the Irish Church as part of that phenomenon called the Celtic Church. Other aspects of the topic addressed in this chapter include history, theology, asceticism, radicality and how each of these facilitates the future analysing of the primary sources. Chapter 2 analyses the Irish penitentials that traditionally, and often today, have been seen as harsh and inflexible.

---

1. The significance of this word will be explored in chapter 1 of this work. X. L. Dufour, *Dictionary of the New Testament* (London: G. Chapman, 1980) has details on the use of this word.

Chapter 3 analyses the monastic rules[2] of some early founders and demonstrates that they are a call to a radical lifestyle for those committed to the religious life, compared with the ordinary demands of the Christian *evangel*. In chapters 4 and 5, the lives and writing of ColumCille and Columbanus are treated. The Sermons of Columbanus are the primary material used in chapter 5.

The conclusions of this work are that the radicality in the monastic rules, penitentials and the *Vitae* of some of the prominent founders[3] reveals that all the practices were designed to promote personal growth in the spiritual life and were not primarily focused on punishment. They were about an inner transformation that enhanced one's personal, spiritual and human well-being rather than a humiliation and belittling of the person. Present-day psychology and the behavioural sciences in general would affirm the wisdom of the fundamental belief inherent in Cassian's *contraries*,[4] which underpinned the injunctions in both the monastic rules and penitentials. The evidence deduced from many of the injunctions in the extant penitentials is that of a balanced presentation of the ideals of asceticism, which were a guide for the inner transformation of the person. Both the penitentials and the monastic rules also point to the emphasis on individuality that is evident in much Irish secular writing. The injunctions of the extant rules make it clear that their asceticism was, through prayer, sacrifices or mortification and work, to aid in the transforming of the energy of self-denial into a spiritual power. The asceticism thus recommended in these primary sources of the sixth- to eighth-century Irish monastic movement was not harsh and inhuman, for the radicality of their lives depended on the fact that it was deliberately and personally chosen by the monks. They were captured by the beauty of their newly-found faith in the Christian God, incarnated in Jesus whose life they contemplated in the daily recitation of the Canonical Hours and whose presence surrounded them in the totality of creation.

---

2. U.Ó Maidín, *The Celtic Monk: Rules and Writings of Early Irish Monks* (Massachusetts: Cistercian Publications, 1st edn, 1996), discusses all the rules that will be addressed in Chapter 3 of this work. However, since this study was begun before this publication, the source for these rules is an earlier publication, which is missing some of the rules included in this 1996 publication. The publication being used is U. Ó Maidín, 'The Monastic Rules of Ireland' *CS* 15 (1980), pp. 24–38.

3. Only the rules of male founders will be used, though there is some traditional belief that three foundresses, Brigit, Ita and Monenna/Darerca (see chapter 1, fn 22, for reference to two of these women) had many followers in monastic establishments prior to the foundations of the now famous monastic communities of Ciarán, Kevin, ColumCille and Columbanus, to name but a few of the early founders.

4. This fundamental aspect of both the rules and penitentials will be treated in greater detail in later chapters.

Acknowledgements

Many people assisted me during the course of this research. Thanks are due to people overseas: the Librarians of the University of Glasgow, particularly the late Mr Henry Heaney, chief librarian. Librarians of Aberystwyth, Cambridge and Oxford made available their valuable resources. The Celtic Studies Library at Edinburgh University was also free for my use at any time, due in large part to Dr Mary Low, a very helpful companion during my stay in that city. Most particularly helpful were Orna Somerville and Siobhan de hOir at the Royal Society of Antiquaries in Dublin. Oine Keegan at University College Dublin and other staff, too many to mention, need acknowledgement for their painstaking assistance to me over a period of precious months.

Dr Michael Herity gave valuable insights into the archaeology of the Christian and monastic west of Ireland, particularly Cahir Island, and clear evidence for the 'co-habiting' of pre-and post-Christian symbols. Fr Sean O'Duinn OSB from Glenstal Abbey spent valuable time sharing his speculative ideas about the same links between the pre- and post-Christian traditions in Ireland. Fr Eion de Bhaldraithe OSC from Bolton Abbey must be credited with being the most prompt respondent to my cries for help. Not only did he manage to make available translations of two obscure sixth-century monastic rules, but he also read a chapter of the work and promptly sent an article that he thought would enhance the discussion on the penitentials. Some of the participants at the Conference in Maynooth in July 1994 shared insights into many aspects of this topic.

In Scotland, during my two periods of study leave, I could not have achieved so much without the friendship and hospitality of Mr B. McGettrick, his secretary Linda Sanders, Pat Lock and countless members of staff, including the chaplain Fr Noel Woods, of the former St Andrews College, Bearsden. Fr Noel O'Donoghue, when I first met him, was a recently retired Lecturer in the Divinity Faculty of Edinburgh University. He is an inspirational author of works on philosophy and theology, particularly as evident in his native Irish and adopted Scottish people. After initial hesitation, he became my constant sounding board and a true friend with his profound philosophic and theological insights into the meaning of what it is to be Irish and how this is influenced by the pre-Christian as well as the Christian context. His warnings about *syneisaktism* have proved very wise indeed. My debt to Noel and to other wonderful Scots can never be adequately repaid.

In the United Kingdom, many friends were always solicitous about the research and how it was progressing. Mention must be made in particular of

Dr Margie Tolstoy in the Divinity Faculty of Cambridge University, and Dr Richard Mason, philosopher at the same University, whose house in Cambridge became my second home when I was using the Library. Others include Dr David Cornick of Westminster College, Cambridge who read a chapter and commented constructively. Professor Bryn Rees of Cardiff, though ill, has been helpful and his book on Pelagius started my thinking on this Celt and his place in the theology of Irish Christianity. Professor Davies of Jesus College, Oxford gave me valuable insights into the role of the penitentials in the lives of the Celts, and even though it was Christmas Eve when we spoke he did not appear to see me as an intrusion. His comment that I was asking good questions was followed by the more realistic comment, 'but you will probably not find the answers!' His encouragement to keep asking the questions has stayed with me.

Colleagues over the past 25 years have contributed much to this work: Dr Gideon Goosen, past head of the Religion Department where I first worked, was constantly encouraging me to continue research. Maria Sacco of Sydney University, Truc Nguyen of Australian Catholic University and Lyn Raftery could not be thanked enough for their brilliance with computers and programmes. To these women I owe a great debt. Dr Rosa MacGinley was important initially in the whole process of writing this work. Finally, Dr Gideon Goosen and Dr Mary Sheather as supervisors were painstaking in their reading of the text and suggesting changes to be made. They must be given credit for their meticulous and constant work on my behalf. My debt to them is indeed enormous.

Sarah Douglas, who I worked with initially at T&T Clark, was most enthusiastic about this project and when she moved to another position Rebecca Vaughan-Williams took over and continued her concern. Rebecca was most prompt in her replies to my constant questions. I am deeply grateful to them both for their assistance to me throughout this project.

To the Religious Leaders in the NSW Province of the Sisters of St Joseph, in particular, more recently, to Srs Anne Derwin and Judith Sippel, my heartfelt thanks for allowing me time and emotional and financial support to carry out this research over some years. Many of my religious Sisters have been truly supportive over the years of this work's production.

I am deeply grateful to the following people for permission to use their work: Steven Hope for the use of his map of the journeys of Columbanus in Europe; Sean O'Boyle to use the poem describing an early Irish monastery; Fr Clem Hill (retired Lecturer at Catholic Institute of Sydney) and Mr Chris Sanders (Caledonian University, Glasgow) for the use of their photos of the islands of Skellig Michael and Hinba respectively; Floris Books for permission to use parts of a poem from the *Carmina Gadelica*; the Governing Board of the School of Celtic Studies of the Dublin Institute for Advanced Studies for the use of two poems from the *Martyrology of Oengus*; the Penguin Group of publishers for allowing me to use the 'Table of Abbots' from R. Sharpe's work on *Columba of Iona*; and the Board of Trinity College, Dublin for granting permission to use material from the *Book of Kells*; St Brigit's Prayer from *Love of Ireland: Poems from the Irish* by Brendan Kennelly © 1988. Reprinted by kind permission of Mercier Press, Cork. These people and institutions have been acknowledged in detail throughout this work. Any faults with the work are mine alone.

INTRODUCTION

The Genesis of this Study

This book began as a study of the 'suppression' of the Celtic Church by Rome at the Synod of Whitby in 664 CE and its implications for the Australian Church. It was thought that the Roman Church suppressed the Celtic Church because the male hierarchic structure of the former excluded the *femininity* of the latter. It became obvious to me that suppression was not an accurate word for what happened at Whitby: some of the practices intrinsic to the Latin jurisdiction were adopted by sections of the Church in Ireland even before the above-mentioned Synod. As the research progressed it became evident that this topic was very large in its scope and there was an abundance of primary sources. After more detailed and concentrated research in the United Kingdom and Ireland during two periods of study leave the topic became more specifically focused on the ascetical theology and *praxis*[1] of sixth- to eighth-century Irish monasticism. Further, more intense analysis of the monastic rules and penitentials of the period revealed that they seemed to be coming from a distinctive Celtic consciousness that in all likelihood accounts for the radicality of the Irish response to the Christian *evangelium*.

The omission of any foundresses in this work is due to the fact that their lives, if not wholly discredited, are not as authenticated as those of the men. Besides, the lives of some women whom tradition credits with founding monasteries (for example, Brigit and Ita) are either so interwoven with goddess stories (in the case of Brigit) as to be historically questionable or are in what historians call the pre-Patrick era, and as such do not fall within the ambit of this work.

Many disciplines have contributed to the volumes of written material about the Irish Church: archaeology, history, linguistics, law, literature and geography to mention a few. While theology in its present-day understanding cannot be said to have been one of the disciplines employed to elucidate the period, the Irish were undeniably theologizing[2] about the major human and cosmological

---

1. Though this word is generally interpreted as practice, it has in this context, and by virtue of using *praxis*, the added meaning of the reflection on lived experience which leads to particular behaviour. It involves a thought process that is more than that usually associated with the word 'practice'. It is also mainly used in the context of Christian living based on reflection on gospel values and their implications for living.

2. As distinct from the noun 'theology', theologizing is what the person is said to be doing when s/he reflects on life, her/his own in particular, and relates it to a higher being and its relationship with humans.

questions generated by their experience. Since all these disciplines shed valuable light on the topic under discussion, it is not possible to do justice to more than the disciplines of history and theology on which this study will concentrate.

The dilemma implicit in the name Celtic Church,[3] which includes the Irish, Scots, Welsh, Bretons and Manx, has not been solved, in spite of the volumes of literature devoted to it. Nor has its meaning been adequately clear in that, as a nomenclature, it is given by people other than the Celts themselves. Because more Irish sources are extant, and in order to narrow down a mammoth task, this study will concentrate on the Irish group of Christian Celts in the specific period of the sixth to the eighth century, which most reputable historians would call the Golden Age of the Irish Church. This period coincided with the change from the predominantly diocesan ecclesial structure initiated by Patrick. The question regarding Patrick's role as originator of Christianity in Ireland will be referred to in chapter 1. Hesitation is appropriate when speaking about historical eras, as these are mainly in the mind of the historian who needs such distinctions to delineate a period in order to show differences. However, with actual history there is more flexibility between what historians call historical periods or ages. Similarly, in referring to the movement from the diocesan to the monastic period in the Irish Church, hesitation is wise. The penitentials, in particular, have been the victim of much use out of context with a resulting implication that the Irish were obsessed with sex, or that they were particularly prone to hideous crimes. Neither conclusion is correct when the *Sitz im Leben* of all these primary sources is taken into account.

The monastic rules have been viewed within the context of ideal statements about how a particular group expressed its general principles regarding Christian living. Since no era attains its expressed ideals and human beings are prone to selfishness, the penitential practices were appraised as attempts to help human beings, both clerical and lay, to acknowledge personal failings and to take measures to rectify any anti-social and morally reprehensible behaviour. Even thoughts that militated against the ideal of monasticism were seen to be in need of correctives: thoughts beget deeds. While cultural contexts vary and personal consciousness differs from person to person, the pursuit of love and the effort to live fulfilled lives remain constant.

Given that human beings are prone to be inspired by other humans, the lives of two prominent monastic founders of this era have been scrutinized for evidence of virtues motivated by such ideals. In the posthumous treatment of any hero, there is a tendency to idealization, and this has happened with the Irish saints. Removing the encrustations of time is not an easy task, but reading the *Vitae* within their historical context, conscious of the genre and the ancient

---

3. The notion of the Celtic Church as a Patristic Church was flagged at a study week on Celtic Christianity I attended at the University of Wales, Lampeter in June 2004. Dr J. Wooding, 'borrowing' from Canon Allchin, started my thinking about the Patristic nature of the Celtic Church in its developing understanding of itself and subsequent grappling with orthodoxy, authority and identity. More research and time is needed by me on this line of thinking.

Irish sagas that provided a model, can contribute to a more balanced view of these saints and their activities. However, the ever-present *mysterium tremendum* remains whenever one attempts to look at people's religious beliefs and the extent to which their lives exemplify their beliefs.

Context

The context for this study of the ascetical theology and *praxis* of sixth- to eighth-century Irish monasticism is not only the historical setting for the events occurring and the people involved but encompasses the wider intellectual discussion of the broader issues included in this book. Dodds and other earlier writers have succinctly captured a cluster of issues directly pertinent to this study and so their work is being used as a springboard for dialogue about asceticism and the daemonic, the idea of the holy, the relationship of humans with the gods and their incarnation, dreams and an understanding of the cosmos. Of primary importance are the Irish cultural context and the radicality of the Irish response to the *evangelium* within the wider context of the declining Roman Empire. The events include the Christianizing of Ireland and the evangelizing of the continent in the sixth century. The evolution of the Celtic Church is traced and the development of monasticism within the same idiosyncratic Church is a significant focus. In the foreground are the ordinary Irish people from whose ranks arose those 'special' people called the saints, Patrick, ColumCille and Columbanus. These men exemplified the doctrine of *homoiosis*, 'assimilation to God', first stated by Plato. Such men were seen as imitating the perfect goodness of the gods.[4] Using the sources referred to in footnote 4 has shown that integral to any discussion of context is the notion that the work continues the academic debate. This illustrates the fact that the issues of asceticism, sanctity, self-discipline, dreams, the power of the daemonic and their role in human striving for union with God have a perennial attraction. In the background, but not insignificant, is the whole panoply of Irish heroes, druids, poets, kings and other cultic figures.

According to Roman and Greek historians and geographers, the Irish were those barbarians on the edge of the world, not worthy of serious consideration, unless they were to be conquered.[5] Reflections from such commentators as the

---

4. E. R. Dodds, *Pagan and Christian in an Age of Anxiety* (New York: Norton and Co., 1st edn, 1965). Though this book is an early publication it discusses many of the major aspects of asceticism treated in this study. Some aspects of the present study are also prefigured in the works of R. McMullen, *Christianising the Roman Empire, A.D. 100–400* (Massachusetts: Yale University Press, 1984); R. L. Fox, *Pagans and Christians* (San Francisco: Harper and Row, 1988); R. Doran, *A Birth of a Worldview: Early Christianity in Its Jewish and Pagan Context* (Oxford: Westview Press, 1995); R. McMullen and E. Lane, *Paganism and Christianity 100–425 C.E.: A Sourcebook* (Minneapolis: Augsburg Fortress, 1992); S. Benko, *Pagan Rome and the Early Christians* (Indiana: Indiana University Press, 1986).

5. J. F. Kenney, *The Sources for the Early History of Ireland: Ecclesiastical* (Shannon: Irish University Press, 3rd edn, 1968).

Greek Strabo and the Roman Diodorus are to be found elsewhere in the body of this text. So what is to be discussed, as context, though culturally distinctive in the Irish setting, is part of a wider movement from primal religions to Christianity. Because a society is composed of individuals, these will form part of the focus of the following brief discussion. However, people have ideas, adhering to different philosophies, and so the tapestry of context will necessarily be coloured by some of the different philosophies influencing the times.

Apropos of Dodds' treatment of the age of anxiety, where he applies a psychological interpretation to his discussion of the period from Marcus Aurelius to Constantine, the statement that appears most pertinent to the work at hand is one he has borrowed from Rostovtzeff. After examining the social and economic history of the Roman Empire, Rostovtzeff 'expressed the view that a change in people's outlook on the world was one of the most potent factors'[6] to be addressed when investigating a society. The exploration of this change is one of the most important and urgent tasks in all periods of history. Change, its origin, speed, impetus, momentum, is important when looking at society and the lives of people prior to our own. The further the society is removed from the period of the 'observer' or historian the greater the need for caution. Change in a person's view of the world is influenced by that person's underlying cosmology, philosophy and 'theology'. These elements could be called the soil from which change draws its nourishment and subsequent growth.

Prior to the sixth century, there was a general understanding of the world, with resulting attitudes culminating in the feeling of humankind's inferiority to the cosmos. This was manifested in a sense of alienation from the vastness of this universe. The activity of humans seemed insignificant as they strove to understand their wider environment and see themselves in relationship to it. Matter was experienced not only as inferior but as a source of evil, according to both Oriental and Greek interpretations, and by extension the body became the object of hatred and therefore in need of taming and controlling. Hence the strong emphasis on self-discipline, asceticism,[7] training the body to feats of endurance. This apparent separation of the body and the self has been expressed in a recently discovered papyrus document where the monk is described as the 'renouncer': renouncer not only of the world but also of his own body and his self.[8]

Such a view permeated the thinking of the time. The examples of those who appeared to have achieved this separation from the body, either in primitive or

---

6. Dodds, *Pagan*, p. 1.
7. P. Hanks, (ed.), *Hamlyn Encyclopaedic World Dictionary* (Middlesex: Hamlyn Publications, 1971), p. 121 ascribes the meaning to the Greek *asketikos* – pertaining to a monk or hermit. Asceticism in its theological meaning the dictionary gives as 'the theory or systematic exposition of the means (whether negative as self-denial or abstinence or positive as the exercises of natural and Christian virtues) by which a complete conformity with the divine will may be attained'. This notion will be further explored in chapter 1 and evident in most of the chapters of this work.
8. G. Gould in J. Loades, (ed.), *Monastic Studies: The Continuity of Tradition* (Bangor: Copycat, 1990), pp. 1–10.

Christian lifestyles, gave rise to the movement for exclusive concentration of the energies of one's life on this task. Examples of ascetic groups include the Essenes in Palestine, Therapeutae near Lake Mareotis and the Neo-Pythagoreans in Rome. Emulation of such persons is fundamental in the purpose of what is called hagiography. This initially was a celebration of the lives of the saints within a liturgical setting, particularly on the day of the saint's feast.[9] However, later an understanding of the term was much wider in its meaning.

What will be evident in the discussion of these related issues in sixth- to eighth-century Irish monasticism is that a shift was occurring. Celtic consciousness did not fully reflect the Roman and Greek model. The cosmos, a strong part of Celtic cultural awareness, was sensed as bringing the deity into intimate contact with the human. Far from a dichotomy between matter and spirit, the Incarnation[10] enfleshed the deity in such a way that an intimate relationship with the divine reality became the end-point of existence. Some ascetic principles were revealed in the monastic rules and penitentials and manifested in the lives of ColumCille and Columbanus and their followers. Actions viewed from outside the person can be inaccurately assessed if the observer does not know the motivation. The intentionality of the Irish monks of the sixth to the eighth century is clearly spelled out in the sources used in this work: love of God and neighbour as oneself. Simple as this sounds, it is the task of a lifetime and is intrinsic to the radicality that is the focus of this book.

In the slow evolution towards a Christian society, one persistent element was the power of the daemonic. Plato thought of the daemonic as intermediaries between God and mortals in that they communicated with mortals. By gods, Homer had meant 'divine powers, the *daimones* which accompany virtuous people, which share their life and in the same charming image hold their hand'.[11] Maximus of Tyre, using the Homeric suitor's lines on the gods as 'spies in disguise',[12] points to the possibility that there could be a malignant side to the gods.

What both Plato and Homer acknowledge is that there is a spirit world with a capacity to communicate with the human world. In Christian experience this communication is seen to be principally the work of the Holy Spirit. In the Hebrew Scriptures angels and archangels were the messengers between God and humans. Some of the early Christians, including the Irish, would have agreed with Plato that the divine communicated with them when they were asleep. In their dreams both primal religious adherents and Christians were in close

---

9. It will be seen in chapter 4 of this study that this was precisely the reason for Adomnán's writing the *Life* of ColumCille.

10. Dodds, *Pagan*, p. 23 discusses the incarnation as punishment and he gives the ancient sources for this belief. It must be noted that the Irish, in the period under discussion, did not so much emphasize the incarnation as Incarnation, meaning Jesus Christ, God's living presence on earth, but as more akin to panentheism, as the omnipresence of God in creation.

11. Fox, *Pagans*, p. 129.

12. Fox, *Pagans*, p. 129.

contact with gods.¹³ Much of the Irish *Vitae* of the period under discussion used the dreams or other spirit communication of their heroes as evidence of their holiness and closeness to God. It was only later in Christian history that such daemonic communications were attributed to satanic possession.¹⁴ The experience of the spirit world sometimes had the effect of momentarily releasing the recipient of such encounters from the body in what was often called a mystical experience. The resultant energy gave the mystic new vitality and often insights into life. The mystics nonetheless did not shed their humanity. It was still as fragile, limited human beings that they had to continue to live their mortal lives. This 'reality test' sometimes helped distinguish the genuine from the false holy person or saint. The Christian Scriptures and the early Fathers used *pneumatikoi*, 'filled with the spirit' to describe such persons. If it were truly the Holy Spirit who was the source of the mystical experiences, which often were manifested in prophecy,¹⁵ then the Church more easily listened to the mystic. Dodds maintains that the need for such persons and their pronouncements arose from the 'insecurity of the times'.¹⁶ Ironically, it was this spirit of prophecy that Irenaeus fought to retain in the early Church. Its devaluing gave way to the dictate of Ignatius of Antioch, 'Do nothing without the bishop.' In Ireland, on the contrary, particularly in the monastic period, the prophetic and charismatic appear to have been favoured over episcopal dictate. Bishops were essentially sacramental functionaries and were, in all other aspects, subject to the abbot of the monastery in which they resided.

So close was the relationship of the two worlds, pre-Christian and Christian, it is understandable that a group of people emerging from absorption in primal religions would still have residual beliefs and practices that, at times, were inseparable from the incoming Christian beliefs and practices. Moreover, even in the centuries prior to the focus of this work, both persons and philosophies supposedly distinguished as primal and Christian were so often not only not in contention, but were two sides of the one coin. Both approaches to life were seeking 'assimilation to God'. Both were concerned with the salvation of the individual rather than making the world a better place.¹⁷ Both Christians and neo-Platonists largely subscribed to the same standards of ethical behaviour. However, an important difference was that the Christians based their ethical behaviour on the revelation of God through Jesus Christ, and the neo-Platonists did not. Origen's education was indebted to a pagan philosopher called

---

13. Fox, *Pagans*, p. 150.
14. A. A. Barb in A. Momigliano (ed.), *The Conflict between Paganism and Christianity in the Fourth Century* (Oxford: Clarendon Press, 1963), pp. 100–25 for a treatment of the relationship between magical arts, often associated with the daemonic and Christianity.
15. Dodds, *Pagan*, p. 53 and the corresponding footnote, discusses the many names and meanings given to the word 'prophet'.
16. Dodds, *Pagan*, p. 57.
17. This work stresses, as part of the consciousness of the Celts, the individual. The rules and penitentials are focused on the specific needs of the individual and the manner of aiding the healing and spiritual transformation of the specific person. No one could doubt the rugged individuality of the two monastic founders treated in chapters 4 and 5 of this work.

Ammonius Saccas. Both Brigit and ColumCille (called Crimthann by his parents) were born into families with strong primal religious leanings, though their hagiographers do not mention this fact.[18] ColumCille was put into the care of Cruithnechán, who educated him and possibly was responsible for his eventual baptism.

However, the point of this discussion is that residual aspects of primitive religions were evident in Christianity of the later periods and particularly in the lives of prominent persons of sixth- to eighth-century Irish monasticism. The spirit and intention of these people were embodied in the rules and penitentials used as guiding principles for monastic asceticism of the era. The continuity of pre-Christian philosophies, ways of thinking and sometimes practices, could be detected for many centuries and gave way only gradually, if ever fully, to Christian thinking and practices. Given the persistence of these pre-Christian cultural elements, the central theme of this work explores the radicality with which Irish monks responded to the *evangelium*, that corpus of beliefs and ethical behaviours embodied in Christian teaching and lived out within the context of a peculiarly Celtic consciousness.

Meaning of Celtic *Church*

Since it was within the so-called Celtic Church that monasticism, central to the focus of this study, emerged and flourished, it might be important to give a brief overview of how some authors understood the concept of the Celtic Church. Stokes and Bryant are clear about using Celtic to mean all the churches with Celtic cultural links. Lehane seems to be focusing his study of Celtic Christianity on the lives of three saints of the Irish Church, namely Brendan, ColumCille and Columbanus. In doing so he seems to be equating Celtic with Irish while ignoring the Welsh, Scottish, Bretons and Manx. This focus he seems to justify on the grounds that, 'Ireland, in every age, is best known through the lives of individuals – figures sometimes comic, or fanatic or rumbustious or humble.'[19] Most writers on associated topics whose work spans the 1930s to the 1990s are precise about what Celtic means. Stokes gave a series of lectures in 1886 on Ireland and the Celtic Church in which he said:

> I propose to treat of the history of the ancient Celtic church, not merely of the history of the Irish Church. I certainly intend to devote especial attention to the Irish branch of that Church. But Celtic Christianity was both older and more extensive than Irish Christianity.[20]

---

18. R. Sharpe (ed.), *Adomnán's Life of St Columba* (Middlesex: Penguin, 1st edn, 1991), p. 10.
19. B. Lehane, *Early Celtic Christianity* (London: Constable, 1994), p. 3.
20. G. T. Stokes, *Ireland and the Celtic Church* (London: Hodder & Stoughton, 1886), p. 1.

Stokes goes on to explain what he means when he says Celtic Christianity is older and more extensive. He leaves the reader in no doubt that 'Celtic Christianity [was] prior to St Patrick'.[21]

The meaning and identity of the Celtic Church can be further highlighted by considering some differences with the Roman Church. Beresford-Ellis highlights what many historians were saying about the main differences between the Celtic and Roman Church, but his emphasis is more challenging than that of earlier historians. He believed that 'the development of the Celtic Church was therefore due not to the isolation from Rome, but to the conviction that Rome's reforms were wrong, that Rome was "revisionist" and not adhering to the true dating of Easter'.[22]

As far as communication with the continent, and the concomitant possibility of discourse with the Roman Church goes, Bieler says that 'Ireland's (and western Britain's) isolation from the continent was never complete'.[23] Beresford-Ellis reiterates this notion when he says, 'The Celtic Christians were constantly travelling and at no time were they ever isolated.'[24]

Gougaud, however, does not hesitate to apply the word 'insular' to the Celtic Church. His use of the generic title 'insular' has lesser emotive connotations than the reference to the 'particularism' of the Celtic Church. He insists, 'the insular churches display a spirit of pertinacious particularism and inveterate confidence in their own traditions. Hence arose the long and acrimonious controversies on the Easter question and the form of tonsure.'[25] Though this way of speaking about Celtic particularism may seem to be condemnatory, Gougaud softens it later by the wish that they [the Irish] 'had shown in the course of their medieval history greater political insight, and better realised what principle of strength and duration union is'.[26]

Chadwick, while lamenting the loss of the distinctiveness that was Celtic Christianity, believes that 'the disappearance of the idiosyncratic Christianity of the Celtic Church was inevitable . . . but it is impossible to reach the end without a feeling of regret. A Christianity so pure and serene as that of the age of the saints could hardly be equalled and never repeated.'[27]

Mackey, writing at a later date, makes a case for a distinctive form of Celtic spirituality, as some of the authors above make a case for a Celtic Church, with the words 'Celtic Spirituality . . . did exist, and it still exists in part and is in part recoverable'.[28] In the same book, O'Loughlin discusses in detail the controversial issue of an essentially different spirituality particular to the Celtic peoples. This he does before presenting some worthwhile primary sources

---

21. Stokes, *Ireland*, p. 2.
22. P. Beresford-Ellis, *Celt and Saxon* (London: Constable, 1993), p. 130.
23. L. Bieler, 'The Christianization of the Insular Celts', *Celtica* 8 (1968), pp. 118–129 (121).
24. Beresford-Ellis, *Celt*, p. 125.
25. L. Gougaud, *Christianity in Celtic Lands* (London: Sheed and Ward, 1932), p. 387.
26. Gougaud, *Christianity*, p. 424.
27. N. Chadwick, *The Celts* (London: Penguin, 2nd edn, 1991), p. 218.
28. Mackey, in O. Davies (in collaboration with T. O'Loughlin), *Celtic Spirituality* (New York: Paulist, 1999), p. xxii.

from the Irish and Welsh traditions to illustrate the characteristics of the different way to God he delineates. He concludes with

> the relative innocence and freshness of early Celtic Christianity is a discovery that the modern observer, wearied by the abstractions and dualisms of body in opposition to spirit that have dogged the Christian tradition in its more classical forms, may find welcome.[29]

However, it is valid to try to specify in what manner the group of countries of Ireland, Wales, Scotland and Brittany – often called Celtic – had an approach and response to Christianity that was different and distinctive, and a *praxis* that validates the use of the term Celtic.

Methodology

This section on methodology will make a brief reference to the general understandings of hermeneutics, exegesis, the interpretation of history and historico-critical consciousness. Of major importance to this discussion is the whole area of culture and how it is related to all of the above aspects of methodology. As the primary sources utilized in this work are texts, the following discussion will confine itself to text 'understood in a general sense as evidence which may be written, oral, monumental or figurative'.[30] In chapter 1 it is claimed that an historico-cultural methodology would be necessary to understand the whole area of Celtic consciousness. This implies that the broadest possible understanding of culture and history is intended. Later in chapter 1 it is argued that a poly-focal methodology should be used in the overall study, broadening the scope still further to include those aspects of hermeneutics specific to the study of theology, culture and history.

Hermeneutics generally speaking is the study and activity of understanding and interpreting texts.[31] Since some of the texts used in research work are from an era different from the researcher's own it is imperative that certain stances are taken in regard to them. The researcher has to come to an understanding of the period of the text, the cultural context and, if possible, the language of the text.

According to Schökel, author hermeneutics, as practised today, is chiefly represented by the historico-critical method. While recognizing the method's limitations, he goes on to say that it aims 'at understanding texts in their

---

29. O'Loughlin (in collaboration with Davies), *Celtic*, p. 12.
30. B. Forte (ed.), 'Memory and Reconciliation: The Church and the Faults of the Past', *ITC* December, (1999), p. 62.
31. W. G. Jeanrond, *Theological Hermeneutics: Development and Significance* (New York: Crossroads, 1991). Many authors would give similar definitions. Some of these include: L. A. Schökel, *A Manual of Hermeneutics* (England: Sheffield Academic Press, 1998); R. E. Palmer, *Hermeneutics: Interpretation Theory in Schleiermacher, Dilthey, Heidegger and Gadamer* (Evanston: Northwestern University Press, 1969); J. Painter, *Theology as Hermeneutics: Rudolf Bultmann's Interpretation of the History of Jesus* (England: Sheffield Academic Press, 1987).

coordinates of space and time, of which culture is a principal factor'.[32] The essence of this method is evident in the fact that the reader does not try to bring the text into the present but tries to make a bridge between the two eras, the context of the text and the context of the reader. In so doing a reader engages in personal reflection inspired by the text and this process has been given the name of the 'hermeneutical circle'. Painter puts it thus: 'the hermeneutical circle draws attention to the relation of the interpreter to the text to be interpreted'.[33] According to Palmer this dialectical process is used to convert a partial understanding to a fuller one.[34] The matrix of pre-understanding, reader's conceptuality, historical knowledge and tradition all go to make up the movement between the text and the receiver. All of this reflective/interpretative work must be provisional in order for the text to 'speak authentically in its own voice'.[35]

How then does one interpret the past from the viewpoint of historical knowledge or historical consciousness? The complexity of the process has firstly to be acknowledged. The past is the past and in no way could be easily transported to the present. The mediation of language (which itself is historically determined but does not thereby determine the interpretation of the text) is often the most immediate tool to be used in interpretation. However, in some cases language is not used in recording the past. This was the case with a prominent group treated in the study, namely the druids.[36] We find that, while able to write, they chose not to do so, for to commit to words the story of the clan would devalue the meaning or lead to misinterpretation. However, it also meant that their lives, worship and actions were not understood by those whose minds were not open to their important role in society and the culture of the times.

If the above points regarding hermeneutics are present in every hermeneutic act, 'they must also be part of the interpretative process within which historical judgement and theological judgement come to be integrated'.[37] However, the difference between the interpretative process for 'ordinary' texts and the process for 'faith' texts is based on 'the unifying action of the Spirit and on the permanent identity of the constitutive principle of the communion of the faithful, which is revelation'.[38] There is, therefore, in the theological hermeneutic the indefinable element of faith out of which people speak, write and act. This faith can be seen in actions and words, as with other historically determined texts, but cannot be judged in the same sense that purely historical texts can be judged.

---

32. Schökel, *A Manual*, p. 40.
33. Painter, *Theology*, p. 64.
34. Palmer, *Hermeneutics*, p. 25.
35. Painter, *Theology*, p. 65.
36. See S. Piggott., *The Druids* (repr. 1968, London: Thames and Hudson, 1991), pp. 91–122, for details of these people in classical and vernacular texts.
37. Forte (ed.), *Memory*, p. 62
38. Forte (ed.), *Memory*, p. 62

In this work then, a variety of methodologies is utilized in different combinations in different chapters. That is why the way of looking at the primary texts of the era, the sixth to the eighth century in Irish monasticism, is said to be poly-focal. It utilizes history and historical consciousness, culture, exegesis, interpretation, reflection and, above all, analysis. Throughout the following chapters, apart from chapter 1, there is an examination of the historical setting and persons involved in formulating the texts. There is an attempt to come to some decision about the authenticity of these sources. The texts are then analysed and their message about the ascetical theology that underpinned the *praxis* evident in the lives of the monks of the sixth to the eighth century in Ireland is heard with as much objectivity as is possible given the time differences.

In spite of the many methodologies utilized, culture remains a constant backdrop for the investigation. Culture cannot be divorced from historical consciousness and the genre of hagiography. The primary texts have to be evaluated in the light of the evidence available about authors, linguistic peculiarities, society's expectations and the predominance of the clan. Interpretation and analysis flowed from the above, and the conclusions arrived at can only be valid if the reader is aware of the gap between the two periods: that of the text and that of the reader.

1 Towards an Understanding of the Major Aspects of Irish Monasticism in the Sixth to the Eighth Century

> Christianity has entered into the stream of human history and the process of human culture. It has become culturally creative, for it has changed human life and there is nothing in human thought and action which has not been subjected to its influence, while at the same time it has suffered from the limitations and vicissitudes that are inseparable from temporal existence.[1]

Introduction

As a preamble and in an attempt to focus the above statement on the Irish situation, a few comments will be made on the conversionary process. 'Conversion was not an imposition of a monolithic ideology upon a cultural void, but an interactive process, in which Christianity assumed distinctive regional forms.'[2] Professor Mbiti, head of theology in Uganda, claims that

> Christianity is a universal and cosmic faith. It was universalized on Calvary, and cosmicized on the first Easter day. Our duty is now to localize this universality and cosmicity ... It belongs to the very nature of Christianity to be subject to localization, otherwise its universality and cosmicity become meaningless ... Localization means translating the universality of the Christian faith into a language understood by the peoples of a given region ... The localization of Christianity cannot be carried out effectively without reference to traditional religiosity.[3]

---

1. C. Dawson, *The Formation of Christendom* (New York: Sheed and Ward, 1st edn, 1967), p. 35; P. Cherici, *Celtic Sexuality: Power, Paradigms and Passion* (London: Duckworth, 1st edn, 1994), throughout this work keeps referring to the Celtic paradigm which interpreted the culture and informed people's behaviour towards each other. The Celtic paradigm, not only in the sexual sphere, was subsumed into Christian culture when it emerged in early fifth-century Ireland; P. Brown, *Society and The Holy in Late Antiquity* (Berkeley: University of California Press, 1st edn, 1982), p. 3, has a pertinent discussion on history.
2. S. Hollis, *Anglo-Saxon Women and the Church: Sharing the Same Fate* (Suffolk: The Boydell Press, 1992), p. 16.
3. Richter, in Edel (ed.), *Cultural Identity and Cultural Integration: Ireland and Europe in the Early Middle Ages* (Dublin: Four Courts Press, 1st edn, 1995), p. 118.

Edel says that cultural integration was effected in Ireland in two phases, Christianization and literization.[4] Further she expressed the specific process thus:

> an intensive dialogue between existing [pre-Christian] culture . . . and that of the new Faith, a dialogue that led, after fundamental mutual influencing, to integration in the end. For the sake of this dialogue Irish Scholars made efforts to raise their native tradition to the level of a fully-grown partner in the communication with the newly imported learning. Thus they made, so to speak, the archaic dynamic.[5]

Stevenson believes that the evolution of the Irish as a Christian culture was different for the early Irish from the familiar model of other cultures.[6]

In order to discuss the ascetical theology and *praxis* of sixth- to eighth-century Irish monasticism as a radical response to the Christian *evangelium*[7] the aspects that will be treated in this chapter include: Irish pre-Christian social consciousness, culture and history, the shaping of the Celtic Church, monasticism, theology, asceticism/*ascesis* and radicality. The latter point is pivotal as it is the focus on radicality which forms the basis for a good deal of discussion of the penitentials, monastic rules, literary works of Columbanus and the *Vita* of ColumCille in this study. Because a specific cultural group's degree of self-awareness, to a large extent, determines all aspects of its culture, and its national manifestation in art, literature, socio-political organization, religious formulations and rituals, the concept of culture will be discussed first. Culture, the catch-all phrase for the above elements of a nation's consciousness, will be explored for any evidence of a distinctive Irish awareness being manifested in cultural forms differing from those of other peoples living according to the same Christian *evangelium*. Kathleen Hughes' treatment of the Irish notion of history[8] will be used to set the scene in which the development of the Celtic Church and its manifestation in an idiosyncratic monasticism emerged. Theology, the formulation of how a group sees its relationship with the divine or the Other, and its more specific expression of asceticism will be treated in

---

4. Edel (ed.), *Cultural*, p. 7.
5. Edel (ed.), *Cultural*, p. 168.
6. Stevenson, in Edel (ed.), *Culture*, p. 11.
7. See the Abstract for source of this word. X. l. Dufour, explains

the Gospel must be proclaimed to all the earth. Its preachers are 'evangelists' charged with announcing the inbreaking of the Rule and, above all, the Easter victory of Christ: therein lay the only true gospel, *evangelium*. Their proclamation of it was efficacious: with God's concurrence it stirred up faith and brought about salvation. It was only in the second century that the word designated the written accounts of the life of Jesus, that is, books.

8. It is to be noted that the period under discussion does not have the present-day notion of empirical history as its main methodology, though historians do point to Bede's *Ecclesiastical History of the English People* as being very close to such a methodology. Kathleen Hughes is still the person whose reading of the sources of Irish history is given most credence.

tandem with the relationship between history and theology. The question 'just how radical was this Irish response to the Christian *evangel*' will be treated last.

What will be evident in the logic of this sequence is that while monasticism was widespread in the Christian world of the period under discussion, the particular manifestation of this form of commitment in Ireland and the lands evangelized by Irishmen such as ColumCille and Columbanus was sufficiently different in *praxis* to merit such a study as this. Both Mackey and O'Loughlin discuss the fact that claiming aspects of Irish monastic *praxis* as distinctive is quite controversial. Nevertheless both sustain their arguments to the conclusion that there is such a phenomenon as Celtic (Irish in the context of this work) theology and spirituality. Hopefully the differences noted in all the primary sources utilized in this work may lead to similar conclusions concerning not only the distinctiveness of such a theology and spirituality but also that this very distinctiveness gives validity to the claims of this work. In the discussion of the theology and *praxis* of sixth- to eighth-century Irish monasticism, while we acknowledge its culturally specific monastic organization and experience, no questioning of the orthodoxy[9] of the theology that underpinned the *praxis* is implied.

Just as culture manifests differences in art and other material aspects of a society, so does it explain why certain societies (the Irish Celts in this particular discussion) approach different elements of the Christian *evangel*, such as the Scriptures, with a specific methodology of both appropriation and articulation.[10] More will be written later in this work about the intrinsic place of Scripture, and particularly the psalms, in the lives of Irish monks.[11] However, since Scripture was almost the sole source of their prayer one may need to know at the outset how the Irish interpreted Scripture and to ask the question: was their understanding different from that of their Western continental counterparts? Bradshaw points to the 'predilection of Celtic scholars for the literal-historical method of biblical exegesis, against the tide in favour of the spiritual-allegorical method'.[12]

---

9. There was a law of 418 CE, which had as its purpose the exile of those found guilty of heresy. In relation to the 'heresy' of Pelagius, which some writers would say was never taken too seriously by the British and the Irish, some see the sending of Palladius to the Irish as safeguarding the orthodoxy of Irish Christianity. D. Dumville (ed.), *St Patrick A.D. 493–1993* (Woodbridge: Boydell Press, 1st edn, 1993), p. 8, quoting the words of Prosper's *Contra Collatorem*, said the point of sending Palladius was 'to make the barbarian Island Christian'. Barbarian is the nomenclature given to the early Irish tribes by the Romans.

10. The hermeneutic of suspicion has characterized the feminist critique of Scriptures in the latter part of the twentieth century and illustrates the point that different historical periods and people with differing perceptions do tend to approach Scripture from new vantage points which often lead to new articulations.

11. J. Ryan, *Irish Monasticism: Origins and Early Development* (London: Longmans, Green and Co., 1931), p. 377 holds that 'the Holy Scriptures were the chief course of study, and theology was not neglected . . . the mastery of the Latin language . . . [was] useful in the understanding of the sacred text'.

12. B. Bradshaw, 'The Wild and Woolly West: Early Irish Christianity and Latin Orthodoxy', *SCH* 25 (1989), pp. 123–34.

McNamara begins with the earliest texts[13] and gives a comprehensive survey of the same literal-historical approach to Scripture. He makes the point that there is a singularity in the Irish historical approach in that it has a twofold dimension:

> We find reference to a multiple (or twofold) historical sense in the introduction of both the *Eclogae* and the Psalter section of 'Das Bibelwerk' – both Hiberno-Latin works roughly contemporary with the *Old Irish Treatise*. Furthermore, the twofold historical sense is worked out in great detail in the exposition of Ps.I, both in the *Old Irish Treatise* and in 'Das Bibelwerk'.[14]

In conclusion McNamara believes that this particular style of interpretation of Scripture of the early Irish monks arises from a 'confluence of two independent historical traditions of interpretations'.[15] This literal interpretation is applied by McNamara to a particular piece of Irish literature about the affection of Mael Isu Ua Brollchain for a Psalter. However, other scholars would see this poem applied to a lady and as evidence of *syneisaktism*,[16] or 'co-habiting' in an English translation of the word.

---

13. M. McNamara, 'The Psalter in Early Irish Monastic Spirituality', *MS* 14 (Advent, 1983), pp. 179–205 (180) cites these sources thus:
> What is probably the oldest specimen of writing from Ireland (outside the Ogham) is evident on tablets, now in the National Museum of Ireland, Dublin were found in Springmount Bog, County Antrim, and were probably originally used as school exercises to initiate students through the psalms. They date from about 600 CE. Somewhat later is the Gallican Psalter known as the *Cathach of St Columba*; others are glosses in Latin.

Notable are the important double Psalter texts of the *Gallicanum* and the *Hebraicum* on facing pages, written in Ireland in the tenth century. Other authors who treat the exegetical practice of the Irish in the early days of Christianity include: Sharpe (ed.), *Ireland*, chapters 17 and 18; J. Mackey (ed.), *An Introduction to Celtic Christianity* (Edinburgh: T&T Clark, 1st edn, 1989, pp. 414–30); B. Ramsey, *Beginning to Read the Fathers* (London: SCM, 1993), pp. 22–41, where he describes the two basic methods of scriptural exegesis; and M. Maher, (ed.), *Irish Spirituality* (Dublin: Veritas Publications, 1981), pp. 37–41 and also chapter 3, where he refers to the particular kind of scriptural exegesis of the Irish monks, though he says that he is concentrating on the modern Irish use of Scripture in spirituality. All authors acknowledge that the classic work on the different approaches to scriptural exegesis is Origen's *On First Principles*. An excerpt from this document in which he explains in detail the differences between literal-historical and allegorical-spiritual exegesis is found in M. Wiles and M. Santer (eds), *Documents in Early Christian Thought* (Notre Dame: University Press, 1975), pp. 138–45. M. Smyth, *Understanding the Universe in Seventh Century Ireland*, (Indiana: The Medieval Institute, 1984), pp. 11–35 refers to many early medieval Irish manuscripts which are strongly scriptural in content or exegetical in intent. Two sources are: *De Mirabilibus Sacrae Scripturae*, of which she claims 'that owing to the fascination of the Irish Augustine with the Great Easter Cycles, the text can be dated with certainty to 654 or 655 CE', p. 12, and the Anonymous Commentary on the Catholic Epistles, written in the style of Pelagius.

14. McNamara, 'The Psalter', p. 199.
15. McNamara, 'The Psalter', p. 199.

How Christianity arrived in Britain[17] and its neighbouring insular territory of Ireland is still the cause of conjecture, with varying historical theories gaining current acceptance.[18] However, that Christianity was introduced into Ireland before the arrival of Patrick,[19] purported to be Ireland's founder of Christianity, is evident from Prosper's *Chronicle* revealing that Pope Celestine sent Palladius as Bishop 'to the Irish who believe in Christ'.[20]

16. See Appendix 1 A for the poem.
17. L. Laing, *Celtic Britain: Britain Before the Conquest* (London: Routledge and Kegan Paul, 1st edn, 1979), p. 151 makes a case for Christianity being brought to northern Britain and Wales by the army. Since it was thought that no such Roman invasion occurred in Ireland, other sources must be sought. Recent debate, however, over the archaeological finds (1985 but reported in 1996) at Drumanagh, north of Dublin, have archaeologists divided on the claims for authenticity of those who used the artefacts to claim that a Roman fort was established there. Professor Michael Herity is one of those who claims that the site was Celtic; Dr Peter Harbison tends to agree with those archaeologists who say that it was a Roman fortification, thus putting a whole new perspective on the Iron Age history of Ireland; see also N. Constable, *Ancient Ireland* (London: Promotional Reprint Co., 1996), p. 38.
18. Sherley-Price (ed.), *Ecclesiastical History of the English People* (London: Penguin, rev. edn, 1990), has a version of how Britain became Christian; P. Beresford Ellis, *Celtic Inheritance* (London: Muller, Bond and White, 1st edn, 1985), p. 25 gives a variety of possible theories about how Christianity came to Britain and Ireland; Richter, *Medieval*, p. 349 discusses the beginnings of Christianity in Ireland; L. de Paor, *Saint Patrick's World: The Culture of Ireland's Apostolic Age* (Dublin: Four Courts Press, 1st edn, 1993), in chapter three discusses Christianity in Gaul and Britain. These references reiterate the fact that scholars are still divided on precisely how Christianity came to Britain and Ireland.
19. N. D. O'Donoghue, *The Mountain Behind the Mountain* (Edinburgh: T&T Clark, 1993), pp. 7–10 makes the point, 'There may have been Christians in Ireland before Patrick, but it was Patrick, the slave, who first brought the Good News of a God with a human heart, a God of tears', to the Irish. The dates of both the commencement of Patrick's missionary work in Ireland and his death have been the cause of much debate, particularly when supposed anniversaries were to be celebrated. The latest, and no doubt the most scholarly work is that of Dumville (ed.), *St Patrick*, where a variety of authors go over the previous research and make a very cogent case for placing the beginning of his ministry nearer 493 CE than the usual date of 431 CE.
20. *Chronica Minora* (ed. Mommsen, 1.473 Prosper, Chronicle, s.a. 431) states: *Ad Scottos in Christum credentes ordinatus a papa Celestino Palladius primus episcopus mittitur* (Consecrated by Pope Celestine, Palladius is sent as the first Bishop to the Irish who believe in Christ); T. M. Charles-Edwards, in Dumville (ed.), *St Patrick*, sees the sending of Palladius as closely allied to the sending of Germanus to Britain: in both instances, 'Celestine's energy in defence of the faith was demonstrated by having rescued Britain from heresy and Ireland from paganism', p. 7, J. B. Bury, *Tirechan's Memoirs of St Patrick*, EHR 17 (April, 1902), pp. 235–63 (245), Tirechan's version of this event introduces the dilemma of the two Patricks, but his wording is not so tied to heresy: 'In the thirteenth year of the Emperor Theodosius Bishop Patricius is sent by Bishop Celestine, the Pope of Rome, for the teaching of the Irish ... Bishop Palladius is sent first, who was named Patricius with another name, who suffered martyrdom at the hands of the Irish' v 56, pp. 164–7; Bury, *Tirechan's*, p. 235; 'Itinerary of Patrick in Connaught', Pro R.I.A. xxiv c (1903), pp. 153–68; *Life of St Patrick*, 1905, pp. 248–51, pp. 358–60; *Annals of Innisfallen*, translation Mac Airt, 45, V 389–91; cf. above pp. 39–43. De Paor, *St Patrick's*, p. 21, makes the point, using the letters of Pope Celestine, that 'A bishop shall not be supplied without consent. Both the assent and the request of clergy, laity and people in authority are required.' De Paor goes on to say that the numbers of Irish Christians must have been sufficient to warrant the appointment of a bishop. This was also required by canon law at the time. His claim seems, however, to assume a more organized Church than could have actually existed. Some scholars put the population of Ireland in the sixth century at 700,000 and we do not know what

Early Irish Monasticism

Monasticism has been an integral part of Christianity since the Eastern mystics and hermits of the desert. The movement from the eremitic to the coenobitic lifestyle was accomplished in the eastern Mediterranean by the fourth century. Anthony began as a hermit seeking God in the isolation and solitude of the desert. As the numbers of his followers increased, he was forced to accept the fact that seeking God in this way was attractive to other people as well, and so the coenobitic lifestyle evolved. Monasticism as it was manifested in both Christian and non-Christian traditions has been able to accommodate both the hermit and the person who prefers to live in a community. As a response to the Christian *evangel*, forms of monasticism eventually were found throughout the known world. It is not surprising then to find that in Britain and remote Ireland this form of Christian living was also practised. Some historians even point to the presence of monasteries[21] before Patrick's time.[22]

What is this Christian *evangel* that Irish monasticism was thought to live so differently? It can be directly defined from its etymology, *evangel* meaning the 'good news' preached by Jesus in first-century Palestine and promulgated by his followers before their deaths. It can be seen as a particular view of the ambit of human experience expressed initially at a specific time, in a specific locale, by particular central individuals. It is a message of life about life and as such it is far from an abstract philosophy. Philosophers did contemplate the phenomenon of life in the early years of Christianity, but theirs was a human view of the ultimate meaning of things that we observe. Their view may or may not include a deity, depending on the convictions of the philosopher regarding

---

percentage of these were Christian or what percentage, according to canon law, warranted a bishop.

21. While the existence of monasteries was evident in both Britain and Ireland in the early Middle Ages, most writers would caution against an over-simplification of the organization and living styles of these establishments. That they had monastic rules and that the penitentials articulated the asceticism of the monastic life, and were intrinsic to it, is not denied. However, both Hughes, *Early*, p. 69 and *The Church*, pp. 32–5, pp. 50–2, pp. 79–81 *et passim* and Sharpe, 'Some Problems', pp. 233–51, remind the reader to be wary of too great a generalization about an homogeneous form of monasticism.

22. Brigit of Kildare and Darerca (Monenna) of Killeedy both founded monasteries and if one is to take the most recent research of Dumville, *St Patrick*, pp. 39–43, who places Patrick in the 490s rather than in the 430s as earlier historians believed, then these monasteries were pre-Patrick; Darerca/Monenna died in 517 and Brigit (452–524 CE) earlier according to Cogitosus' life. Both the *AU*, translation by de Paor (*St Patrick's*, p. 120), and the *AFM*, translation by de Paor (*St Patrick's*, p. 130), (in which the following verse accompanying the reference to her death indicates her age and character: 'Nine-score years together, according to rule without error, without folly, without evil, without danger, was the age of Moninne') refer to Monenna or Darerca as she is often called; de Paor, *St Patrick*, pp. 46–50, has a chapter entitled 'Women Founders of Churches', in which he treats of these foundresses. Kenney, *The Sources*, p. 366, gives details of the lives, successors and hymns in her honour. Ryan, *Monasticism*, reprinted 1992, p. 136, gives a full account of Monenna. She is also called Edana, according to W. F. Skene, *Celtic Scotland: A History of Ancient Alban* (2, 3 vols; Edinburgh: David Douglass, 2nd edn, 1887), pp. 36–8, where he speaks about the three legends concerning Monenna and, using the Bollandist sources, gives more details of her life

the possibility of human knowledge of the supernatural, concerning which there is a debate even among theologians. What is basic to this *evangel* is the belief in a creator God. A belief in Jesus as Son and Saviour bringing hope and purpose; an acknowledgement of the all-pervading Spirit who constitutes the third person of the Trinity and of whom the Irish Christians had an abiding consciousness; finally a belief in salvation from the selfish potential of the human person and an all-embracing love and purpose drawing and impelling the human person's journey forward.

The *evangelium*, as it is responded to, lived and incorporated within a culture, seeks articulation through the media of that culture: its literary tradition and forms; its thought patterns, its philosophic understandings, its manifestation in art, its patterns of socio-political organizations. One of the questions to be explored in this work is: did Irish monasticism of the sixth to the eighth century, in its theology and *praxis*, put flesh on this historical period's understanding of the *evangelium*? Another could be: is such a living of this *evangelium* so distinctive in the Irish context to make a case for its being singularly different from other manifestations of monastic *praxis*? It is probable that the Irish developed idiosyncratic practices because they were located in the remotest part of the Western world in the early years of the Christianizing of the Roman empire,[23] or maybe the differences were due to something more peculiarly Irish. The former seems to have been accepted, the latter remains to be explored and 'proved'.

Celtic Consciousness and Culture

What constituted the essence of this consciousness? Here one has to try to come to terms with the culture of the Celt within the context of the sixth to the eighth century. Stevenson holds that, as evident in the development of literacy, the Irish have a cultural self-confidence which sets them apart from other 'barbarian' civilizations of the West.[24] This is best understood in an historico-cultural methodology where the interplay of history and all facets of the lives of the people are so interwoven that it is difficult to abstract components in isolation. What is evident to an observer are the cultural dimensions of a given society, which are deeply embedded in its historical experience and revealed in the chronology of events which shape its evolution.

A very brief and cursory look at Irish society in the pre-Christian era would indicate that the basis of society at the time was rural, with the *Túatha*, called

---

in Scotland and the many churches she is purported to have founded.

23. The official Christianizing of the Roman Empire dated from 313 CE with the Edict of Toleration by Constantine. Ireland, never part of the Roman Empire, had, however, been penetrated by Christianity by 400 CE.

'petty Kingdom',[25] being the important social unit.[26] The leadership of the group was vested in the *ri* or king.[27] Early Irish society was hierarchical and non-egalitarian and this was clearly reflected in the laws regarding the importance of rank.[28] The education system was a continuation of the oral tradition of the druids with the poets or *filid*[29] occupying a place of pre-eminence. These elements of their pre-Christian milieu strongly influenced the Celts when they began to write.[30] The different native literary sources of this lived and living experience, according to Kelly, include law texts, wisdom texts, sages, histories, praise-poetry, annals, genealogies, saints' lives, religious poetry, penitentials and monastic rules.[31] Though there are sometimes divergent and

24. Stevenson, in Edel (ed.), *Cultural*, p. 17.
25. F. Kelly, *A Guide to Early Irish Law* (vol. 3; Dublin: Mount Salus, 1st edn, 1988), p. 3.
26. According to Stevenson, in Edel (ed.), *Cultural*, p. 17, Patrick experienced how an alien was not accepted: *Confessio*, 'And all the time I used to give presents to the kings, in addition to paying wages to their sons who travel with me; and nonetheless they seized me with my companions, and on that day they were keen to kill me but my time had not yet come.' Kinless wanderers were treated with suspicion in early medieval Irish history.
27. Byrne in Kelly, *A Guide*, p. 4, says that on the evidence of genealogies and other sources there were about 150 kings at any one time between the fifth and twelfth centuries. *Totius Scotiae regnator* (36b) is how Adomnán, *Vita Sancti Columbae: Adomnán's Life of Columba*, ed. A. O. and M. O. Anderson (London: Thomas Nelson and Sons, 1961), refers to Diarmait son of Cerball who he claims was ordained by God as ruler of all Ireland. Kelly, *A Guide*, p. 18, claims that 'though the idea of a kingship of the whole island had already gained currency by the seventh century, no Irish king ever managed to make it a reality, and most law-texts do not even provide for such a possibility'.
28. Kelly, *A Guide*, p. 8. He also points to the fact that the Roman principle of everyone being equal before the law was never subscribed to by native Irish law. He further maintains that in the introduction to the main collection of law-texts, the *Senchas Már*, it is stated that the world was in equality until the coming of this law, which introduced the distinction between different ranks of people. 'This claim is of course untrue', according to Kelly.
29. O'Curry, *Lectures*, p. 462, explains the qualification of the *filid* thus:

He exhibits his compositions to him, that is, to an Ollamh [a Master of the arts of poetry etc.]; and he has the qualifications of each of the seven orders [of poets]; and the king confirms him in his full degrees, and in what the Ollamh reports of him as to his compositions, and as to his innocence and purity; that is to say, purity of learning, and purity of mouth [from abuse or satire], and purity of hand [from blood shedding], and purity of union [marriage], and purity of honesty [from theft and robbery and unlawfulness], and purity of body – that he have but one wife, for he dies [in dignity] through impure cohabitation.

30. There was a form of writing called Ogham script which was used mainly in funerary worship and notation but was not used for communicating ideas. It is credited to ogmios, Celtic god of speech and poetry. S. Costley and C. Kightly, *A Celtic Book of Days* (London: Thames and Hudson, 1998) January 30, states, 'Examples have been found in Ireland, particularly in the south, Wales, in the Isle of Man and in Scotland. A version has been found on some of the Western Isles. There are also one or two in western Britain, and one in southern England. Each letter corresponds to a tree or a climber and a calendar month.' A great deal of Ogham script is found on the Irish monument in the Waverley cemetery in Sydney. See Appendix 1 B, for ColumCille's name written in this script. See also O'Curry's, *Sources*, pp. 464–72. Green in Edel (ed.), *Cultural*, p. 129, holds that to all intents and purposes the Celts were illiterate though she does acknowledge that Caesar in *De Bello Gallico*, V1. 14, maintains that the druids could and did write.

disagreeing interpretations of these sources they do nevertheless display an essential unity, complementing each other such as in the case of legal rules illustrated in saint's lives. Also this complementary aspect is evident in some events in the sagas as they are explained in reference to some law-text.[32] The Brehon law and ecclesiastical law benefited from the fact that clerical and secular lawmakers were involved in the formulation of both codes.[33]

Sometimes exaggerated claims are made for the place of women in early Irish life. According to Kelly, a woman such as Queen Medb in the Táin Bó Cúailnge is presented as the real leader of Connacht and occasionally she is involved in the fighting. In the Mythological Cycle of Tales, Otherworld women are seen as important and aggressive. However, in real life, their power is more restricted.[34] From the Triads of Ireland we see most accurately what qualities women are to display: reticence, virtue and industry. In Triad 180 women are reminded of the need for 'a steady tongue, a steady virtue, a steady housewifery'.[35] Sexual failings by women were the most frowned upon and the practice of polygamy seemed to flourish in spite of the Church's condemnation of it. Bretha Nemed déidenach notes a special position in society for nuns, 'at a certain age a girl should be betrothed to God or to a man' and the betrothal to God carries legal rights not given to laywomen.[36] Perhaps this elevated role of nuns could be attributed to the influence of Christianity. Cáin Adamnáin is thought to have given women more respect, for in paragraph two it states, 'Cumalack, (a derivative from cumal, a female slave, bondmaid) was the name for women till Adomnán came to free them.[37] However, Cherici makes the

31. Kelly, A Guide, p. 1.
32. Kelly, A Guide, p. 2.
33. R. Finnane, 'Late Medieval Irish Law Manuscripts: A Reappraisal of Methodology and Context' (unpublished MA Thesis, Celtic Studies Department, University of Sydney, 1991), pp. 51–53, discusses the relationship between Brehon and Canon law.
34. Kelly, A Guide, pp. 68–69. Quoting from actual texts he claims that in Serglige Con Culainn, two green-clad women from the Otherworld beat the hero Cú Chulainn with whips until he is nearly dead. In the voyage-tale Immram Curaig Maíle Dúin, one of the Otherworld islands on which Máel Dúin lands is ruled over by a beautiful queen with 17 daughters. Since her husband has died she has to give judgments and settle disputes of her subjects.
35. Kelly, A Guide, p. 69.
36. Kelly, A Guide, p. 78. He says this legal status of a nun extends to her giving evidence, though the evidence of a woman is not normally entitled to be accepted.
37. K. Meyer (ed.), Cáin Adamnáin: An Old-Irish Treatise on the Law of Adomnán (Oxford: Clarendon Press, 1st edn, 1905), p. 2. However, T. Newlands, 'The Changing Position of Women in Early Christian Ireland', ACJ 111 (1990–91), pp. 38–55, claims that this is not so. She compares the position of women in secular law and that of the post Cáin Adamnáin era, and shows that 'the change claimed to have been brought about was greatly exaggerated to justify clerical involvement in a potentially lucrative area'. To my knowledge there has not been any refutation of this thesis, so the conclusions still require some more scholarly debate. Cherici, Celtic Sexuality, chapter 5 in treating the predominant images of women in pre-Christian Celtic culture, makes the point that the paradigms of Celtic culture recognized the triple aspect of mother, lover and hag. Of these paradigms, Cherici, Celtic Sexuality, p. 51, explains, 'the accepted paradigms were the models or thought patterns which the Celts relied upon to make sense of events'. Some of the earlier writers spell Adomnán as Adamnáin, but in future when not quoting from these sources the former spelling will be used.

point that Gaelic and British women were not merely wives but had their own areas of responsibility. As evidence of what he calls a matrilineal descent,[38] he says that, 'heroes [were] often known as the son of such and such a woman'.[39] Some women in the Old and Middle Irish Literature, Banshenchas, participated in warfare[40] and owned property in their own right.[41] The Goddess was held in very high regard and it is still a point of contention if Ireland's first female saint, Brigit,[42] honoured along with Patrick and ColumCille as the founders[43] of Irish Christianity, was an actual person or the embodiment of the Goddess.[44]

38. Cherici, *Celtic Sexuality*, p. 48, makes the point that the 'matrilineal society of the Celts traced ancestry through the mother since the exact identity of the father could not be proved'.

39. J. Markale, *The Celts: Uncovering the Mythic and Historic Origins of Western Culture* (Vermont: Inner Traditions International, 1st edn, 1978), p. 146.

40. Kelly, *A Guide*, p. 68 in a footnote calls this twelfth-century collection, edited by M. E. Dobbs, of genealogical lore about women unique in European literature: RC 47 (1930), pp. 283-339; 48 (1931), pp. 163-234; p. 49 (1932), pp. 437-89. See reference from Kelly above regarding Connacht's Queen Maeve. Celtic Britain's Queen Boudicca, Queen of the Iceni tribe, according to Tacitus, killed 70,000 Romans before she was defeated. Cassius Dio in Constable, *Ancient Ireland*, p. 42 gives a description of her

'In stature she was very tall, in appearance most terrifying, in the glance of her eye most fierce, and her voice was harsh; a great mass of the tawniest hair fell to her hips; around her neck was a large golden necklace; and she wore a tunic of diverse colours over which a thick mantle was fastened with a brooch. This was her invariable attire. She now grasped a spear to aid her in terrifying all beholders.

This is a very minute description of a woman the Romans would only have 'seen' in battle. One wonders about the authenticity of most descriptions of the Celts given by Roman historians and geographers.

41. Cherici, *Celtic Sexuality*, p. 21, claims that 'generally women in Celtic mythology enjoyed full control of their sexuality dispersing their favours as they saw fit. Women could contract, bear arms, become druids and engage in politics.'

42. Cogitosus' *Life a*nd the many other lives are divided on the veracity of the sources. The fact that her feast is celebrated on February 1 very clearly links her with Brigit the Irish Goddess of childbirth and one of the pre-Christian festivals of *Imbole*. Traditionally, in the minds and hearts of the people, she was a real person. See also O'Riain, in Edel (ed.), *Cultural*, pp. 151-6 for an interesting treatment of Brigit as an instance of 'Pagan example and Christian practice'; also Smyth, in Edel (ed.), *Cultural*, p. 34 where she addresses the two aspects of Brigit: paganism and festivals.

43. These three saints are often referred to as Trias Thaumaturga; M. E. Cusack, *The Trias Thaumaturga, or Three Wonder-Working Saints of Ireland* (London: J. G. Murdock, 1890s). This story of the lives of Patrick, ColumCille and Brigit recounts their lives and deeds, but in the preface the author explicitly claims that the book is written for Catholics. He refers often to the contemporary debates when Ussher and others, Todd in this instance, were making claims for the Church of Ireland being the authentic Patrician Church. While Cusack, *Trias*, p. 10, acknowledges the scholarship of Todd he insists on his sectarian bias.

44. De Paor, *St Patrick's*, p. 29 claims that, 'goddesses appear in every part of Ireland as spirits of place – whole territories, or hill-tops, rivers and springs – and as divinities of natural forces of motherhood, fertility, growth and destruction. They were often triple in character (reiterating the fondness of the Celts for three). War Goddesses in the form of ravens often presided over the battlefield'; de Paor, *St Patrick's*, p. 47 seems to believe in the existence of the person called Brigit for he states: 'Brigit the church foundress certainly existed'. The nature and importance of Kildare for many centuries are indisputable testimony to the foundation of Kildare but not necessarily of a personal Brigit.

There is evidence for the positive role Christianity played in elevating the position, increasing the honour-price, of some members of Irish society. Children seem to have been one such group for, according to *Bretha Crolige*, the honour-price (díre) of a child between baptism and the age of seven is the same as that of a cleric. Consequently an injury to a child merits a heavy penalty regardless of the social class of the child.[45] In the Christian era there is also evidence for an interesting role carried out by women during the Eucharistic celebration and some have seen this as evidence for a positive role of Christianity in the lives of women. However, not all would see some roles assumed by women as a positive contribution to the life of the emerging Christian community. A sixth-century letter written by the bishop of Tours to two Celtic priests regarding women, called *conhospitae*,[46] distributing the chalice at the Eucharist is a case in point. The fact that a letter was written at all may indicate that the practice was more widespread than with the two Gallic priests.

To say that Christianity has anything in common with primal religions strikes fear into the hearts of some Christians. However, it is clear that there would be no dialogue between religions if there were not some points on which they could 'converse'. It is one of the strong points being made in this study, particularly in regard to the *Vitae* and writings of the two prominent founders of Irish monasticism, that the relationship between Celtic Christianity and its predecessor religions was not one of conflict in any overt sense. It may have been subconscious but the strength of the Celtic consciousness out of which it grew, or on to which Christianity was grafted, allowed for a somewhat smooth transition. If primal religions are the first religious forms to arise in human culture then historically and psychologically they have to make an impact on other religions that come after them. Tanner refers to the meeting point of Christianity and primal religions as the 'boundary'. She expresses this process as follows:

> the distinctiveness of a Christian way of life is not so much formed *by* the boundary as *at* it; Christian distinctiveness is something that emerges in the very cultural process occurring at the boundary, processes that construct a distinctive identity for Christian social practices through the distinctive use of cultural materials shared with others.[47]

Hatch, in the introduction to the Hibbert Lectures of 1888 holds that, 'the religion of a given race at a given time is relative to the whole mental attitude

---

45. CIH 923. pp. 3–4 states, *id comdíre macríg mac aithig co cenn .uii. mbliadnae* translated as 'the son (7) of a king and the son of a commoner have the same honour-price up to seven years'.

46. This word is often coupled with, and in some instances used as synonymous with, the word *syneisaktism* and is thought to have been practised in the early Celtic Church. It was the practice of celibate women living with celibate men before the establishment of monastic settlements. See Appendix 1 C for a translation of the letter.

47. K. Tanner, *Theories of Culture: A New Agenda for Theology* (Minneapolis: Fortress Press, 1997), p. 115.

of that time. It is impossible to separate the religious phenomena from the other phenomena.'[48]

How does one speak about 'the whole mental attitude' of sixth- to eighth-century Irish monks? An 'insider' expresses what he sees as four dimensions of this consciousness.[49] In the first place he sees a unity with nature that is linked with a powerful sense of the omnipresence of the unseen world.[50] Pre-Christian Ireland had at its heart a deep and constant sense of an invisible world continuous with the visible world.[51] Two other aspects associated with this consciousness were a feeling of human immortality and a love of learning. The latter is exemplified in the monastic schools that received scholars from all over Europe in the sixth century. The Irish love of learning is further manifested in the central role of the storyteller who keeps alive the sense of wonder; a love of words that blossoms in poetry and rhetoric.[52] All of these elements of Celtic-Irish

---

48. A. M. Fairbairn (ed.), *The Influence of Greek Ideas and Usage upon the Christian Church* (London: William and Norgate, 1907), p. 2. Hatch actually wrote the work but died before publication.

49 O'Donoghue, *The Mountain*, p. 4, treats this Celtic consciousness based on his own experience of growing up in the south-west of Ireland over seventy years ago. Because of his strongly philosophic and theological training he weds the two disciplines well. In chapters 7, 8 and 9 of the same book, O'Donoghue treats a sense of cosmogenesis which he links with nature and Irish imagination, an integral part of Irish consciousness. See also Smyth, in Edel (ed.), *Cultural*, pp. 23–44, for more discussion of the cosmic aspect of Irish consciousness.

50. See M. Low, *Celtic Christianity and Nature: Early Irish and Hebridean Traditions* (Edinburgh: Edinburgh University Press, 1996), for a comprehensive discussion of nature and the sacred in early medieval Ireland and the Hebrides. She treats with close reference to primary sources land, mountains, water, birds, trees, fire and sun and culminates with the chapter on the God of the elements.

51. O'Donoghue, *The Mountain*, p. 8. This is evident in the sagas, poems and *Vitae* of the early Irish saints; de Paor, *St Patrick's*, p. 29, sees the primal Irish as 'living and breathing with one foot in this world and one foot in the otherworld: the two worlds interpenetrated'; this visible world also includes an understanding of cosmology that Smyth, in Edel (ed.), *Cultural*, p. 23, claims to be evident in two documents: *De mirabilibus sacrae scripturae* which is a theological treatise by an author known as the Irish Augustine, the other, *Liber de ordine creaturarum*, a treatise once attributed to Isidore of Seville, but shown to be a product of seventh-century Ireland. Her whole chapter discusses lucidly the arguments for a specifically Irish worldview. She claims that

> in the Irish texts . . . one senses a genuine interest in the universe for its own sake, not merely as a sign of some higher truth . . . even more importantly, they [the Irish] absorb this knowledge [from the texts] making it their own and integrating it into a consistent system. It was not as complex as a cosmology of the classical world . . . but it was coherent.

She also makes the point that it was out of this cosmology and understanding of the cycle of nature that a monastic cycle for calculating time and giving a pattern for the Canonical Hours emerged, pp. 27–28.

52. O'Donoghue, *The Mountain*, pp. 4–5. Since the early Irish monks had access to the classics, for which their writing gives evidence, they were no doubt used to rhetoric and used it in the writing of the monastic rules and penitentials and in the *Vitae* of the saints. Augustine, in his *De doctrina christiana*, made a deliberate attack on those who misused rhetoric. By the ninth century all debates about rhetoric had ceased. A recent work, Lapidge (ed.), *Columbanus*, involved various authors who raised questions about his facility with Latin and his classical learning. This question of facility with Latin could also be applicable, no doubt, to other Irish writers of the time.

consciousness will be shown to be present and operating in the monasticism of this period under discussion.

Initially the term culture, in the classical designation for the process, in the seventeenth and eighteenth centuries, referred to intellectual and spiritual development based on the assumption of continuous improvement as a conscious goal or ideal.[53] It is now seen as an integral whole or configuration incorporating the awareness that symbols play a vital role in our understanding of culture.[54] In keeping with this conviction, Cote has proposed a model for analysing culture. The model is that of an iceberg with the two enduring and influential elements of a group's dynamic myths and values hidden deeply in the subconscious. It is a contention of this study that the iceberg model could be applied to the lifestyle and *praxis* of sixth- to eighth-century Irish monasticism to which they gave rise: the tangible elements of the monastic rules and penitentials are the external manifestations of the deeply embedded values of commitment and radicality that were articulated so distinctively by the Irish in the era under discussion.

A significant aspect of the Celtic culture within which Irish monasticism developed and which contributed to its essence is what Mary Schmiel calls a metaphorical mindset:

> The Celtic mind acknowledged no real dichotomy between reality and fantasy, between this world and the world 'beyond'.[55] It is because of this mindset so different from the literalism of the Levant of that time, that the 'letter' and 'spirit' of the law never diverged in Celtic Tradition.[56]

---

53. Tanner, *Theories*, pp. 3–24.
54. R. G. Cote, Revisioning *Mission: The Catholic Church and Culture in Postmodern America* (New York: Paulist, 1st edn, 1996), p. 90.
55. This reiterates what O'Donoghue has said in the quotation on the previous page.
56. M. Fox, *Western Spirituality: Historical Roots, Ecumenical Routes* (Indiana: Fides, 1979), p. 170. P. Sheldrake, *Living Between Worlds: Place and Journey in Celtic Spirituality* (Massachusetts: Cowley, 1996), uses the metaphor of a membrane to show the fluidity with which the Celts can move from one 'world' to the 'other' and feel equally comfortable in each. This fact also helps to understand why the 'letter' of the law, viz., the issues at the forefront of the Synod of Whitby, tonsure, date of Easter and Baptismal practices, were seen as insignificant to the Irish because the 'spirit' or theology was orthodox. Moreover, the dualism so prized by Platonic philosophy and the later Roman Church was never a part of the Irish Church or its consciousness. J. O'Donohue, *Anam Cara: Spiritual Wisdom from the Celtic World* (London: Transworld, 1997), p. 16, believes that 'the Celtic mind was not burdened by dualism. It did not separate what belongs together ... The dualism which separates the visible from the invisible, time from eternity, the human from the divine was totally alien to them.' Dodds, *Pagan*, p. 9 makes a reference to the classical Greek dichotomy between the self and the body which eventually became the dualistic world of matter and spirit: he goes on to claim that the body and self dichotomy was 'the most far-reaching and perhaps the most questionable, of all her gifts to human culture'.

The dichotomy of 'letter' and 'spirit' in the context of the above quotation seems never to have entered into the Irish calculation.[57] While law was important for the functioning of a society, it was not to be a crippling of the spirit that pervaded life. Moving this notion of spirit to another level of discussion, to the theological, one finds the Holy Spirit of Christian revelation. In the Irish consciousness this Spirit was much honoured and was evident in their reverence for all of creation that to them was a manifestation of the creator God. 'This unity with nature was felt rather than consciously expressed.'[58] As an aspect of this being immersed in nature, there was the awareness of the unseen world as more friendly than malignant. Even the 'little people',[59] the *Túatha Dé Danann, leannawn shee*, people of the goddess Dana or Danu, confined to the nether world, were somehow continuous with the angels and the faithful departed in Christian theology.[60] As a consequence, the Celtic consciousness had intimations of its own immortality and so traditionally did not fear death to the extent that modern Western consciousness reflects.

Another aspect of this worldview was the Irish tendency to put great value on imagination, 'at once a vision and a way of life'.[61] It can also be called an 'attunement' that sets up an environment within which the perceiving subject can be at home with aspects of life and awareness, events and experiences that defy description except in the language of love and poetry. This is not an attempt at glorification of imagination to the extent that the darker side of this faculty, evident in the Irish race, is not addressed. O'Donoghue calls it the *feminine* aspect and as such 'she' needs her 'brothers', *thought* and *observation*, to help 'her' put a rein on what could otherwise be unbridled living in an unreal world.[62] Modern literature and particularly drama often presents the literary world with evidence of this: Brian Friel's two plays, *Dancing at Lughnasadh* and *Philadelphia Here I Come*, are two such depictions of this over-riding imaginative capacity which without thought could lead to an incapacity to

---

57. Stevenson, in Edel (ed.), *Culture*, p. 13, refers to law introduced by the Church as 'the law of the letter', but this was because this kind of law was only supplementary to oral law. She is in no way referring to the letter of the law in the same sense as the duality indicated in Schmiel's comment.

58. O'Donoghue, *The Mountain*, p. 4.

59. W. Evans Wentz, *The Fairy-Faith in Celtic Countries* (England: Gerrards Cross, 1977) Introduction by Kathleen Raine discusses these people. It is interesting and significant that in Irish monastic writing, unlike Eastern monastic literature of the time, there is minimal reference to Satan. So the unseen world was not malignant but friendly. No wonder the Irish of this period had no word for Original (or birth-transmitted) Sin in their language.

60. O'Donoghue, *The Mountain*, p. 5.

61. O'Donoghue, *The Mountain*, p. 5; O'Donohue, *Anam Cara*, p. 16, speaks of Celtic imagination as '[embracing] nature, divinity, underworld and human world as one'. Lehane, *Early Celtic*, pp. 39–41, discusses Irish imagination in the context of its paradoxical nature.

62. O'Donoghue, *The Mountain*, 86. The duality, absent in the early Celtic Church, was 'imposed' with the Synod of Whitby in 664 CE and later when the Roman Church sought to make the Irish Church conform to Roman attitudes.

come to grips with the reality of life at the present moment. The former points to the missionary's problem when returning home to Ireland: he has inculturated the gospel message to the indigenous culture of Africa, but when he is confronted with the duality of an unintegrated primal past and Christian present of his relatives, he is treated as a madman. When thought and observation are working with imagination a balance is maintained in life and living.[63] Brown would also agree that a balance is required when dealing with imagination. He actually says, 'imagination itself must go to school', meaning that it must be subjected to discipline in order to be really effective and useful: 'not to mock, not to lament... but to understand'.[64] What other than a fertile imagination, a heart in love with Christ and a restless quest to share the *evangelium* with others could have impelled both ColumCille and Columbanus to undertake their *peregrinatio pro Christo*: away from family and clan almost in defiance of the Celtic *raison d'être* of familial rootedness and belonging?

One strong manifestation of imagination in the Celtic consciousness was that which flowered in poetry.[65] Maybe this explains why the psalms, those classic poems of the Hebrew Scriptures, and an integral part of the Psalter recited daily at set hours by the monks, were constantly on their lips and were enjoined on them sometimes as part of their monastic penances. Only a fertile and playful imagination[66] would conjure up the illuminations of the Book of Kells and

---

63. O'Donoghue, *The Mountain*, 86. These aspects are described in detail in chapters 8 and 9 of his book. This notion of balance, borrowing from Cassian who developed his theory of *contraries* from the Pythagoreans, is treated elsewhere in this work; Mackey (ed.), *An Introduction*, p. 3 fn 1, has a lengthy discussion of the value and intrinsically Celtic preference for memory-retention and oral-transmission in continuation of the druidic tradition.

64. P. Brown, *Society and the Holy in Late Antiquity* (Berkeley: University of California Press, 1st edn, 1982), p. 21.

65. While ColumCille is remembered as the founder of many monasteries, he is also credited with the writing of poetry, no doubt making for a more balanced character. Not only were the poets valued in early Irish society, they also acted as a kind of social critic in the person of the druids. So much did ColumCille value the place of the poets in Irish society, that he is thought by many of the earlier writers to have come back to Ireland for the meeting at Druim Cette where his intervention helped to maintain the poet as integral to Irish society. Sharpe's editing of the latest English translation of *Adomnán's Life of Columba* would question the usually held belief of ColumCille's presence at the meeting at Druim Cette. Chadwick, *The Age*, p. 90, refers to poetry, that flowering of intellectual activity, as one of the characteristics of the Irish Church of the period; she treats the poetry of the period on pp. 104–18.

66. A. Cremin's review of Megaw's book on Celtic Art in *ACJ* (1990–91), p. 62, reiterates this point about the playfulness of early Celtic art and manuscripts. She comments on the cover of the book being reviewed: it is a magnificent example of mixed art

> an S shape with animals heads at either end. It can be viewed upside down (after reading this book one automatically turns everything around to seek out the hidden image) and is equally charming either way. An unusual choice, but one which admirably demonstrated the *ingenious wit* [emphasis mine] of Celtic jewellers.

similar manuscripts:[67] playfulness seen especially in the vignette of the two rats watched by two cats fighting over the host in the Incarnational Initial, also known as the Monogram Page of the Book of Kells.[68] One would not expect such 'irreverence' from the dour non-Celtic monks! For all the wild possibilities of this aspect of Irish consciousness and imagination, tending towards extravagance, O'Donoghue maintains that, 'it surely is the life-blood of all real philosophy and theology'.[69]

Allied with the poet's competence for verse is the capacity to tell stories. It is in the telling and re-telling of the stories of the clan and the Christian community that the synthesis of the past, present and the future occurs. These two aspects of Irish culture are manifested in the *Vitae* of saints, collected in the *Acta Sanctorum*.[70] The specific genre of these *Vitae* borrowed from the earlier *Vitae* of Hilary of Poitiers and Martin of Tours provided a pattern for the early hagiographers of the Irish tradition.

Dreams, those fanciful states of imagination, or prophetic vision, were also an intrinsic part of the lives of Irish monastic founders. Patrick's *Confession* recounts a dream about his being called to evangelize the Irish among whom he had been a slave:

> In the moment I saw the sun rise in the heavens; and while I was crying out 'helias' with all my might behold the splendour of the sun fell upon me, and at once removed the weight from me. And I believe I was aided by Christ my Lord, and his Spirit was then crying out for me.[71]

---

67. This is not the way Brown, *Society*, pp. 216–21, sees the illuminations and the concomitant theology of the Book of Kells. He refers to them, in comparison with Mediterranean and Byzantine illuminations as '[ways] of seeing the world [that] remained recalcitrant of incorporation into a 'method of theology', p. 218. Smyth, in Edel (ed.), *Cultural*, p. 43, however, would probably apply her reference to analogy in the linguistic field in this area also and come to the same conclusion:

> A Culture in which such mental gymnastics were habitual would encourage the scholar confronted with some tricky intellectual situation to resort to analogy, and this would help explain *the independence of mind* [my emphasis] and the surprising willingness to tackle problems by some of the early texts under discussion.

68. See Appendix 1D. P. Brown (ed.), *The Book of Kells* – selected and edited by P. Brown, librarian of Trinity College, Dublin, 34R, p. 19. This is said to be the most elaborate page in the entire book and perhaps the most elaborate piece of calligraphy ever executed. Chadwick, *The Age*, p. 224 makes the point that a similar engaging inclusion can be seen on the Cross of Muiredach at Clonmacnoise, where a couple of cats are depicted licking their kittens directly under the depiction of the apprehending of Christ.

69. O'Donoghue, *The Mountain*, p. 5.

70. C. Plummer (ed.), *Vitae Sanctorum Hiberniae* (2 vols, London: Oxford University Press, 1st edn, 1910). Plummer was an important writer in the history of Christian hagiography. It must be stressed that the *Vitae* are not intended as history, a very different genre from hagiography. They do express larger truths about the saints and so draw readers to growth in self-awareness and ultimately to God, if readers are so disposed.

71. *Confessio*, V 20 (ed. and trans. O'Donoghue, p. 106).

The two founders ColumCille and Columbanus were the subjects of their mothers' dreams.[72] ColumCille, in his life recorded by Adomnán, had many dreams as a result of which he saved the lives of others or 'foretold' events to happen. Dreams, like the imagination, were so much an intrinsic part of Irish consciousness that their presence in hagiographical writing is expected. The fact that Jungian theorizing was not developed until the early twentieth century did not mean people before Jung were not dreaming or guiding their lives by such intimations.

Archaeology[73] points to another facet in the manifestation of Irish consciousness: the powerful and all-pervasive presence of the sea.[74] The major monastic sites[75] all attest to the irresistible drawing power and numinous nature of the sea for the early monastic founders. Not only was the sea[76] the setting, either alongside or surrounding, for their most rugged monastic sites (called *inis* in the native tongue and meaning: 'island sanctuaries') in which the most extreme of the ascetics lived,[77] but it took them far from family and friend. Theirs

---

72. A. O'Kelleher and G. Schoepperle (eds), *Betha Colaim Chille – A Life of ColumCille*, compiled by M. O'Donnell (Illinois: University of Illinois, 1st edn, 1918), p. lviii. The editors have pages called 'A Table of Matters', where they tabulate the differing aspects of the life of ColumCille and they have a section called 'Of Visions foretelling the Birth of ColumCille' and 'Of Matters before his Birth', where seven such visions are recorded.

73. Herity, 'The Buildings', pp. 247–315; K. R. Dark, 'Celtic Monastic Archeology: Fifth to Eighth Centuries', *JMS* 14 (Advent, 1983), pp. 17–29.

74. One would have to note here the powerful presence of holy wells in the spiritual life of the pagan (*sic*) and Christian Celts. Green, in Edel (ed.), *Cultural*, p. 137, treats water in its many aspects in the religious lives of the pagan (*sic*) Celts.

75. Nendrum on Strangford Loch; Clonmacnoise, the home of Ciarán; Innisboffin, on the west coast of Ireland, the refuge of the fleeing monks of Lindisfarne; Glendalough, in the Wicklow hills with its upper and lower lake; Bangor on the sea, the formative place for the later Columbanus; Skellig Michael, on the remote rocky outcrop off the west coast together with Cahir Island, to mention some of the most famous. The last mentioned is discussed, together with Rathlin O'Birne, Donegal, by M. Herity, 'Two Island Hermitages in the Atlantic', *JRSAI* 125 (1995), pp. 85–128. Herity, 'The Buildings', p. 85 makes the point that Rathlin O'Birne dates from the sixth century and Cahir Island from the seventh century. No doubt, these places of refuge can also be identified as *crannogs*, occupation sites on islands or lakes which were another part of the psyche of the Irish and had their origins as far back as the Neolithic age; see L. Laing (ed.), *Studies in Celtic Survival* (British Archaeological Reports, 1977), p. 90. Archaeological research on Loch Tay in Scotland shows at least 15 crannogs previously existed on the loch, now they are mostly submerged.

76. The *Navigatio* of Brendan is the first recorded account of an Irishman's encounter with the sea. T. Severin, *The Brendan Voyage: An Epic Crossing of the Atlantic By Leather Boat* (Australia: Hutchinson, 1978) certainly is convinced that the voyage was a reality. He concludes his spectacularly detailed and splendidly photographed journey in the book with the 'forensic' comment, 'Whatever the answer, there is plenty of room for speculation and further investigation, particularly now that *Brendan* [referring to his boat] has shown that one group of suspects could certainly have reached the scene (the west coast of USA) of the 'crime' at the time alleged', p. 279. Whether the trip is fanciful or not, the fact remains that in the psyche of the Irish their closeness to the sea and its potential for eliciting a God-awareness, are attested to.

77. N. Chadwick, *The Age of the Saints in the Early Celtic Church* (London: Oxford University Press, 1st edn, 1963), p. 95.

was literally a marginal world of seagulls[78] and seals where difference is often misunderstood, misinterpreted and, so, isolated. When marginal people call those at the 'centre' to integrity and wholeness they can become more marginalized. However, ironically in the persons of ColumCille and Columbanus, the two archetypal monastic founders discussed in this work, Europe and its peoples were to be put on a Christian footing deeply indebted to the spiritual and cultural energy[79] of the marginal and idiosyncratic Irish *peregrini*.

The Irish Notion of History

No theological understanding or interpretation stands alone, unaffected by the human condition. Christianity, like the Judaism to which it is heir, lies in an historical understanding of human experience and destiny.[80] Humankind is on a journey and travels through the ever-evolving historical landscape which is human society. The only context within which human experience can be apprehended, reflected upon, 'theologized' about, is in constant interaction with its environment, understood in its deepest sense. Christianity is a religion of historians according to Bloch: 'the religious historian had to look at every aspect of a society, and all it produced to understand it'. It was, he continues, 'necessary for a good theologian to know and practise the discipline of history, as it was important for the historian to be able to operate knowingly within the world of theology'.[81]

Intrinsic to this experience is the pervasive notion of culture: a set of meanings and values that informs our way of life. In this sense culture is not something that is outside the person, but an atmosphere which permeates all that one does and is. This empiricist model of culture implies that a person is cultured by being socialized within a particular society.[82] That is essentially why a poly-focal methodology has been chosen as the most relevant in this study of sixth- to eighth-century Irish monasticism and *praxis*.

Intrinsic to any attempt to understand the sixth- to eighth- century Celtic environment and consequently Celtic consciousness is an exploration of their notion of history. Hughes sees it as clearly focused on the individual[83] and based

---

78. Smyth, in Edel (ed.), *Cultural*, p. 36, looks at birds and the role they play in Irish culture and cosmology. Low, *Celtic Christianity*, pp. 105–17.

79. O'Donoghue, *The Mountain*, p. 1.

80. Hollis, *Anglo-Saxon*, p. 27, again in relation to the conversionary dynamic, makes the point that 'the form Christianity assumes at any given place or time represents the foregrounding of one among the many possibilities offered by its constituent texts'.

81. M. Bloch in T .O'Loughlin, 'Theologians and Their Use of Historical Evidence: Some Common Pitfalls', *TM* (January, 2001), pp. 30–35 (30).

82. S. Bevans, *Models of Contextual Theology* (New York: Orbis Books, 1998), p. 5. Lonergan is quoted in Bevans as making the distinction between classical and empirical models of culture. He distinguishes the classical as universal and permanent.

83. K. Hughes, *The Early Celtic Idea of History and the Modern Historian* (Cambridge: Cambridge University Press, 1977), p. 3. Kierkegaard's comment at the beginning of chapter 3 on monastic rules, where the relationship between the individual and the community is treated.

upon lived experience. Lehane claims that 'Ireland, in every age is best known through the lives of individuals – figures sometimes comic, or frantic, or rumbustious or humble, never as coldly motivated as an abstract of national trends would suggest them to be.'[84] Gougaud, quoting Fournier, says that the Celtic genius was for stimulating the individual: 'The Irish race has always been fertile in individualities, but susceptible of organisation, and again it has been observed that the Celt [was] better suited to win converts than to train and manage them when won.'[85] Dallen, seems to be blaming the individualist spirit of the Irish for divorcing penance from the worshipping community.[86] This is very different from the empirical basis of much present-day academic historical interpretation.[87] When Le Goff, a French medievalist, in his groundbreaking work on medieval civilisation, stresses the importance of the people as opposed to the institutions, he also seems to be reiterating the importance of people and their lived experience. This, he maintains, is the fertile ground for studying society. These lived experiences can be seen in the art, literature, myths and behaviour of people. Some people and societies are particularly imaginative in their approach to life and living. Others value order and regulations. Le Goff seems to be asserting the importance of imagination in the creativity and lasting influence of people who allow themselves to use this imaginative faculty which draws on the experience of the common people of an era. Burke, borrowing from Le Goff, calls this 'history from below'.[88]

The Irish word for history is *senchas*,[89] which means 'old tales', traditions about the past, and it is applied specifically to genealogy, place-names, legends

84. Lehane, *Celtic*, p. 3.
85. Gougaud, *Christianity*, p. 425.
86. J. Dallen in A. W. Sadler (ed.), *The Journey of Western Spirituality: The Annual Publication of the College Theological Society* (Chicago: Scholar Press, 1981), p. 90.
87. Hughes, *The Early*, p. 3, describes the post-medieval idea of history thus: '[it is] based on a critical and exhaustive examination of source-material, the date, where the author obtained his information and how reliable it is likely to be, his prejudices, why he wrote, what his style shows of his associations and milieu'.
88. P. Burke, (ed.), *New Perspectives in Historical Writing* (Pennsylvania: Pennsylvania University Press, 1991); Le Goff, *Medieval Civilization* (Oxford: Blackwell, 1997), p. viii. In the preface to this work, he states that it has two important points, the second of which is expressed as:

On the other hand, even more than others, perhaps the society of the medieval west can be understood only if one shows how its material, social and political realities were penetrated by symbolism and the imaginary world. Only the study of how people represented themselves alongside the study of the way in which they thought and felt can allow us to understand this world which we lost not so very long ago and which still permeates our minds and our imaginations.

It really has to be noted here that Burke is a public devotee of Le Goff whereas Pierre Bourdieu, Roger Cartier and Peter Brown all have some reservations about what Le Goff had to say in terms of understanding history.

89. Stevenson, in Edel (ed.), *Cultural*, p. 13, using the ancient law text *Senchas Már*, asks,

The *Senchas* of the men of Ireland, what has sustained it? The joint memory of the old men, transmission from one ear to another, the chanting of the *filid*, supplementation from the law of the letter, strengthening from the law of nature, for these are the three rocks on which are based the judgement of the world.

and legal records.[90] Such history was learned and cultivated by a specific group, the *filid*, a word usually translated as 'poets'. These were the Bardic families in which the skills of the *filid*,[91] those keepers of the memory of the culture, were nurtured, and those who aspired to this learning underwent stern training in schools where the boys and young men learned to memorize, and to compose in a dark room lying on a couch without writing materials.[92] This lengthy training with its concomitant isolation from the community not only enhanced the vitality of the *senchas* but also prolonged the belief and the ennobling of the memory and imagination that was so much a part of the druidic tradition.

Hence the peculiar emphasis and focus of Irish history would explain why the monastic system with its powerful *Túatha*[93] identity resonated with these early Irish Christians. It was in the clan that the person received and developed a sense of personal identity. When he entered a monastic settlement, a similar sense of identity as a member of a Christian/monastic clan was inculcated. The predominantly oral, druidic tradition of education emphasizing the affective (poetic) as opposed to the cognitive illustrates the approach to scriptural exegesis. That Irish monasticism did not develop a 'theology' of its own as understood in the systematic sense,[94] stems from this anthropology and related philosophic outlook.

---

90. The many *Annals* from which much of the early Irish history is culled, while contradictory in some instances, do attest to the very early recording of significant people and events in their history. The balance evident in these personalized histories suggests that society put much store on this personalized aspect of life; see also Finnane, 'Late Medieval', pp. 90–94, where she maintains that the study of law in early Ireland was always in the context of the study of history and poetry, such a study increased one's honour-price: 'The broader one's learning, the higher one's honour price.'

91. Carey, in Edel (ed.), *Cultural*, p. 46, comments: 'All of the past lives are in the minds of these masters of memory, and it is this possession that justifies their exalted status'; Stevenson, in Edel (ed.), *Cultural*, p. 16, makes the point that in contrast with druids, *filid* continue to flourish and to forge an excellent relationship of mature trust and understanding with the Christian Church.

92. Hughes, *The Early*, p. 3.

93. The *Paruchia*, distinctive in Irish monasticism, was evidence of this. The monastic leader or abbot was usually a member of the same clan as the Founder. In many cases it was the specific clan that endowed the monastery with the land. It is said that twelve of the earliest abbots of Iona were members of ColumCille's clan. The chart of these abbots and their relationship with the clan is in Appendix E. This issue is treated in the whole article by C. Etchingham, 'The Implications of Paruchia', *Eriu* 44 (1993) pp. 139–62 (xliv); R. Sharpe, 'Some Problems Concerning the Organisation of the Church in Early Medieval Ireland', *Peritia*, 3 (1984), pp. 230–70, also addressed the issue.

94. Bradshaw, 'The Wild,' p. 22, claims that the early Irish 'did not engage in formal theology, in structured inquiry, development analysis of the content of divine revelation, in systematising'; O'Donoghue, *The Mountain*, pp. 15–16, claims that 'the Celtic mind was neither discursive nor systematic. Yet in their lyrical speculation [they] brought the sublime unity of life and experience to expression.' Hughes, *The Church*, p. x comments on the Irish lack of formal theology in these terms: 'it is possible that the highly individual character of the early Irish Church

The Celtic Church and its Relationship with Irish Monasticism

If this pattern of monastic living was begun in the East in the early years of the Christian era and spread among diverse peoples, then what is so distinctive about the Irish form of monasticism?[95] To answer this with any degree of adequacy, one has first to look at the phenomenon called the Celtic Church for it is because of the peculiar socio-cultural system it gave birth to that Irish monastic development came to wield so much influence in the sixth to the eighth century, not only in Ireland but also on the continent when Columbanus embarked on his *peregrinatio pro Christo*. O'Donoghue maintains that Europe, from Charlemagne to the present day, rests squarely on the spiritual and cultural energy of Irish monasticism.[96] Being Irish he may be forgiven for claiming this, but exaggerated though this may sound, there maybe is a case to be made for the distinctive contribution made by the Irish monks on the continent even if only in the penitential changes that they initiated.

Here it is necessary to return to the concept of Celtic Church before discussing its nature and distinctiveness, as many historians hold that there is no such thing as a Celtic Church.[97] The ambiguities of the meaning of 'Celtic Church' have already been mentioned in the Introduction. Kenny sees the Irish Church as the quintessential Celtic Church[98] but with little justification. Stokes, besides making the unequivocal statement that 'Celtic Christianity was older and wider than its Irish form'[99] leaves a reader in no doubt that 'Celtic Christianity [was] prior to Patrick'.[100] Bieler differs from Stokes in that he holds

---

may have encouraged practical experiments, for though her clerics produced little speculative theology, she seems to have been distinguished by certain innovations in church discipline'. Chadwick, *The Celts*, p. 210, maintained that since their doctrines had never been called into question, the Irish writings would be primarily personal and not deeply concerned with theology or religious speculation for which she holds 'their facilities may have been limited'. G. V. Murphy, 'The Place of John Eriugena in the Irish Learning Tradition', *JMS* 14 (Advent, 1983), pp. 93–107, takes issue with J. F. Kelly in P. NiChathain and M. Richter, *Ireland and Europe in the Middle Ages* (Stuttgart: Klett-Cotta, 1st edn, 1982), p. 552, about his contention of conservatism in Irish learning. He holds that it is possible to propose an unorthodox and eclectic learning in Ireland but he concludes that it is not so easy to discern a tradition of speculation. He goes on to state, as does Kelly, that 'another uniquely Irish source was imagination', for they constantly fill in gaps in texts – hence the creative glosses. However, Murphy concludes that such creativity would surely lend itself to speculation. Later in the article, p. 97, he contends that there could be a speculative philosophic tradition in early Irish learning.

95. This comment does not ignore monasticism in major world religions, e.g., Buddhism, that pre-date Christianity. The tenets of monasticism are similar but are lived out within different cultures with the natural differences which, however, do not alter the basic monastic rationale.

96. O'Donoghue, *The Mountain*, p. 1.

97. Some of these authors have been discussed in the Introduction of this work.

98. Kenny, *Sources*, p. 156. See Richter, in Edel (ed.), *Cultural*, fn 38, for many references to the Celtic Church.

99. G. T. Stokes, *Ireland and the Celtic Church* (London: Hodder & Stoughton, 1886), p. 1.

100. Stokes, *Ireland*, p. 2.

that the designation Celtic Church is associated with a 'peculiar form of religious life and ecclesiastical organisation'.[101] Here he is in agreement with Nora Chadwick, who also identifies the Celtic Church with monasticism: 'Its place was taken in the sixth and seventh centuries by the "Celtic" Church, in which the diocese gave way to the federation of monastic communities, each with its *paruchia* under the supreme jurisdiction of the "heir" (*conarb*) of the founder-saint.'[102]

Meissner asks a similar question to the one posed at the beginning of this discussion of the Celtic and Irish Church. The answer he gives, while possibly not satisfying some historians, is worth referring to in passing. He deduces from his reading of the records of Patrick's life, '[that Patrick] was assisted in his mission in Ireland by many clergy from Gaul and from both the Romanised and Celtic-speaking districts of Britain'.[103] However, when they died and were not replaced,

> the Church of Ireland[104] was perforce left to herself during the earliest years of her existence, when she was totally unfit to govern herself, and was thus early cut off from the advice and guidance of Western Christendom [and so developed] that peculiar system known to us as Celtic Christianity; and when the darkness begins to lift from the history of early Irish Christianity, we find that the predominant influence in the Irish Church is that of the non-Romanised, Celtic-speaking districts of Britain.[105]

Is this perhaps why later at the Synod of Whitby in 664 CE the Roman Church, with Wilfrid as spokesperson, found the differences in *praxis* of the Celts, and specifically the Irish Church, so much a cause of disturbance?[106] Those who defended the Irish Church's date of celebrating Easter did so in view of the fact that the particular date was handed down to them from their ancestors, and

---

101. L. Bieler, 'The Christianization of the Insular Celts', *Celtica* 8 (1968), pp. 118–29 (122).

102. Chadwick, *The Celts*, p. 203.

103. Meissner, in W. A. Phillips (ed.), *The History of the Church in Ireland from the Earliest Times to the Present Day* (Vol. 1; London: H. Milford, 1933), p. 120.

104. To a modern reader this way of referring to the Church in Ireland may be confusing. The term *Church of Ireland* is used today to refer to the Anglican communion in Ireland, while the Church in Ireland means what it says: the Church on the island of Ireland. However, at the point in history under discussion, namely the sixth to the eighth century, there is no *Church of Ireland*, only the Church in Ireland.

105. Meissner, in Phillips, *The History*, p. 129. Moreover, the point that Meissner and many authors in this time, and even as early as Ussher, are endeavouring to make is that the modern Church of Ireland is in a direct line of descent with the original Celtic Church, founded by Patrick. F. Ó Briain, 'The Expansion of Irish Christianity to 1200: An Historiographical Survey', *IHR* Part 1, *IHS*, Vol. 3, 11 March (1943), pp. 131–63 (243), uses Meissner as an example of a researcher who failed in the heuristic stage of his work on double monasteries.

106. As this is not the place to go into details of the Synod of Whitby, suffice it to say that the theological and *praxis* difference that were discussed may have been more a matter of political differences between feuding kings in Britain, rather than a specifically religious matter. Smyth, in Edel (ed.), *Cultural*, p. 34, explains the dating of Easter, the most controversial aspect of the Whitby Synod discussion, in terms of the Irish notion of cosmology.

no Roman Church was as important to the Irish as were their ancestors.[107] In the 1920s Lucy Menzies,[108] writing about the life of ColumCille, prefers to use the term Columban Church specifically in relation to the above-mentioned Synod. It was the beliefs and *praxis* of the Church under the leadership of ColumCille on Iona that perpetuated and promulgated the practices that were the matter for discussion at Whitby: the Roman date of Easter was already being observed in parts of Ireland before the Synod.

In spite of the fact that there were contacts between the Church of Britain and the Roman Church as early as the Synod of Arles, 314 CE,[109] it is probably important to conclude with the comments of Hardinge, with which this writer is inclined to agree: 'Rome was ignorant of these differences till the opening decade of the seventh century. It seems reasonable that the Celts were also ignorant of the usages and beliefs of Roman Christians.'[110]

Writers of the calibre of Hughes down to the most recent, Sharpe, make clear that in the lands called Celtic, including Scotland, Ireland, Wales and Brittany, there was not one form of Church organization. Specifically Hughes asks in relation to the title Celtic Church:

> ... [it] must mean that the various branches of the Celtic Church had certain features in common – ideas like penance and pilgrimage, styles of building and carving and manuscripts illuminations, comparable libraries and intellectual training. Most obvious of all, they must have shared the same peculiar ecclesiastical organization, based on monastic *paruchia* – but did they?[111]

107. This is not to say that the Roman Church and the bishops of Rome were not much honoured and loved by the Irish Christians. Columbanus' letters to two popes, Gregory the Great and Boniface, and one pope-elect, written sometime after 591 CE when he arrived on the continent of Europe, attest to the Irish affection for the bishop of Rome. All his writings are to be found in G. S. M. Walker (ed.), Scriptores Latine Hiberniae: *Sancti Columbani* (Dublin: Institute for Advanced Studies, 1957). His final letter to Boniface specifically refers to the Irish, their orthodoxy and their relationship with the bishop of Rome thus:

> For all we Irish, inhabitants of the world's edge, are disciples of Saints Peter and Paul, and of all the disciples who wrote the sacred canon by the Holy Ghost and we accept nothing outside the evangelical and apostolic teaching; none has been a heretic; none a Judaiser, none a schismatic; but the Catholic Faith, as it was delivered by you first who are the successor of the holy apostles, is maintained unbroken. (p. 39)

And to the bishop of Rome himself, 'To the most fair Head of all the churches of the whole of Europe, the estimable Pope, the exalted Prelate, the Shepherd of Shepherds, the most revered bishop' (p. 37). See also P. Beresford-Ellis, *Celt and Saxon* (London: Constable, 1993), pp. 125–30; K. Hughes, in D. Dumville (ed.), *Church and Society in Ireland 400–1200* (London: Variorum Reprints, 1987), pp. 1–28.

108. L. Menzies, *St Columba: His Life, His Times and His Influence* (Felinfach: J. M. F. Books, facsimile reprint, 1992).

109. De Paor, *Patrick's*, p. 54 records the signatures of those attending the Synod, including bishop Eborius [Aeburius, Eburius, Euortius] of the city of York in the province of Britain; bishop Restitutus of the city of London in the above province; bishop Adlefius [Adelfus] of the city of Lincoln; also the priest Sacerdus [the bishop Sacerdos, the bishop Sacer] and the deacon Arminius [Menius]. Probably other bishops from Britain were also present at the Synod of Rimini summoned by Constantius in 359 CE.

110. L. Hardinge, *The Celtic Church in Britain* (London: SPCK, 1st edn, 1972), p. 28.

111. Hughes, in Dumville (ed.), *Church and Society*, p. 1.

Her answer is an unequivocal 'no'. For each of the Celtic regions, Irish, Scottish, Welsh and Breton manifested a distinctiveness that meant that while the theological orientation was similar the *praxis* was different. This can be illustrated by the fact that in the Welsh Church leadership was a socially sought-after lifestyle. Gildas maintains that Welsh bishops were not necessarily celibate and not the husband of one wife.

> They exercise hospitality, but their motives for doing so are wrong. They and the other clergy are worldly, attending public entertainments and story-telling. They do not know much about apostolic decrees; but they are exceedingly well-versed in secular affairs.[112]

It seems that only the Irish had a passionate devotion to the concept of pilgrimage as a form of mortification. In addition the notion of monastic *paruchia* seems to be peculiar to the Irish also. So while the Irish had elements in common with other Celtic peoples, the Irish Church and its monastic *paruchia* were sufficiently distinctive in their development and impact on Christianity to merit a specialist study.

Theology

Reference has been made earlier in this chapter to the fact that the Irish of this period did not have a theology in the sense that Christians in Antioch and Alexandria did. However, like all Christians they did have their beliefs and practices that arose from what could be called an all-pervasive belief structure. Both Mackey and O'Loughlin, among others, argue about whether this was a specifically Irish belief structure. Mackey claims that at its simplest the general theology of Celtic Christianity thinks of the divine being and act, the divine power and presence, 'flowing in and through what can only be described as an extended family'.[113] Mary, he claims, is the person through whom this divine power flows. But not only through her. He goes on to list other channels of the divine such as angels, 'the great holy men and women of the Celtic Christian Community, the sacral kings and right down to the natural elements'.[114] Like the Celtic notion of history, theology too is strongly linked to persons: it is a very concretely mediated divine presence.[115]

---

112. Hughes, in Dumville (ed.), *Church and Society*, p. 3.
113. Mackey, in Davies, *Celtic*, preface, p. xvii.
114. Mackey, in Davies, *Celtic*, p. xviii.
115. Mackey, in Davies, *Celtic*, p. xviii, would try to defend the Celts from the charge of magic in their invocations, springing from the immediacy of the divine by saying that

> it [magic] is the mentality that invokes the power immanent in creatures and uses the corresponding prayer, particularly in its ritual forms as if that power could be automatically activated. It is against this mentality that thereby attempts to bypass God's gracious will and thus in effect treats the immanent power as other than the free creative grace of the one true God.

Sometimes such a charge is levelled at the stories of the *Vitae* treated in chapters 4 and 5 of this work. In the light of the *intentionality* treated in this chapter, this claim cannot be sustained.

Theology has been described as 'the ordered effort to bring our experience of God to the level of intelligent expression'.[116] It has also been spoken of many centuries ago by St Anselm as 'faith seeking understanding'. However neither of these definitions specifically mentions the role of culture in theology. Today, words like 'enculturation', 'inculturation', 'contextualization' and 'indigenization' have become commonplace in discussing the nature of theology due to the recent appreciation of the origin, nature and functioning of culture in society. Thus we now have emerging feminist, eco, buffalo, black, African, dalit, Han and many other kinds of theology, all of which reflect local culture. Lonergan highlights the importance of culture in his definition of theology thus: '[theology] is what mediates between a cultural matrix and the significant role of religion in that matrix . . . [it] is the way religion makes sense within a particular culture'.[117]

The inculturation principle, to which Lonergan refers, states that Christianity, like most other religions, inevitably influences the shape of the culture in which it is born or to which it travels.[118] But the local culture also influences Christianity. There is thus a symbiotic process, a two-way movement of influences between culture and religions. Some of the Irish literature bears this out:

> I'd like to give a lake of beer to God
> I'd love the heavenly
> Host to be tippling there
> For all eternity.
> I'd sit with the men, the women of God
> There by the lake of beer.
> We'd be drinking good health forever
> And every drop would be a prayer[119]

So the Celts seem to have developed a thoroughly this-worldly theology because of the pre-existing religious culture. This intimate relationship between culture and religion underscores the importance of coming to grips with the cultural context of sixth- to eighth-century Irish monasticism in order to appreciate better why the practices of the monks not only attracted so many aspirants but persisted for so many centuries.

Of its very nature theology presupposes a belief in God who, as creator of all, is in control. This statement in no way denies the existence of freedom in the human person. It simply makes the point that theology has to do with God and how the human person perceives the relationship between the self on the one hand and God, others and the material world on the other. Alternatively, it embraces the human response to an experienced awareness of God. This

---

116. R. McBrien, *Catholicism* (San Francisco: Harper and Rowe, 1st edn, 1981), p. 1258.
117. Lonergan, in Bevans, *Models*, p. 5.
118. Mackey, in Davies, *Celtic*, p. xix.
119. There are many translations of this poem, attributed to St Brigit, but this one is from *Love of Ireland – Poems from the Irish*, translated by B. Kennelly, used on a CD *Vox de Nube*, Glenstal Monks, Gael-linn, Merrion Square, Dublin, 1989.

experience is either affective or intellectualized, both of which dictate that we behave in a particular way that emerges from our understating of the truth of ourselves and the corresponding understanding of the truth of who God is for the human person. Therefore the primary environment of Christian theology is the world of human truth and human love, both of which are seen manifested in the chapters on monasticism and penitentials where profoundly human persons strive to respond to the *evangelium* within the truth of who they are and drawn on by the love they have both for the deity and sustainer of human existence and humankind itself.

More specifically, theology can be described as a study of God. Given the nature of God this study for Christians is focused on Jesus, God incarnate as he is manifested in the Gospels: the Christian *evangelium*. This understanding of theology is concerned with the divine activity in history or more particularly with the person of Jesus Christ rather than a revelation of ideas.[120] This approach seems to capture a 'down-to-earthness' in theology. While not dismissing the transcendent nature of the divine it somehow takes seriously the reality of God becoming man in what is properly called incarnational theology. Moreover, unlike the theology of Barth centuries later, it seems not to be overawed by the finiteness of the human in the presence of the divine. This emphasis on a relationship with the divine makes it possible to live with the awesomeness and immanence simultaneously. Hence the emphasis on the *praxis* of Irish monasticism which manifested this relational quality of their theology.

Theology further, in a second-step process, reflects on the lived experience of faith and so interprets, mediates and translates the experience into an intelligent and systematic articulation of human experience about God and the Kingdom of God. This articulation seeks to clarify this understanding about God and the Kingdom and its implications for the person's response to life in a Christian milieu. Theology therefore is primarily concerned with giving lived expression to a mystery which essentially cannot be fully understood or adequately expressed in human language. Theology neither seeks to contain the mystery, nor to replace it, but it attempts to move people into an experience of the truth it contains. In this sense it has an educative and even a prophetic function and acts as a channel aiding the movement between Christian faith and life. Christian faith and its lived expression in both theology and life are inextricably linked. In Irish monasticism this link is clearly evident in the practice of asceticism. O'Loughlin correctly maintains that the Christianity which developed in Celtic countries during the early Middle Ages 'is characterised by a strongly incarnational theology, with an emphasis in diverse ways on physicality and materiality that supports both asceticism and sacramentality'.[121]

---

120. O'Loughlin, 'Theologians', p. 30.
121. O'Loughlin, in Davies, *Celtic*, p. 11. The poem quoted above could also be an example of the materiality and this-worldly theology that underpins the *praxis* of the period under discussion.

Asceticism

An indispensable component of the monastic lifestyle, nay the rationale for this way of living the *evangelium*, is to be found in the practice of asceticism or *ascesis*. Brown speaks about asceticism in the life of the holy man (referring specifically to Syria in late antiquity) as being 'marked by so many histrionic feats of self-mortification that it is easy, at first sight, to miss the deep social significance of asceticism as a long drawn-out, solemn ritual of dissociation – of becoming the total stranger'.[122] While there is something of this social significance in Celtic asceticism, many students of asceticism would not go to the extent of calling it, 'becoming the total stranger', for the purpose of Celtic asceticism was the transformation of the inner energy of self-denial to a higher level of energy to be used in the service of others. Later, Brown puts forward another function of asceticism: 'the holy man wielded the harsh surgery of the ascetic . . . renunciation of the world: for many, total death to the world was regarded as the only remedy for sin'.[123] Fundamentally the word, taken from the Greek *askesis*, means a form of exercise or training: it was initially associated with the training required for athletic performance.[124] Implicit in this is the contention that the athlete has a goal in mind, is committed to the exercises and is willing to engage in them for the sake of the goal. Its Christian usage stems from Paul who says he trains his body for the 'Christian warfare' against the powers of darkness.[125] Dodds refers to the Greek meaning of the word, asceticism, as stemming from hatred of the body. He claims that there were other motives for *askesis* not associated with body-hatred. These were: as a means of ritual purity (usually temporarily); as a means of strengthening one's *mana*; as an exercise to fortify the will.[126] The driving force of asceticism, according to Chadwick, is 'a renunciation of success in this world'.[127] On whose terms is success evaluated? Is it in the sense of a successful business, a successful profession, or a successful marriage? This way of defining asceticism hardly seems appropriate as a way of understanding the motive for such a lifestyle as witnessed in the centuries of monasticism's growth and spread. A more appropriated way of coming to grips with this term and more in accord with its original Greek meaning is as 'an exercise undertaken to live the Gospel more faithfully'.[128]

Asceticism then, in this context, applies to the exercises that a person performs in order to become more like the God who is perceived to be in relationship with each person. In terms of the preceding definition of *askesis*, the goal of the

122. Brown, *Society*, p. 131.
123. Brown, *Society*, p. 145.
124. Dodds, *Pagan*, p. 30 fn 1. The Latin form of *ascesis* is the one adopted by most writers on ethics and moral theology in the Roman Catholic tradition. Scripture references include: 1 Cor. 9:24–27; 2 Tim. 4:7; Acts 24:16.
125. Paul, 1 Cor. 9:24–27 *Jerusalem Bible* (London: Darton, Longman & Todd, 1966), p. 221.
126. Dodds, *Pagan*, p. 30.
127. H. Chadwick, 'The Ascetic Ideal', *SCH* 22 (1984–85), pp. 1–23 (2).
128. McBrien, *Catholicism*, p. 1258.

exercises is a closer relationship with God. The assumption is that the person performing the exercises is a willing participant, otherwise the exercises are simply punishment of self for no valid reason.[129] The juxtapositioning of bodily taming and asceticism, though often evident during a superficial reading of the texts to be addressed in future chapters, is not necessarily a part of the understanding of Celtic asceticism. O'Loughlin maintains that,

> Running through a number of the texts (for the sixth to the eighth century, concentrating on Irish and Welsh) is the awareness of the body as the focus of human existence, not subordinate to the mind in a tortuous relation of subjection and culpability, but thematised as the locus of penance, where penance itself is not self-inflicted mutilation but the reception of new life and the beginning of the transformation that leads to glory.[130]

He quotes a poem from the Welsh tradition, the *Loves of Taliesin*, which exemplifies this notion of penance leading to glory:

> The beauty of the virtue in doing penance for excess,
> Beautiful too that God shall save me,
> The beauty of a companion who does not deny me his company,
> Beautiful too the drinking horn's society
> (other beauties are specified).
> Beautiful too doing penance for sin.
> But the loveliest of all is covenant
> With God on the Day of Judgment.[131]

Unlike the metaphysical asceticism of the early, highly Origenist monastic texts of the East, which in many instances were influential in the Celtic lands, the Celtic monks enjoyed what O'Loughlin calls 'a monastic environment rich with heroic values within a straightforward asceticism more congenial than the philosophical abstractions of Hellenistic theology'.[132]

So it is these exercises explicitly enjoined by the founders of monastic institutions, and undertaken by those who choose to live according to a monastic rule, that are part of the subject of this study. The performance of these exercises and the wholehearted dedication to their practice in part constitute the radicality of

---

129. An underlying assumption is that the person so engaged in ascetical practices is not part of the Manichean brotherhood who sees the human person as bad and in need of punishment almost regardless of its possible detrimental effects. In medieval terms they are a pathology and a distortion of the reality of the human person who needs to attend to aspects of self that are non-material. They have to do with the notion of psychic energy, to use a modern concept. St Augustine was tainted with this theology of the person for some time in his life. His development of the theory of Original Sin, formulated over against what he perceived as the Pelagian 'heresy', can be seen in this light.

130. O'Loughlin, in Davies, *Celtic*, p. 24.

131. O'Loughlin, in Davies, *Celtic*, p. 283. Excerpts from *Celtic Spirituality*, from *The Classics of Western Spirituality*, translated and introduced by Oliver Davies, with the collaboration of Thomas O'Loughlin, Copyright © 1999 by Oliver Davies, Paulist Press, Inc., New York/Mahwah, NJ. Used with permission of Paulist Press, *www.paulistpress.com*.

132. O'Loughlin, in Davies, *Celtic*, p. 14.

the way of living the call to discipleship. These exercises, to a later observer, can be inadequately and even wrongly evaluated. They have been seen as harsh, inhuman and, when read with a later twentieth-century mentality, destructive of the human person. Even within the ideal situation of monasticism there was still room for abuse, but this was not the ideal for which the exercises were intended. The ideal was to transform the energy of discipline to a higher order of energy. Anyone who understands that kind of energy, especially the spiritual kind, knows that it is never lost but can be transformed and put to another use.[133] It is in this understanding that one can say the persons entering into the ascetical life sought transformation into their better selves. What this study intends to show is that, given an aware and willing espousal by monastic practitioners, the inner transformation is effected. Its import is evident in the transformation of Europe from the incorrectly called Dark Ages to the Golden Age of Medieval Christianity.[134]

The inner transformation that such practices are designed to bring about in the person who willingly enters into such a lifestyle is the goal of monastic life. An assumption in all this is that a pre-existing religious faith is necessary for such a lifestyle to bring about the desired result. If Cote's iceberg image has any validity, then the upper layers of behaviour/*praxis* of the Irish monastic culture manifest the deeply held values and myths[135] of the culture. That they are radical vis-à-vis the general response of most Christians to the *evangel* is the contention of this work. But how is radicality understood in this context?

Radicality

Etymologically the word is interesting. Its meaning ranges from 'free-floating' in regard to atoms, to 'excessive', 'fundamental', 'wholly', 'non-conformist', 'original', 'inborn' and 'enthusiast'. One need not take each word and try to make the point that the Irish *praxis* of the period under discussion embodied each. However, a link can be tentatively made between the word 'excessive' and the way in which some observers saw the penitential practices. 'Non-conformist' is certainly how the Roman authorities saw the Irish, particularly in relation to the issues discussed at the Synod of Whitby. 'Original', 'creative' and 'enthusiastic' could be applied to how the sources reveal the lives and lifestyle of many of the predecessors of the Irish who flocked to the monasteries in the early stages of the Christianization of the island. Their extant manuscripts, the literary glosses that contain their theology, undoubtedly could also be designated 'original' and 'creative'.

133. E. Kennedy, *Tomorrow's Catholics Yesterday's Church: The Two Cultures of American Catholics* (Missouri: Ligouri, 1995), p. 164.

134. This is not said by way of idealizing these people or their impact on Europe in unawareness of the very human limitations they displayed. Aspects of the limitations of both ColumCille and Columbanus are addressed in chapters 4 and 5.

135. Myths correctly understood as those stories of the culture that contain deep truths with universal meaning and significance.

Rahner[136] uses the word radical often in his chapter on guilt. His meanings can be summed up as 'a very immediate way and at a clear and tangible level of consciousness;'[137] 'radical partnership with and immediacy to God in what we call grace and God's self-communication;'[138] freedom he calls radical in that it is 'the capacity to do something final and definitive;'[139] he also speaks about the 'radical importance of freedom'[140] and 'the real message of Christianity as the radical interpretation of the subjective experience of freedom'.[141] It seems from the above that inherent in his use of the word is the consciousness of the person and the freedom of the person to act. He also seems to be saying that intrinsic to radicality is the awareness of the gulf between the transcendent Other and the limited and finite human person. So radical in this sense implies that in responding to the call to live the Christian life there has to be awareness and freedom. There is also a presumption of faith and some concept of the greatness of the divine being and the fallibility of the human person. Radicality then may be seen as the response of interiorization of the *evangelium* as it has been heard and allowed to interact with the deepest values of the person within a particular culture. So using radical here does not imply that other cultural responses to Christianity were not radical. It simply states that the Irish response was made by aware persons acting faithfully to their culture with a freedom and finality which bore fruit over a period of centuries. Later, in the discussion of the monastic rules and penitentials the texts will reveal that those who became monks did so freely and ever conscious of their own limitations. Nevertheless, relying on the all-powerful God, they embarked on the pilgrimage which was truly *peregrinatio pro Christo*. All of the above facets of radicality will be shown to be present in the discussion of the four primary texts to be used in the remainder of this work.

This conformity of a culture (Irish in this context) however, can be said of all cultures that embraced the monastic form of Christianity in the early days of its evangelization. What was distinctive about the Irish response to this call? The previous discussion in this chapter has highlighted the aspects (e.g., a singularly Irish understanding of history and the role of the sea in Celtic consciousness) that are seen, among many others, to be peculiarly Celtic/Irish. They will be explored in future chapters in some primary texts to see if there is any substantial evidence for their presence in these texts. So the radicality used here is making the modest claim that these dimensions of the Celtic/Irish psyche, if manifested in the selected texts, can validate the claim that the Irish response to the call of the *evangelium*, while employing some of the universal behaviours of the monastic life, are sufficiently different to allow one to speak of a singular and radical Irish response.

136. K. Rahner, *Foundations of Christian Faith: An Inroduction to the Idea of Christianity* (London: Darton, Longman and Todd, 1978).
137. Rahner, *Foundations*, p. 91.
138. Rahner, *Foundations*, p. 93.
139. Rahner, *Foundations*, p. 95.
140. Rahner, *Foundations*, p. 105.
141. Rahner, *Foundations*, p. 105.

Another dimension of this radicality is that the response of those who called themselves 'religious' was markedly different from those who lived within the monastic enclosure but were not called 'religious'.[142] That this response was striking and noteworthy seems to be attested to by historians, theologians, sociologists, linguists and modern-day researchers. Particularly in its penitential reforms, taken to the continent in the latter part of the sixth century by Columbanus, the Irish Church can claim to have introduced a unique form of penitential practice which of itself would give it a claim to having made a valuable and influential contribution to the life of the Church in the sixth century. It was valuable in that it enabled people to form a relationship with God not based on fear of public exposure for human failings. It was influential in the sense that the Universal Church later adopted the practice. This contribution towards a private form of penance stems from the distinctive role of the *anamchara* in Irish monastic life. Each monk had a soul-friend, *anamchara*, to whom he went for counsel. This interaction, at times, included discussion of the monk's failings and the imposition of a penance. So the beginnings of private 'confession' as opposed to 'public confession' can be seen as making a substantial contribution to the inner life of the early Irish Church and indeed later to the Universal Church.

Response to the *evangelium*, then, is basic to the following discussion of the rules, penitentials and lives of the two saints treated in this study. Each cultural form of Christian monasticism, Egyptian, Basilian, Russian, Benedictine, has shown this. All share a common apprehension: the role of prayer, of asceticism, of service, of work, of silence as conducive to intimate dialogue with God. Work, being another form of prayer, has a unique transformative energy. That is why it is seen, in the Irish monastic rules, as an integral part of asceticism.

The practices of asceticism in the monastic context and from an ordinary human viewpoint include prayer, corporal penances and silence, all of which need to be rationalized. Earlier, O'Loughlin reminded us of the valuable understanding of the body as the locus of penance and not as something needing to be tamed. The forms of this corporal penance were threefold: fasting, ascetic immersion and pilgrimage. Fasting was undertaken on Wednesdays and Fridays and to show how intrinsic to the culture was the notion of fasting, the Gaelic words for these days point to fasting: *cétáin* meaning 'first fast' was the word for Wednesday and *âin diden* meaning 'last fast' was the word for Friday.[143] *Betha Máedoc Ferna* reminds a reader that fasting was also used by couples wanting a child.[144] Elsewhere in the sages it was seen as a way of humiliating an opponent or enemy as the offended one would fast publicly outside the

---

142. The composition of monastic enclosures is discussed in the chapter on monasticism. The designation monk is different from the accepted understanding and is also discussed later. How the word 'religious' is used in this work is also discussed in the chapter on monasticism.
143. W. Stokes and J. Strachan, *Thesaurus Palaeohibernicus*, Vol. 2 (Cambridge: University Press, 1st edn, 1903), 1 4, 11 32; L. Gougaud, *Devotional and Ascetic Practices in the Middle Ages* (London: Burns Oates and Washbourne Ltd, 1st edn, 1927), p. 147.
144. Gougaud, *Devotional*, p. 152.

opponent's house. The law books gave many cases of this practice and how it affected the punishments stipulated. More serious punishments were imposed if the fasting person died while performing the fast. Another form of maceration was ascetic immersion. The lives of saints attest to the almost universal practice of this form of penance. In the *Vita Brigidae* we are reminded that God did not wish such a penance, so in order to prevent Brigit from her daily ritual he dried up the pool.[145]

So fasting and other monastic ascetic practices can be apprehended as a form of spiritual work. By the law of the known universe, work, as understood in the science of physics, transforms energy from one form or manifestation to another. By a perceived analogue psychic energy operates similarly, its driving motor being *intentionality*. Whoever consciously *intends* good achieves good. In the world's mystery, and as yet only dimly understood, this is perceived in the struggle between good and evil, between positive and negative powers and between constructive and destructive initiatives. We do not understand the ultimate dimensions of these forces but are caught up in them. In this lies our need for salvation, our preservation from evil. So the many and varied macerations of Irish monasticism were part of this attempt to facilitate the triumph of good in the human person.

Conclusion

As Hollis claims in relation to the conversionary dynamic, the 'localisation of Christianity cannot be carried out effectively without reference to traditional religiosity'[146] and the added claim of the foregoing discussion is that not only the religiosity but the whole content of the culture (of which religiosity is a part) of a group must be taken into consideration. So the previous discussion has traced some of the elements of the cultural context of pre-Christian Ireland and through reference to sagas, law-texts, archaeology, poetry, art has made the point that when Christianity came to Ireland (and the debate is still going on about by whom and when this occurred), it was these cultural aspects that acted as the tree on to which the incoming Christianity was grafted. The distinctive aspects of Irish society – the tribal kingship, the place of the druids, the honoured role of the poet as a class, nature and its formative place in the culture – all shaped the way Christianity integrated into the pre-Christian culture.

Celtic consciousness dictated that what emerged after the Christianizing of the Irish was singularly different from other forms of Christianity. Unlike the Roman Christians of the time, the Irish Christians did not succumb to the duality of the philosophies of the East. Their metaphorical mindset indicated that rather than a rational approach to what they heard as the *evangelium*, they made a poetic, imaginative and creative response. Their God-awareness arose from their pre-Christian consciousness of the divine being in the created world.

---

145. Though one of the earlier Lives gives this story, Cogitosus' most ancient *Life* does not.
146. Hollis, *Anglo-Saxon*, p. 16.

So the Christian doctrine of the Incarnation, God present in the person of Jesus, seemed natural to them. The dichotomy of 'letter' and 'spirit' never entered their awareness. They lived within such closeness to the Otherworld that the dead and spirits were their constant companions.

The Irish notion of history was congruent with the emphasis on the individual in the society. However, it also had to be understood within the all-pervading understanding of *Túatha*, clan. It was clearly associated with ancestry and was allied with the poet tradition. These *filid* were the keepers of the stories of the group. They had an honoured place in society. But this society was within a particular era and context, so any reading of history had to take into consideration this important aspect of Irish society. Theology itself was also influenced by and influenced the reading of history.

One distinctive aspect of the emergence of Christianity in Ireland of the sixth to the eighth century was the monastic nature of the Church. It has been said that the Celtic Church was distinguished by its monastic structure. During the formative stages of Patrick's time a diocesan structure was paramount but later the distinctive structure of the monastic *paruchia* emerged as more in keeping with the rural and clan roots of the society. It was in the strength of the monastic founders that the different notion of history was evident. The Irish saw history as 'old tales' and applying to genealogy, place-names, legends and legal records. Another aspect of it was its emphasis on individuals and experience. Sometimes these individuals were unique in that their lives, as recorded for posterity in *Vitae*, were unbelievable by modern standards. They apparently allowed themselves to be governed by their dreams and performed miracles which were meant to inspire those who read about them. Hence the central place in this monastic tradition of the founders of the *paruchia*. They not only wrote the rules and penitentials that are the matter for discussion of chapters 2 and 3, but their tribal or clan group gave the lands on which the monasteries were established. In some cases, especially Iona, the leadership of the monastery for at least the first ten abbots rested with members of the clan that bequeathed the land.

Though the Irish of the period under discussion did not develop a 'theology' in any systematic sense they did have a belief structure and a religious sense which was distinctive. Mackey refers to the general theology of the Irish as that of an extended family with the divine being and act as central to it. He then sees this action being transmitted through a series of levels with Mary first, then angels, holy women and men and finally created things being conduits through which this divine being communicated with human persons.[147] He calls it a very concretely mediated divine presence. If all aspects of the society are the matter of culture then theology also manifests some aspects of the society in which it is functioning. Other writers have claimed that Irish theology of this period is very this-worldly. O'Loughlin specifies what this means when he says it emphasizes physicality, materiality and supports sacramentality and asceticism.[148]

147. Mackey in Davies, *Celtic*, p. xviii.
148. O'Loughlin in Davies, *Celtic*, p. 11.

Monastic asceticism in the Irish tradition was not unlike its Eastern forebears in the fundamental tenets, but was coloured by the distinct culture of its pre-Christian influence. It sought through intentionally disciplined human urges to place the resulting 'spiritual energy'[149] at the service of good. Paul strongly advocated this very form of energy transference when he challenged the Corinthians to discipline the body and bring it into subjection so that it may win the crown of glory. As will be discussed in the chapter on the Irish penitentials, this employing of the principle of *contraries*, borrowed from Cassian, uses the energy of apparent negation to bring about a positive energy which can be used in the service of others.

Where Irish asceticism differed from other forms of monastic discipline is in its understanding of the body. O'Loughlin claims from the texts of this period that the body is the focus of human existence and as such is 'not subordinate to the mind in a tortuous relation of subjection'.[150] He sees is as the 'locus of penance, where penance itself is not self-inflicted mutilation'. Far from being merely the mortal shell for the soul, the body has the honoured role of being the instrument that beckons the person on a journey of 'transformation that leads to glory'.[151]

The radicality of sixth- to eighth-century Irish monastics is a product both of their cultural milieu and a concomitant of the initial response to the *evangelium* as they heard it, filtered as it was from the East, through the Gaul of Martin of Tours. Particularly in its penitential reforms, stemming from the distinctively Celtic/Irish practice of the *anamchara* relationship, can the Irish monastic tradition claim to have made a valuable and influential contribution to the life of the Church. The radicality can also be understood as the difference between religious and lay responses to the *evangelium*. It can be understood in the light of the initial acceptance by the monastic novice of a lifestyle that attempts to answer deeply felt universal questions and desires.

So it was with the founders of Irish monasticism of the sixth to the eighth century. From deep within their Celtic cultural consciousness they took up the challenge of the *evangelium* and founded many monasteries in their native Ireland. They set out rules of life that were in keeping with their Celtic consciousness and within the genre prevalent at the time. These monastic rules were to enhance their response to the message of the gospel. In order to tame self-centred natural instincts the founders set out penitential practices that drew on the wisdom of the Pythagoreans and they elevated the medieval notion of *contraries* to the spiritual domain. They set out on what was uniquely

---

149. Green, in Edel (ed.), *Cultural*, p. 129, says that intrinsic to pagan Celtic religion was their belief in the omnipresence of gods; thus they were surrounded by supernatural energy which could do humankind good or evil and thus needed to be controlled or neutralized. This controlling is seen in the lives of the *Irish Thaumaturges*; 'controlling' in the sense that their miracles manifested their control of the forces of nature and also in the power they displayed in getting God 'on-side'. All this is seen, in the eyes of their followers and later devotees, to be a result of their closeness to God.
150. O'Loughlin, in Davies, *Celtic*, p. 24.
151. O'Loughlin, in Davies, *Celtic*, p. 24.

called *peregrinatio pro Christo* and set aflame the continent of Europe with a commitment to living the *evangelium* that lasted for centuries and gave rise to an age labelled the Golden Age of Monasticism. Because of the nature of human beings only other persons can inspire them to such lifestyle commitments. The lives of ColumCille and Columbanus will be explored to see how they manifest this same Celtic consciousness, using the *Vita* of ColumCille and the Sermons of Columbanus.

2 THE ASCETICAL THEOLOGY AND PRAXIS OF THE EARLY IRISH PENITENTIALS

The penitential literature is in truth a deplorable feature of the medieval Church. Evil deeds, the imagination of which may perhaps have dimly floated through our minds in our darkest moments, are here tabulated and reduced to a system. It is hard to see how anyone could busy himself with such literature and not be the worse for it.[1]

Introduction

In this chapter we are dealing with a select number of the Irish penitentials and two other primary sources, the *First Synod of Patrick* and the *Canones Hibernenses*,[2] that resemble penitentials. The penitentials utilized are those of Vinnian, Columbanus and Cummean. The aim of the chapter is to describe and analyse the ascetical theology that underpins these primary sources and the *praxis* that flowed from this theology. However, it is important first to make some general comments on differing assessments of the penitentials, the origins and their relationship to druidism. Next their connection with ancient Brehon law will be addressed. This will be followed by a discussion of the purpose of the penitentials and how this is evident in the documents being treated in this chapter.

In the ecclesiastical legislation of the Irish Church in the Old Irish period[3] there were three sets of documents: first, the *canons*[4] were promulgated by synods of the sixth to the seventh century and can be used to elucidate some fundamental facets of Irish ecclesiastical history during the period of its rapid

---

1. Plummer, in J. T. McNeill and H. Gamer, *Medieval Handbooks of Penance* (New York: Octagon Books, 2nd edn, 1965), p. 47.
2. The debate about dates, language, which was the original penitential text and the degree to which each borrowed from the other is acknowledged but will not be entered into as scholars of the calibre of Kenney, Bieler, Binchy, McNeill and Gamer, Watkins, Oakley, Hughes and most recently Connolly have done that hard work.
3. There are two periods called Old Irish and Middle Irish relating to texts. The Old Irish texts were based on canon law, according to Kelly, *A Guide*, p. 233.
4. These are called *Canones Hibernenses* and *Collectio Canonum Hibernensis*. The former, synodal decrees in Latin include regulations relating to penance, as well as canons and secular laws. The latter is based chiefly on biblical and patristic sources, but also contains elements of native Irish legal tradition.

development.⁵ Second, the *cana*, generally attributed to particular saints (the Law of Sunday was an exception) were about keeping peace and order and protecting non-combatants from violence. A gloss puts it this way: 'The four chief laws of Ireland, the law of Patrick, and of Daire and of Adomnan and of Sunday. The law of Patrick,⁶ now, not to slay clerics; the law of Daire, not to steal cattle; of Adomnan,⁷ not to slay women; of Sunday, not to travel.'⁸ Third, the penitentials, sixth- and seventh-century documents, were written in Latin and on a superficial level were seen as being used for assigning penances to particular sins. That they have another more complex purpose is part of the contention of this chapter. Since all three sets of documents were being codified contemporaneously they were seen as a support for each other.⁹

This present work is concerned only with the two primary sources and penitentials specified above and how they were extensively used in the monasteries of Ireland, Britain and on the continent when Columbanus left Ireland in the sixth century. Given that the aim of monastic living was to transform selfish human tendencies, by way of prayer, the practice of Christian virtues and self-denial, into spiritual energy to be used in the service of God and others, the penitentials were obviously an integral part of this commitment. They became an equally integral part of the development and practice of private penance.

Negative and Positive Assessment of Penitentials

McNeill, among others, appears to use the opening comment above from Plummer to justify the negative press the penitentials have had, in popular perception, throughout history. Nora Chadwick also sees them as less than positive and she seems to have grave doubts about the authenticity of the cases cited. She comments: 'we may be sure that many of these cases are the webs spun in the casuistry of the monkish brain . . . thought up in the cloister by the tortuous intellect of the clerical scribe'.¹⁰ However, McNeill does make the point that 'but for these crude instruments of discipline it is very questionable whether we should have reached the stage of Victorian culture and restraint which makes it possible for Dr Plummer to utter this verdict'.¹¹

5. Hughes, *Early Christian*, p. 67. One of these canons will be treated later in this chapter.
6. In the *AU* the record for the year 736 states, *Lex Patricii tenuit Hiberniam*, the law of Patrick took effect in Ireland.
7. The reader is referred to a comment about the *Cáin Adamnáin* in chapter 1, fn 37.
8. Stokes and Strachan, *Thesaurus*, p. 306; Hughes, *Early Christian*, pp. 80–82, treats these *cana* and addresses the vexed nature of their function.
9. Hughes, *Early Christian*, p. 86, holds that the penitentials would have supported the secular law, implying that the secular law tracts were written before or concurrently with the penitentials. The secular laws were actually being codified in the Celtic and Germanic world at the same time as the penitentials were being developed, according to McNeill and Gamer, *Medieval Handbooks*, p. 37.
10. Chadwick, *The Age*, p. 148.
11. McNeill and Gamer, *Medieval Handbooks*, p. 47.

Hughes on the other hand, while acknowledging that Plummer is a great historian, does not agree with him in his appraisal, and moreover she does 'not think that the penitentials are likely to have a morally harmful influence on anyone'.[12] Charles-Edwards makes the point that 'the penitentials make rather depressing reading, yet their desire to prescribe a penance for each and every shameful deed is only a consequence of the wish to show that no sin is so terrible or so despicable that it is beyond the mercy of God'.[13] Unlike some more contemporary readers Hughes thinks of them as 'possibly extremely boring'.[14] If the sins catalogued in the various penitentials are a true record of people's behaviour, then they do not paint a very pleasant picture of society in the sixth to the eighth century, both on the continent and in Britain and Ireland.[15] McNeill does not believe that the writers of these penitential books invented the sins so listed.[16] Besides, social historians and the Irish epics would give evidence for the savagery and brutality that marked this period of history.[17] Eion MacNeill, however, cautions those who would talk simplistically about civilization and barbarism or brutality when he says:

> Civilisation and barbarism are matters of degree ... Men are barbarous in the degree to which they are dominated by their non-human natural surroundings, and are civilized in the degree to which they succeed in dominating these, including among these all that lower nature within themselves that men have in common with animals. A wholly barbarous man or society has yet to be discovered and some degree of barbarism, with the seeds of more, is always present in the most complete civilization.[18]

Defective as the penitentials are when viewed from the standpoint of modern ideals, a sound historical judgement will ascribe to them a civilizing and humanizing role of no small importance.[19]

---

12. Hughes, *Early Christian*, p. 84.
13. T. Charles-Edwartds in J. Blair and R. Sharpe (eds), *Pastoral Care Before the Parish* (London: Leicester University Press, 1992), p. 74.
14. Hughes, *Early Christian*, p. 84.
15. A reader of an earlier draft commented that there could be another possibility regarding the list of sins: they may have been included to cover every possible case even if it never happened. This is not 'fabrication' as some people may think. It is considering hypothetical cases. Educational institutions still set such cases for discussion in moral theology, in counselling courses and pastoral training.
16. McNeill and Gamer, *Medieval Handbooks*, p. 21.
17. Among many works, the following treat this aspect of Celtic society: C. Eluere, *The Celts First Masters of Europe* (London: Thames and Hudson, 1st edn, 1993), using primary historical documents stresses the warrior nature of the Celts; S. James, *Exploring the World of the Celts* (London: Thames and Hudson, 1993); H. Hubert, *The History of the Celtic People* (London: Bracken Books, 1993). Both the Sagas and general mythology of these people also provide evidence of this aspect of society as does J. Markale, *The Celts: Uncovering the Mythic and Historic Origins of Western Culture* (Vermont: Inner Traditional International, 1st edn, 1978); M. Green, *The Gods of the Celts* (Avon: The Bath Press, 1993); T. W. Rolleston, *Myths and Legends of the Celtic Race* (London: Constable, 1986). Sharpe (ed.), *Adomnán*, p. 300.
18. E. MacNeill, *Early Irish Laws and Institutions* (Dublin: Burns Oates and Washborne Ltd, 1935), p. 48.
19. McNeill and Gamer, *Medieval Handbooks*, p. 47.

Unlike Plummer, McNeill sees the penitentials in a far more positive light: he sees them as the intimate revelations of man and society as it struggles with life, and of the attempts by monastic and ecclesiastical authorities to help in the guidance of souls.[20] They form, therefore, 'a priceless record of one important stage of the perennial conflict of ideals with realities which marks the progress of man towards the attainment of a moral culture'.[21]

Referring to life, and specifically life in the early church and society of the time, McNeill believes that the reality was found in primitive brutality but the ideal was to be found in monastic asceticism.[22] However the lines of demarcation are not so clearly drawn. Society, of which monasticism was an integral part, contained both potentially brutal and potentially saintly people. How each person chose to act within their human limits and the profound awareness of the omnipresent divine is partly what constituted the radical response of the Irish of this period.

In aspiring to attain an ideal these penitentials, along with the rules of life of the monks, can be seen as radical in a threefold way: first getting to the root of what it is to be fully human; second, aspiring to the best that is in the human person while acknowledging the darker side of our nature; and third, taking the measures that history and the ancient sciences[23] suggest for the gaining or regaining of a state of equilibrium. This tripartite process is fitting for a people like the Celts who from the earliest days of their history had a fondness for triads.[24]

Origins of Penitentials

A system of penitential discipline had been enforced in the Christian Church from primitive times. Characteristic of this discipline was public exclusion from religious services for varying periods of time. This system of public penance was not so rigorously enforced in Western Europe as in the East, and it is doubtful if it was enforced at all in the British Isles.[25] It seems certain that one of the features of the strict and enthusiastic Irish monastic Church of the sixth and seventh centuries, which contrasted with the more lax Christianity of the continent, was the emphasis laid on confession and works of penance. Historians are not dogmatic about where and how private penance emerged, but it is undeniable that the Irish Church in the monastic period made it a general practice. Some

---

20. McNeill and Gamer, *Medieval Handbooks*, p. 3.
21. McNeill and Gamer, *Medieval Handbooks*, p. 3.
22. McNeill and Gamer, *Medieval Handbooks*, p. 3.
23. Reference is made to the Pythagoreans and the Methodists who initially put forward the principle of *contraries*. 'Methodists' refers to the school of medicine that dominated the Roman period and the early Middle Ages.
24. H. Connolly, *The Irish Penitentials and Their Significance for the Sacrament of Penance Today* (Dublin: Four Courts Press, 1st edn, 1995), p. 5 has a detailed discussion of this notion of threeness in relation to the druids and Irish society in general.
25. Kenney, *The Sources*, p. 238.

writers emphasize the theory and practice of penance as a medicine for souls. Columbanus, in his penitential, expressed the medicinal aspect this way: 'For the doctors of the body also compound their medicines in diverse kinds; thus they heal wounds in one manner, sickness in another . . .. So also should spiritual doctors treat with diverse kinds of cures the wounds of souls.'[26]

Since the introduction of private penance was a prolongation and intensification of the soul–friend relationship, it stands to reason that the individual penitent would be known by his *anamchara*.[27] The state of his soul, his motivation and intimate thoughts and deeds, if they were unfaithful to the *evangelium*, could be counteracted by an appropriate penance. In this way, just as a doctor treats each individual patient and disease differently so the Irish soul–friend relationship laid the foundation for a more personal, as opposed to public, approach to sin and its forgiveness. These penances were not only for the medicinal benefit of the individual but were also seen as reconciling community members with each other and with their God.

Connolly reiterates what McNeill has said, for he believes that, given the prominent role of the *anamchara* in the Irish monastic setting and its[28] relationship to penitential practice,

> it is only in the context of the healing dialogue that a theological reading of the Irish penitential literature can properly take place. To make the criticism, as some commentators have done, that the penitential books were mechanical and impersonal, is, I think, to ignore their true *Sitz im Leben* and thus to read them out of context.[29]

Part of the context of the penitentials must be the druidic tradition of Ireland. This product of the primal society and culture (often referred to as a pagan institution)[30] was all pervasive and an integral part of Irish life. Some writers

---

26. Penitential Section B (ed. and trans. Walker, *Sancti Columbani*, p. 171). It is also instructive to recall that the principles of *contraries* used in the curing of souls were adapted from a medicinal principle.

27. See chapter 3, for a discussion of the soul-friend, *anamchara*, in Irish monasticism.

28. The reason why the masculine pronoun is not used here is that in the areas of northern England where the Celtic monks had been there was an established practice of women acting as *anamchara* (Abbess Hilda of Whitby is a case in point) and even going to the extent of 'hearing confessions' in the technical sense; McNeill, 'Medicine for Sin as Prescribed in the Penitentials', *CH* 1 (1932), pp. 14–16 (26), points to Ita of Cluain Creedal as the confessor of Brendan; Columbanus in his youth also obtained spiritual advice from a saintly woman. E. Sellner, *Wisdom of the Celtic Saints* (Indiana: Ave Maria Press, 1993) and 'A Common Dwelling: Soul-Friendship in Early Celtic Monasticism', *CS* 29 (1994), pp. 1–21, writing on this topic of the role of the Irish *anamchara* said, in personal correspondence, that women actually did assign penances.

29. Connolly, *Irish Penitentials*, p. 16.

30. This word is used deliberately with the original meaning: that of the people from the countryside. To use 'pre-Christian' may be seen to devalue the elements of the primal religions. In the case of this particular Irish tradition, there are a wealth of positive aspects which have been incorporated into the later Christian tradition. J. Minahane in *The Christian Druids: On the Filid or Philosopher-Poets of Ireland* (Dublin: Sanas Press, 1993), reveals evidence for the lack of hostility and a positive appreciation of this group from the fifth century to the present day.

would say that it did not present a problem for the incoming Christianity as is evident in a lack of open conflict with druidism.[31] According to the *First Synod of Saint Patrick* oaths were sworn in the presence of druids, so it would seem that they retained some power. However, the progress of Christianity did reduce the druids' role in society. Though many could read and write they chose an oral mode of communication and so there is a dearth of written documents. Other accounts of their activities could therefore be prejudiced or based on ignorance. In Reeves' edition of the *Life of ColumCille* there is a hint that ColumCille was educated partly in the druidic tradition.[32] An integral part of this tradition was the notion of conversion[33] which was also one of the main purposes of the penitential practices of the emerging Christian religion. Chadwick comments that it has been claimed that druids believed in metempsychosis, the expiation of sin in other bodies after death, but 'there is little evidence of any kind that the Celts believed in sin and punishment'.[34] Druids did, however, have a strong belief in the afterlife which was evident in their gravesites. Though the superstructure of this druidic tradition appeared to have been dismantled, the deeper layer of its foundations was possibly still flourishing in the minds and hearts of the Irish converts.

There were many canons warning against druidic ritual practices included in the penitentials. Maybe the very human need to wean people from the practices that were thought to be antipathetic to their fledgling belief in a loving God was taken seriously by the framers of the penitentials and so this could account for these anti-druidic inclusions. That both Patrick and later Columbanus did not hesitate to use primal religious structures for their churches and monastic settlements points to the fact that they were not overly superstitious or reluctant to be seen using primal buildings or sites.[35] It is instructive to see that the magical powers and seeming control of the forces of

---

31. Minahane, *Christian Druids*, p. 127, quoting O'Curry, makes the point that,

from all the ancient records we have reason to believe . . . that St Patrick found before him on his arrival many men among the people of Erinn of cultivated mind, sharpened by study, capable of appreciating new ideas, quick to recognise the sublime truths of Divine revelation in preference to the unsatisfactory mysteries and secret ceremonies of their ancient mythology, however venerable it had become in their eyes.

32. W. Reeves (ed.), *Life of Saint Columba: Founder of Hy*, Facsimile reprints (Dyfed: Llanerch, 1st edn, 1988), p. 20, refers to ColumCille's going south into Leinster and placing himself under the instruction of an aged bard called Gemman. In the ancient Life of ColumCille preserved in the *Leabhar Breac* in the Irish Academy it is stated that his mother even consulted a druid as to the proper time to put him to the work of his education; that this druid was in fact his first tutor. Minahane, *Christian Druids*, p. 126.

33. Connolly, *Irish Penitentials*, p. 10.

34. Chadwick, *The Celts*, p. 150.

35. However, it could also be seen as replacing primal religions with Christianity and as such trying to eliminate the former because of a strong belief in its inferiority to Christianity; according to some historians this is an inappropriate use of power. However, such a criticism implied in the last sentence is to impose a 'presentist' interpretation to a former age and as such it cannot be justified in this context.

nature that were an integral part of the druids' stock in trade were, in a sense, some of the elements that were incorporated in the later *Vitae*[36] of the early Irish saints proposed for the edification and imitation of the new Irish converts. Whether this incorporation was from deep within the Celtic consciousness or in imitation of the earlier continental *Vitae* cannot be definitively claimed. However, in the context of the thrust of this study one would opt for a combination of both forces, with emphasis being placed on the former.

This importance of the druidic culture highlights the more deeply embedded sense of the Celtic consciousness and culture that underpins the penitentials. Aspects of this deeply ingrained Celticness include: a stress on the individual as recalcitrant and unorthodox, with a theology that is eclectic and pragmatic.[37] Most of these facets of Celticness have been treated as aspects of the radicality that is understood in this work. The remainder of this discussion will show that the penitentials emerged from the myths and values that were specific to the culture of the Irish Christians as they responded to the challenge of the *evangelium* filtered through their understandings of what it was to be Christian in their particular era.[38] What needs to be remembered is that conversion/commitment is not a once-for-all total change of lifestyle at the moment of conversion. It is a gradual process of internalization and integration. The act of commitment may be total in its proclamation but the implementation and integration is slow and subject to variation. Because this response was sufficiently different from that of people in surrounding cultures, these penitentials can be said to be a part of the radical response of the Irish monks of the period under discussion.

Relationship with Ancient Laws

A passing reference to the relationship between the Irish Brehon law, largely based on custom, and the penitentials would not be amiss here.[39] Unlike the secular laws, the ecclesiastical laws were far from a homogeneous group. Given that the purpose of the ecclesiastical laws was healing of the soul, their intention went beyond the secular law: a fact which constituted a major difference between the two. Secular law enforcement was concerned with protecting rights and penalizing transgressions while penitential law concentrated on moral evil

---

36. This will be discussed in chapters 4 and 5.

37. The understanding of the lists of sins as possibly hypothetical cases for discussion also highlights the facts that penitents were seen as individuals and so required an approach that took this important aspect into consideration. Practically speaking, if the purpose of penitentials was healing of the person then this was the only logical approach.

38. Hence the importance for any readers of this material to be sparing of blame for what they perceive as harsh, inhuman or even perverted, for society in each era is different and its evolving understandings of important components of its life and living have to be seen precisely in its evolving nature.

39. D. O'Corrain, L. Breatnach and A. Breen, 'The Laws of the Irish', *Peritia* 111 (1984), pp. 382–438, argue for a clerical background for the secular laws.

and how it could be cured and the sinner reinstated in the community.[40] Hughes says that the secular lawyers were schematizers,[41] but McNeill maintains that this passion for schematism was characteristic of early law-makers regardless of whether they were jurists or metricists or clerics.[42] Binchy saw the main motive of the early law-makers as a need to preserve as much as possible of traditional Irish law in the face of the encroachment of Christian ideals and organization.[43] Oakley thought that this relationship of the Brehon and ecclesiastical codes was so significant that he devoted a whole chapter to it in respect of the Anglo-Saxon laws and their provisions on penance. He holds that the penitentials strengthened the enforcements of the secular law.[44]

Kelly goes to great lengths in citing specific laws to show that it is not easy to assign particular laws to particular people. As an example he says that there is an assumption that all Old Irish law-texts were composed by clerics. But *Cáin Adamnáin* and *Cáin Domnaig* use substantially the same legal terminology as other texts.[45] It would explain why secular topics such as those treating of dogs appear in the Irish *Canons*, a specifically ecclesiastical text. The fact that their authors were clerics would no doubt explain why *Críth Gablach* asks: 'Who is nobler, a king or a bishop? The bishop is nobler, for the king rises before him on account of the Faith. The bishop raises his knee before the kings'.[46] However he goes on to say that in actual fact the two *Cána* mentioned above display quite different legal principles from other law-texts. In the *Cáin Adamnáin* women should be put to death not only for murder but also for arson or breaking into a church while the *Senchas Már* consistently recommends reparation rather than the death penalty for murder and other serious offences. The law of Sunday, *Cáin Domnaig*, has a ban on grinding corn on the Lord's day and is different from other laws; *Coibnes Uisci Thairidne*, for instance, allows for the mill to operate seven days a week.[47] While the precise authorship of law-texts is debated, Kelly maintains that on the whole they are humane and fair. They contain many stipulations aimed at protecting the weaker members of the community. The authors are well informed about the topics of the law. So while there might still be some doubt about the authorship of individual texts, both ecclesiastical and secular, they are sound guides to early Irish institutions.[48]

Compensation, firmly enshrined in the secular law, is also operating in the stipulations of some of the penitentials, especially those that imposed on the

---

40. J. R. Walsh and T. Bradley, *A History of the Irish Church 400–700 AD* (Dublin: The Columba Press, 1991), p. 121.
41. Hughes, *Early Christian*, p. 82.
42. McNeill, in D. A. Binchy, 'The Old-Irish Table of Penitential Commutations', *Eriu* 19–20 (1962–66), pp. 47–72 (55).
43. Binchy, in Kelly, *A Guide*, p. 233. In this and following pages he discusses in detail the arguments about these two law systems and who was responsible for formulating them.
44. T. P. Oakley, *English Penitential Discipline and Anglo-Saxon Law in Their Joint Influence* (New York: Columbia University, 1st edn, 1923).
45. Kelly, *A Guide*, p. 234.
46. Kelly, *A Guide*, p. 234.
47. Kelly, *A Guide*, p. 237.
48. Kelly, *A Guide*, p. 236.

sinner a loss of rank for the period of the penance. Therefore there was a need to look at more aspects of the offence than the deed itself. So the element of intentionality as evident in the penitentials needs to be addressed. This set them apart from the usual codes of secular law. With the introduction of the element of motivation in the penitentials and the concomitant attempts to rehabilitate the sinner, the historian and theologian see a departure from the secular law. One wonders if the penances as stated in the penitentials were ever actually enforced in all their rigour. There was an injunction suggested by some of the framers of monastic rules that the monks should go to confession every day even if the fault was only trivial. This act of humility, as an aid in aspiring to selflessness, could enable the sinner to come more easily to self-awareness and so be led to depend more on the mercy of God.

The distinctively Irish notion of commutations[49] revealed a people not solely bent on punishment, or breaking the human spirit, but on healing personal and communal conflicts in relationships as speedily as possible. The fact that commutations were in existence shows that the penances were being attempted in spite of their harshness. Ironically it was the system of commutations that later laid the Irish penitentials open to the charge of being 'soft' on sinners.[50] McNeill concludes that it is 'probably a matter of high historical importance that the secular and ecclesiastical disciplines effectively supplemented each other'.[51]

Purpose of the Penitentials

In the preface to the *Old Irish Penitential* we get a strong indication of the purpose of the penitentials:

> The venerable of Ireland have drawn up from the rules of Scriptures a penitential for the annulling and remedying of every sin, both small and great. For the eight chief virtues, with their subdivisions, have been appointed to cure and heal the eight chief vices, with whatsoever springs therefrom.[52]

---

49. To commute a penance meant that the actual penance was increased; simultaneously the length of time given to it was decreased. Initially this was in keeping with the medicinal/healing purpose of the penitentials in the Irish tradition. Binchy, 'Old Irish', p. 55 discusses in scholarly details these peculiarly Irish aspects of penance. He explains that they are later than the penitentials as such and are more part of the reform movement led by the monastery of Tallaght and its Abbot Máel-Rúian.

50. Connolly, *Irish Penitentials*, p. 170, states that the 'practice of commutations marked a serious deterioration of the original ideal'. He bases his comments on an article of Binchy, 'Old Irish', p. 55. However, Binchy says, 'Whether the performance of penance by substitute, which ultimately became a serious abuse, derives from this type of *arre*, I am not competent to discuss, but it seems to me not improbable.' In coming to this conclusion Binchy is quoting Schmitz who was extremely pro-Roman in his stance. With this attitude it is understandable that he might see Irish penitentials open to abuse even if the abuse did not exist.

51. McNeill and Gamer, *Medieval Handbooks*, p. 37.

52. L. Bieler (ed.), *The Irish Penitentials* (Vol. 5; Dublin: Institute for Advanced Studies, 1963), p. 259.

Not only is the intention to 'annul' the sin but the rules of the Scriptures are applied so that there can also be a remedying process. Annulling in the basic meaning of the term is not possible, however, for it means that the sin never existed. The application of the principle of contraries, *contraria contrariis curare*: curing contraries by contraries, while acknowledging the existence of sin, forms the basis of most of the major penitential systems. One cannot apply a remedy if one denies the existence of the 'disease'. The octade[53] of Cassian is set in operation so that where a sin occurs the opposite virtue is suggested as the remedy. He therefore utilized the pre-existing philosophy to fashion an efficient mode of Christian reconciliation.[54]

The notion of asceticism or ascetical theology being used here is that which looks to the inner transformation of life. This transformation involves the practices adopted to facilitate it. The intention that accompanies it, the lengths to which people will go to achieve it and the 'power' it exercises on those who encounter it in others. Once the healing purpose is established with the principle of *contraries* as basic, we are dealing with an external notion of penance. The penitential presumption therefore laid down an ascetic regime as the means to sustain, nourish and strengthen one's monastic life. The three staples of this regime were prayer, fasting and almsgiving, all of which at one time or another could be part of the penitential practices of the Irish monk.

The radicality of this way of living gets to the roots of what it is to be human and the desire of those who follow such a way of life to be totally caught up in the pursuit of holiness and wholeness.[55] It implies a freedom on the part of the monk to choose this lifestyle. Though an incarnational theology, basic to Irish Christianity, it nonetheless does not detract from the awareness of the gulf between the divine and the human person. That it was the lifestyle of few in the Irish Church, despite the fact that some historians tell us that there were up to 3000 persons in one of the monasteries at the height of this ascetical movement,[56] points to the other notion of radicality that is intended here,

---

53. Of all the writers who use this term only one, Bieler, used *ogdade*, which is the Irish form.

54. Though to Cassian is sometimes attributed the 'creation' of this schema, in fact, he was borrowing from the Pythagoreans (who borrowed from the Babylonian sources) who in turn used the information in the foundation of Greek medical literature from Alkmaion of Croton (500 BCE). Detailed discussion of the development of the principle of *contraries* is found in J. T. McNeill, 'Medicine', pp. 14–26.

55. Vinnian actually uses the word 'whole' in this sense – to be discussed later.

56. O. D. Watkins, *A History of Penance: Being a Study of the Authorities* (2 vols; New York: Burt Franklin, 1st edn, 1920), Vol. II, p. 607, quoting from E. C. Quiggan, 'Ireland, Early History', *Encyclopaedia Britannica* (ed. Quiggan), p. xi, claims that 'no less than 3000 students are said to have received instruction at the same time' in the monastic school of Clonard. He goes on to say that Quiggan may have been mistaken in counting 3000 and assuming that they were all monks. Kenney, *The Sources*, would also make this claim about Clonard. M. M. Dubois, *Saint Columban: A Pioneer of Western Civilization* (Dublin: Gill and Son, 1st edn, 1961), p. 13 claims that it was at Bangor that this number of monks lived. If population statistics were as available then as they are today, it would be easier to check the credibility of these figures. However, it may be a more metaphorical expression. There were undoubtedly great numbers of people living in the monastic settlements of this period.

namely, that the distinction between monks and non-monastic lay persons was based not only on the commitment to monastic life of the former but on the decidedly more radical lifestyle followed by them. This in no way is meant to demean the laity and their commitment to Christianity. It is simply clarifying the notion of radicality used in this discussion. It remains true to say that for all forms of radicality, they characterize the lifestyle of the relatively few.

In discussing the Irish penitentials of the sixth to the eighth century to discern the underlying ascetical theology contained therein, it is important to acknowledge briefly the Irish indebtedness to the earlier Welsh penitentials. Those whose influence is most notable are the Preface of Gildas (*Prefatio Gildae*), the Synods of North Britain (*Sinodus Aquilonaris Britaniae*) and Grove of Victory (*Sinodus Luci Victoriae*) and the Book of David (*Excerpta de libro Davidis*). The task at hand is to distil the underlying asceticism that shaped the formulations of the penitentials of the Irish Church of the sixth to the eighth century. In passing it may also indicate different degrees of *ascesis* contained in the different penitentials. This will, of necessity, include the penitential of Columbanus because it is undeniable that his penitential was gestated in Ireland[57] and expressed with the vigour and uncompromising zeal of the Irish Church from which he came and to whose cause he was irrevocably committed.[58]

In terms of the basic ascetical principle of monasticism, it is clear to see why the Cassian[59] octade is utilized by all the penitential writers. It was used by Columbanus and Cummean but was first enunciated in Vinnian's penitential.

> But by contraries, as we said, let us make haste to cure contraries and to cleanse away the faults from our hearts and introduce virtues in their places. Patience must arise for wrathfulness; kindliness, or the love of God and of one's neighbour, for envy; for detraction, restraint of heart and tongue; for dejection, spiritual joy; for greed, liberality.[60]

Its significance lies in the underlying tenet that selfish tendencies are replaced with virtues. In addition they train the mind, heart and body in the opposite virtues to the selfishness that caused sins. Practising the virtues strengthens the will to act honourably. Ascetical practices enjoined by the penitentials and stemming from the theory of *contraries* enable the aspiring ascetic to gain a

---

57. His indebtedness to Comgall the Abbot of Bangor where he resided for a number of years will be treated in a later chapter. See Appendix II A for the Rule of Comgall of Bangor from the Antiphony of Bangor.

58. See chapter 1, fn 107 for evidence of this in the letter he wrote to Pope Gregory the Great defending the orthodoxy of the Irish and their devotion to the bishop of Rome.

59. The teaching of Cassian is to be found in the original in *De Institutis coenobiorum et de octo principalium vitiorum remediis libri XII*, specifically Books 5–12. Also in E. C. S. Gibson, 'The Works of John Cassian', in *Nicean and Post-Nicean Fathers* (2nd series, Vol. 2, repr. W. B. Eerdmans 1964, Oxford: James Parker and Co., 1894).

60. Canon 29, Vinnian, (ed. and trans. McNeill and Gamer, *Medieval Handbooks*, p. 92).

balance between sinful tendency[61] and the fundamental ideal of monasticism. The penances intrinsic to the penitentials consist of doing hard labour, sometimes as composition[62] for a crime committed, refraining from food and drink for a specified period of time, limiting the intake of certain foods, again for a certain number of days, weeks or years as the case may be. Exile or pilgrimage is the penance for some more serious crimes. Others include loss of rank, particularly for the clergy with its concomitant embarrassment and loss of gratuity, and finally withdrawal from the Eucharist, which is virtually ostracism, or non-canonical excommunication from the worshipping community. The last of these is imposed rarely but is an important component of the penitential disciplines of the Irish, and later continental Church. All are part of the ascetic regime designed to effect conversion.

Only The First Synod of Patrick (*Synodus S.Patricii* – 450 CE) will be referred to in this discussion and even this is not strictly speaking a penitential. However, it does have more than half of its canons imposing a penance and so can be said to be about church discipline. Part of its importance and use here is that it gives some insights into the Church of the period, a 'Church that is neither in the first flush of mission nor yet fully integrated into the host society'.[63]

Of these penances over one-third impose excommunication (canons 1, 17, 19, 20, 27, 31, 32), or its equivalent as in 'exclusion from the church' (canons 10, 22). Other expressions that equate with excommunication are referred to as: 'outside the church' (canon 8); 'removed from the church' (canon 6); 'cut off from the church' (canon 26). Intentionally or not, these canons point to the basic community orientation of the Irish monasteries. Being cut off from the *Túatha* or Christian community is profoundly alienating. Three canons refer to the punishment of being made a 'stranger' (canons 7, 21, 24) that may also be a synonym for excommunication. Seven others are simply given a penance or punished with no specifics recorded (canons 11, 14, 15, 18, 28, 33, 34). Seventeen of the canons apply to clerics, seven to lay people and ten apply to both. The ones that apply to the clergy give insights into the status of some of the clergy. When they enforce surety or use violence against defaulters this suggests that they are of noble rank in the society since enforcing surety (*Naidm*) was reserved for the nobility.[64]

---

61. Some spiritual writers, especially Augustine, would attribute the sinful tendency to Original Sin but the Irish had no word for Original Sin and neither did Pelagius. The Pelagian debate of the fourth century regarding Original Sin and grace has been revived by one Creation Spirituality writer today: M. Fox, *Original Blessing: A Primer in Creation Spirituality* (Santa Fé: Bear and Co., 1983).

62. Composition is understood, in the context of the penitentials, as the compensation a person makes to the offended one in terms of payment to relatives in satisfaction for murder or injury. The notion of *talio* in the sense of retaliation is evident in some penitentials: Cummean III, Columbanus B 21, Vinnian 23, Columbanus B 1. Composition therefore 'marks an advance on the still more primitive customs of retaliation and revenge, reversion to which was more frequent in the early Middle Ages'. See McNeill and Gamer, *Medieval Handbooks*, p. 35, for more details of this practice.

63. O'Loughlin in Davies, *Celtic*, p.17.
64. O'Loughlin in Davies, *Celtic*, p.17.

The canons abound in references to primal practices and this is possibly because at this point in time the embryonic Church is 'outside' society and acts as a foil for the aspects of the society that it sees as contrary to the Christian *evangelium*. In the case of canon 12 the text of Bieler uses 'Christian' whereas the *Canones Hibernenses* uses 'cleric' and the conclusion seems to be that Christian is the most likely rendering of the intended sense, for the canons were designed for all Christians not only for the clerics. Moreover, if clerics were to be addressed there would usually be a separate section dealing with them. Later canons will reveal a much different Church that has become integrated into the society but nonetheless has a structure markedly different from that of Patrick's 'diocesan' model. The emerging Church structure is monastic.

The initial principle expressed in the First Synod, 'we deem it better to forewarn the negligent rather than to condemn accomplished deeds',[65] embodies the underlying care for the rehabilitation of the sinner that is so often lost in the preoccupation with the excesses of the sins delineated. Since these canons are addressed primarily to 'priests, deacons and all the clergy',[66] and considering that the church of Patrick's day was, not solely, but predominantly, a diocesan one, Patrick, Auxilius and Iserninus, from whom the Synod dictates come, are probably addressing those churchmen not living in monasteries. Nevertheless, it is significant that the first virtue recommended is obedience in relation to collecting money for captives without permission: submission of the will and heart was regarded as the most likely to effect the inner transformation that was basic to an ascetical lifestyle.

A particularly 'modern' concept is evident in canon 6 where it is obvious that a married clergy is being warned about dress codes and hairstyles that should conform to the Roman pattern. Even the wife of the cleric is not to go unveiled lest they both incur the contempt of the laity.[67] It seems that some kind of differentiation is implied here where the cleric and his wife are expected to give good example to the laity. Maybe a greater degree of conformity with church rules is expected of the cleric than is expected of the lay person. These expectations can be expressed in terms of a more total commitment to Christian values. Not only do those in the clerical state hear this stricter call but also it is taken up by them and is manifested in a behaviour that is qualitatively different. The exemplification of this comment will be seen when the different penances expected from the two groups are highlighted in the discussion of each penitential. Social history and reflected-upon human experience attest to the fact that response to the *evangelium* is heard differently in each age and responded to within the uniqueness of each age and culture.

Those historians who adhere to the belief that *syneisaktism*[68] was a practice in the early Irish Church might well find the following words of Patrick a

---

65. Prologue, 'First Synod of Patrick' (ed. and trans. Bieler, *The Irish*, p. 55).
66. Prologue, 'First Synod of Patrick' (ed and trans. Bieler, *The Irish*, p. 55).
67. Canon 6, (ed and trans. Bieler, *The Irish*, p. 55); the Pauline Epistles contain similar warnings: the committed Christian is to give good example.
68. For details of this practice and the historical evidence for it see chapter 3, fn 90.

condemnation of such a practice: 'A monk and a virgin, the one from one place, the other from another, shall not take lodging in the same inn, nor travel in the same carriage from village to village, nor carry on prolonged conversations together.'[69]

As the context hints, it was the scattered, rural nature of the fledgling Irish Church that would necessitate the wandering of clerics for pastoral reasons. Because there were not, as yet, many established convents for women[70] who wished to live the coenobitic life, it is understandable that they would attach themselves to some cleric, for safety and for formation in the ascetic life. If the monastic rules warn against too much conversation which would distract the mind and heart from its primary purpose of communing with God, then Patrick's warning may be seen in this light. The ascetic life was the goal[71] of diocesan priests as well as of monks.

Penitential of Vinnian[72]

Most commentators on this penitential, *Poenitentiale Vinniai*, would attribute it to Finnian of Clonard, the distinguished founder of the greatest Irish monastery of the period who died in or about 500 CE.[73] As the first of the Irish penitentials, the work of Vinnian holds an important place in the literature. It uses Scripture, reference to Cassian's *contraries* and some of the early Irish canons but, on the whole, it is original or based on sources not able to be discovered by any of the penitential scholars.[74] McNeill claims that there is no evidence that Vinnian was conscious of originating a tradition and maybe he is merely codifying practices that were already operating in the Irish Church of his day.[75]

---

69. Canon 6 (ed. and trans. Bieler, *The Irish*, p. 55).
70. Chapter 1, fn 22, for discussion of monasteries founded by females in Ireland.
71. This is not to deny the dual function of the priest in the Irish Church: that of personal commitment and pastoral care of others.
72. Commentators on the penitentials include: Bieler, Kenney, McNeill, Connolly, and Wasserschleben. H. J. Schmitz, according to Kenney, *The Sources*, p. 239, makes an unconvincing case for the Roman origin of the Irish penitentials. This is part of what Kenney sees as the continuation of the often polemical debate arising from the differing perceptions of Irish historical events, namely Protestant and Roman Catholic orientations.
73. This is the date given by McNeill and Gamer, *Medieval Handbooks*, p. 86. However, Connolly dates the penitential at 590 CE. B. Lehane, *Early Celtic*, p. 223, also has Finnian's dying in 550 CE. The strong support for the author being Finnian of Clonard, and not Finnian of Moville, comes from a letter of Columbanus to Gregory the Great in which he refers to 'Vennianus auctor' who asked advice of Gildas, the Welshman, on some unstable monks. Columbanus himself was the pupil of two of Finnian's own monks at Clonard namely Sinell and Comgall. Since the later penitential of Columbanus draws heavily on Vinnian it seems to add weight to the above assertion about authorship.
74. McNeill, 'Medicine', p. 87; Kenney, *The Sources*, p. 241; Connolly, *Irish Penitentials*, p. 32.
75. McNeill and Gamer, *Medieval Handbooks*, p. 87.

Generally speaking the 53 canons of this penitential can be divided into two parts: one which deals with clerics and one which addresses the laity and the married state. Further division can be seen in the different penances allotted to these two groups of people. What is highlighted in this and all the Irish penitentials is the importance given to private penance. In the Western Church of earlier centuries penance was a public affair,[76] with reconciliation also being witnessed by the whole community. Bieler's edition of this work prefaces it with four rather odd canons which are found only in the Vienna manuscript. The nature of these inclusions gives rise to the negative perception of the penitentials and adds fuel to the comments made by Plummer at the outset of this discussion. McNeill and Gamer's rendition does not include them. What one could call an epilogue to the work has some points of interest. Vinnian is said to have addressed these canons 'to the sons of his bowels, by occasion of affection or of religion', in order that 'by all means all the evil deeds of men might be destroyed'.[77] Maybe this figurative language is Vinnian's way of expressing his care and love for his fellow monks. On the other hand it may be indicating that he is one of the married monks who shared the monastic settlement with the clerical monks. The former is the most likely meaning because those who were leaders of monastic communities were predominantly in the clerical state and committed to the evangelical councils.

The first four canons speak about sins of thought and deed. In these canons there seems to be a gradation of seriousness. If thought only (canon 1) then the penance is less severe than if the thought is actually embodied in a deed. A nuance is detected in canon three where the evil thought has been deprived of the opportunity of fulfilment: 'it is the same sin but not the same penalty'.[78] This distinction and gradation are addressed also in the sins of the clerics in relation to fornication: 'if one who is a cleric falls miserably through fornication he shall lose his crown,[79] if it happens once (only) and it is concealed from man but before God'.[80] Further distinction is made if the cleric is in the habit of sin: if he 'falls to the depths of ruin and begets a child and kills him',[81] the sin is a compound of fornication and homicide. If the child is not killed 'the sin is less, but the penance is the same'.[82] Theft is also subject to the graded penances: if a cleric commits theft once or twice he does penance for an entire year and shall

---

76. Both Watkins and Oakley do not believe that public penance, meaning all three aspects of the sacrament, confession, penance and absolution were of universal occurrence in the Western Church. The distinction needs to be made that while penance, the performance of the penitential acts and absolution or reconciliation may have been public, the actual confession of one's sins was still performed in private.

77. Penitential of Vinnian, Epilogue (ed. and trans. McNeill and Gamer, *Medieval Handbooks*, p. 97).

78. Canon 3 (ed. and trans. McNeill and Gamer, *Medieval Handbooks*, p. 88).

79. Canon 10 (ed. and trans. Bieler, *The Irish*, p. 77), says this is a symbol of virginity, whereas McNeill and Gamer, *Medieval Handbooks*, p. 89 fn 11, translate it as place of honour in reference to his public function.

80. Canon 10 (ed. and trans. Bieler, *The Irish*, p. 77).

81. Canon 12 (ed. and trans. Bieler, *The Irish*, p. 77).

82. Canon 13 (ed. and trans. Bieler, *The Irish*, p. 77).

restore fourfold to his neighbour.[83] Here one sees an element characteristic of Irish law, the notion of composition[84] where the offender is bound to restore to the offended party a proportion of the damage, either in kind or in time, especially if the crime deprived the offended one of a person, such as a child or spouse.[85]

Similar distinctions are made in regard to the cleric in his relationships with women (canons 14–19). Simply being on familiar terms with a woman, neither cohabitation with her or engaging in lascivious embraces,[86] carries the penance of refraining from communion and doing penance for forty days on bread and water.[87] What is significant in terms of the remedying of this behaviour is that the cleric is admonished to 'tear out of his *heart* his fellowship with the woman'.[88] Not merely avoiding her company but conscious of the closeness of mind and heart, and the linking of the mind, heart and affection, the cleric is cautioned to make the break by ridding his heart of this woman. The heart is seen to be significant where merely lusting in his heart merits a penance of seven days on bread and water.[89] However, if the familiarity is more intense but he has preserved himself from ruin, he is to do penance for half a year on bread and water and another half a year refraining from wine and meat. After this he can be restored to the altar.[90] Indeed this conforms to human experience. If one thinks negative thoughts then it is highly probable that negative deeds will follow. But if one can prevent the thoughts from taking root then the deeds have been circumvented. However, in the case of the Irish there is the added power of the mind and thoughts to be considered. These two faculties have been given such pre-eminence from the days of the druids and poets, and so were intrinsic to how the activities of such faculties were seen to impinge on, or contribute to, one's choices in life. The gradings show the distinction between habitual and one-off sins. The importance of this means that all sin is not the same and if healing is the aim of the penitentials then such considerations bear out the purpose of these penitentials, namely healing of the individual.

Other canons highlight the role played by the heart in sin and repentance and, in addition, the notion of the difference between lay and clerical sins and penance is highlighted. For the homicide of a neighbour, first germinated in the heart of the offender, the punishment is half a year on bread and water and

---

83. Canon 25 (ed. and trans. Bieler, *The Irish*, p. 83).
84. McNeill and Gamer, *Medieval Handbooks*, p. 35, see the whole issue of composition as an advance on the more punitive, secular notion of retaliation. Oakley, *English Penitential*, p. 69, calls it secular composition for crimes or restitution according to secular law and makes the point that there is stern insistence upon obedience to such secular laws in addition to penance.
85. Canon 23 (ed. and trans. Bieler, *The Irish*, p. 83), gives details of this as do Brehon law regulations.
86. Canon 14 (ed. and trans. Bieler, *The Irish*, p. 79).
87. Canon 14 (ed. and trans. Bieler, *The Irish*, p. 79).
88. Canon 14 (ed. and trans. Bieler, *The Irish*, p. 79).
89. Canon 16 (ed. and trans. Bieler, *The Irish*, p. 79).
90. Canon 15 (ed. and trans. Bieler, *The Irish*, p. 79).

another whole year abstaining from wine and meat.[91] However, if the offender is a lay person, 'he shall do penance for a period of seven days';[92] 'since he is a man of this world, his guilt is lighter in this world, and his reward less in the world to come'.[93] In the mind of a modern reader of these injunctions many questions could be raised: Is his guilt less because the expectation placed on the lay person is not the same as that on the cleric? Is his guilt less because the same *evangelium* does not call him so radically? Is he seen as weaker, thus more prone to sin? Or is the gospel injunction, 'To whom much is given, of him much will be expected', the basis of this different theology of holiness? In the context of these penitentials as guides for Christian living in the sixth- to the eighth-century Irish Church, the distinction made between lay and committed religious persons was a real one. It would appear that the above injunctions do bear out the fact that a more radical response was expected from persons committed to religious life.

Thinking of this nature would have been widespread in early Christianity and would have taken as its justification the scriptural affirmation that those who have left father or mother or lands for the sake of the gospel will receive a hundredfold in this life and everlasting life in the world to come. It is in the light of this, and other canons to be discussed, that the notion of the radicality of the clerical lifestyle vis-à-vis the lay person is seen as fundamental in monasticism in general and of Irish monasticism of the sixth to the eighth century in particular.

Later in his penitential, the heart is seen again to play a vital part in the case of envy, backbiting, greed or despondency. These failures Vinnian calls capital sins for they slay the soul and cast it down to the depth of hell.[94] However, they can be eradicated from the heart through the help of God and through one's own zeal. Like Pelagius[95] before him, Vinnian lays stress on the personal effort which must accompany God's grace. Brown says something profound by way of explanation about the differences between Augustine and Pelagius regarding personal choices made under the guidance of grace. He claims that the language both men use highlights differing attitudes. Augustine's fascination with babies and their helplessness conditions how he sees the relationship of the person with God: one of total dependence. Pelagius, by contrast, was contemptuous of babies. 'There is no more pressing admonition than this that we should be called sons of God. To be a "son" was to become a separate person.' No longer dependent on the father, but one who takes responsibility for one's own actions.[96]

91. Canon 6 (ed. and trans. Bieler, *The Irish*, p. 77).
92. Canon 7 (ed. and trans. Bieler, *The Irish*, p. 77).
93. Canon 7 (ed. and trans. Bieler, *The Irish*, p. 77).
94. Canon 29 (ed. and trans. Bieler, *The Irish*, p. 85).
95. There is a great deal of discussion about whether Pelagius was an Irish Celt. Initially Augustine admired Pelagius for his asceticism and his writings on Scripture. Later he was responsible for the strong backlash against his teachings. At certain periods in the debate the misunderstandings may have been due more to political than theological reasons; B. Rees, *Pelagius: A Reluctant Heretic* (Suffolk: St Edmundsbury Press, 1988).
96. See O'Donoghue, *Angels*, p. 125, where he gives the full text of Brown's comment.

One aspect of radicality used in this work, implies the freedom to choose and act on that choice. The principle of *contraries* is introduced here with the admonition that these faults can be cleansed from our hearts by introducing the heavenly virtues in their place.[97] As an example of this principle detraction is replaced with 'restraint of heart and tongue'.[98]

Given the overall medicinal intention of the penitentials,[99] and the clear declaration 'there is no crime which cannot be expiated through penance',[100] the stipulations of some canons seem to be contradictory. 'If one has sworn a false oath, great is the crime; it can hardly, if at all, be expiated, but none the less it is better to do penance and not to despair: for great is the mercy of God.'[101] In an earlier canon, magic[102] is said to be a monstrous sin that, however, can be expiated by penance.[103] The medicine of immediate penance is recommended with the injunction that 'first, he must never in his life take an oath',[104] for to do so is to call on God to witness that what one states is true and this, to Vinnian and his fellow monks, is worse than fornication and homicide. Even covetousness is called a great crime, for it is seen as idolatry and in this historical setting the person to whom all honour and worship is due is God and God alone. The fundamental asceticism of monasticism is orientation towards God and, if one places another person or thing in this central position, one is not living up to the monastic ideal. This constant reminder of the central or sole focus of the life of the Christian is reiterated in many of the penitentials. The endurance of such penances was always for a higher good and the healing of human weakness.

Clear indications of the different penances for lay and cleric are seen in the different Christian virtues expected of the lay person. In canons 7 and 9 both cleric and lay persons are allotted penances vastly different in duration and severity for the same crime. For canons 31 to 48 virtues of the married state are treated and the penances for failure in this area are allotted. The issue of contributing funds for the redemption of captives is addressed only to the laity, and pilgrims are to be welcomed,[105] a stipulation that would apply equally to the monks, as they had sections of their monasteries specifically set aside for this work.

If a layman defiles his neighbour's wife the penance is one year. If the woman is a virgin the penance is two years.[106] On the one hand it may seem

---

97. Canon 29 (ed. and trans. Bieler, *The Irish*, p. 85).
98. Canon 29 (ed. and trans. Bieler, *The Irish*, p. 85).
99. Since Vinnian's penitential is the model on which later penitentials are based, this medicinal element recurs. Its meaning is explained in more detail in Columbanus' penitential.
100. Canon 47 (ed. and trans. Bieler, *The Irish*, p. 93).
101. Canon 22 (ed. and trans. Bieler, *The Irish*, p. 81).
102. Magic, seen as a constant reminder of the druidic past of the Irish, is to be guarded against. Canons 18, 19, 20 all treat of this.
103. Canon 18 (ed. and trans. Bieler, *The Irish*, p. 79).
104. Canon 22 (ed. and trans. Bieler, *The Irish*, p. 81).
105. Canon 33 (ed. and trans. Bieler, *The Irish*, p. 87).
106. Canon 36 (ed. and trans. Bieler, *The Irish*, p. 87).

that the hardship of the woman is the consideration here. Such injunctions suggest that the writers of the penitentials were reasonably enlightened and possessed a heightened sense of justice. On the other hand, the above stipulation regarding the defiling of a woman may be out of consideration of the bride-price that would be less for a deflowered bride. Marital fidelity is treated with the respect one would expect today and, given the society in the context of which these penitentials were written, it would seem to be further evidence of an enlightened treatment.[107] Another canon exhorts 'that there be continence in marriage, since marriage without continence is not lawful, but sin'.[108] In concluding the discussion of Vinnian's penitential, it seems clear that in providing penances for the sins of all ranks of people, one and the same manner of administering penance applies whether the penitent be a monk, lay person or cleric. However, the penance allotted to each is different for persons of different rank.

Penitential of Columbanus[109]

Watkins, in his *magnum opus* on penance, says that the first feature to emphasize in relation to this work is that 'it is from start to finish the outcome of the Keltic monastic system'.[110] He takes issue with Wasserschleben who places it with those he calls Frankish.[111] Connolly, like McNeil and Gamer, places its composition in the first decade of the seventh century. It was to have a far wider influence given that it was formulated on the continent and thus disseminated to a wider group of monasteries and, as a consequence, had a more profound influence on the theory and practice of penance.[112] Kenney, while asserting that the document is stamped with the personality of Columbanus and as such is logical, severe, and displaying considerable intelligence, good judgement and a sense of justice and proportion, nonetheless has some doubts about its authorship.[113] T. M. Charles-Edwards notes all the

---

107. Canon 41 (ed. and trans. Bieler, *The Irish*, p. 89). Warren, *The Liturgy*, in fn 151 gives some instances regarding marriage that reiterate the point that this penitential was indeed enlightened. He makes the point that the *Canones S.Patricii*, ii Synod xxv–xxviii show a harsher attitude to marriage in early Irish history. The question of incest in the mss in St Gall probably is a question of necessity of the times rather than indicative of any special degradation in the morality of Ireland.
108. Canon 46 (ed. and trans. Bieler, *The Irish*, p. 91).
109. M. Lapidge (ed.), *Columbanus: Studies on the Latin Writings* (Suffolk: The Boydell Press, 1st edn, 1997), pp. 217-39 is the most recent scholarly work, to my knowledge, on this penitential.
110. Watkins, *A History*, Vol. II, p. 615.
111. Watkins, *A History*, Vol. II, p. 615.
112. Connolly, *Irish Penitentials*, p. 33.
113. Kenney, *The Sources*, p. 200 citing Seebass, McNeill and Wasserschleben comes to the conclusion that the author, while probably Columbanus, is hardly beyond dispute. He believes that it contains considerable interpolations. Walker's detailed discussion is also informative; T. M. Charles-Edwards, in Lapidge (ed.), *Columbanus*, pp. 217-239, has no doubt about its author being Columbanus.

difficulties encountered by earlier authors. However, he maintains that the Columbanus' penitential, 'stands close to the most fundamental single change in the tradition of the Celtic penitential, a change which may be expressed as the divide between the period before Cummian (sometimes spelled Cummean) and the period from Cummian onwards'. He claims that those prior to Cummian addressed monks or clergy or laity, and post-Cummian were more systematic in that they were based on Cassian's octade. These two eras he calls 'particular' and 'comprehensive'.[114] He has no doubt about its author being Columbanus. The work will be taken here as that of Columbanus or emanating from his influence.[115]

With the penitential, as with the monastic rules and all of the literary works of Columbanus, what becomes transparently clear is that it is personal faith not philosophy that is the guiding force of his life and the lifestyle he proposes for his followers. It seems that human life, 'as *peregrinatio* alienated from a heavenly *patria*', was very present in his writing, especially in his sermons.[116] His initial response to the call to leave mother and motherland shows a man of action who is obsessed with the search for Christian perfection regardless of the personal hardship. His lifestyle gave concrete evidence of the ascetical theology that underpinned it: an ascetic regime that included prayer, fasting and behaviour that 'incarnated' these values and practices. Like many of his Celtic forebears, his view of life is that of a battlefield[117] and so the spiritual quest is easily seen as a battle in which the foe is the selfish human spirit, and the weapons are the penances and ascetical practices. The goal is mystical union with Christ the redeemer who has gone before in the fight and has conquered.[118] This imagery of battle not only has its origins in the monks' Celtic consciousness but after their conversion the image resonated also with the scriptural references from Paul, who himself used the imagery of the battle as a model for the spiritual journey. A feature of all the Irish penitentials, but more significant given the continental milieu of Columbanus, is the rapid accessibility of private and repeated opportunities for penance made possible by the growth of monasticism and the pastoral dimension afforded by its lifestyle. Walker goes so far as to claim that the readiness of access and the privacy of confession '[worked] a revolution in the old forms of pastoral supervision'.[119]

The penitential is seen by some as composed of two penitentials, with Part A comprising canons 1–12 and concluding with a statement of *contraries*,

---

114. T. M. Charles-Edwards, in Lapidge (ed.), *Columbanus*: p. 218.

115. Walker (ed.), *Sancti Columbani*, liii, alludes to other people in the debate, viz. Schmitz, whom other writers agree had a different agenda when it came to the penitentials and their authorship and source of inspiration.

116. Charles-Edwards, in Lapidge (ed.), *Columbanus*, p. 219.

117. Epistle iv. 6 (ed. and trans. Walker, *Sancti Columbani*, p. 31); the sagas so full of battles and warfare were not simple stories but the embodiment of the Celtic tradition and spirit.

118. Sermon 13 (ed. and trans. Walker, *Sancti Columbani*, p. 115).

119. Walker (ed.), *Sancti Columbani*, p. lii.

similar in structure to the canon 29 of Vinnian already discussed. Part B is more lengthy but, in structure, forms a parallel with Part A in that the issues and penances apply to the sins of the laity, where those of Part A refer to similar sins of monks. Here is where the different length, duration and severity of penances for a lay person vis-à-vis clerics are clearly spelled out and reinforce one of the aspects of radicality used in this work.

True penance, according to Columbanus, 'is not to commit things worthy of repentance'.[120] It is, in other words, to live the Christian life perfectly in such a way as not to have to atone for transgressions from this narrow path. Christian life itself is true penance, for it is a life-long commitment to living like Christ. It is, like the life of a warrior, being on guard at all times. However, if one succumbs, one is advised to 'lament such things as have been committed'[121] since most of the human race is prone to being selfish. Elsewhere in the writing of Columbanus this life task is given credence because he sees the conquest of sin as being the opportunity for greater good. Hence the measure of penances, or the scheme of penances, must be known and obviously put into practice. Simply knowing is not enough. To be truly radical the person must freely choose to act on this knowledge.

His acknowledgement of his indebtedness to the holy fathers[122] has been seen by Walker, in particular, as evidence that Columbanus was not original in his thinking.[123] But is this not another instance of the Celtic regard for ancestors and their tendency to guide their present by inspiration from the past? This is the interpretation that is favoured here. At this early stage in his penitential there is a hint of the equilibrium and even a sense of justice that is hoped for as a result of submitting to the following penances, for 'in accordance with the greatness of the offences the length also of the penance should be ordained'.[124] Justice and those who administer it are safeguarded in both Church and secular Irish law. A frequently repeated dictum of the *Corpus Iuris Hibernici* is: *cach brithemoin a báegul* ('to every judge his error'), meaning that each judge must be responsible for any mistakes he makes. Moreover, his judgment is not valid unless he swears on the Gospel. He pays fines, sometimes in silver, if he makes an incorrect judgment or fails to look at both sides of the case. Kelly gives more details about the effort to which early Irish law goes to ensure that justice is done, even to detailing the punishments meted out to unjust judges.[125]

---

120. Canon 1 (ed. and trans. Walker, *Sancti Columbani*, p. 169).
121. Canon 1 (ed. and trans. Bieler, *The Irish*, p. 97).
122. Canon 1 (ed. and trans. Bieler, *The Irish*, p. 97).
123 Walker (ed.), *Sancti Columbani*, p. lxx, cites *Reg. Mon* vii; *Reg. Ceon*.i; *Paenit*.A i and B; Praef., *Epistle* iii. 2.
124. Canon 1 (ed. and trans. Bieler, *The Irish*, p. 97).
125. Kelly, *A Guide*, p. 358, gives a verse from *CIH*, 209, pp. 12–23, about such a punishment:

Sencha judged it in his first judgement
Female entry for male entry
So that blisters were sustained
On his cheek after biased judgement.

So while there appears to be a good deal of effort put into delineating of penances there is, in law, an equal concern for justice and the sense that this will contribute to the smooth functioning of the *Túatha* and the emerging Christian community.

Reminiscent of Vinnian, initially Columbanus discusses sins of thought and deed. A further distinction he makes is that between greater and lesser sins. Some of the greater sins (canons 2–8) include murder, sodomy, perjury, drunkenness, defiling oneself, bearing false witness, and striking one's brother and spilling blood. The penances range from half a year to ten years. In the case of murder or sodomy his penance is ten years; in Part B it is ten years in exile, similar to Vinnian.[126] Perjury carries a seven-year penance in keeping with the belief that perjury is calling on God to witness to a lie. There is a distinction made between greater and lesser penances, examples of the latter being: doing something without asking,[127] simple contradiction of another's word,[128] slander or willing listening to slander,[129] despising one's superior in pride or speaking evil of the rule.[130] This distinction means that these penitential injunctions are, like the monastic rules of this period, guides for life which acknowledge degrees of sinfulness, and in this way make good the belief that the underlying purpose is rehabilitation of the sinner. The individual is enabled to be respected and given the appropriate penance for the sin and so be returned to the community where reconciliation is possible, rather than remaining in a permanent state of alienation and festering resentment.

At the conclusion of his 'preface' to Part B Columbanus expounds his medicinal parallel. There is an unaccustomed tone of humility as Columbanus acknowledges that the gift of understanding the wounds of souls, which he explains as 'to treat them, to restore what is weak to a complete state of health', is given to few. He sets out a few prescriptions [for the healing of the maladies] according to the traditions of our elders, and according to our partial understanding.[131] Exile is introduced into this section. For a cleric who either murders a person or begets a child out of wedlock, the penance stipulated is that he go into exile which is an extreme form of penance typical of the Irish Church. Extreme measures are sometimes necessary: limbs have to be amputated so as not to infect the whole body. One could say that to remove the sinner from the occasion of sin is a way of helping the culprit to amend his ways but this form of ostracism has a more purgative motive. It deprives the sinner of the *Túatha* or community, which to a clan-conscious people is tantamount to death. From a social historian's point of view it could be a means of ridding society of the troublemakers, but the fact that they were to be under the guidance of an abbot or priest in another region is evidence that even in

---

126. Canon 3 (ed. and trans. Bieler, *The Irish*, p. 97).
127. Canon 9 (ed. and trans. Bieler, *The Irish*, p. 97).
128. Canon 9 (ed. and trans. Bieler, *The Irish*, p. 97).
129. Canon 10 (ed. and trans. Bieler, *The Irish*, p. 98).
130. Canon 11 (ed. and trans. Bieler, *The Irish*, p. 98).
131. 'Preface' B (ed. and trans. Bieler, *The Irish*, p. 99).

extreme cases of punishment, the overall motivation of rehabilitation, including the healing of the sinner, is foremost.

Canons 13 to 25 deal with the sins of the laity. It is here that the differences between the penances of the two groups, cleric and laity, are most obvious. Why would the same sin performed by two people of different rank merit different penances? It is important not to interpolate here the mentality of later centuries, but there must have been a differing perception of the role which the cleric, monk, bishop played in the Church in relation to that played by the lay person. Why is murder by a monk given a penance of ten years with exile and the same crime by a lay person given 'three years on bread and water as an unarmed exile'?[132] As mentioned earlier, the attitude may be formed by the scriptural maxim: 'to whom much is given, of him much will be expected'. The exile spoken of had two forms, one with weapons and one without. Indeed in the context of the society in which these penances were given, the harsher may have been the exile without arms. What we do not know is how the two groups perceived these differences. It may have been better, in terms of penance, to be a lay person. If these penitentials were for the use of clergy then they were not at the disposal of anyone other than clerics, so the laity would not necessarily know of the differences. The fact that all penitentials record different penances for different ranks is established. Whether they were actually performed in all their rigour is not known.

Sodomy for the lay person who is married[133] carries a longer penance than for the unmarried person. It would be instructive if this were in consideration for the wife.[134] Similar differences apply to a masturbator who has a wife. For theft that is a habit, Columbanus (and it seems that this is the only time such a recommendation is made) insists, 'further [he should] undertake not to repeat it'.[135] In the case of perjury, out of greed, the sinner is made to take the tonsure and, 'bidding farewell to the entire world, and until death let him serve God in a monastery'.[136] From one of his Epistles it seems that Columbanus believes that the full Christian life is only possible in a monastery.[137] Though this may seem a very strict penance, all penitentials seem to view oath taking, perjury and those sins that call on God to witness to a falsehood, with a greater degree of gravity. The above interpretation is supported by what cultural anthropologists point out. They emphasize that in pre-modern largely

---

132. Canon 13 (ed. and trans. Bieler, *The Irish*, p. 103).

133. Canon 17 (ed. and trans. Bieler, *The Irish*, p. 103).

134. A reader of an earlier draft of this chapter commented that this was indeed in consideration for the wife. This is in line with Jewish tradition, from which Christianity derived many of its ideas, in which sex is not seen as sinful (the permitted 'sin' to achieve procreation; the line Roman Christianity took for many centuries) but as natural and necessary for human flourishing. In this Jewish belief a husband is blessed if he arouses his wife, condemned if he seeks his own pleasure solely. He is twice blessed if he allows his wife to climax before himself. In short, blessing is attached to thinking of the other first.

135. Canon 19 (ed. and trans. Bieler, *The Irish*, p. 103).

136. Canon 20 (ed. and trans. Bieler, *The Irish*, p. 105).

137. Epistle iv.6 (ed. and trans. Walker, *Sancti Columbani*, p. 31).

oral cultures, the taking and keeping of oaths is basic to an ordered society. They would see the survival of the tribe as the basic human instinct and individual life as cheap. They would also highlight that public oath taking was an intrinsic part of the legal system and as such seemed to merit more strict adherence than our particularly modern abhorrence of murder.[138]

Canon 25 B contains a distinctly non-Celtic stipulation that would cause a reader to ask if this is truly a part of Columbanus' penitential. It insists that if a layman should have 'communicated with the Bonosiaci or with other heretics' he should stand with the catechumens, 'separated from other Christians for forty days'. If he did it in defiance, after it had been denounced by the priest, 'let him do penance for a whole year' and after that time he would have to submit himself to the Catholic bishop for 'imposition of the hand'. From the whole text it is clear that the three aspects of this process, public penance, public reconciliation, and with a bishop as minister, are contrary to the accepted Irish practice.[139] This could indicate that maybe Canon 25 B is a later inclusion. That the heresy was operating in southern Gaul would mean that perhaps Columbanus came into contact with followers of the sect. However, given that he was the quintessential Irish Celt on the continent of Europe it seems more likely that this canon was a later inclusion.

The physicality inherent in the penances imposed by Columbanus, including 50 strokes for a 'simple contradiction of another's word',[140] 24 strokes for leaving the enclosure open,[141] 25 strokes for bathing misdemeanours,[142] reinforces some of the perceptions that the Irish monks and their penitential practices were harsh and even sadistic. This interpretation is only possible if one fails to read them in context. What the present-day reader has to remember is that in the period under discussion there were differing attitudes. Violation of the rights of minors, women or the insane was commonplace. Many socially acceptable practices of the times differ from the public norms in Western society today. In particular a level of violence, including physical punishments for legal infringements, was more widely accepted. It may be debatable, but to some historians the coming of Christianity brought a degree of humanity to these attitudes. This opinion is supported by the discussion of Christianity's role in 'civilizing' society in chapter 1 of this work. From the ecclesiastical texts

---

138. In Irish society, it is instructive that the Conference of Druim Cette attempted to devalue the role of the *poet/filid* who, in certain instances, used the age-old form of ridicule to show his disdain for leaders of the tribe, thus undermining the cohesion of the group. Significantly, ColumCille spoke in favour of the retention of the honoured role of the *poet/filid* in Irish society. This is perhaps evidence of emerging Christian values working to improve and supplement the older Brehon law.

139. Watkins, *A History*, Vol. 11, pp. 617–18. In explanation he says that the Bonosiaci were an obscure group of heretics in Gaul in the sixth and seventh centuries and most likely unknown in Britain.

140. Canon 9 (ed. and trans. Bieler, *The Irish*, p. 99).

141. Canon 26 (ed. and trans. Bieler, *The Irish*, p. 107).

142. Canon 27 (ed. and trans. Bieler, *The Irish*, p. 107). These misdemeanours include: bathing alone naked; washing in the presence of brethren, but standing rather than sitting; bathing sitting but uncovering one's knees or arms (canon 10).

it was seen that the rights of children and women in some instances were protected in certain circumstances.

Canon 30 of the present Columban penitential gives us insights into some of the motivations underlying the canons. All these injunctions seem to be geared to preparing the person more worthily to 'approach the altar'.[143] If the end of penance is to rid oneself of 'mental disturbances before going to Mass', inner transformation not only does not take place but is prevented by virtue of the inner disposition or proclivity to sin. As the end of asceticism is mystical communion with God, Communion, being a foretaste of this, must be approached only after a serious attempt at inner transformation. The penitential puts it thus:

> Therefore, just as we must beware of mortal and fleshly sins before we may communicate so we must refrain and cleanse ourselves from interior vices and the sicknesses of the ailing soul before the covenant of true peace and the bond of eternal salvation.[144]

Penitential of Cummean

This is the next Irish penitential in chronological order[145] to be treated and according to Connolly and McNeill and Gamer it was written about the middle of the seventh century.[146] In some sense it is the most detailed and unified in that it treats each of the eight vices in a separate chapter with an introductory prologue giving the scriptural background for the twelve ways in which sins are forgiven. Cummean (if he is the author) calls it 'the health-giving medicine for souls,'[147] reinforcing the overall belief that indeed this cataloguing of sins and penances has as its most fundamental purpose healing of individual sinners and reuniting them to the community of Christians.

The major vices treated include gluttony, fornication, avarice, anger, dejection, languor, vainglory and pride. It is probably informative to note that the sections to which most time and canons are given are fornication and pride. In the case of the former it could be said that in the social milieu of these penitentials this would be, in some aspects, a clearly visible, societal failure and as such was public and scandalous. Pride, on the other hand, is more insidious, possibly masquerading under the guise of acceptable social practices. Its exaltation of the self and its disregard for others is basically contrary to the Christian ethic. More detailed treatment of these two vices will be addressed

---

143. Canon 30 (ed. and trans. Bieler, *The Irish*, p. 107).
144. Canon 30 (ed. and trans. Bieler, *The Irish*, p. 107).
145. McNeill and Gamer, *Medieval Handbooks*, p. 98; Bieler, *The Irish*, p.108 ff.; Kenney, *The Sources*, p. 241, discuss the authorship of this penitential and come down on the side of Cummean the Long ('Foto') who lived about 592–662 CE.
146. McNeill and Gamer, *Medieval Handbooks*, p. 98; Connolly, *Irish Penitentials*, p. 33.
147. Penitential of Vinnian, Prologue (ed. and trans. McNeill and Gamer, *Medieval Handbooks*, p. 99); (ed. and trans. Bieler, *The Irish*, p. 109).

later. If, however, one puts together sections X[148] and II,[149] the reader is confronted with a greater emphasis on sins of the flesh with 54 canons and their respective penances. The significance of this will be explored below. There is a section that treats petty cases, similar to the distinction made by Columbanus between big and small sins. Section X declares: 'Let us now set forth the decrees of our Fathers before us on the (sinful) playing of boys.'[150]

A reading of this penitential after the previous two, with the vivid details of sins, could give credence to the belief that the Irish penitentials were unnecessarily concerned with sins of the flesh and justify Plummer's earlier negative comments. However, like the monastic rules, the more details given indicate that the penitential/rule was of a later origin. The depth and knowledge evident in this document is commended by Connolly,[151] and may be due to its later development, benefiting, as it probably did, from the earlier works of Vinnian and Columbanus. Such details would certainly make allotting penances simpler for the cleric charged with the work of confession and absolution. It could be said, however, that the less detailed accounts of Vinnian and Columbanus are more likely to convince the reader that the motivation is rehabilitation of the sinner because these books were for the benefit of the confessor in allocating penances. Uniformity would be preserved when clerics used the same set of criteria for specific sins but it seems highly unlikely with the Irish that such uniformity existed. Moreover, in dealing with the developing moral conscience it was important that the issue of justice guided the behaviours in the public forum.

One seemingly out of place canon is the one that has to do with the Host, as in Communion. But fundamental to all the injunctions of the penitentials of the period is the belief that persons living in community are striving for union with God and a more charitable relationship with those with whom one shares this journey. Each helps or hinders the others in their quest, by their faithfulness. This faithfulness is fostered and reaches its climax in the communal celebration of the Mass. Hence the healing of sinful tendencies prepared the monk for a more fruitful celebration of Mass and a more worthy reception of Communion and ultimately fostered a more charitable monastic community.

In the first canon in the section on gluttony, there is a phrase which expresses succinctly how the writer sees the monastic vows: they are vows of sanctity.[152] Nothing short of the wholehearted pursuit of that ultimate Christian goal is permitted here. Elsewhere, another expression reiterates this radical commitment, not only to sanctity but also to perfection.[153] It may seem ironic that the catalogue of sins, formulated by people familiar with human foibles

---

148. Section X (ed. and trans. Bieler, *The Irish*, p. 127).
149. Section II 'Of Fornication' (ed. and trans. Bieler, *The Irish*, p. 113).
150. Bieler, *The Irish*, p. 127; Section X (ed. and trans. McNeill and Gamer, *Medieval Handbooks*, p. 112) expressed this same section as '... misdemeanours of boys'.
151. Connolly, *Irish Penitentials*, p. 34.
152. Section I.1 (ed. and trans. Bieler, *The Irish*, p. 111).
153. Section IV.4 (ed. and trans. Bieler, *The Irish*, p. 121).

from their confessional experience, is so horrendous and yet the monks are committed to lives of sanctity and perfection. A positive aspect of this irony is that the dichotomy between what is aspired to, and what is the reality, can more clearly manifest the mercy and compassion of a God to whom these very people are bound.

Because moderation is prized as a monastic virtue, then gluttony can only detract from this ideal. In the details of these canons, there is a statement which illustrates the different penances allocated to the cleric and the lay person: for the former, who fails in this regard, 'Those who are drunk with wine or beer, contrary to the Saviour's prohibition . . . if they have taken the vow of sanctity they shall expiate the fault for forty days with bread and water; laymen, however, for seven days.'[154]

Sanctity, union with God and one's fellow humans, is one of the aims of monastic living and in this regard both monks and lay persons are challenged to respond to this exalted calling. Whether either was aware of the dichotomy evident in the differing penances is not known. What is known is that there were different penances. In view of the claims of this chapter these reveal the radicality of the monks' commitment over against that of the laity.

Avarice is contrary to the search for poverty in the material sense. Hoarding goods contradicts the monk's commitment to giving to the poor and as such merits penances ranging from fasting and almsgiving to penances with a duration of four years. The majority of the penances consist of restitution, silence in the case of one who lies, and reciting psalms. A cleric 'who has an excess of goods' and refuses to give to the poor was to be excommunicated.[155] If he repents, then he is to live in seclusion for the length of time he was recalcitrant.[156] Mathematical restitution is a very strong element in most of the penitential exercises. The seriousness of the commitment to poverty and its failure is seen by the extreme nature of the penance and bears out the underlying tenet that if one commits to a radical lifestyle and one's public behaviour does not bear this out then the consequences are a serious betrayal of the monastic ideal. No lay person is given such a judgment of excommunication. This was how crime and punishment would be regulated in the sixth- to eighth-century monastic setting in Ireland.

Cassian's principle of *contraries* is seen operating, both explicitly and implicitly, in the section on anger and the much briefer sections on dejection, languor and vainglory. If a person deprives another of his life by murder, the offender shall, in the words of the canon, 'die unto the world with perpetual exile'.[157] One who offends another by cursing shall himself 'live secluded for seven days',[158] thereby being deprived of the company of others. In the case of dejection the one who 'harbours bitterness in his heart shall be healed by a

---

154. Section I.1 (ed. and trans. Bieler, *The Irish*, p. 113).
155. Section III.14 (ed. and trans. Bieler, *The Irish*, p. 119).
156. Section III.14 (ed. and trans. Bieler, *The Irish*, p. 119).
157. Section IV.8 (ed. and trans. Bieler, *The Irish*, p. 121).
158. Section IV.12 (ed. and trans. Bieler, *The Irish*, p. 121).

joyful countenance and a glad heart'.[159] The person who is lazy out of a spirit of languor 'shall be taxed with an extraordinary work, and the slothful with a lengthened vigil'.[160] Any person who suffers from instability, 'shall be healed by permanent residence in one place and by application to work'.[161] Boasting about one's good deeds has the effect of depriving the person of the merit accruing since one is acting out of a desire for human glory. Not only are *contraries* operating here, but also there is the ever-present sense of healing and rehabilitation as of prime importance.

Pride, according to section VIII of the penitential, comes in various guises: heresy,[162] censuring others,[163] disobedience,[164] blasphemy,[165] envy,[166] murmuring,[167] being garrulous,[168] offering excuses to the abbot,[169] disdaining to bow to a senior,[170] silence about a brother's sin.[171] Canons 23 and 24 speak about offences against obedience, that submission of one's mind and will to another in imitation of Christ who always did the will of his Father. The monastic rules contend that this is the most important injunction of monastic living. Canon 24 as well as inculcating obedience could also be a warning against *syneisaktism* for it states, 'He who speaks with a woman alone, or remains under the same roof [with her] at night, shall go without supper. If [he does this] after being forbidden, he shall do penance on bread and water.'[172] It should be noted that this canon goes further than the injunction of the First Synod of Patrick about talking to a woman. If as earlier stated, *syneisaktism* (that is, sharing of living quarters by both female and male monks), is intended to 'test' the chastity of the males, then both virtues of obedience and chastity are here seen as of equal value.

Canon 16 is interesting in that the detractor is saved from penance if his motives are any of the following: preventing a person from doing evil; confirming good and blaming evil; sorrowing for the evil. Any person acting thus 'is to be held a physician [of souls]'.[173] The notion of intentionality is seen in this canon as not cancelling censure but as commendable in attending to a wider community good, thus healing both the offender and those with whom he comes in contact. Heresy, the ever-present fear of any communitarian group, is taken as a form of pride. If the offender abjures his own opinions and

---

159. Section V.1 (ed. and trans. Bieler, *The Irish*, p. 121).
160. Section IV.2 (ed. and trans. Bieler, *The Irish*, p. 121).
161. Section IV.2 (ed. and trans. Bieler, *The Irish*, p. 123).
162. Section VIII.1 (ed. and trans. Bieler, *The Irish*, p. 123).
163. Section VIII.3 (ed. and trans. Bieler, *The Irish*, p. 123).
164. Section VIII.4 (ed. and trans. Bieler, *The Irish*, p. 123).
165. Section VIII.5 (ed. and trans. Bieler, *The Irish*, p. 123).
166. Section VIII.7 (ed. and trans. Bieler, *The Irish*, p. 123).
167. Section VIII.6 (ed. and trans. Bieler, *The Irish*, p. 123).
168. Section VIII.14 (ed. and trans. Bieler, *The Irish*, p. 123).
169. Section VIII.17 (ed. and trans. Bieler, *The Irish*, p. 125).
170. Section VIII.18 (ed. and trans. Bieler, *The Irish*, p. 125).
171. Section VIII.19 (ed. and trans. Bieler, *The Irish*, p. 125).
172. Section VIII. 24 (ed. and trans. Bieler, *The Irish*, p. 125).
173. Section VIII.16 (ed. and trans. Bieler, *The Irish*, p. 125).

converts those who were influenced by his erroneous ideas, he will be welcomed back into the community. A similar care for a brother is evident where he who is silent about a brother's sin shall rebuke him with confidence.[174]

Blasphemy, murmuring and envy, all forms of pride, are warned against as they, together with heresy, cause scandal which is destructive to the morale of any ecclesial group. Whether this is because the group will be seen to be fallible human beings or whether there is a tone of idealism and unreality about the Christian pursuit is unclear. Whatever the anthropology of scandal, pride in all its forms goes contrary to that most basic of monastic virtues, obedience. Submitting one's will, mind and heart to the directions of another (the *anamchara* was a pivotal person in monasticism) even today strikes the observer of monasticism as a little short of madness. However, what fundamentally sets the monks apart from the rest of humankind is that they aspire to this radical lifestyle. They fast, abstain from prohibited foods, undertake physical trials, submit their hearts and minds to the abbot, pray without ceasing and most of the time do this in the very human context of their own acknowledged weaknesses and failures. Without their commitment to this lifestyle, these penitentials may never have seen the light of day.

Some of the most recognized penitential canons are those which deal with sins of the flesh. As was mentioned above, if time and space allotted to a topic is any indication of its importance, then this category of sin is important. Fornication is discussed in 33 canons. In both Vinnian and Cummean's penitentials there is an awareness that one-off failures are not as culpable as habitual offences. This is not because the offence is not serious but because habitual sin calls for a more radical application of penance as, it would seem, the proclivity is more entrenched. The longer the habit has been entrenched, the longer the healing will take. In addition to this, entrenched behaviours are not as easily uprooted, as are the more superficial ones. Canon 1 simply states, 'A bishop who commits fornication shall be degraded and shall do penance for twelve years.'[175] When a deacon or presbyter is involved, canon 2 goes into extensive detail about the amounts of food to be taken or foregone, as a penance for sin.[176]

Further evidence of a somewhat enlightened approach is the fact that the notion that the health or strength of the penitent is to be taken into consideration in undertaking fasts. Along with this seemingly lenient attitude on the part of the framer of the penitential, there is the admonition, in keeping with the fundamental tenets of monasticism, that he 'deplore his guilt from his inmost heart, and above all things he shall adopt an attitude of the readiest obedience'.[177] Since the whole end and purpose of penance is to be reconciled with the community, with the person offended and ultimately with God, the fornicator is to be admitted to the Eucharist after a year and a half, 'lest his soul perish utterly

---

174. Section VIII.19 (ed. and trans. Bieler, *The Irish*, p. 125).
175. Section II.1 (ed. and trans. Bieler, *The Irish*, p. 113).
176. Section II.2 (ed. and trans. Bieler, *The Irish*, p. 113).
177. Section II.2 (ed. and trans. Bieler, *The Irish*, p. 115).

through lacking so long a time the celestial medicine'.[178] Not only the person but the Eucharist itself is encompassed in the healing imagery deeply embedded in these penitentials. Canons 3, 4 and 6 all address the different penances for persons of different rank, with those of lower rank receiving lesser penances.[179]

Canons 11 to 25 echo those of Vinnian and, in some cases, those of Columbanus, in that they treat of the difference between sins of thought and those put into action. They also refer to the differences among sins and their allotted penances for different ranks of persons. The defiling of woman, whether she be virgin or not, is the same as in previous penitentials. The linguistic touch, seen later as a poetic device in the monastic rules, occurs where a layman repenting of fornication submits to penances which include 'in all (three years) without wine, without meat, without arms, without his wife'.[180] Another pointed difference is noted where after the birth of a child the father, the only parent explicitly mentioned though both would be involved, is to abstain from sexual intercourse, 'if it is a son, for thirty-three [days]; if a daughter, for sixty-six [days]'.[181] Similar differences are seen regarding girls and boys in the Irish practice of fosterage. The fee for a girl is higher than for a boy. Commentators think that it may be due to the difficulty in rearing a girl or the fact that the girl is less likely to benefit her foster parents.[182]

The Roman historian, Diodorus Siculus, would probably see section X as a valid representation of the behaviour of the Irish, whose ancestors he so soundly decried.[183] The 21 canons of this section deal mainly with homosexuality (canons 1, 2, 3, 4), masturbation (canons 6, 7, 13, 15, 16), bestiality (canon 5), fornication (canon 17), and the pervading dilemma of the relationship operating between sins of thought and deed (canon 17). There are some canons which could be equally applied to sexual sins of both homosexuality and heterosexuality, as the sin and penance are regarded the same. One of these canons[184] stipulates that the victim is to perform a penance, even though he may be only ten years of age.[185] There

---

178. Section II.2 (ed. and trans. Bieler, *The Irish*, p. 115).
179. Section II.2, 4, 6 (ed. and trans. Bieler, *The Irish*, p. 115).
180. Section II.22 (ed. and trans. Bieler, *The Irish*, p. 117).
181. Section II.31 (ed. and trans. Bieler, *The Irish*, p. 117). This difference is also a practice in the Jewish tradition.
182. Kelly, *A Guide*, p. 87.
183. C. Eluere, *The Celts*, p. 141. In the document section of the book, Eluere, while acknowledging the often rather biased ancient accounts about the Celts, forerunners of the Irish, nonetheless quotes the said ancient author in relation to their sexual tendencies.

They abandon themselves to a strange passion for other men. They usually sleep on the ground . . . and tumble with a bedfellow on either side. And what is strangest of all is that, without any thought for a natural sense of modesty, they carelessly surrender their virginity to other men. Far from finding anything shameful in all this, they feel insulted if anyone refuses the favours they offer.

184. Section X.9, states: 'a small boy misused by an older man, if he is ten years of age, shall fast for a week; if he consents, for twenty days'.
185. It has been suggested to me by a reader of an early draft, that the idea of the young victim's doing penance may be similar to the Jewish act of purification rather than penitential satisfaction. This explanation certainly has some validity.

is no specified sense in which the older man is given a penance, unless canon 15 on homosexuality is applicable to him.[186] Three other canons in this section are rather enigmatic in the present context. Canon 18[187] could come from the druidic culture and the severity of the penance speaks for itself. From it we learn that the offender is to be absolved by the bishop and do penance for a whole year. Maybe these canons, underpinned by a Celtic consciousness that stresses the unity of all of creation, come from a theology of the human body which sees it as a temple of the Holy Spirit, and hence the profanity of defiling it in any way. However, these canons are more likely associated with the druidic and primal cultures where such practices were accepted. In this way the stress on them could be from a deep-seated fear of this primal tradition.[188] As stated earlier in this work, the movement from primal religions to Christianity was a gradual process and while this movement was taking place residual practices were likely to be still happening in the lives of some converts. The condition of the healing is that the penances must be entered into with obedience and humility. They exist for the healing of the individual and for the stamping out of those thoughts and desires which detract from wholehearted devotion to God. Only if they truly help the penitent to transfer the focus of his life from the body to the inner spirit and its life, will they bring about the inner transformation intrinsically sought in Irish monasticism.

Finally, as has been said, the last group of canons deals with the Host and how one should approach its reception. The pragmatic nature of these is in keeping with what is essentially part of Celtic consciousness: the desire to help the sinner to sorrow, forgiveness, reconciliation and ultimately union with God. It could be noted here in passing that both the priest and the lay person were encouraged to approach their *anamchara* daily. The clerics too were seen as needing forgiveness. Connolly, in discussing the links between Brehon law and the penitential system,[189] says that the roles of both physician and judge envisage close collaboration between priest and penitent in preparing the penitential pilgrimage back to the virtuous, moral life. Cummean, or Cumminianus as he calls himself in the final statement, seems to be reiterating this while emphasizing the mutuality of this penitential process: 'when thou art such a priest, and such is thy teaching and thy word, there is given to thee the share of those whom thou correctest, that their merit may be thy reward and their salvation thy glory'.[190]

---

186. Section X.15, states: 'Those practicing homosexuality, if they are boys, two years; if men, three or four years; but if it becomes a habit, seven years.'
187. Section X.18, states: 'He who eats the skin of his own body, that is, a scab, or the vermin which are called lice, and also he who eats or drinks his own excreta – with imposition of hands of his bishop he shall do penance for an entire year on bread and water.'
188. In chapter 1 this has been denied because the Celts seem to have been at one with their primal past. Maybe this development has something to do with a societal change in perceptions of what is good for the group. Another explanation could be that because different impressions come from different eras this might be the cause of this apparent contradiction.
189. Connolly, *Irish Penitentials*, p. 158.
190. Epilogue, 1 (ed. and trans. Bieler, *The Irish*, p. 135).

Canones Hibernenses

Of the two collections of Irish Canons, *Canones Hibernenses* and *Collectio canonum Hibernensis*, only the former will be used here as the latter contains little that is of a penitential nature.[191] Kenney, speaking of the latter, says, 'it is doubtful if any of these canons can be of a date later than the first half of the seventh century'.[192] According to all commentators the canons are decrees from various Irish synods. The penances are more severe than those previously encountered in the penitentials already discussed.[193] They appear to be an attempt to put together a collection for ecclesiastical use. Kenney claims that in this collection of canons we meet for the first time provision for payments, in the normal secular unit of value, the female slave.[194] This provision alone would seem to remind the reader of the criticism that Church law was no better than the Brehon in relation to the role of women in the society. However, there are other provisions of both ecclesiastical and Brehon law that give evidence for the opposite treatment of women. The *Canones Hibernenses* is quoted in the Penitential of Theodore[195] and so is significant in that it was sufficiently wellknown that its injunctions were used as the basis of answers given by Theodore on the principles of penance.

The work is divided into six sections, each a compact unit. The detail of section I where penances for polluting water are given points to the Celtic respect for all things natural. The uniquely Irish feature of commutations is found in section II. Fines imposed for injuries to clerics make up section III. Section IV has a code of penalties for inhospitality. This is significant in the climate of Irish monasticism where hospitality was seen as an integral part of the building and overall rationale for monastic living. Section V, on dogs, does not seem to have any ecclesiastical significance and could be evidence that there is still some dispute about authorship of both the ecclesiastical and secular texts. In the case of section V, one can safely assume that it is part of the Brehon law. How it managed to find its way into the ecclesiastical law and more particularly what its significance was for society is a puzzle. The final section, VI, deals with tithes and firstfruits in the pattern of Exodus. McNeill and Gamer hold that this document gives the impression of a laborious, cooperative task. They believe, as do other writers on ecclesiastical and secular law, that both ecclesiastical and secular jurists may have cooperated in the preparation of the canons.[196]

---

191. McNeill and Gamer, *Medieval Handbooks*, p. 139; these two sets of canons are treated in Hughes, *Early Christian*, pp. 67-80.
192. Kenney, *The Sources*, p. 244.
193. Connolly, *Irish Penitentials*, p. 34.
194. Kenney, *The Sources*, p. 244.
195. Theodore was archbishop of Canterbury in 668 CE. He was born in Tarsus and his penitential contains his replies to various persons in Britain who questioned him on the remedy of penance. He is said to have been a brilliant administrator and unifier of the Celtic and Anglo-Saxon factions on the island of Britain.
196. McNeill and Gamer, *Medieval Handbooks*, p. 118.

Section I can be passed over rapidly except for the references to what today would be called the abortion issue, treated in four canons.[197] The prohibition against dirge singing or keening is a reference to druidic practices that were deeply embedded in the pre-Christian society of Ireland. It is perhaps significant to note that they are retained in the present-day funeral tradition of Ireland so the prohibition was not able to dislodge this powerful ancestral practice. It seems that in this set of canons the notion of slaves being used as payment in the penitential process is new and constitutes a rather complicated method of calculating what number of slaves was the equivalent of the crime committed. In summary then, this group of canons gives credence to the fact of the bipartisan formulations of some ecclesiastical laws. They therefore address more than purely religious issues but in doing so they bear witness to the oft-repeated assumption of this work that in the period under discussion the Irish *praxis* conformed closely with the Celtic consciousness of their pre-Christian ancestors.

Commutations

Binchy gives the most detailed treatment of commutations as practised in the Irish Church of the sixth to the eighth century.[198] Since the purpose of this section is simply to detail some of the commutations and not to comment on Binchy's arguments, the reader is directed to follow the logic of his work to his conclusions that 'it seems that a system of commutations [was] designed to shorten (and in some cases . . . to lighten) the traditional forms of penance'. An additional comment of his on the issue of commutations is:

> it seems that the *arre*[199] represents an ancient practice of the Irish Church, possibly one which was originally confined to certain districts or to the houses of a single monastic federation and hence remained unrecognised by the more important communities – this might account for the silence of the Penitentials.[200]

197. Section I.6, 7, 8, 11 (ed. and trans. Bieler, *The Irish*, p. 161) read as follows:
6) The penance for the destruction of an embryo of a child in the mother's womb, three and a half years.
7) The penance for the destruction of flesh and spirit, seven and a half years on bread and water, in continence.
8) The life price for the destruction of the embryo and the mother, twelve female slaves.
11) The penance for a mother's destruction of her own child, twelve years on bread and water.
198. See Binchy, 'Medicine', in which he compares the Rawlinson B 512, ff.42c–44a (referred to as R) with the text of 3 B 23 (referred to as B) and comes to the conclusion that despite the defects of B, it is 'closer to the original for two reasons'. First, it has a much more intimate link with the well-known Latin treatise *De Arreis* (and Binchy goes on to detail the links and comes to the stance that B 'must represent an older and fuller translation of which R is a shortened version'). Secondly, he gives textual proofs that with R for example omitting some of the statements there is a lack of coherence and meaning.
199. Binchy, 'Medicine', p. 47, gives a detailed explanation of this word.
200. Binchy, 'Medicine', p. 54.

Briefly Binchy says that *arr(a)e* means a commutation of penance. The penance itself is usually shorter and more intensive. *Arr(a)e*, in later orthography *arra*, is the verbal noun of *ar-rem*, which means, 'pays for, pays instead of'. All later versions are derived from this original old Irish word. In section 11 of *Canones Hibernenses* the Latin term *arreum* is used.

The text itself gives four reasons, enumerated by the sages, why the commutations were practised. They clearly reinforce the overall motive given throughout this discussion, of healing and rehabilitation of the penitent. These reasons are: 'for a speedy separation from the sin with which one has been united'.[201] This is wise, as the 'cohabitation'[202] with sin only makes it harder to overcome the sinful tendency. It seems like the short, sharp shot to eradicate it as soon as possible. Second, the sages wish to rid the penitent of the 'fear of adding to his sins in the future'.[203] One weakness leads to others and the sooner the original fault is conquered the easier will be the rehabilitation. The third reason: 'for fear that one's life be cut short before the end of the penance decided by a soul-friend'.[204] This anxiety seems to go contrary to the uniquely Irish notion of intentionality that marked one of the differences between secular and ecclesiastical law. If one intended to perform a penance, did it make any difference if one died before the penance was completed? The answer is most probably yes in the prevailing mentality. The final, and probably the most important reason, for it is treated in two of the penitentials already discussed, is to free the sinner to approach the Body and Blood of Christ without restrictions.[205]

Since the twelve *arrum* of the *Canones Hibernenses* are an abbreviated form of the original ones given in the translation by Binchy, they will be used here. In the *arre* the list of sins that are not entitled to any remission include kin-slayings, homicides, and secret murders. In addition to the foregoing are brigandage, druidism, satirizing.[206] Further sins include adultery, incest, perjury, heresy and violation of [the duties of one's ecclesiastical] grade.[207]

The harshness of these commutations would have to be assessed in the light of the reasons given by the sages above. The first is to rescue a soul from hell and hence,

> three hundred and sixty-five Paters and three hundred and sixty-five genuflections and three hundred and sixty-five blows of the scourge every day for a

---

201. Penitential Commutations, referred to as PC in future, V 6 (ed. and trans. Binchy, 'Medicine', p. 59)
202. Binchy, 'Medicine', p. 59 has an interestingly intimate literal translation: 'sin . . . with which one has been united' as 'after cohabitation with', which nonetheless points to the power of sin to infect every facet of one's life.
203. PC, V 6 (ed. and trans. Binchy, 'Medicine', p. 59).
204. PC, V 6 (ed. and trans. Binchy, 'Medicine', p. 59).
205. PC, V 6 (ed. and trans. Binchy, 'Medicine', p. 59).
206. This sin is interesting given the comments made earlier in relation to the poets or *filid* and their role in satirizing or ridiculing people in the tribe and the destabilization of the society this brought about.
207. PC, V 5 (ed. and trans. Binchy, 'Medicine', p. 59).

> year, and a fast every month. For it is in proportion to the number of joints and sinews in the human body that this commutation to save a soul which has merited torments [while] in the body has been devised.[208]

In keeping with the belief that the different lifestyle expectations of the cleric and the lay person merit different treatment in relation to sin and penance, verse 7 states that,

> As there is a difference between laymen and clerics and between nuns and laywomen, so too there is a difference between the [kind of] mortification and penance due from them, as well as between the commutations which may properly be performed by them.[209]

The first commutation proper to these lay persons is, 'spending the night in water or on nettles or on nutshells, or in a grave with a dead body... for it is not usual for [them] not to have some part in manslaughter'.[210]

Verse 27 also suggests standing in water, for one night, or on nettles or on nutshells as part of the commutation for a year's penance. The other part is 'a black fast for three days without drinking, eating or sleeping'.[211] This conforms to the belief that though the length of time was commuted the severity was greatly increased.

Another specifically Irish penance was the *crosfigell*, which tested the endurance of the whole body through the adoption of a cruciform position. This form of commutation is cited in six different verses.[212] Thirteen is the commuting of a three-day fast to one day with (for him who reads) 'reciting the three fifties and their canticles standing and celebrating each canonical hour, twelve genuflections with arms outstretched towards God each canonical hour and diligent concentration upon heaven'.[213]

This last comment, 'diligent concentration upon heaven', is interesting in that it would be impossible for anyone except the penitent to evaluate this. Was it included for the purpose of reiterating that inner transformation was the aim of all these penances? It would seem so. Verse 19 is the 'commutation of a week's strict penance on bread and water: seven *Beati* [recited] in a properly performed cross-vigil, with a Credo, a Pater, and *Hymnum dicit* after each *Beati*'.[214] For those sinners who cannot read verse 20 is intended. Reminiscent of the monastic rules, given the toughness needed to live by them, the framers of these penitential commutations nonetheless were conscious of those who were not able, either by ill-health, infirmity, age or educational deficiency, to conform completely. This commutation then suggests, 'seven hundred properly

---

208. PC, V 1 (ed. and trans. Binchy, 'Medicine', p. 59).
209. PC, V 7 (ed. and trans. Binchy, 'Medicine', p. 61).
210. PC, V 8 (ed. and trans. Binchy, 'Medicine', p. 61).
211. PC, V 27 (ed. and trans. Binchy, 'Medicine', p. 67).
212. These six verses include: 13, 18, 19, 20, 31 and 32.
213. PC, V 13 (ed. and trans. Binchy, 'Medicine', p. 61).
214. PC, V 19 (ed. and trans. Binchy, 'Medicine', p. 63).

made genuflections and seven hundred properly administered lashes, and a cross-vigil after each hundred until they are weary'.[215]

The weariness, like the physical aptitude, points to the fact, stressed elsewhere, that the purpose was healing and rehabilitation and so there was no reason to break the spirit. Another commutation called for a single fast or possibly a triduum to 'chant the twelve *Beati* in cross-vigil without lowering the arms while doing so'.[216]

'A commutation of fifty nights of strict penance capable of being performed in a single day',[217] is how another is expressed. This comes with the recommendation of Mobi Clarenech (d. 580 CE), ColumCille and even with the counsel of the Archangel Michael. All of the psalms are carefully spelled out with seven genuflections at the end of each psalm and sundry other brief prayers. Finally, a later verse reduces a year's strict penance to three days where the penitent spends

> three nights in a grave with a dead body without drinking, eating or sleeping; [in addition the person makes] earnest confession to God and every man at every hour of the day and night, together with resolution to abandon all sin under the direction of a pious soul-friend.[218]

Added to this the penitent is 'to chant the three fifties each day and keep each canonical hour'. Again the concession to one who cannot read, 'he prays in his heart with mental ardour, with tears and repentance'.[219] The rationale for such commutations is the speedy separation from sins, lessening of potential for future sinning, being prepared for death and worthiness to approach the Eucharist. That the soul-friend, *anamchara*, was consulted in these commutations is understandable and that they accepted some of the penitential burden themselves is not always acknowledged. However, as this practice was distinctively Irish it added to the overall belief, specified in many of the penitential injunctions already addressed, that at root these penitentials and commutations were a genuine attempt to heal the sinner and reconcile them with the community. This understanding of the asceticism of monastic penance conforms with the overall contention of this study that the *praxis* of the sixth to the eighth century, as a radical response to the *evangelium*, was specifically influenced by the Irish and their cultural context. In this healing and rehabilitation aspect of penance, here was a sense of balance not always evident in other forms of monastic penance.

---

215. PC, V 20 (ed. and trans. Binchy, 'Medicine', p. 63).
216. PC, V 31 (ed. and trans. Binchy, 'Medicine', p. 67).
217. PC, V 24 (ed. and trans. Binchy, 'Medicine', p. 65).
218. PC, V 26 (ed. and trans. Binchy, 'Medicine', p. 65).
219. PC, V 26 (ed. and trans. Binchy, 'Medicine', p. 5).

Asceticism as geilt

When one remembers the purpose of these penitentials and the subsequent commutations, one cannot but be impressed with the detail and the underlying care for the sinner, his health and rehabilitation that is included in these regulations. However they are judged by present-day readers (and Plummer is not the only person who has read these penitentials with a negative response), the rules, penances, commutations were congruent with the age, an age characterized by brutality but also by high aspirations. This was the period that came to be regarded later as the golden age of the Irish Church and was called the Age of the Saints. Saints were those who took up the challenge to live the counsels of the gospel as perfectly as humanly possible. Many did so, some in very extreme ways, with a fervour that resembled madness. Actually Nora Chadwick says that the most extreme form of asceticism was madness, captured in the Irish word *geilt*. The word is usually translated as 'lunatic' or madman' and in the Irish literary tradition is influenced by a sixth-century saga about a certain Suibhne. This sixth-century king saw a vision during the battle of Moyra, 637 CE, after which he fled human society, abandoning his kingdom, led a wandering life alone with wild nature subsisting solely on a vegetarian diet.[220] Hence those who saw visions, fled to monasteries and lived austere lives were equated with Suibhne. Their lives were seen as models of a penance that attempted to confront human frailty.

As if intending to show that the Irish, as a race, were deeply penitential, Walters maintains that not only in the penitentials, but also in the *Carmina Gadelica*[221] does one find attitudes to human frailty that pervade the Celtic tradition.[222] Whether the *Carmina* is authentically Celtic cannot be asserted with any certainty. However, what is clear in many of the prayers is a balance between awareness of personal sinfulness and the omnipresence of a forgiving God. This excerpt from one of Carmichael's prayers culled from the Celtic

---

220. Chadwick, *The Age*, p. 105. Another reference to him is found in an early Irish codex known as the *Book of Aicill* where he tells us that there were many other men in Ireland who lived ascetic lives as hermits, recluses and who were similarly *geilt*.

221. Carmichael, A., *Carmina Gadelica: Hymns and Incantations*, (Edinburgh: Floris Books, 2nd edn, 1994), p. 7. Carmichael spent many years collecting these prayers, incantations and hymns which he says in the preface of the one volume (there were actually six volumes, with the original preface repeated in the abridged version) are

> religious texts which with their strange blend of pagan and Christian imagery, witness to the spirituality of a vanished age. Their complement of mysterious word and phrases, apparently unknown outside this repository of incantations, and their dignified, almost liturgical style fascinate the reading public.

O'Loughlin in Davies, *Celtic*, p. 23, claims they 'remain strongly Celtic in kind and are a reminder of the extent to which an oral and minority culture can conserve elements from an earlier tradition'. Given the lengthy discussion in the 1994 edition of this work, perhaps the searcher for Celtic prayers could more profitably be directed to those translated by O'Loughlin in Davies, *Celtic Spirituality*, pp. 259-307.

222. Conference attended in Edinburgh, November 1994, where Dyffed Walters gave a paper on the Irish penitentials and subsequently sent me a copy.

people of the Outer Hebrides, gives us some idea of this balance that was ever present in their acknowledgement of sin:

> To condemn myself at the chair of confession
> Lest I be condemned at the chair of judgement;
> Jesus give me strength and courage
> It is easier for me to go under subjection for a brief while
> Than to go to death during eternity.[223]

Many instances of such prayers, hymns and incantations are claimed to underscore the theological basis for Irish, Celtic in the broader sense, Christianity in the sixth to the eighth century. A reader needs to be wary of some of these anthologies for, as Sheldrake claims, the picture they present 'is at best one-dimensional and at worst positively misleading'.[224] This difficulty sometimes stems from the lack of a historical and cultural perspective. They may come from a disillusionment, as O'Loughlin claims,[225] with institutional religion. The Celtic world and its religion may also appear, as was thought when this work was commenced, to be less patriarchal and more in tune with the feminine. What is probably one of the main reasons for the attractiveness of things Celtic is its 'embrace [of] a more contextual, grounded, varied yet uncomplicated, messy, even chaotic faith and spirituality than the conventional, institutional forms'.[226]

Conclusion

Irish society, like that of most groups of the period, was developing from one state to another and so the transition was marked by attempts to guide behaviour in codified texts. No person or society is completely civilized nor is it completely brutal or barbaric. So, growing in awareness of the potential for both modes of behaviour, the leaders of society try to specify acceptable behaviour and to indicate how unacceptable behaviour would be punished within the context of the particular society's emerging self-perception.

Because of the spread of Christianity in early Irish society both secular and ecclesiastical law-makers were involved in formulating codes of behaviour. The discussion about the authorship of the penitentials analysed in this chapter shows how each code supported the other. Both codes were fair and humane. The authors of both were well informed about the issues being codified. In the case of the penitentials the conclusion arrived at was that they were balanced in the penances assigned for they took into account whether the penitent could read, was too old or infirm to perform them, and whether it would be

---

223. Moore (ed.), *Carmina*, p. 275, used with permission of Floris Books.
224. Sheldrake, *Living*, p. 3.
225. O'Loughlin, in Davies, *Celtic*, Introduction.
226. Sheldrake, *Living*, p. 3.

more beneficial to commute them in order really to achieve the purpose for which they were formulated.

It is evident from statements in all the Irish penitentials treated here (Vinnian, Columbanus and Cummean) that the primary purpose was to heal the penitent and to return the sinner to the community and community worship. The grading of penances acknowledges that some transgressions are more serious than others. Some behaviours require more concentrated work as they are more entrenched. While transgressions, on the whole, are in the public arena, the motivation and seat of the problem may be more deeply rooted in the heart. There is ample evidence in the penitentials that the heart needs to be involved if true conversion is to be effected.

The whole notion of conversion is deeply ingrained in the Irish psyche as it was an integral part of the druidic tradition and in most aspects was continued in the penitential stipulations. Druids held a place of honour in the society of the time. They, with the poets, *filid*, were the keepers of stories of the *Túatha*. They had a certain kind of power in the community. In a similar way the soul-friend, *anamchara*, of the Irish monastic tradition knew in minute detail the stories of the monks who came to them for advice. They knew that healing was the primary purpose of the penances they would suggest and so did not take advantage of the 'power' they had.

Intrinsic to this penitential regime was the ancient principle of *contraries*, utilized by Cassian but standing in a long line of ancient practices that highlighted the healing nature of true penance. Even today it is sound to suggest that one changes behaviour that is unacceptable by performing the opposite behaviour; when one has overindulged with food the best way of counteracting the effects of this is to perform some kind of fast. Throughout the Irish penitentials this principle is seen time and time again.

In the penitentials analysed in this chapter, the reader gets an insight into the attitudes that pervaded the ecclesial society of the sixth to eighth century in Ireland. The practices spelled out in such detail and the underlying spirit or attitude that accompanied them leave the reader in no doubt that uppermost in the minds of the Irish framers of these penitentials was the desire to be at one with the creator whom they saw as working in and through creation. By extension, the same divine presence is encountered in and through the penitential stipulations of the lifestyle they had chosen. These practices were seen as healing the individual and, in the process, enabling the monks and ultimately the ecclesial community to live more in keeping with the Christian call to holiness.

The monastic tradition, within which these penances were performed, was for the monks the most perfect fulfilment of the call of the *evangelium* to wholeness and holiness. While the expectations were different for the clerics and the lay members of the monastic settlements, all saw communion with God and service of others as the goal of their life on earth and hence the dynamism towards emulation exercised by those who committed themselves to live this life more radically. The austerity of the penances, whether they were performed in all their rigour or were subject to frequent commutations, have to be balanced by the ever-present recommendation of all penitential writers that the penances were to be performed subject to the health, work expectation and temperament of the penitent.

The idea that penances could be commuted initially was in consideration for the penitent, and in the period under discussion this motive was paramount. In the ancient text, *De Arreis*, there are four specific reasons given for commutation: speedy separation from sins, lessening of potential for future sinning, being prepared for death and worthiness to approach communion. Such commutations were in the hands of the *anamchara* to grant and who better to know the penitent than the soul-friend. However, later in history (and there is no evidence to indicate that this occurred in the sixth to eighth century) this practice did eventually degenerate into paying someone to do one's penance. A peculiarly Irish Christian practice was for the 'sinner' to make compensation (composition) to the wronged person or family by being available to them to perform the tasks that the dead or injured person would perform. This was an advance on the practice of *talio* or retaliation, a primitive custom that was present in the society of the time. The bulk of the commutations are contained in a specifically ecclesiastical text *Canones Hibernenses*.

When one reads these penitentials for the first time it becomes obvious that such expectations about one's behaviour are readily understood by people who are committed to a different lifestyle from the general population. They would only be undertaken willingly. In all their severity, they could be seen as extreme and bordering on the bizarre. Some observers of these monastic penances have called them *geilt*, the Irish word for madness. What has been maintained throughout this chapter is that primarily the penitentials were designed for the healing of both monks and lay people with differing penances assigned to each. They could be commuted in conversation with one's *anamchara*. Degrees of transgressions were noted and the motivation for behaviours that militated against the smooth running of the community was found in the heart. Hence the many times heart is mentioned in relation to conversion in monastic living.

The three penitentials used in this chapter have points in common. Both Vinnian and Columbanus divide their work into two parts. With the former the division shows that the first part deals with the clergy and the second part with the laity and the married state. In Columbanus' penitential the division is clearly marked (part A and B) with similar emphasis: part A addresses sins of the monks and part B those of the laity. Both have references to Cassian's *contraries* throughout. Cummean's work is more clearly using the *contraries* as the basis for its discussion of sin and its remedy. His sections revolve around eight vices and the remedy for each with an introductory Scripture message. The combined message of these penitentials is that they are intended for all the inhabitants of monastic settlements. They are to be suited to the individual penitent and they aim to bring the penitent closer to God and restore them to the community and its worship.

Initially, the aggregations of like-minded people in monastic settlements did not require a rule of life, but as the number of members of monastic institutions increased, the founders, or their immediate followers, wrote simple rules which took the form of principles rather than minute stipulations for living. These rules like the penitentials have to be read with the cultural context in mind. Some of these rules are the subject of the next chapter of this work. Unless the cultural context is in the forefront of the mind of the reader the subject being addressed is liable to be a source of confusion and the era is doomed to be misunderstood. Both the monastic rules and the spirit of the founders in whose name they were written contribute to the fact that in the minds of later historians, linguists and theologians, this period in Irish history is called the *Golden Age*.

3 Irish Monastic Rules Of The Sixth To The Eighth Century

Romantic individualism has been explored by many writers, including Kierkegaard. The chaotic nature of frenetic personal striving in those who become their own objective reality highlights the futility of such self-focused absorption. Only when the ego of the individual has been focused on others can true community develop. Kierkegaard believed that, 'the preparatory work must be done in the soul of the individual, where all the decisive battles are fought and permanent foundations laid'.[1]

Introduction

The latter part of the above comment underpins the belief inherent in most of the primary sources used in this study: the individual, vital as s/he may be, nonetheless is predominantly a social being who is primarily 'in relationship' and, as such, these two aspects of the person, individual and communal, are seen as the two sides of the one coin. Each is different yet complementary in that the whole coin would not exist without both sides. They reveal different aspects of the coin but contribute to the wholeness thereof. The dilemma and tension this identifies and the resolving thereof are an important endeavour of monastic striving. Kierkegaard comments that 'it behoves us to have respect for the monastic movement' because it highlights 'monasticism's passionate commitment to God, the "absolute *telos*" of human existence'.[2]

This chapter will look at the general notions of monasticism, membership of Irish monasteries and the basic ascetic principles that guided these establishments. This will be attempted in the context of the sixth to the eighth century. Discussion of the monastic rules, their number and nature, of each of the prominent founders of monasteries will follow. The chronological order of the rules given by O'Curry with the inclusion of Columbanus' rule will be

---

1.   G. Connel, and C. S. Evans, *Foundations of Kierkegaard's Vision of Community: Religion, Ethics and Politics in Kierkegaard* (New Jersey: Humanities Press, 1993), p. 193.
2.   D. R. Law, 'Kierkegaard on Monasteries', *DR* Vol. 114, No. 396 (July, 1996), p. 185. However Law goes on to say that despite the praise noted above, Kierkegaard insists on criticizing monasticism because it 'is based on an inadequate understanding of human existence'. After analysing the comments of Kierkegaard, Law concludes with a rejection of the arguments for 'far from being an escape from the world, the monk takes the world with him into the monastery in the form of his spiritual struggle with himself and his worldly desires and urges', p. 190.

utilized and an analysis of the ascetical theology that emerges from each of them will constitute the main focus of this chapter.

The following dialogue says something about an aspect of monastic life as perceived by the two most important founders of the reform movement in Ireland. Máel-Rúain of Tallaght said, 'As long as my injunctions are observed in this place, the liquor that causes forgetfulness of God shall not be drunk here.' Dublitir of Finglas replied, 'Well my monks shall drink it and they shall be in heaven along with yours.' However, Máel-Rúain seems to have had the last word: 'Anyone of my monks who harkens to me and who keeps my rule, shall not need to be cleansed by the fire of Doomsday . . . Your monks, however, shall perchance have something for the fire of Doomsday to cleanse.'[3] While this little exchange may or may not have taken place, it is about differing perceptions of what constitutes monasticism[4] in general and an aspect of monastic asceticism in particular. In this dialogue there is a link between the monastic rule, the way of life and the hereafter. Others see evidence that the purpose of the rule is to inculcate a way of life in order to avoid the horrors of Doomsday. The incompatibility of 'worldly' goods with asceticism may be another way of understanding this exchange. It could also be about two abbots boasting of the superior asceticism of their adherents. Maybe it is a pointer to the preoccupation of Máel-Rúain with the *eschaton*. Another aspect of monastic life under scrutiny could be the question of the beverages that the monks drank. The quoted dialogue also shows that each monastery had different rules sometimes about what might be called mundane matters. That Máel-Rúain points to keeping the rule as equivalent to the purgation needed before enjoying the Beatific Vision and implies that Dublitir's monks fail this test simply by having a beer or mead[5] could lead the reader to imagine that only external observance was required for achieving the monastic ideal. All this could not be determined, however, by looking at only one exchange rather than at the whole literature of the monastic world of this period, but we do not have the whole literature, only what survives. However, all the above aspects are important in any study of monasticism and some of them will be evident in the following discussion of the major rules of the period.

---

3.   Hughes, *Early Christian*, p. 92. It could be inferred from these comments that Dublitir's theology is nearer to that described in chapter 1, than is Máel–Rúain's.

4.   Some general articles on the theme of Irish monasticism in this period include: C. Bourgeault, 'The Monastic Archetype in the *Navigatio* of St Brendan', *JMS* 14 (Advent, 1983), pp. 104–22, who while acknowledging the difficulty with the text maintains that the *Navigatio* is monastic to the core and goes on to show how it is an archetype of monasticism; G. Carville, 'The Road from Camus to Moone – Advance a Step Each Day: An Expression of Celtic Monasticism', *JMS* 14 (Advent, 1983), pp. 161–78; A. Firey, 'Cross-Examining the Witness: Recent Research in Celtic Monastic History', *JMS* 14 (Advent, 1983), pp. 31–49; Ryan, *Irish Monasticism*, remains the classic work on Irish monasticism.

5.   A distinction is made in the translations of the rule of Ailbe between 'mead and rich beer' (Hennessy and O'Looney, 'Notes on the Life of Brendan', *IER* 8 (1871), p. 43, pp. 179–90 (186) and 'mead or princely malt', in J. O'Neill, 'The Rule of Ailbe of Emly', *Eriu* 3/4 (1907–10), p. 35, pp. 92–115 (105).

Ó Duinn cites a poem, in archaic Irish, in which the monk Manchán describes his ideal monastery:

> I wish, O son of the living God, eternal ancient King,
> For a hidden little hut in the wilderness that it might be my dwelling.
> All-grey shallow water beside it, a clear pool to wash away sins through the grace of the Holy Spirit.
> A beautiful wood close by, surrounding it on every side,
> For the nurture of many-voiced birds, for shelter to hide them.
> A few young men of sense, we shall tell their number,
> Humble and obedient to pray the King.
> Four threes, three fours (to suit every need) two sixes in the church, both north and south.
> Six couples in addition to myself ever praying to the King Who makes the sun shine.
> This the farming I would undertake and openly choose,
> Genuine fragrant leek, hens, speckled salmon, bees –
> Raiment and food enough for me from the kings whose fame is fair, to be seated for a time, and to pray to god in some place.[6]

This poem highlights three principal aspects of all monasticism: the recitation of the Divine Office (the numbers and north and south directions indicate this), work and some study. Benedictine monasticism would also stress these: *Opus Dei*, work and *Lectio Divina*. What is omitted about monastic life though is the important component of asceticism, unless work is seen as an aspect of asceticism. This is particularly the case in the later discussion of monastic rules. Being immersed in nature is to be expected of the Irish monks. Obedience is the only 'vow' mentioned, implying that this is the paramount virtue. This last aspect of monastic life will be discussed in more detail later in this chapter.

Since ascetical principles spring from the *evangelium*, why are the monastic rules under discussion so different in form? Ascetic principles rather than detailed legislation formed the legacy of the early monastic founders. Ryan comments that monasteries were ruled more by custom than by law. Hence each abbot made, even if subconsciously, his personality felt in a very effective way.[7] Rules, as their name implies, were statements about the essence of what it was to follow Christ in the monastic life. They were not written down in the early days of like-minded people coming together under the leadership of a charismatic person. This could be due to the oral tradition of early Celtic life both secular and religious. It is more likely that 'what was written was lost at the time of the Norse invasion'.[8] However, as adherents increased and the number of monastic establishments (*paruchia*) multiplied, there was need for some rules to be written for living based on the ascetic principles espoused. These 'rules' are not to be understood in a modern sense. They varied in

---

6. Quoted in S. Ó Duinn, *Where Three Streams Meet: Celtic Spirituality* (Dublin: Columba Press, 2000), p. 194. Ó Duinn gives the Irish original text citing Murphy, 1956 as the translator.
7. Ryan, *Irish Monasticism*, p. 411.
8. Ó Maidín, *The Celtic*, p. 9.

length, depending on the person or group for whom they were intended, whether the solitary life of the monk or the communal life of the monk (see the differences noted in Appendix III C, D). These rules reflected the personality of the formulator and were always based on the perception of how the *evangelium* was to be lived out by these people, within their locale and given their cultural ambit.

According to Uinseann Ó Maidín, there are eight ancient monastic rules.[9] There were another eight rules that have not been preserved but they are referred to here, in passing, to give a fuller picture of the extent to which, it would seem, the monastic founders were intent on laying down guides for living.[10] Like Ó Maidín, this researcher, too, hopes that 'somewhere, sometime, one or other of these rules may be found in some corner of a library'.[11]

The extant monastic rules are mainly in metrical form ensuring an ease of memorization that accorded well with the Irish love of poetry and facility for memorization. They were given the names of prominent founders of monasteries, not to claim that they necessarily wrote them but, as one author has said, to give lustre to their rendition of the rule,[12] as was the case with the Gospels. Kenney says that the names assigned to the rules are 'either guess work of the redactors, or perhaps in some cases indication that the rule was derived from the community of which the saint in question was the founder'.[13] According to Ó Maidín, the linguistic evidence proves that the persons named could not have written them.[14] Though this may be the case, most of the extant rules are close enough to the person named as the 'author', and the spirit that permeated their monastic establishments, for them to be a faithful rendition of their 'spirit'. So some of the famous founders of monasteries in the era and the rules ascribed to them are used in the chapter.

Eoin de Bhaldraithe, in his work on *Irish Monastic Rules*, gives not only names but also the monasteries in chronological order of foundation with approximate dates and the number of verses of each rule.[15] O'Curry gives a slightly different listing, which he claims to be in chronological order of the death of the saint who is purported to have established the monastery. He includes one rule not mentioned by de Bhaldraithe.[16]

Symptomatic of the hesitation needed regarding the authorship of ancient documents in general and these rules in particular, all four commentators on the rules, O'Curry, de Bhaldraithe, Ó Maidín and Kenney in his *Sources,* have questions about which Ciarán is referred to in the rule bearing his name. There are two possibilities, Ciarán of Saighir or Ciarán of Cluainmacnois

---

9. See Appendix III A.
10. See Appendix III B.
11. U. Ó Maidín, 'The Monastic Rules of Ireland', *CS* 15 (1980), pp. 24–38 (24).
12. Ó Maidín, 'The Monastic', p. 24.
13. Kenney, *The Sources*, p. 469.
14. Ó Maidín, 'The Monastic', p. 24.
15. See Appendix III C.
16. O'Curry, *Lectures*, p. 374. See Appendix, III D.

(Irish spelling). O'Curry says, 'I am not at present able to decide.'[17] De Bhaldraithe puts a question mark in his schema of the different rules and Ó Maidín says that it is generally assumed that the 'author' is Ciarán of Clonmacnois who died of the plague in 549 CE. He goes on to claim that 'linguistic evidence proves beyond all shadow of doubt that this is in fact a late seventh-century composition'.[18]

It is interesting to note that O'Keeffe gives the Old Irish and English translation of a rule he calls the Rule of Patrick,[19] whereas none other of the authors who write on the monastic rules calls it a rule. Undoubtedly in the T.C.D. codex H.3.17 there appears a fragment called the *Riagail Pádriac*,[20] interpreted as the Rule of Patrick. However, this fragment will not be used here as an instance of a monastic rule. Maybe it is more fittingly put with the canons or penitentials in the sense that it addresses behaviours and the penances that accrue to transgressions. There is, however, an interesting link, repeated a couple of times in this rule, between the 'law of their belief and of their faith'[21] which requires some discussion later in terms of the relationship between faith, belief and *praxis*. The rules of each of the different founders will be looked at briefly, in the order given by O'Curry with the inclusion of Columbanus, and then the ascetical theology underlying each will be discussed.

Membership of Irish Monasteries

Before discussing the individual rules it is important to explore the nature of Irish monasticism and the people it attracted. Irish monasticism, as is well known, differed from the Benedictine form. It was more akin to the ancient form found in the Eastern desert. De Bhaldraithe compares the rules of Ailbe and Aphrahat,[22] a Syrian about the time of the Council of Nicea 340–350 CE, and shows striking similarities between his and Ailbe's rule. Similarities are evident both in the stress on asceticism and the absence of specific legislation. As Hughes shows from the *Sources*, there were 'some monasteries where the whole community led an ascetic life; others where some men, supported by the monastery, lived a religious life'.[23]

From Bede's account it seems that the schools of the Irish monasteries formed an essential part of their monastic system, although students need not necessarily become monks.[24] Ascetics seem to have been in Orders and as

17. O'Curry, *Lectures*, p. 374.
18. Ó Maidín, 'The Monastic', p. 24.
19. J. G. O'Keeffe, 'The Rule of Patrick', *Eriu* 1–2 (1904–1905), pp. 216–24.
20. O'Keeffe, 'The Rule', p. 216.
21. Rule V 2, 9 (O'Keeffe, ed., pp. 221–23) 'For the tribe and the nation which have not bishops for the works (specified in V 1 of the rule) the law of their belief and of their faith dies.'
22. E. de Bhaldraithe, 'Two Rules of Ailbe and Interpolated Verses', *Conference paper*, Maynooth (June, 1995), pp. 1–27, (p. 9).
23. Hughes, *Early Christian*, p. 93.
24. G. Bonner, (ed.), in *Famulus Christi* (London: SPCK, 1976), p. 215.

such probably became the *anamchara* of other members of the monastery settlement. They also may have been part of the monastic administration, though not necessarily so. The term 'monk' (*manach*, pl. *manaig* in Gaelic) is confusing as it has a variety of meanings. The Latin word for monk, *monachus*, sometimes means one following a religious life commitment, as the word is understood today. In another form, *monach* means a monastic 'client' though not in the Benedictine sense of a tenant. They lived outside the monastic family while the Irish *manach* lived within the enclosure.[25] Hughes further elaborated, pointing out that these men were married laymen who supported the monastery by their labour and taxes and were the recipients of spiritual guidance and education for some of their children.[26] In the case of some *paruchia* they provided the *comarbs*.[27] Chadwick claims that this notion of *comarb* is associated with privately owned churches of the Celtic-speaking countries and *comarb* is the 'most interesting characteristic institution of the Celtic Church'. Stated simply she explains that 'the land granted by a chief to a saint was a personal grant to himself and his heirs, who were originally drawn from the kindred of the original founder, who became his 'heir', 'inheritors', *com-arbae*'.[28] So the Irish monastery[29] should be seen as a diverse community, governed by abbot, vice-abbots or *seniors* as the rules call them. There were cooks and stewards, again mentioned in the rules, ascetics, scholars and *manaig*, married laymen who lived within the monastery and without whom the monastery could not function.[30] In future references to the word, a monk (some present-day writers use the word monastic for monk) in the context of discussing the monastic rules will mean a celibate person committed to the religious life, living in a monastic enclosure that catered for both eremitical and coenobitical lifestyles.

25. Hughes, *Early Christian*, p. 94.
26. Hughes, *Early Christian*, p. 94.
27. Often spelled variously *coarb, conarb, comarb*; it means a member of the family or tribe, who endowed the land on which the monastery was built. In the case of ColumCille and Iona there were about twelve succeeding abbots who were descendants of the royal house of Niall of the Nine Hostages. Hughes, *The Sources*, p. 73, holds that on Iona abbots six and ten were not of the same kindred; see Appendix 1 E for diagram of these *conarbs* of ColumCille. The system of *com-arb* is explained in J. Barry, 'The Erenagh in the Monastic Irish Church', *IER* 5th ser., 89 (1958), pp. 424–32 (424); Chadwick, *The Age*, p. 64, has some fascinating references to the *conarbs* of Moninna taken from the *AU* in 517 CE which contains her successors from the fifth to the fifteenth abbess: 'the thirteenth abbess was the daughter of Foidemnn, king of Conaille Muirthemne around Dundalk, in which Killeevy lay. Her sister and daughter were successively abbesses here. The eighth abbess was granddaughter of the fifth, and the ninth and tenth were sisters, nieces of the eighth.'
28. Chadwick, *The Age*, p. 63.
29. Two informative works on these are: A. Gwynn and R. N. Hadcock, *Medieval Religious Houses: Ireland* (London: Longman, 1970) with a splendid map and appendix of early sites; M. Herity, 'The Buildings', pp. 247–315, where the specifically archaeological aspects are highlighted.
30. Hughes, *Early Christian*, p. 94; Sharpe (ed.), *Adomnán's*, pp. 34–43, also treats ColumCille's successors.

The prayer life of the monastery seemed to frame all other activities. Regarding Ailbe's rule Ó Maidín comments that the text seems to make a distinction between *iarmeirge*, 'prayer after rising' and *midnocht*, 'midnight prayer', highlighting his belief that 'the composition and times of the hours of prayer in early Ireland are difficult to establish with certainty.'[31] The Canonical Hours, judging by later monastic practice, were thought to be at fixed times of the day. According to Columbanus the night Hours lengthened in winter and shortened in summer.[32] The monks seemed to have been in their cells till Terce either at prayer or work.[33] Between Terce and None the time was given over to work,[34] sometimes in the fields and at other times in occupations specified in later rules. Colgan has an interesting interpretation on verse 39 of the rule of Ailbe relating to where the monks prayed and the Hour of None: 'From the eight day of kalends of April until October the rule prescribes that the hour of None should be said in an open place.' If his interpretation is correct then we must conclude that the liturgical Hour of None is celebrated out of doors.[35] After Nones the main meal of the day was eaten.[36] At the conclusion of the evening meal each monk went to his cell for reading or private prayer till Vespers.[37] From this regime is can be inferred that, in all probability, Prime and Compline were recited by the monks in their own cells. An interesting practice in many monasteries was for two monks to remain on vigil in the church for the whole of the night hours. This seems to have been a 'rostered' event and cannot therefore have been to do with any personal penance for sin.

What, however, was the relationship of the ascetic community to the wider community of the monastery in the Irish tradition? Sheldrake saw the monastic enclosure as 'simply a privileged space within which a particular vision of the world could be lived out'.[38] This did not exclude any person, as monasteries often housed, in the tradition of being a place of refuge, criminals who were part of the order of penitents.[39] 'Professional' ascetics were not the only inhabitants of such monastic enclosures. Education, agriculture, copying of scriptural texts and other forms of art were part of the everyday occupation. 'Within

---

31. Rule V 19, 'There should be thirty psalms every hour, and twelve at midnight' (ed. and trans. Ó Maidín, p. 22).
32. Walker (ed.) *Sancti Columbani*, p. 128.
33. O'Neill (ed.), 'The Rule of Ailbe', p. 101.
34. MacEclaise (ed.), 'Rule of Carthage', *IER* 4th ser., 27 (1910), pp. 495–517 (510). MacEclaise is the pen-name used for this translation. It is not clear whether it is a pen-name for the journal or for the authors Meyer and O'Curry; Ó Maidín, *The Celtic*, p. 60.
35. Ó Maidín, *The Celtic*, p. 25 fn 42, Colgan's interpretation, *Ab octavo Kalendis Aprilis, simul cum sua Regula legant nonam in loco patenti usque ad Octobrem*.
36. Rule V 28 (ed. and trans. O'Neill, p. 102).
37. MacElaise (ed.), 'Rule of Carthage', p. 514.
38. Sheldrake, *Living*, p. 39.
39. Ryan, *Irish*, p. 321, claims that there were at least two penitential settlements at Iona, one on the island of Hinba and the other at Tiree. At Luxeuil the *mendicamenta paenitentia* were as eagerly sought as the means of restoring bodily health as is a modern hospital. Jonas, in his *Life of Columbanus*, gives many instances of this attitude.

[such] enclosures there took place, ideally speaking, an integration of all elements of human life, as well as of all classes of human society.'[40]

To those people living within the enclosure the ascetics were fellow searchers and workers in the field, pray-ers in the monastic church and spiritual guides.[41] In the minds of those outside the enclosure, no doubt, the same roles were assigned to the ascetics. The pastoral duty[42] of the monks was firmly established early in the history of monasticism. The majority of monks were dedicated to the pastoral care of those both within and outside the monastic enclosure. Sacramentally the bishop, not the abbot if he were not a cleric, was the important person. However, in all other aspects of life he submitted to the abbot as his superior. Bishop, abbot or abbess formed around them an inner circle, while other monasteries were more like villages. This has been said of Kells, which even today is an integral part of the local area.[43]

Ascetical Theology and Praxis in the Irish Monastic Rules in General

Maybe a brief exploration of the image of the 'mirrors of perfection',[44] as Kenney calls the monastic rules, will reveal something more about this distinctive way of life. Mirrors are meant to show us ourselves as we are. This is not always a pleasant experience. But, depending on the clarity of the mirror, we do see the 'truth'. However, if it is a mirror of perfection is it not meant to be showing us how we could be? Is it not holding up the image (brought to completion by ascetical practices) of the person the monk desires to be? In the place of the person looking into the mirror, sometimes the image reflected back is that of other persons, holy persons, who are held up for the monk's emulation. Otherwise why would one subject oneself to an ascetical regime if one did not have perfection in mind?

It may be important to remind the reader of the understanding of theology and asceticism, earlier enunciated. McBrien says that theology is 'the ordered effort to bring our experience of God to the level of intelligent expression'.[45] Mackey, reflecting on the Irish notion of theology, naturally sees the divine presence and act in terms of clan, with the power being mediated through a hierarchy beginning with Jesus, God incarnate, then Mary, holy people, kings and the natural elements.[46] However, as the bulk of chapter 1 of this work is claiming, culture and its manifestation in all facets of a society means that theology, to be true to the *evangelium* that it strives to articulate, is of necessity coloured by different groups' rendering of it. That is, the cultural matrix of different groups will, to a large extent, determine how that group brings lived

40. Sheldrake, *Living*, p. 39.
41. This is treated later in this chapter when the rule of ColumCille is discussed.
42. Blair and Sharpe (eds), *Pastoral Care*, discuss this topic in detail.
43. Sheldrake, *Living*, p. 40.
44. Kenney, *The Sources*, p. 198.
45. McBrien, *Catholicism*, p. 1258.
46. Mackey in Davies, *Celtic*, p. xviii.

experience to bear on its understanding of religion and this, in turn, defines how that religion is lived out in all the facets of the life of the group. The negation of success in the world is called the driving force of asceticism.[47] However, a more positive understanding of asceticism is the 'exercises undertaken to live the Gospel more faithfully'.[48] It also implies that such exercises are undertaken willingly by people conscious of the freedom they have to choose such a lifestyle. Ascetical or spiritual theology, McBrien claims, 'focusses on the inner transformation effected by the presence of faith and grace in the human mind and heart'.[49] What will be sought in the rules to be discussed in detail is evidence of practices that seek to bring about this inner transformation of human energy, based on the faith and grace that moves not only the mind but also the heart in response to the gospel call to follow Christ in the light of the cross.

While this Christological dimension is the focus in the following discussion, it does not preclude acknowledging the fact that asceticism is not a uniquely Christian concept. As Chadwick says, 'asceticism looks different in various religious frameworks'.[50] This follows from the essential difference in each religious tradition's understanding of the nature, purpose and destiny of the human person. It also includes differing perceptions of the 'nature and significance of the mystical experience'[51] in each of the major world religions. In addition, one needs to heed the warning from Chadwick that such an observation must remind us of the possibility of similar variations within the Christian tradition and, in the present discussion, in different monastic rules.

Those to be treated in the remainder of this chapter are in the order given by O'Curry with the inclusion of Columbanus for the reasons given earlier. O'Curry's quasi-chronological order will be followed because, if there is any sense in which these rules contain the spirit of the founder whose name they bear, a gradual movement from general principles to specific regulations will be evident. However, any organization, even one aspiring to such exalted ideals as monastic perfection, tends to lose sight of the originating vision and needs renewal after a time. It seems that the minute regulations of the later rules bear witness to the fact that the original charism of the founder faded and so the rules had to be more prescriptive. The reasons for the omissions from O'Curry's list will also be addressed later. Likewise in the discussion of individual rules those aspects of each which distinguish them from each other will be highlighted.

---

47. Chadwick, 'The Ascetic', p. 2.
48. McBrien, *Catholicism*, p. 1238.
49. McBrien, *Catholicism*, p. 57.
50. Chadwick, 'The Ascetic', p. 2.
51. Chadwick, 'The Ascetic', p. 2.

Rule of Ailbe[52]

O'Curry says this rule was addressed to Eugene, son of Saran. As regards content it consists of lessons on the duties of a priest, an abbot, and a monk, and on the rules by which their lives ought to be regulated.[53] As regards authorship there is some contention. Ó Maidín comments that as Ailbe is a contemporary of Patrick there can be no doubt that the rule is the actual composition of the saint.[54] This seems to be a *non sequitur*; why does Ailbe's[55] contemporaneity with Patrick, whose mission is purported to have begun in 432 CE,[56] make it unquestionable that the rule is 'the actual composition of the saint'?[57] Kenney, when making comments on the metre and language of the rule, refutes this. He concludes that 'authorship by Ailbe is, therefore, out of the question'.[58] Like O'Curry and Ó Maidín, Kenney says the rule whose Irish title is *Riagol Ailbi Imlecha oc tinchosc Eogain mic Saráin*[59] was composed for Eoghan Mac Sarain, abbot of Cluain Ceolain, in County Tipperary. The date of the composition has been tentatively put at 850 CE.[60] Maybe Ó Maidín means that it was composed by Ailbe, but only 'discovered' in the ninth century. So the question of authorship and date remain open. The topics Ó Maidín identifies in the rule can be summarized as: prayer, perseverance, silence, mutual service, the sacraments, reverence, food, and mutual dependence. His overall impression of the rule is that it 'is one of great moderation, of concern for the well being of the monks, concern for prayer, and indeed for all the monastic values'.[61]

At a Maynooth conference in June 1995, de Bhaldraithe presented a paper in which he discussed the two rules of Ailbe, the one referred to above, and

---

52. Ó Maidín says there are four extant copies of this rule in manuscript. No doubt he had derived this information from Kenney's *Sources*. The following are the four: (i) 5100–4 Bibliothèque Royale, Brussels; (ii) 20 N 10 Library of the Royal Irish Academy, Dublin; (iii) 23 p 3 R.I.A. Dublin; (iv) H.I.II Library of Trinity College, Dublin, which is dated 1752. Also in Ó Maidín, 1996, 17–27. The version used here is that utilized at a conference in Maynooth by Eion de Bhaldraithe O.S.C., 1995, pp. 1–27.
53. O'Curry, *Lectures*, p. 374.
54. Ó Maidín, 'The Monastic', p. 25.
55. De Paor, *St Patrick's*, p. 227, says that according to the *AI* and *AU* an Ailbe died either in 527 or 528 CE. Others claim he was born in 420 CE.
56. The plethora of scholarly work on things Patrician questions this date. As it is not pertinent to this present work to discuss the research, I will simply point the reader to the latest of the most serious scholarly work: that of D. Dumville (ed.), *Saint Patrick*, pp. 39–44, where the date 493 CE is favoured as the more accurate date for the commencement of the Patrician mission.
57. Ó Maidín, 'The Monastic', p. 25.
58. Kenney, *The Sources*, p. 315.
59. Kenney, *The Sources*, p. 315 gives this in Irish and an English translation – Rule of Ailbe of Imlech for the instruction of Eoghan Mac Sarain.
60. De Bhaldraithe says 860 CE and Kenney between 700–950 CE.
61. Ó Maidín, 'The Monastic', p. 26.

the other titled 'A Community Rule of the Monastery of Emly'.[62] These two rules do not seem to be the same and the interpolated verses for both rules[63] make it clear that de Bhaldraithe is talking about two distinct rules. Kenney, in calling this the best of Irish rules, makes the claim because,

> it is a reasonable hypothesis that the poem originally written by, or rather at the command of, the *comarba* of Ailbe at Emly to Eogan on the occasion of his elevation to the headship of Cluain-Coilain, contain[s] more exhortations and some account of the customs and practices of his own monastery. In later times an attempt was made to expand this into a monastic rule by incorporating extracts from other somewhat similar sources.[64]

These extracts are, no doubt, the interpolations spoken of by de Bhaldraithe.

O'Neill's analysis of the rule of Ailbe,[65] predominantly a linguistic analysis, concurs with the above authors in regard to the person to whom the first rule of Ailbe was addressed. The person *Eogaian mic Saráin* (Irish spelling) is mentioned in the martyrology of Donegal[66] but his relationship to Emly is less clear. He may have been transferred to Emly from Cluain Coelain before Cashel superseded the See. That Coglan does not mention him in his list of the abbots who succeeded Ailbe at Emly[67] poses a problem. The translation by O'Neill is from the *Old Irish*. So while the actual format of the rule is ambiguous, there is little confusion about the person whose spirit it embodies. Ailbe's life translated by Liam de Paor[68] gives valuable insights into the character of the purported author of this rule.

Hennessy and O'Looney give an earlier translation of the rule of Ailbe.[69] O'Neill acknowledges that he did not know of its existence when he wrote his paper on the Rule in 1907. Unlike those of both O'Neill and de Bhaldraithe, this translation seems to be from the Latin version of Coglan and is vastly different from the other two. It is obvious that this version of the rule of Ailbe

---

62. De Bhaldraithe, conference Paper, p. 4; this paper had been published in *Hallel*, Vol. 15 (1987), pp. 53–61.
63. De Bhaldraithe has three sets of interpolated verses, each with a different metre which he aligns with the specific metre of the two rules he draws on. There is a third set of seven interpolated verses with varying metres which he does not assign to either of the two rules. In the final form of the rules, by both O'Neill and Hennessy and O'Looney, most (with the exception of two verses) of these interpolations are incorporated into the rule which each calls the Rule of Ailbe.
64. Kenney, *The Sources*, p. 315.
65. O'Neill (ed.), 'Rule of Ailbe', pp. 92–115. In this translation O'Neill makes one rule out of the two, plus interpolations, that de Bhaldraithe used at the Maynooth Conference, 1995. O'Neill has a rule of 56 verses whereas de Bhaldraithe has one of 31 verses (the poem) and the second, 'A Community Rule for the Monastery of Emly 7+5 Metre', comprised 21 verses. No doubt, this is what Kenney is referring to when he comments on the exhortations and customs that are inserted into the original poem to make it a monastic rule.
66. O'Neill (ed.), 'Rule of Ailbe', p. 95.
67. O'Neill (ed.), 'Rule of Ailbe', p. 95.
68. De Paor, *St Patrick's*, p. 227.
69. Hennessy and O'Looney, 'Notes'.

is more a general rendition than one based on a close study of the linguistic, metrical and phonetic aspects of the work.

In discussing the asceticism underpinning the rule of Ailbe, no distinction will be made between the de Bhaldraithe and O'Neill translation, as they draw on the same source, ultimately the *Old Irish* original, and show no great discrepancies. However, the translation by Hennessy and O'Looney seems to be taken from Coglan's Latin version and shows some marked differences of expression. It will be used in comparison with O'Neill and de Bhaldraithe.

Much of the rule of Columbanus is peppered with Scripture quotations but Ailbe's rule has not one direct scriptural quotation. It appears to lay stress on silence, the Canonical Hours, work (briefly), hospitality, perseverance in the one monastery and the use of bells and food. All three translators use the Irish poetic form 'without' for the vices to be avoided, as in:

> Without pride, without sin of perversity, smiling without levity, without laughter;
> Without vindictiveness towards anyone, without proud arrogance, without pomp.
> Without weeping, without crying for prosperity . . .
> Without a fringe of red Parthian leather, without blue, without red, without finery.
> Without cheating or defrauding anyone, without failing in watchfulness.
> Without revenge for evil in the heart, without hate for anyone not a friend.[70]

Hennessy and O'Looney do not refer to work but O'Neill and de Bhaldraithe see it as a serious duty and a part of the vow of obedience: 'If they go by obedience to work together, this is a serious duty.'[71] It is a duty because tilling the soil helps to keep the monastery in food and allows the monks to give of their excess to those who may need it. But it is more that this. It is also part of the asceticism of subduing the body that tends to opt for the easy life, but it is not subjection for its own sake. It is, in the earlier discussion of asceticism in the Irish tradition, a means to an end. Finally, work conforms the monk to Christ who, apocryphal literature and pious traditions teach, laboured as a craftsman in imitation of, or in conjunction with, his foster-father, Joseph. While this aspect of the monk's life seems not so different from the work performed by the tenants of the monastic establishments, the difference lay in the inner transformation that such work was intended to effect in the lives of these monks. This transformation would be evident in the virtues all translators mention:

> Let him be sedate without haughtiness,
> Let him be a wise, devout sage,
> Vigilant against anger;
> Austere, humble, gentle.
> He should be mild, reserved, active;
> He should be modest, generous, bountiful;

---

70. Ailbe's rule, V 4–6 (ed. and trans. de Bhaldraithe, p. 1).
71. Rule, interpolated Verse 27b in the metre of the Second Rule of Ailbe (ed. and trans. de Bhaldraithe, p. 7).

Against the darts of the world he should be watchful;
With the world's bounty he should be generous.[72]

The distrust of the world, spelled out in the above reference to the 'darts of the world', against which the monk should be watchful, was an important component of the monastic lifestyle. The monk should at all times be alert, 'against the torrent of the world . . . against the brood of the world vigilant'.[73] In the stanzas that follow in the original text the world is personalized with the use of the words 'offspring' and 'brood', which, to the Celts, posed a potent challenge. Offspring were a prolongation of the self. They embodied their parentage where they represented the continuation of the clan. Without them the clan would cease to exist. Yet the Irish monk is challenged to make a distinction between earthly and worldly clan and those who threaten the very ideals to which the monk is committed.

Withdrawal from this world was signified in the apparel of the monks, their tonsure, the situation chosen for their monastic establishments and in their silence, penances and overall preoccupation. The fact that they located their guest rooms, an integral part of all monasteries, far from the main cloister of the monks indicated that they wished to be of service but that the guest master was the only one to be in contact with the guests, to save the monastic community from the distractions of the world. However, the world was not shunned in its entirety, for any of its bounty that came to the monastery was to be shared with the laity of the place and the people in need to whom the monks ministered.

Silence enjoined on monks is referred to in the rule of Ailbe as consisting of two-thirds piety.[74] It is recommended to enhance piety. It is also seen as more than a lack of words, 'fewness of words, not talkative'.[75] Refraining from words is the prerequisite for a growth in piety. Indeed it nurtures piety. Since communing with God is the primary task of the monk, anything that distracts from this, even people and pious conversation, is to be avoided. The mystique surrounding this aspect of the life of the monk was a source of puzzlement to outsiders at the same time as it encouraged people to trust them as intermediaries with the divine. Blessings were sought and received from these monks. Not only did this practice set them apart from the others of the monastery community but also eventually it became a source of power that could be

---

72. Rule V 7–8 (ed. and trans. Hennessy and O'Looney, p. 181); a slightly different version in V 3, 7, 8 (ed. and trans. de Bhaldraithe) reads:

Let him be steady without any weakness
Let him be steady, let him not be restless,
Let him be gentle, close and zealous.

73. Rule V 8 (ed. and trans. de Bhaldraithe, p. 54); elsewhere 'brood' is translated as 'offspring'.

74. Rule V 47 (ed. and trans. Hennessy and O'Looney, p. 187); V 38 (ed. and trans. O'Neill, p. 105).

75. Rule V 2 (ed. and trans. de Bhaldraithe, p. 53).

dispensed or withheld. The rule of ColumCille, discussed later in this chapter, illustrates this particularly well.

Because the monk is part of a community and therefore part of that constant raising of the voice to God in prayer, 'the perfect observance of the Canonical Hours is reckoned the chief rule'.[76] Intrinsic to this *Opus Dei* is the Psalter, which is usually recited in the order found in the Hebrew Scriptures rather than according to a theme.[77] As a matter of fact, it is the boast that every hour of the day is sanctified by an *Hour*. Throughout the day and night, monks are called to prayer by the bell: 'The striking of the little bell should be long',[78] giving time to those who live at a distance from the Chapel, so that 'each may take upon himself the step of obedience with keenness, and humility with pleasantness'.[79] No place here for the sluggish or the reluctant monk. The rule enjoins the Canonical Hours and even in the middle of night and during winter, alacrity of step is expected of one who has chosen this way of life. Some of the more physical ascetical exercises that accompany the reciting of the Canonical Hours are: 'A hundred genuflections for him at the *Beati* at the beginning of the day; A hundred genuflections every matin;[80] A genuflection thrice, earnestly, after going in past the altar-rail.'[81]

The fact that these injunctions are in a number of the rules under discussion points to the influence of the reform movement embodied in the *Céli Dé* or Culdees and probably reinforces the contention that some of the rules were committed to print at a later date than that of the foundation of the monastery of the saint whose name they bear. While these practices are confined to the Canonical Hours and other liturgical functions, there are other ascetical practices that are proper to hours of the day not specifically canonical hours: 'With fighill and prayers; With frequent confessions; Obeying the gospel'.[82] This fighill, in the above quotation, is translated by both O'Neill and de Bhaldraithe as 'vigil' while Hennessy and O'Looney in a footnote explain that it was 'a special form of devout prayer, performed kneeling or prostrate on the ground, with the hands extended in the form of the cross'.[83]

Whether it is called *fighill*, vigil or *crosfigell* as Walker refers to it,[84] the motivation is surely the same: praying in such a way as to discipline the body as well as the mind. Or to discipline the body in order to effect discipline for the mind. This was in imitation of Moses in supplication to God on the mountain of Horeb. Not only did the Irish monks chant the psalms but they attempted to imitate the behaviours of Old Testament characters in order to

---

76. Rule V 22 (ed. and trans. Hennessy and O'Looney, p. 183).
77. Stevenson, in Lapidge (ed.), *Columbanus*, p. 215, says that this manner of recitation was the basic feature of the monastic Canonical Hours or *Opus Dei*.
78. Rule V 30 (ed. and trans. Hennessy and O'Looney, p. 184).
79. Rule V 27 (ed. and trans. O'Neill, p. 101).
80. Rule V 17–18 (ed. and trans. O'Neill, p. 99).
81. Rule V 25 (ed. and trans. O'Neill, p. 101).
82. Rule V 26 (ed. and trans. Hennessy and O'Looney, p. 184).
83. Hennessy and O'Looney, fn 184 of their text.
84. Walker (ed.), *Sancti Columbani*, p. xiii.

bring about the same results. There is no doubt that this cruciform position had the effect of reminding the monk of the person whose life he strove to emulate and in whose sufferings he chose to share with the same hope of salvation and ultimately resurrection.

Of the three vows of the later monastic tradition,[85] only scant reference is made in Ailbe's Rule to obedience, none to chastity and most to poverty. The translation by Hennessy and O'Looney does have a line which reads: 'Obeying the rules of the gospel; And the chaste rule of the monks',[86] but this is not the translation of O'Neill and de Bhaldraithe who call it 'the gentle rule of the monks'.[87] Lehane, *Early Celtic*, p. 60, has some interesting comments to make about chastity in the Irish tradition and particularly as evident in the penitentials. He claims that chastity, implying sexual restraint, would have been difficult for a people accustomed to free sexual morality. However, he maintains that the Christians, in this issue of chastity, had 'extended a practice kept by Roman Vestal Virgins, priests of Diana, and sects and religious officials in every society, of subliminating physical love in a dedication to a deity'. So there was a precedent for the Christian ideal of vowed chastity, and what made the difference in practice in Christianity was that some people vowed this for life whereas the ancients practised it either on a part-time basis or after one's childbearing activity had been accomplished. This is much as the Sanyasans do in Buddhism.[88] Regardless of the different nuances of the translation, it was obedience to the *erenagh*,[89] abbot, which counted as heroic virtue and constituted an important aspect of the radicality of the monk's life assuming that the obedience was freely chosen by the monk. As these rules represent guidelines, not specific instructions, it is understandable that there is a vagueness about the vows. Moreover, the evolution of vows as known later in monasticism was slow. That *syneisaktism*[90] as a form of testing the chastity

85. Ryan, *Irish Monasticism*, p. 239 fn 3, comments at length on the possibility of vows being a part of the monastic tradition at Lérins. 'It must be said that profession under vow was not universal when Lérins was founded. Palladius, writing about AD 420 and purposing to give a faithful account of contemporary monasticism, praises Lausus for his good sense for avoiding oaths and vows, and thus saving himself the danger of perjury'.
86. Rule V 26 (ed. and trans. Hennessy and O'Looney, p. 184).
87. Rule V 25a (ed. and trans. O'Neill, p. 101); V 25a (ed. and trans. de Bhaldraithe, p. 58).
88. Lehane, *Early Celtic*, p. 60.
89. De Bhaldraithe, 'Obedience', pp. 63–83; J. Barry, 'The Erenagh', pp. 424–32.
90. Many references to this practice exist, not least in the church documents commencing with the Council of Nicea in the fourth century, with at least seven other councils in Europe and four councils in Spain up to the seventh century condemning the practice. The first scholarly reference made was by Henry Dodwell, *Dissertationes Cyprianiae*, iii (Oxford, 1682) but the most detailed is found in H. Achelis, 'Agapetae', *Encyclopedia of Religion and Ethics*, Vol. 1 (1908), pp. 177–80. R. Reynolds, 'Virgines Subintroductae in Celtic Christianity', HTR 61 (1968), pp. 547–66, renewed the debate. The synonyms used for this practice are many, including *virgines subintroductae*, which, together with *syneisaktoi*, was used in a pejorative sense referring to celibate women who shared domestic arrangements with celibate men. Others include *Agapetae*, similar to *syneisaktoi* but with the added suggestion that both parties were animated to keeping the vows they had taken. *Mulieres* was

of the monks in a spirit of penance was part of the Celtic monastic tradition is attested to by the many references in church synods condemning it. That it was either widespread or reprehensible is still not agreed upon. Reynolds maintains that the 'Irish Scholars have been slow to publish ancient Celtic source materials and slower yet in the publication of source material relating to *syneisaktism*'.[91] Ryan himself comments, 'Some curious and often disedifying tales are told of the successful tests to which Irish monks exposed their virtue, but stories of this kind need not be taken too seriously.'[92]

To be unbelieving about the possibility of such a practice in the Celtic Christian tradition means that one does not really understand or comprehend the radical monastic *praxis* in this era of church history.[93] Enthusiasm for the practice of the Christian *evangelium* led to extreme forms of ascetical testing.

Another important component of monastic life was moderation. However, the concept needs to be seen against the big picture of those times. With the collapse of the Roman Empire came a disintegration of its social system and the concomitant lifting of social restraint. The barbarian invasions, coupled with the principle and practice of social discrimination, added to the chaos. In this state of confusion the Church assumed many of the roles of a state. As one commentator expressed it: 'monastic missions tamed the more savage instincts of [people]'.[94] In this atmosphere moderation was not seen as a social virtue.

more frequently used up till 543 CE. Tertullian called the female ascetic who lived with a man his *uxor spiritualis*. They were given honoured positions in the community as Brides of Christ; *sisters* and *adopted sisters* were also words used to describe this practice. *Conhospitae* was the name given to women who helped clergy distribute the chalice at the Eucharist. See Appendix I C for a translation of a sixth-century letter from a bishop in Gaul to two Irish missionaries about the use of *Conhospitae*. Colloquially, the Welsh use the term *bundling* for a similar practice. The notion of *Spiritual Marriage* has been treated in D. Elliott, *Spiritual Marriage* (New Jersey: Princeton University Press, 1st edn, 1993) giving the names, dates and instigators of this practice commencing with the third century through to the sixteenth century. While this notion of spiritual marriage is not specifically what is being referred to in Celtic monasticism, the fact that a similar ascetical practice being pursued by married couples was widespread over such a long period of time means that it is possible that such a practice could equally have been a feature of the wandering Celtic monks' lives. Lehane, *Early Celtic*, p. 60, in speaking about the practice condemned by the Council of Nicea, does call it spiritual marriage and holds that it 'may have been continued in Brigit's foundation in Kildare'. L. Gougaud, 'Mulierum Consortia: Etude sur le Syneisaktisme chez les Ascètes Celtiques', *Eriu* 9/10 (1921–28), pp. 147–56 also treats the topic. The most celebrated account of *syneisaktism* in the Celtic tradition is found in the *MO*, the Culdee. See Appendix III E for a version of this. Another example of this practice is evident in the words, written in the ninth or tenth century, by Sean O'Faolain; see Appendix III F for a translation.

91. Reynolds, 'Virgines Subintroductae', p. 547.
92. Ryan, *Irish Monasticism*, p. 249. He does refer the reader to the *MO* 14, but does not comment on its veracity. It is said that Gandhi also used this kind of 'test'.
93. One could say that such is the case with any conversion to any tradition, particularly religious. The neophyte cannot see any problem with taking on the whole and extreme elements of the tradition.
94. T. P. Oakley, *English*, p. 13. Some of the evidence for 'legalized immoral connections' according to Ryan, *Irish Monasticism*, p. 249, can be seen in the *Cáin Lánanma* tract in *Senchas Már*, Vol. 11, pp. 342–408.

However, in monasticism great emphasis was placed on the ascetical practices relating to prayer, hours of sleep, obedience and charity. There was scope for similar asceticism in the matter of the food the monks consumed. Moderation was counselled but, as the opening exchange between Máel-Rúain and Dublitir attests, some saw refraining from strong drink as virtuous and others saw strong drink as not unvirtuous. In the *spirit* of Ailbe's monastery, 'if the *erenagh*[95] be wise, his rule shall not be harsh, as the food shall be, so will the order be'.[96]

Many verses are given over to discussing the nature and amount of food and the frequency of eating. The cook should be 'generous, fair, and strong, whether his repast be salt meat or flesh, whether it be mead, curds, or warm milk'.[97] Details such as 'a cake of thirty ounces, in measure by twelve inches, is correct unless a famine take it from them. The brethren should get it at about Nones.' For sages there is a different fare: 'Whether it be mead or princely malt, though it be the desire of a rich man, it is dry bread, it is cress, which is pure (food) for sages.'[98]

There are in Ailbe's rule a few images that tell us something about the writer's perception of monastic asceticism. The anvil of the O'Neill and de Bhaldraithe translations symbolizes the strength and personal discipline required for perseverance: 'a striking of the anvil into the block, to be there until death'.[99] This reference to the virtue of stability, of staying put, is interesting in view of the fact that Irish monks of the period were not bound to stay in one monastery. Another image that counsels perseverance uses a different metaphor: 'Make not a fire of fern; then its extinction is high.'[100] The wandering proclivity of the Irish monks was a source of some consternation later in Europe. Hence the admonition for the abbot to be compassionate and keep a good pantry in order to entice the monks to stay. This does not appear in any of the other rules under discussion here. Nor do the references, no doubt borrowed from Scripture and applied to the monk: 'Let him be a serpent with its deftness, let him be a dove with its filial affection.'[101] As all animals are part of creation both symbolize the sureness of faith and childlike simplicity of it.

---

95. Both de Bhaldraithe and O'Neill use this word for abbot while Hennessy and O'Looney use *Airchinneach*. Barry, 'The Erenagh', says the term *erenagh* is derived from the Irish *airchindic* and *airchinneach* and literally means a person in a position of authority and in late Viking times was most frequently applied to the head of a monastic establishment. The *airchinneach* appears to have held the same position as the earlier *abbas*.

96. Rule V 1 (ed. and trans. de Bhaldraithe, p. 56); This same wording is found, V 32 (ed. and trans. O'Neill, p. 103).

97. Rule V 34 (ed. and trans. O'Neill, p. 105).

98. Rule V 28 (ed. and trans. de Bhaldraithe, p. 55).

99. Rule V 20 (ed. and trans. de Bhaldraithe, p. 58).

100. Rule V 5 (ed. and trans. Strachan, p. 194).

101. Rule V 9 (ed. and trans. de Bhaldraithe, 'A Review', p. 54). It is interesting to note that the serpent, in Celtic mythology a symbol of the Goddess, is identified with deftness which is positive, and only in later centuries did this attribute become negative when Christianity reinterpreted the Genesis story to put blame on the serpent for the fall of humankind.

This first of the Irish rules discussed in this chapter emphasizes three integral aspects of all monasticism: *Opus Dei*, the recitation of the Hours, manual work and *Lectio Divina*. Ailbe also makes reference to perseverance, silence and mutual service. Finally, it embodies one of the important points being made in this work: namely, that among the many apparently strict injunctions regarding behaviour, there is nonetheless a genuine concern for the well-being of the monks. Later in this chapter this is noted as a sense of balance.

Rule of Ciarán[102]

Ó Maidín says, regarding the rule of Ciarán, that the 'linguistic evidence proves beyond all shadow of doubt that this [rule] is in fact a late 7th century composition'.[103] To the present writer's knowledge there are no other commentators on this rule with which to compare his claim. The earlier discussion as to which Ciarán is being quoted still remains unclear, with the preference for Ciarán of Clonmacnoise. All commentators attest to the difficulty of the text. The corrupt nature of the text and its metrical structure make the analysis difficult but not impossible. While O'Curry says that the rule treats of clerical and devotional matters,[104] Ó Maidín says that the beauty of the rule lies in the fact 'that it treats of nothing other than purely monastic virtues'.[105] This he calls a 'theology of community living',[106] stressing again the relationship between the individual person's pursuits of holiness within the context of a community of like-minded persons.

In looking at the rule of Ciarán of Clonmacnoise and its concomitant ascetical theological underpinning, one has to be conscious of the fact that its age and the enigma surrounding it are factors calling for hesitation in interpretation. However, Ó Maidín claims that 'nevertheless the teaching it contains is too precious to be completely ignored'.[107] Just what is this teaching? It is expressed as aspects of work, silence, discipline and fraternal correction; the last is a feature not found in Ailbe's rule.

The significance of the rule to Ciarán is that it is a shield to protect the monk: 'No one can captivate a person who willingly submits to the rule.'[108] This belief is followed by the statement that one can bear witness only to what one

---

102. Ó Maidín says that there is only one extant copy of this rule. It is to be found in 23 P 3 of the Library of the Royal Irish Academy. It was published in restored form by Strachan in *Eriu* (1905). However, in 1996 I was forwarded a copy of this rule translated by U. Ó Maidín, included in his book, *The Celtic*, pp. 43–7.
103. Ó Maidín, 'The Monastic', p. 29.
104. O'Curry, *Lectures*, p. 374.
105. Ó Maidín, 'The Monastic', p. 9.
106. Ó Maidín, 'The Monastic', p. 29.
107. Ó Maidín, notes on the rule given to me in personal correspondence, July 1996. Also Ó Maidín, *The Celtic*, pp. 43–47; as this book was published after I received the personal translation and the verses are the same in both I will continue to use the earlier copy.
108. Rule V 6 (ed. and trans. Ó Maidín, p. 2).

has experienced. And the captivation that is primary in a monk's life is to be captivated by Christ. However, even with the importance of personal experience there is an acknowledgement that what stands in the way of this total captivation is selfishness, so the monk is instructed: 'make full confession of your sins if you really appreciate the rule'.[109] Confession is not simply getting rid of sins, but it is an exercise in self-knowledge, in humility, (another virtue prized by monks), and is a submission to one's *anamchara* without whom the monk cannot hope to progress in the interior transformation. Obedience to one's soul-friend is like obedience to the abbot, a virtue highly thought of in this life of dying to self in order to be associated with the humble Christ.

Withdrawal from the world into the silence of the cloister could seem like heaven in a frenetic world. The motivation, however, for such a withdrawal in the early days of Irish monasticism, as it was in its Eastern predecessor, was to commune more easily with God. Hence the many references in these early precepts in Ciarán's rule make a great deal of the virtue and practice of silence. One such reference states, 'There are three or four faults common to otherwise virtuous persons, such as, being given to drawing others into endless chatter.'[110]

Other facets of the failure to value and practise the virtue of silence are: 'belittling the efforts of others',[111] and 'false witness [and] murmuring'.[112] It is not only the lack of fraternal charity that is at stake here (though the reference to the 'pollution of water by mire'[113] could be a reference to the waters of Baptism that binds the monks together in the Christian community), but also the time spent in chattering, murmuring, and belittling others is time taken from the monk's foremost task, communing with God. The realism and human immediacy of these rules point to the pragmatism of the Celtic spirit and the fact that these are living rules, devoid of abstract spiritual theory: 'Fasting and penance should have primacy among your bodily habits. In Christ's eyes they are truly clerics whose hands are calloused.'[114]

The monk is to fast and do penance not only for the sake of the body but also to discipline the mind and heart, for 'heaven is the reward of the one who, for the sake of all, disciplines his own heart'.[115] As well as he being the beneficiary of this personal penance, 'for the sake of all' indicates that a part of the monastic rationale is that others will benefit from the monks' lives of mortification and self-discipline. Work, undertaken by monks, indicated by the calloused hands, is not only a necessity for daily sustenance, but is part of the penance, part of the service to the community, including the tenants and those in need. However, it is the motivation that sets them apart from those ordinary folk who till the soil and perform similar tasks. They are committed to imitate the servant Christ who became flesh to live among people with the intention

109. Rule V 16 (ed. and trans. Ó Maidín, p. 3).
110. Rule V 4 (ed. and trans. Ó Maidín, p. 3).
111. Rule V 11 (ed. and trans. Ó Maidín, p. 3).
112. Rule V 14 (ed. and trans. Ó Maidín, p. 3).
113. Rule V 14 (ed. and trans. Ó Maidín, p. 3).
114. Rule V 3 (ed. and trans. Ó Maidín, p. 3).
115. Rule V 7 (ed. and trans. Ó Maidín, p. 3).

of making up for the offence done to the Creator by the selfishness of humankind.

Though no specific reference is made in the rule of Ciarán to the Canonical Hours which involve a good deal of the monk's waking hours, there is a rule which insists that they 'Do not profane the Sabaoth of the Son of God', and 'On Sundays meditate on the Scriptures, read them aloud and make copies of them'.[116] O'Donoghue poetically describes this activity thus: 'These men, and in less inaccessible places women carried the fuel for [their] soul-fires around with them in the form of Psalters and Bibles, and some of them spent a lifetime's love and care in illuminating these books by way of line and colour.'[117]

This instruction to meditate on the Scriptures reminds one of the training of the *filid* who was put into a room to memorize the sagas in order to be able to repeat them before a gathering. To memorize something of importance to the clan or group was to be a keeper of the story of that group. In the oral stage of a culture such a task was a truly noble one. In the case of the Scriptures the story being memorized was not that of a single clan but of the whole Christian family from the beginning to the present. With this injunction to copy the Scriptures, there was a movement from the honoured role of the poet to that of the scribe. The Scriptures were to the newly converted Christian what the sagas were to the pre-Christian Irish. The same heroic deeds inspired them. The same miracles sought to inflame their love and devotion. Scriptural poetry, particularly of the psalms, accorded well with the Irish love of verse. In the *Vitae* of prominent people there is a similar pattern to this kind of writing. It was the heroism of this lifestyle and a response to the recently heard *evangelium* that was a source of admiration and, in many cases, imitation by those who sought entry into the monasteries. The author of Ciarán's rule reminds the monks of Clonmacnoise that 'It is dangerous to form the habit of leaving one's monastery unless it be to visit a church, to consult the wise or to make the round of the cemeteries.'[118]

Not only are these activities part of the pastoral care enjoined on the monks, they also point to an important aspect of the Celtic consciousness out of which the Irish monastic tradition operated. Visiting the church and the wise *anamchara* have been treated earlier in this work. The activity contained in the last of the above reasons for leaving the monastery is one that is still a feature of pious Irish life today. 'Doing the rounds' is an ancient custom involved in following a time-honoured path left and right, with prescribed pausing places where prescribed prayers were recited. A poem well known to Irish people sums it up: 'All men know it: the three best footsteps that any man shall ever walk are the step to visit the sick, the step of a pilgrim, the step to the church.'[119]

The place of pilgrimage and its association with martyrdom will be treated later in this chapter. What is even more important in the verse of the rule quoted

116. Rule V 10 (ed. and trans. Ó Maidín, p. 3).
117. O'Donoghue, *The Angles*, p. 12.
118. Rule V 9 (ed. and trans. Ó Maidín, p. 46).
119. Ó Maidín, *The Celtic*, p. 46.

above is the reference to the round of the cemeteries. Here were buried the ancestor who impinged on the life of the Irish at every moment. The practice connected the devotee with the spirit world as in ancient days of the primal religions. Both the ancestral spirits and the spirits of the elements were integral to the consciousness of these people. They were constantly consulted and their resting place was not a sad abode but the place of the resurrection, the ante-chamber to eternal glory. Ciarán's rule then, though much mutilated in its manuscript, contains a few very worthy aspects of monasticism. It stresses being captivated by Christ and this assures the monk of salvation. What looks like a very modern notion is contained in the stress on the contention that one needs to experience before one can witness. Confession, a daily requirement, is linked with experience in that this is seen as a way to self-knowledge. Silence and the violation of it by murmuring, giving false witness and belittling others is recommended to enhance the primary monastic purpose of communing with God. Fasting and penance should have primacy in the life of the monk. Finally, stability is insisted upon though it was not as much a part of monasticism in this era as it eventually became.

Rule of Comgall [120]

Part of the significance of this rule, called the Rule of the Lord (*Riagul in Choimded*) and located, according to Kenney, 'maybe at the end of the eighth century',[121] was that it gives an insight into one of the most important monastic establishments in Ireland, namely Bangor. Not only was this monastery one of the earliest in the north of Ireland but it provided the formative influence in the education of Columbanus,[122] who with ColumCille provide the outstanding leadership of the ascetical movement of the Irish Church. Bangor, founded by

---

120. There are three different spellings of the name of this saint; O'Curry, *Lectures*, uses Comhghall. Ó Maidín, 'The Monastic', uses Comghaill in both *old Irish* and English renditions while de Bhaldraithe uses the anglicized Comgall. This is the form I shall use. Four manuscripts exist: (i) 5100–4 Bibliothèque Royale, Brussels; (ii) 23 N 10 Library of Royal Irish Academy, Dublin; (iii) 23 p. 3 Library of Royal Irish Academy; (iv) H.I.II Library of Trinity College, Dublin, 1996, 29–36. Three of the manuscripts carry no signature but (i) carries a note, written on or about 1630, in the hand of Michael O'Cleary OFM, attributing the rule to Comgall of Bangor. It is instructive to note that in Plummer's edition of *Vita S.Comgalli*, quoted by Stevenson in M. Lapidge (ed.), *Columbanus*, p. 205, the comment is made that 'when the time of death was approaching for the most blessed old man Comgall, he was tormented by immense and various infirmities . . . some people said that such great infirmities were visited on him by God on account of the rigour and harshness of his rule over his monks'. One wonders if this man, abbot at the time of Columbanus' stay at Bangor, was not partly the 'inspiration' for Columbanus' own reported harshness in his rule.
121. Kenney, *The Sources*, p. 475.
122. In stressing the formative role of Bangor, this is not meant to diminish the principal role of the monastery of Finnian of Clonard (founded 530 CE) which is said to have been the best of the monastic schools at the time and the one which gave 'birth' to many of the luminaries in the Irish missionary tradition. Lehane, *Early Celtic*, p. 113.

Comgall (517–615 CE),[123] was an early sixth-century foundation. O'Curry says the rule is addressed to abbots, monks and devout Christians. Most of the commentators on the monastic rules devote much time to the discussion of their linguistic characteristics. Strachan says that 'from linguistic considerations, and in particular, from the treatment of final vowels, the poem (Comgall's Rule) can hardly be put later than about 800 AD'.[124] He also admits that there is difficulty in understanding some of the verses.

The sentiments of Máel-Rúain quoted at the outset of this discussion find echoes in the first verse of this rule: 'Preserve the Rule of the Lord; therein thou runnest no risk. It is better that thou transgress it not, as long as thy life lasts.'[125] Not only is the life-long commitment to living the rule a preventive for life's risks but also, unlike Máel-Rúain, whose verbal focus is on keeping 'my rule' and 'my injunctions', the focus of this rule is the Lord. It is interesting to note that only Comgall stresses this aspect of monastic life. The cliché 'keep the rule and the rule will keep you' seems to have come from sentiments such as these. However, it is not a mindless keeping of the rule, for the author goes on to specify the reason for this fidelity and how it can be accomplished. Moreover, given that one aspect of radicality discussed in chapter 1 was the freedom of choice of the person committing to this lifestyle, then one would expect a ready response to these rules.

The essence of the rule is 'Love Christ, hate wealth; piety to thee towards the King of the sun and smoothness towards men.'[126] Nothing could be more simply said. Nothing could be more radical. Here is a paradox: the goods of the earth are to be cherished, valued and cared for but the monk is to hate wealth that is the accumulation of these very goods. This, no doubt, is the motive for divesting oneself of any superfluous goods, as with superfluous food in Ciarán's rule treated above. 'What thou carries off over and above thy sufficiency, thou shalt give to the poor.'[127] Even the necessities of life are to be had in moderation, to be denied on occasions, as part of the readiness for martyrdom on this journey of pilgrimage. Desire itself is to be tempered with patience, 'that in every desire which thou desirest thou shouldst exercise patience'.[128]

---

123. These dates, like so many dates for the early Irish saints and monasteries, differ from one historian to another. Even the dates in the *Annals*, with their complicated computation system, cannot be taken at face value. The dates used here differ from Lehane, *Early Celtic*, who specifies the following dates for Comghall: born 516 CE, founded Bangor 558 CE, died 601 CE. De Bhaldraithe claims that Comgall died in 602 CE. O'Curry has Comgall dying 552 CE, before Lehane says he founded Bangor. It is probably safe to say that while O'Curry's work is a thorough treatment of the manuscripts available in 1878, the more recent writers may have the benefit of recent research, which leads one to favour Lehane's dating over O'Curry's.

124. Strachan, 'An Old Irish Metrical Rule', *Eriu* 1/2 (1904–1905), pp. 191–208 (192) give or take a few years, Kenney, *The Sources*, would agree with this.

125. Rule V 1 (ed. and trans. Strachan, p. 192).
126. Rule V 2 (ed. and trans. Strachan, p. 193).
127. Rule V 21 (ed. and trans. Strachan, p. 199).
128. Rule V 12 (ed. and trans. Strachan, p. 196).

There seems to be a keen knowledge of human nature's need for guidance, since the follower of this rule is admonished to have 'a devout sage to guide thee, 'tis good to avoid punishment. Though great thou deem thy firmness, be not under thine own guidance.'[129] Here, as in other rules, the *anamchara*, soul-friend, is to be sought and followed, provided he is a 'devout sage'.[130] De Bhaldraithe makes the point that in this rule there are references to penance (verses 9, 10, 23, 27). Lent, that liturgical season *par excellence* for penitential practices, recommends strokes on the hand to 'turn aside every evil consequence of our guilty pride'.[131] Elsewhere it suggests that penance during Lent is helpful, for 'every proud act of the hand deserves a blow'.[132] In mentioning penance de Bhaldraithe is reminding the reader that on the continent there was an 'order of penitents' whose regulations were often embodied in rules that sometimes engender confusion between the penitential order and the monastic state.[133] However, penance was an integral part of all monastic establishments and would be included in all rules either overtly or covertly.

Unlike the briefer rule of ColumCille, Comgall's rule recommends, nay insists on, some specific ascetical practices[134] that may seem exaggerated to later readers but which help underscore the totality of the commitment of these Irish monks and their preoccupation with things other than the worldly:

> A hundred prostrations to Him at the *Beati*[135] morning and evening . . .
> Every morning at the time let him bow down promptly thrice . . .[136]
> Three hundred prostrations every day, and three at every canonical hour . . .[137]
> Two hundred prostrations every day to the Lord with a diligent booklet . . .[138]
> Two hundred blows on the hands in every Lent, it will be a help . . .[139]

These practices[140] are performed so that the monk will constantly be conscious of the presence of God and be in a perpetual state of penance. In so acting he

---

129. Rule V 15 (ed. and trans. Strachan, p. 197). It is interesting to note that this same principle of guidance is insisted on by the Eastern mystics today. They hold that the journey into self-knowledge should not be undertaken without a *guru*.
130. Rule V 15 (ed. and trans. Strachan, p. 197).
131. Rule V 13c (ed. and trans. Ó Maidín, p. 34).
132. Rule V 27a (ed. and trans. Ó Maidín, p. 35).
133. De Bhaldraithe, 'Two Rules', p. 49.
134. These are actually more Culdee practices and give credence to the belief that the rules were written later than the person whose name they bear.
135. This is the psalm *Beati Immaculati*, which was commenced at *Prime* and ended at *None*, Hennessy and O'Looney, fn 182.
136. Rule V 3b (ed. and trans. Strachan, p. 193).
137. Rule V 13a (ed. and trans. Strachan, p. 196).
138. Rule V 13b (ed. and trans. Strachan, p. 196).
139. Rule V 13c (ed. and trans. Strachan, p. 197).
140. With the reform of monasticism under the direction of Máel-Rúain of Tallaght in the eighth century the accumulation of such practices increased with the belief that they would keep the monk's mind fixed on God. They also had the added advantage of being a way of disciplining the body and focusing on the externals of monasticism. The majority of the monastic rules under discussion were written in the 'spirit' of the founders but in the time of the reform they can be expected to have elements of these external practices.

will make reparation in order that '[his] soul will not be at the judgment of the King on the day of Doom'.[141] In addition, they will enable him to experience that 'Light, wonderful and mild [which] is the yoke of the Lord.'

There is a one-verse full reference to that most basic of all ascetic principles, the notion of *contraries*, expounded by John Cassian.[142] In verse 27a (quoted in part above) this principle is hinted at. Since this aspect of asceticism has been explored in the chapter on the Irish penitentials, suffice it here to say that human nature and all of the universe seek balance and equilibrium and hence the wisdom of this reminder: 'The eight chiefs of the vices which slay the soul of every man, I know virtues which extinguish them all.'[143] Ó Maidín's slightly different translation is similar to that of Strachan in meaning: 'Eight shameful vices can destroy the soul of any person, but I know of eight virtues that can destroy these vices.'[144] It seems that all the focus of this rule was to remind the monks of human and eternal truths, encourage them to follow the practices that facilitate the development of these virtues, or habits of mind and heart and so to challenge them to a radical response consequent on their acceptance of the *evangelium*. Besides, Comgall's instruction counsels, 'though great injuries come to thee, lament not thereat: because they are not more abundant than those of the King who sends them'.[145] If this model of life does not facilitate inner transformation, then the monk labours in vain.

In summary then, Comgall's rule succinctly states: Love Christ, hate wealth, piety towards God and kindness towards others. The goods of the earth are to be cherished as is all creation but they should not be kept if superfluous. Moderation is important. Specific penances are suggested which could indicate the rule is of later origin. A passing reference is made to Cassian's *contraries* with the major stress on the eternal and human values that are integral as a response to the monastic life.

Rule of ColumCille[146]

Ó Maidín gives some interesting sources about two rules of ColumCille. John Colgan, writing in or about 1630, claimed that ColumCille 'wrote another rule for hermits or one for the brothers dwelling in the desert, which I have in my possession'.[147] He goes on to cite two other sources that can verify the fact of

---

141. Rule V 13a (ed. and trans. Strachan, p. 196).
142. McNeill, 'Medicine', p. 19. Cassian was following in the footsteps of the Pythagoreans who took from the Babylonians a table of contraries of which they made use in philosophy and medicine.
143. Rule V 11 (ed. and trans. Strachan, p. 195).
144. Rule V 11 (ed. and trans. Ó Maidín, p. 32).
145. Rule V 17 (ed. and trans. Strachan, p. 98).
146. There are two extant manuscripts, according to Ó Maidín: (i) 5100–4 Bibliothèque Royale, Brussels; (ii) B 512 fol. 40 b. s. of the Rawlinson Collection in the Bodleian Library of Oxford, 1996, pp. 37–41.
147. Ó Maidín, *The Celtic*, p. 37.

the existence of such a rule. One Jacobus Varaeus claims that ColumCille 'wrote a monastic rule which is extant and commonly the Rule of ColumCille'.[148] The Prior of Affinghem (Belgium), D. Benedictus Haftaens, in high praise of ColumCille whom he called the patriarch, referred to the saint's community, namely St Columba's, as the Most Excellent Fellowship.[149] Therefore it seems there were, at one time, two rules attributed to ColumCille, one for a whole monastic community and one for those monks who chose to live alone. Unfortunately the only one extant is the latter and it is this one that will inform the following discussion regarding the ascetical theology implicit in it.

ColumCille, the most famous monastic founder in Ireland and Scotland, has given his name to a rather brief rule that is specifically directed to one who preferred to 'be alone in a separate place'.[150] In keeping with the intention of rules, ColumCille's is brief because the minutiae of community living need not be addressed. In this rule relationships with others is at a minimum and the brevity helps sharpen the focus of the hermit whose sole intent is communing with God. When analysing this rule, de Bhaldraithe sees similarities with the Rule for a Recluse written by St Aelred some four hundred years after ColumCille's rule. He has a sense that the writer of the rule 'is not too happy about the hermit form of life but he left it to the conscience of the individual monk'.[151] This is a point of significance for understanding the shift in the theology of monasticism and asceticism between ColumCille and Columbanus. Ó Maidín focuses on three virtues emphasized in the rule: prayer, silence and poverty. The reference to the three kinds of martyrdom is dealt with in more detail later in this chapter.

In highlighting the physical set-up of the hermitage, O'Curry gives us an insight into what archaeologists have since discovered in many former monastic sites in Ireland.[152] The predominance of the beehive-shaped cells is a source of admiration and awe when one confronts them on Skellig Michael. A contemporary record of the experience expresses this awe thus:

> To step out on the spit (the vantage point above the hermitage) and look at the drifting clouds, the heaving ocean below, and the birds sailing above is to become deeply conscious of the primeval forces ruling the world. If one stands there on a summer evening as the sea mist rolls in . . . [one] gives way to wonder at the beauty of the scene.[153]

---

148. Ó Maidín, *The Celtic*, p. 37.
149. Ó Maidín, *The Celtic*, p. 37.
150. Rule V 1 (ed. and trans. Skene, p. 508). Since Skene's edition of the rule has no numbering of verses I have used my own.
151. De Bhaldraithe, conference paper, p. 62.
152. Thomas, *Celtic Britain*, p. 151, following the lead of many other archaeologists, including Ann Ross, has pictures of the restored beehive cells on Illauntannig Island, off Co. Kerry.
153. O'Donoghue, *The Angles*, p. 13. See Appendix 111 H for personal photo by Fr Clem Hill from Sydney of the approach to the beehive cells on the Skellig.

The island of Hinba[154] in the Hebridean group of islands with its cluster of stone cells likewise fills the observer with a sense of the presence of the Otherworld and its inhabitants.

The dwelling places of the hermit are to be placed 'near a chief city',[155] not necessarily literally but within walking distance of the common place of prayer. Given that the recitation of the Canonical Hours was so important in the lives of the monks it is understandable that they would need to be close to the church for rising and being present at Office throughout the hours of the day and night. For hermitages, then and now, are intended for those who choose to live apart for a period of time and not necessarily for the whole of one's life, unlike the monks in community.

In the rule of ColumCille, brief though it is, there is ample evidence for theory and practice of a radical lifestyle. The rule naturally focuses on the individual whom the writer addresses as one whose 'conscience is not prepared to be in common with the crowd'.[156] By this stage in monastic history the Eastern desert anchorite or hermit had given way, in general, to the coenobitic way of life where a modified community life existed. The fact that ColumCille's rule is so singularly focused points to his capacity to allow the individual to follow his conscience or the call of God, and so sets out general principles to that end. However, on this sacred pilgrimage one must never go alone. An intrinsic part of this call of God is the role played by the monk's soul-friend, the *anamchara*.

The penitentials, monastic rules and *Vitae* of early Irish monasticism all clearly show a preference for mentoring or spiritual guidance. Hence the importance of the *anamchara* or soul-friend. This, no doubt, flows from the central role of the clan in Celtic consciousness. In the *Túatha*, relationships were important, all pervasive and transformative. These spiritual guides need not necessarily be older than the person being guided: 'holiness, not age, was the criterion'.[157] Fosterage, so prevalent in Celtic education (ColumCille himself was in fosterage to Cruithnechan), could be seen as an offshoot of the central role of the *anamchara*. These soul-friends need not even be human, for many

---

154. There is much discussion about this island off the coast of Iona where there was located the 'Island of the Women', J. Marsden, *The Illustrated ColumCille*, (London: Macmillan, 1991), p. 96. Another name for this island is Eileach an Naoimh on the Garvellachs. See Appendix 111 G for photos of Hinba and beehive cell taken by Mr Chris Sanders of Glasgow Caledonian University. Maybe these are not the same island. However, there are beehive cells and a monument on Hinba purporting to be the grave of Eithne, the mother of ColumCille. Similar stone constructions to Eithne's gravesite are found in the Westport region on the west coast of Ireland. These constructions, archaeologist Professor M. Herity said, during an excursion in 1995, are the constructions used to mark the resting place of founders of monasteries.

155. Rule V I (ed. and trans. Skene, p. 508). Ó Maidín, *The Celtic*, p. 39 translates, *i fial primh cathrach* as 'the seat of a bishop'.

156. Skene, *Celtic Scotland*, p. 508. In this appendix Skene comments that a translation by O'Curry in the Appendix to *Primate Colton's Visitation of Derry* preceded the one by Haddan and Stubbs. I presume it is the latter that this translation follows.

157. Sellner, 'A Common', p. 26.

of the Celtic saints had angelic *anamcharas*. What was important in the Celtic consciousness, and a natural component of Irish monasticism, was the fact that one had someone with whom one could converse and through whom one was helped to encounter the God to whom one's whole life was committed.

Removing oneself of one's own volition from the normal mode of monastic commitment was not even a choice one could make unilaterally for it had to be approved by one's *anamchara*. One's vigils were also performed with the expressed permission of one's soul-friend: 'let thy vigils be constant from eve to eve, under the direction of another person'.[158] What could possibly motivate a person to submit to another even in the choice of how one responded to a basic commitment? An answer may lie in the totality of the personal response of conversion to Christianity. It could also be seen in the perception of the role of the soul-friend as the person who helped one avoid self-deception, aided one in the fight against the wiles of Satan[159] or acted as a bulwark against the multi-faceted attractions of the world. Moreover, it was one of the fundamental 'rules' of Irish monasticism that all such choices had to be discerned with one's *anamchara*.

Nakedness, more metaphorical than literal, is recommended early in the admonition of the rule: 'Be always naked in imitation of Christ and the Evangelist.' This is clarified a few lines later when with reference to possessions of clothing and drink, and later on to property, nakedness is recommended as the way of attaining the 'Love of God with all thy heart and all thy strength.'[160] Nakedness, metaphorically, is required if one is sincerely to lay bare one's soul to one's *anamchara*. Moreover, literal nakedness actually was a part of the Irish monastic asceticism, particularly when, in a spirit of penance and in consultation with his soul-friend, the monk submerged himself up to his neck in frozen water. This was not merely subduing the body, for in Irish theology the body was the vehicle through which one attained glory, and these injunctions were experienced as the beginning of such a transformation.[161]

A constant thread in all the rules of the Irish monastic tradition is the use of the Scriptures, particularly the recitation of the psalms.[162] ColumCille instructs his monks to converse with each other on days of solemnity about the 'narra-

---

158. Rule V 12 (ed. and trans. Skene, p. 59).

159. It is instructive to notice that there are very few direct references to Satan in these Irish rules, except where Scripture is being quoted, while such references abound in the monastic rules of the Eastern desert fathers. Even with the omnipresence of the *Túatha De Danann*, people of the Goddess Danu, in the consciousness of the pre-Christian and no doubt Christian Irish, this awareness of Satan is lacking in these 'mirrors of perfection'. Maybe the explanation lies in the fact that the *Túatha De Danann* were experienced as more benevolent than malevolent. This same absence of the devil or Satan is also noted in secular Irish literature.

160. Rule V 20 (ed. and trans. Skene, p. 509).

161. O'Loughlin, in Davies, *Celtic*, p. 24.

162. Ryan, *Irish Monasticism*, reprint of 1931 edition, p. 338, discusses at length the Canonical Hours and details the number of psalms for each Hour. He also stresses that 'All lessons were from Holy Writ', p. 339, which is not the case with all the lessons in the Canonical Hours later on.

tives of the Scriptures'.[163] This highlights the preoccupation he wishes to see practised by his monks even on hol[y]days. If holy days were highlights in the liturgical calendar then it is only fitting that these days would be enhanced by a sharper or more intense focus on Scripture. As regards the Testament he recommends, '[Have] a few religious men to converse with thee of God and His Testament . . . to strengthen thee in the Testaments of God.[164] Abide in the Testaments of God throughout all times.'[165] This citation emphasizes the importance he places on the constant reflection on the covenant of God with the people as exemplified in the Old Testament stories and in the individual covenant that each monk makes with God at his profession. The word could also mean conversation with God but the notion of covenant, so rich in its connotations of the intimacy of the relationship between Yahweh and the individual in community, is more in keeping with the overall spirit of monasticism.

The easy converse of the poet, the *filid* and ordinary people was an integral part of the nourishment of the Irish psyche. For the monk to deny this aspect of his converse, as he is instructed to have 'a few religious men to converse with thee of God and his Testament',[166] means that maybe the poetry of the Scriptures was meant as spiritual nourishment enough. Perhaps the denial of this aspect of his Celtic cultural life was worth the sacrifice for the following of Christ. The recluse was to shun the person 'who would talk with thee in idle words, or of the world; or who would murmur at what he cannot remedy or prevent',[167] because all this activity would hinder the monk from responding to the main call to commune with God.

The aspect of the rule which treats of the person with whom the monk can and cannot speak would be puzzling if it were not for the knowledge of the primary purpose of the monk's life: this was to leave aside the world and concentrate totally on one's relationship with God, whether through prayer, work or exercises of penance. If one is constantly using idle or worldly words, or is conversing with others 'who murmur at what [they] cannot remedy or prevent',[168] then one is shifting one's focus and so being unfaithful to the profession of the monk. This, of course, is not the attitude expected of the lay people who eventually came to form part of the monastic settlement. Moreover, the spirituality of the committed monk is not necessarily that of others who share the monastic enclosure. Such a 'profession' was hardly regarded as normal for all the Irish of the sixth to the eighth century.

Equally serious was the admonition that the monk was not to admit to his cell[169] the 'tattler between friend and foes'.[170] Such a person should be given the

---

163. Rule V 4 (ed. and trans. Skene, p. 508).
164. Rule V 4 (ed. and trans. Skene, p. 508).
165. Rule V 21 (ed. and trans. Skene, p. 509).
166. Rule V 4 (ed. and trans. Skene, p. 508).
167. Rule V 5 (ed. and trans. Skene, p. 508).
168. Rule V 5 (ed. and trans. Skene, p. 508).
169. This would be difficult in places where there was more than one monk to a cell.
170. Rule V 5 (ed. and trans. Skene, p. 508).

Irish Monastic Rules of the Sixth to the Eighth Century 105

monk's benediction 'only should he deserve it'.[171] This withholding of a blessing needs to be seen in the light of the historical period. Giving a blessing was an exercise of charity. In the name of charity sinners were to be admonished. Those responsible for the morality of the community were asked to make judgments and to act accordingly. If it were seen that withholding a blessing would challenge the would-be recipient to more self-reflection, then in this case the radicality of the monks' lives impinged on the lives of others who saw no difficulty in being called to live the Christian life by those who professed it in a more total way.

Equally radical are the maxims of the latter part of ColumCille's rule:

Follow almsgiving before all things.
Take not of food till thou art hungry.
Sleep not till thou feelest desire.
Speak not except on business.[172]

The first of these maxims is an extension of the initial counsel to be always naked: be ready to give of all your material possessions, your time and your talents in the cause of being divested of all for the sake of the higher good. Undoubtedly personal discipline is at the heart of asceticism, and even the issue of the basic needs of the human person, food and sleep, is not exempted. However, what motivates the monk? 'The love of God with all thy heart and all thy strength.'[173] This is of greater importance than the actual practices. It is this intention that transforms apparent human deprivation into spiritual effectiveness both for the monk and those to whom he ministers. Silence, that deep inner quiet, should precede conversation either with God or with others. Conversation is hollow, in monasticism, if it is not surrounded by an atmosphere of silence.

Not only is the one living apart from the community to be abstemious in these basic necessities, but he is cautioned to have 'a mind prepared for red martyrdom. A mind fortified and steadfast for white martyrdom.'[174] Martyrdom, from earliest times, was rooted in its intimate connection with the death and resurrection of Christ. To be a martyr, which literally meant to be a 'witness', was to 'experience ahead of schedule the final eschatological event'.[175] As monastic life was modelled on the foundational myth of Christianity, then to die in order to rise in union with Christ, was the highest form of living. The *eschaton* was a culmination of, and a reward for, the 'daily dyings' inherent in the ascetical life and *praxis* of the Irish monk. This ultimately led to resurrection. In Irish life and monasticism, cemeteries were called the place of resurrection; with no dichotomy between the now and the hereafter, between the present and the future, one could live with confidence

---

171. Rule V 5 (ed. and trans. Skene, p. 508).
172. Rule V 15, 16, 17, 18 (ed. and trans. Skene, p. 509).
173. Rule V 20 (ed. and trans. Skene, p. 509).
174. Rule V 8 (ed. and trans. Skene, p. 508).
175. McBrien, *Catholicism*, p. 1060.

and hope. Naturally then a vital component of Irish monastic living was the readiness for martyrdom that was not only about self-denial but was perceived as a step on the road to resurrection.[176]

The secular history of the Irish coming to Christianity was not marked, as was the birth of Christianity in other lands, with the blood of martyrs. They therefore came to see a threefold martyrdom which, while not as immediate and final as giving one's physical life in the cause of the *evangelium*, was even more courageous and radical, for this form of martyrdom extended over a longer period, namely one's whole life. The two colours assigned to the notion of martyrdom mentioned by the writer of ColumCille's rule are red and white. It is informative that ColumCille insists that the mind was to be prepared for red martyrdom (giving one's life). No act of martyrdom is an accident: it is intrinsic to the act of self-giving that it is intended. The mind had to be fortified and steadfast for white martyrdom, the *hireath* as the Irish call it, meaning the extreme yearning for home that one had when one went on *peregrinatio pro Christo*. ColumCille's own choice of this kind of pilgrimage only adds to his stature as the courageous warrior monk.[177] This is because it is a greater challenge to be steadfast over a longer period of time than for the usually swifter red martyrdom. White martyrdom, according to early Irish Church teaching was 'to undertake the self-immolation of the ascetic life'.[178]

---

176. The earliest reference to martyrdom is in the Old-Irish Prose, *The Cambray Homily*, where it states in a footnote, 'Now there are three kinds of martyrdom which are counted as a cross to man, that is to say, white martyrdom, and green martyrdom, and red martyrdom . . . These three kinds of martyrdom are comprised in the carnal ones who resort to good repentance, who separate from their desires, who pour forth their blood in fasting and in labour for Christ's sake.' Stokes and Strachan (ed.), *Thesaurus*, pp. 246–47. The same source reveals that the Arabians had a similar notion in referring to white, black, green and red death.

177. Much early history of ColumCille's life has him being sent on pilgrimage, but my reading of the sources convinces me that he actually chose this pilgrimage as white martyrdom. Sharpe, following Herbert, would add a political reason for his departure from Ireland. M. Robinson, *Sacred Places, Pilgrim Paths: An Anthology of Pilgrimage* (London: HarperCollins, 1997), takes excerpts from sources as early as the Hebrew Scriptures to the very modern authors. In his introduction he treats such aspects of pilgrimage as: the holy, the heavenly city, the origins of Christian pilgrimage, the monastic connection, pilgrimage extended, pilgrimage as penance, and pilgrimage as metaphor. A comment from Karen Armstrong, 'A Passion for Holy Places', quoted in Robinson, *Sacred Places*, p. 33, is interesting in the context of this work, as it picks up some of the ambivalence I refer to in relation to the Irish penitentials and she applies it to pilgrimage:

> The spectacle of pilgrims walking barefoot . . . on their knees can cause dismay . . . bizarre behaviour seems obsessive and fanatical . . . perverse survival of a credulity that kept people ignorant . . . Even religious people can find pilgrims an embarrassment . . . The Protestant Reformation abolished pilgrimage with its cult of shrines and saints . . . But Protestantism is unique in its rejection of pilgrimage . . . The veneration of holy places seems to have been a primordial religious experience. The monotheistic religions gave us a religious geography dividing the world into sacred and profane areas. Some places were radically different because they were closer to God.

Maybe it is more precise to say they have the capacity to draw pilgrims closer to God.

178. Bradshaw, 'The Wild', p. 12.

Since this usually entailed some form of pilgrimage, to the clan-conscious Irish it could be truly a death to self. The martyrdom not mentioned in ColumCille's rule was '*glas* (blue), which is the mortified state of the penitent',[179] and is treated throughout the chapter on the penitentials.

Integral and distinctive to the Celtic consciousness of the Irish was the notion of pilgrimage as a form of penance.[180] Despite the hardship, the Irish strongly believed in the curative effect of pilgrimage which brought unexpected blessings, healing of soul and body ('there never was a pilgrim who did not come back to his village with one less prejudice')[181] and an intimacy with God that far outweighed the deprivation entailed. Patrick himself in his *Confession*, encouraged his monks: 'Whence came to me that gift so great, so salutary, the knowledge and love of God so intense that I might part with fatherland and relations?'[182]

Sometimes pilgrimage was imposed by one's *anamchara*, sometimes by one's confessor if he were not the soul-friend, and, in a celebrated case (namely ColumCille), by himself. In the life of ColumCille, this latter form of martyrdom is exemplified in the sense that he took on himself the life-long pilgrimage in penance for the battle of Cuil Dreimme in which 3000 people were killed. The victory, according to the *AU*, was due to the fact that 'they prevailed through the prayers of ColumCille'.[183] The mythology says that so deep was the sense of guilt and so extreme and imperative was the need to make recompense for so heinous a crime[184] that he undertook neither to look on Ireland again nor to set foot on Irish soil. However, in Sharpe's edition and notes on the Life of ColumCille, he would not claim this as a reason for ColumCille's move to the west of Scotland.

As we saw in the other rules, work was an integral part of monastic life and 'valuable as [it] was from the point of view of charity towards the brethren,

179. Bradshaw, 'The Wild', p. 13. C. Stancliffe, 'Red, White and Blue Martyrdom', in Hughes, *Studies*, pp. 21–46, where she, by using linguistic comparisons, clearly shows that where other writers prefer to translate *glas* as green, (she maintains that) blue is the correct translation of the Irish word. To my knowledge these are the only two authors who use blue as the third type of martyrdom.

180. It has to be noted here that in the Irish context of the early centuries the later notion of pilgrimage as going to a place such as Jerusalem or Rome was not intended. *Peregrinatio pro Christo* meant literally 'wandering for Christ'. Though the present-day word 'pilgrimage' comes from the *peregrinatio*, pilgrimage for the early Irish, such as Brendan and other travellers, was not to a place, but at the call of Christ without a destination and under the guidance of the Spirit. It was more the cutting oneself off from homeland and clan as an ascetic discipline with the hope of finding the Promised Land but not in the sense of a real destination.

181. J. J. O'Riordain, *A Pilgrim in Celtic Scotland* (Dublin: The Columba Press, 1997), p. 112. The final chapter of this book is on the tradition of pilgrimage.

182. Patrick, *Confession*, p. 36.

183. MacAirt and MacNiocaill (ed.), *The Annals*, p. 81.

184. Sharpe (ed.), *Adomnán*, pp. 12–15, appears not to give much credence to any of the earlier theories about ColumCille's departure and motivation. He seems to take sides with Marie Herbert who sees ColumCille's departure from Ireland as stemming from his royal lineage and his wish not to be involved in the political negotiation of his royal family connections.

it was equally valuable . . . as a splendid ascetical exercise'.[185] In the rule attributed to ColumCille, it is equated with labours that include prayer, work and reading. The physical work is also divided into three kinds: first dealing with 'the work of the place, as regards its real wants; second, thy share of the brethren's work; last to help the neighbours'.[186] Not only are these aspects of work a meritorious way to engage with others, but the rule also shows the variety of ways in which these works may involve the hermit. These ways speak of the diversity of the monastic commitment.

Working, in another sense, at one's spiritual growth also includes the notion of striving for the gift of tears. This gift is not given to all Christians but it was a sign of special 'graces' and so the hermit is instructed to work assiduously for such evidence of divine approval:

> Thy measure of prayer shall be until thy tears come;
> Or thy measure of work of labour till thy tears come;
> Or the measure of thy work of labour, or of thy genuflections, until thy perspiration often comes, if thy tears are not free.[187]

Another understanding attached to 'tears' or the lack thereof is closely associated with 'dryness'. That is, the spiritual condition which sometimes assails people who strive for holiness. Though it is unpleasant and implies a need to work at it (labour or genuflections in the present discussion) 'to the point of perspiration',[188] its presence is often experienced as rejection by God. It is part of the purgative way mentioned by spiritual writers, and can be experienced equally by those in the illuminative way. Its presence may also be a form of martyrdom, as it causes extreme suffering to those who experience it. What can be said without equivocation is that all these counsels, while being radical in the sense that they are not the ordinary precepts by which all Irish Christians lived in the sixth to the eighth century, were equally not totally self-centred or introspective. The help given to the neighbours was suggested as 'instruction, or writing, or sewing garments, or whatever labour they [the neighbours] may be in want of'.[189] So the primacy of withdrawal from the community, which occasioned the writing of this rule, has to be balanced by the ministry to those who seek help.

Integral to any living of the monastic life was the Divine Office[190] which brought the hermit, clerics and monks alike from their beds, work and reading, at six[191] times of the day and night to chant the praises of God. Deep in the

---

185. Ryan, *Irish Monasticism*, p. 361.
186. Rule V 13 (ed. and trans. Skene, p. 509).
187. Rule V 19f. (ed. and trans. Skene, p. 509).
188. Rule V 22 (ed. and trans. Skene, p. 509).
189. Rule V 13 (ed. and trans. Skene, p. 509).
190. An element of monastic praying closely linked with the strong emphasis on the prayerful reading of the Scriptures was known as *Lectio Divina* – ruminating over Scriptures as a method of meditation.
191. Ryan, *Irish Monasticism*, p. 336 says that with Prime the number became seven.

psyche of the Irish was the consciousness of the ancestors. ColumCille's rule cautions 'fervour in singing the office for the dead, as if every faithful dead was a particular friend of thine'.[192] It is not the mere recitation of the Hours but the fervour (cf. tears) with which this task was undertaken that made the difference. It was not simply abstaining from the beer or mead that Máel-Rúain seemed to be praising in the dialogue recorded at the beginning of this chapter. It was the inner transformation fundamental to the meaning of asceticism that elevated the mundane into the meritorious and which enabled the rare to be seen as radical.

ColumCille's rule, though specified for an individual, has many of the precepts included in the rules for communities. It stresses obedience to one's *anamchara*, links the two aspects of pilgrimage and martyrdom, and stresses the gift of tears and dryness as part of the penitential dimension of monastic life. As with other rules, he makes much of the Scriptures and the promptness required in responding to the call to prayer.

Rule of Columbanus

Of the four commentators referred to in this chapter, only Kenney mentions the rule of Columbanus. It is of vital importance to include it in discussion of the ascetical theology that underpins the monastic rules because of Columbanus' significance to the whole ascetical movement on the continent.[193] Kenney claims that 'it is the only monastic rule of Irish origin, written in the Latin language, which still survives, and is the earliest and most informing of all the rules which can be regarded as Irish'.[194]

Not only the dominating and inflexible character of Columbanus, but the circumstances in which he found himself on the continent, gave rise to a Rule exemplifying the radicality of his lifestyle, and so it is seen by later readers as a particularly rigorous[195] and even puritanical programme of living. Few people would deny that Columbanus was the most striking presence of the Celtic monastic spirit on the continent. The text of the rule is in two parts. The *Regula monachorum*, Monks' Rule, covers such aspects as obedience, silence, food and drink, overcoming greed and vanity, chastity, choir office, discretion, mortification. All the foregoing were designed to achieve perfection.[196] It could be put,

---

192. Rule V 11 (ed. and trans. Skene, p. 508).

193. The reader is referred to chapter 2 on the Irish penitentials where Columbanus is portrayed as the single most significant person affecting the asceticism on the continent in the sixth and subsequent centuries, through the uniquely Irish form and *praxis* of private confession.

194. Kenney, *The Sources*, p. 198.

195. *Versiculi Familiae Benchuir*, from the 'Antiphony of Bangor', fo 30r, ed. Warren (ed.), *The Antiphony*, Vol. 11, 1895, 11.28 [no. 95] speaks about the rule of Bangor as stricta, sancta, sedula/summa, justa, ac mira; it is no wonder that Columbanus' own life and rule could be said to be similarly strict and rigorous.

196. Walker (ed.), Sancti Columbani, p. 124.

in the words of chapter 1, as a way of life which purports to transform the energy derived from personal self-denial into a form of spiritual energy to be used in the search for God and the service of others. In his rule Columbanus shows where some of this energy is directed in the intercessory prayers he recommends.[197] This is followed by the *Regula Coenobialis* that is given in two parts: the *Regula Patrum* for the fathers[198] and the *Regula Fratrum* for the brethren.[199] Kenney maintains that the last chapter is an extract from Jerome not found in any of the extant manuscripts. He further believes that 'no reasonable doubt exists that the rest of the document, except the points of detail, is the work of Columbanus'.[200] Kenney calls Irish rules, especially that of Columbanus, a 'Mirror of Perfection'[201] or the guidance of monks rather than practical regulations for the organization and administration of the monasteries as such.

This rule of Columbanus, the quintessential son of Erin on the continent in the sixth and seventh centuries, 'has the teaching style and intellectual command of his sermons'.[202] Columbanus, according to Kenney, wrote a rule that 'we may feel certain . . . is a true product of the Irish Church',[203] and was, like other Irish Rules, a sure guide to living a life of perfection.[204] Kenney goes on to say that 'acceptance with unflinching logic of the precepts of Christ as preserved in the New Testament is its essential characteristic'.[205] According to Walker's translation and division of the section on Rules, there are three parts: the Monks' Rule, *Regula Monachorum*, Communal Rule of the Brethren, *Regula Coenobialis*, and the Penitential.[206] However, on reading these three sections, it is clear that only the first, *Regula Monachorum*, Monks' Rule, is a rule in the strict sense of the word. The Communal Rule of the Brethren is so bound up with penances assigned for faults that it must be classed as a penitential. Maybe the faults that are catalogued give an insight into the

---

197. *Regula Coenobialis* (ed. and trans. Walker, p. 130):

. . . our elders have appointed for us three psalms at each of the day Hours, on account of the interruption of work, together with an addition of versicles of intercession, first for our own sins, then for all Christian people, then for priests and the other grades of the holy people consecrated to God, then for the alms-givers, then for the peace of the kings, and lastly for our enemies.

Having previously commented, see fn 120, on the apparent influence of Comgall on Columbanus, it is instructive to note that the list of intercession practised at Bangor, in the seventh century, included not six but sixteen groups of people.

198. Walker (ed.), *Sancti Columbani*, pp. 143–5.
199. Walker (ed.), *Sancti Columbani*, pp. 145–79.
200. Kenney, *The Sources*, p. 198.
201. Kenney, *The Sources*, p. 198.
202. Hughes, *Early Christian*, p. 90.
203. Kenney, *The Sources*, p. 198.
204. Kenney, *The Sources*, p. 198.
205. Kenney, *The Sources*, p. 198.
206. Rule, prologue (ed. and trans. Walker, pp. 123–81); Ó Maidín, *The Celtic*, does not treat this rule.

virtues that are recommended. This would be in keeping with Cassian's principle of *contraries*.

The Monks' Rule, *Regula Monachorum*, begins with the now famous fundamental scriptural reference: to love God with the whole heart and the whole mind and all our strength, and our neighbour as ourselves.[207] This rule of Columbanus according to Hughes states the philosophy that underlies Irish ascetic practice. It is a three-stage process, beginning with 'nakedness and disdain of riches, to be satisfied with the small possessions of utter need'. Following is the second admonition, 'the purging of vices', and the third, 'the most perfect and perpetual love of God, which follows the forgetfulness of earthly things'.[208] Hughes claims that this is the aim of monastic life.[209] The initial Scripture reference actually sets the pattern for each of the ten sections of the rule, as they have at least one and sometimes more than one direct Scripture reference. This contrasts markedly with the other rules discussed which do not have more than a couple of references to Scripture in the whole rule. Even in the two very brief sections of Columbanus' rule the one on vanity has the apt quotation: 'I saw Satan like lightning fall from heaven',[210] and the other on chastity contains the succinct warning: 'He who looks on a woman to lust after her has already defiled her in his heart.'[211] So of all the rules, Columbanus' clearly shows that Scripture is the foundation and inspiration of his articulation of Irish monasticism, more so than Ailbe's, Ciarán's, Comgall's and ColumCille's rules.

Community living is given an interesting rationale in section 10, which some commentators say comes directly from Jerome. However, the author of this rule no doubt saw the wisdom of its first principle and incorporated it into his rule. It reads: 'Let the monk live in a community under the discipline of one father and in company with many, so that from the one he may learn lowliness, from the other patience. For one may teach him silence and another meekness.'[212]

This wisdom raises the question evoked by ColumCille's rule for one person. Does the hermit therefore not learn patience and lowliness because he lives alone? Hardly. Even more fundamental than community is the injunction that self-knowledge, often gained in community, but not impossible living as a hermit, is basic to humility. This virtue locates the monk in right relationship to God and others and therefore living alone can equally encourage the virtues of lowliness and patience. These monastic virtues of lowliness, patience, meekness and silence are also prized by other formulators of rules.

A more difficult virtue is that which comes later, but is still part of the primary outcome of silence: 'Let him keep silence when he has suffered wrong.'[213] Who does not wish to speak out in defence of themselves? But the

207. Walker, (ed.), *Sancti Columbani*, p. 123.
208. Rule V iv (ed. and trans. Walker, p. 127).
209. Hughes, *Early Christian*, p. 90.
210. Rule V v (ed. and trans. Walker, p. 129).
211. Rule V vi (ed. and trans. Walker, p. 129).
212. Rule V x (ed. and trans. Walker, p. 141).
213. Rule V x (ed. and trans. Walker, p. 141).

monk is taught that to keep silence is more heroic than to defend. And so it is, but it goes against the natural instincts and this is precisely what is basic to the understanding of monastic asceticism in the third, sixth and later centuries. This reiterates the point of the transformative function of monastic rules and penances. Not that natural instincts are not God-given and therefore good, but they need to be transcended in the interest of a higher good, namely the imitation of Christ and the smooth functioning of the monastic community

Obedience, at the first word of a senior, is equated with obeying God and, if one dares to answer back, he opens the way 'of answering back for others; [such a monk] is to be regarded as the destroyer of many'.[214] Strong words these, but the horror of scandal and its possibility of damnation for the scandal-giver and receiver were the motivation for the warning. Not only does living in community afford the possibility of being edified by good people; the equally strong possibility exists of being influenced by the less good, and this is to be avoided at all costs.

Other references to monastic vows contain language that is equally strong. Greed, a violation of poverty, is called a 'leprosy for monks',[215] and even to want superfluities is reprehensible.

> Thus then nakedness and disdain of riches are the first perfection of monks, but the second is the purging of vices, the third the most perfect and perpetual love of God and unceasing affection for things divine which follows on the forgetfulness of earthly things.[216]

Chastity is judged by the monk's thoughts and presumably these can be known only to one's *anamchara* or confessor, if these are not the same person. A warning is given that the eyes can be 'full of wantonness and adultery', warned against in the Scripture text quoted earlier. The final challenging question on this subject is: 'What profit is it if he be virgin in body, if he be not virgin in mind?'[217] Virginity is a total consecration of the whole person. Since the will is the seat of love, activity and all aspects which make the human person God-like then its single-mindedness is vital in any asceticism. A mind–body unity enables the person to make choices about the ideals for which one strives. These are then accomplished by the body/person.

This idea of the unity of the body/person can be related to earlier times. In pre-Christian druidic culture the mind and imagination were highly prized. The mind being so valued in this rule can be seen as a prolongation of the pre-Christian valuing of the mind and imagination. The inherent power of the *filid* and druids who would not commit to paper the treasured parts of their story is another aspect of the Celtic regard for the mind as the repository of cultural treasures. In preparing for this honoured role in society, the *filid* spent time in the dark with the body in a state of quiescence to allow the mind to work. Far

---

214. Rule 1 (ed. and trans. Walker, p. 125).
215. Rule V iv (ed. and trans. Walker, p. 127).
216. Rule V iv (ed. and trans. Walker, p. 127).
217. Rule V vi (ed. and trans. Walker, p. 129).

from a dichotomy between mind and body the monk's chastity is to be an embodiment of this unity. Since God is simple, having no parts, then the chastity of the monk is likewise to be a response of the whole person with no separation of mind and body.

The whole notion of discretion treated in section VIII (ix) of Columbanus' rule reveals the deep Irish reverence for the Spirit who is the source of the virtue of discernment from which discretion gets its name.[218] The author claims that it is 'in Christ Jesus we were created', and the virtues that are a result of this creation are 'goodness, innocence, righteousness, justice, truth, pity, saving peace, spiritual joy'. These are the 'fruit of the Spirit – all these with their fruits are good'.[219] It is God as Father who is credited with the task of creating nature, the universe, animals and humans. Christ Jesus is the one in whose likeness we are made and guided by the Spirit who is in us 'a light of true discretion to illumine our [way]'.[220] So discretion and discernment involve the Celtic Irish in relationship with a Trinity for whom their whole culture, both pre- and post-Christian, had a fondness. Theophanies, understood as encounters with the deity, were a matter of everyday occurrence for the Celts and, when they embraced Christianity with its trinity of 'persons' in the deity, they naturally experienced these theophanies as triune. Or, more precisely, they acknowledged different 'persons' of the deity in different religious experiences.

The belief in Celtic consciousness was that this Spirit within all of creation is both intimate and proximate. Since the human person is part of that creation, the Spirit must be within the human person. This awareness could not help but lead to a wholesome regard for the human person as an en-fleshed spirit. There is here no duality or separation of spirit and flesh. Jesus in his enfleshed state (Incarnation) makes God present. The Christian ideally makes the Risen Christ present in the Spirit.[221] The Platonic dichotomy evident in Greek monasticism gives way to integration in the Celtic monastic tradition. Nature itself makes its own demands and since the human spirit, and more so the Celtic human spirit, lives within this ambit of nature, it too has to conform to nature's way of being.

---

218. Rule VIII 15 (ed. and trans. Walker, p. 135); Sherley-Price (ed.), *Bede*, p. 151, in referring to Aidan as the suitable person to answer the call of King Oswald to preach the gospel in Northumbria, says Aidan was the choice because 'he was particularly endowed with the grace of discretion, *the mother of all virtues*' (my emphasis).

219. Rule VIII 30 (ed. and trans. Walker, p. 135).

220. Rule VIII 10 (ed. and trans. Walker, p. 135).

221. Recent theological works by: D. Edwards, *The God of Evolution* (New York: Paulist, 1999) and *Jesus and the Cosmos* (New York: Paulist, 1991); T. Berry, *The Great Work: Our Way into the Future* (New York: Bell and Tower, 1999); S. McDonogh, *To Care for the Earth: A Call to a New Theology* (London: Cassell, 1986) treat God and the cosmos differently from previous centuries. Hildegaard von Bingen's writings are at present being hailed as pertinent to those who wish to reclaim the integration of the human person with the whole of nature. She is reported to have said, 'The earth forms not only the basic raw materials for humankind, but also the substance of the incarnation of God's son.' *The Woman's Prayer Companion*, compiled by Carmelites, Indianapolis, 1994, p. 162.

Faith also makes demands and so the maxims of their monastic rules facilitate the Irish monks' attempt to be faithful to the *evangelium* within the inherited and experienced parameters of their cultural and spiritual tradition. That these demands appear at times to expect the impossible is understandable. That they are perceived to be harsh is also within the realm of possibility. However, that they were adhered to by great numbers of monks in the sixth to the eighth century can be given as evidence that they were not only livable but also enhanced the Christian life of those who inhabited the monastic enclosure and left a heritage of ideals and *praxis* for future generations. If *syneisaktism*[222] was practised, and this researcher is firmly convinced that it was a widespread practice, then the very human limitations and pragmatism of this behaviour in Irish monasticism should make it worthy of high regard and not incredulity. Faith is not necessarily absent when the human person is acting in accord with its cultural dictates.

While the Canonical Hours are to be performed 'in accordance with the nature of man's life and the succession of the seasons',[223] the writer of this rule still wished to lay down specific guidelines with the wonderful balancing statement that they 'must weigh our watching according to our strength'.[224] Awareness of the differing capacities of the monks in his care led Columbanus to elaborate further:

> the true tradition of praying is that the capacity of the man devoted to this work[225] should be realised without wearying of his vow, whether the excellence of his capacity allows this, or whether his mental grasp or physical condition could allow it, considering his limitations, and that it should be realised as far as the zeal of each demands.[226]

There is no doubt the *Regula Coenobialis*, the Communal Rule of the Brethren attributed to Columbanus, gives the impression that the way of life he established for his monks was puritanical and harsh. The evidence in this section of the overall rule, however, shows that the writer had an understanding of the mental, physical and intellectual capacity of the men in his monasteries. There is strong support for the harshness in the Communal Rule if the penances are an indication of how people were chastised for minor faults. However, as has been stressed throughout this work, the intention or motivation is the most

---

222. The pragmatism of this practice is seen in groups of committed people living together as part of their peripatetic lifestyle. Charismatic preachers naturally attracted followers of both sexes. Ideally separate abodes would have been temporarily desirable, even if only to give a semblance of 'respectability', but this is putting a twentieth-century slant on a sixth-century practice. Commitment to their newly found faith was paramount and so behaviours that could be seen as questionable to observers may not even have entered the consciousness of these early medieval monks.
223. Rule V vii, 25 (ed. and trans. Walker, p. 131).
224. Rule V vii, 15 (ed. and trans. Walker, p. 131).
225. Both ColumCille and Columbanus call prayer work, implying that it is not necessarily an easy task and that it required a similar commitment for it to be 'successful'.
226. Rule V vii, 5 (ed. and trans. Walker, p. 133).

important element in this type of commitment. If one does not understand this, then one is likely not to understand anything about the whole of monasticism.

This last statement is not meant to be a monumental withdrawal from the debate about the value of monastic commitment, but when one tries to evaluate a lifestyle with criteria that are inadequate, convincing validation is sure to fail. It is like asking an infant to understand the stance taken by an adult in relation to some issue of justice. The life experience is not present; the capacity to rise above one's psychological self-centredness has not been attained. In the area of developmental psychology it is said that one can understand and appreciate behaviour only a couple of stages above one's own level. So it is with attempts to understand the radical asceticism of Irish monasticism of the early Middle Ages. If one cannot understand the issues involved and appreciate the motivation, it may not be the fault of monasticism but a problem of perception. The transcendental nature of this lifestyle, in all generations, is doomed to be misunderstood the more a society moves away from the founding message deeply embedded in the *evangelium* of the Christian Scriptures.[227] However, because life is cyclical and the element of change is ever-present, history shows us the many resurgences of this lifestyle, and the changing perception can be seen to come full circle when society begins to ask again the major questions of life, its purpose and meaning.

No specific mention is made, in Columbanus' *Regula Monachum*, Monks' Rule, of those penances that are evident in some of the other Irish rules of this period. They are, though, seen in Columbanus' *Regula Coenobialis*, Communal Rule of the Brethren, and include punishments for specific faults. However, what is referred to here are those practices that with a pure heart and steadfast mind form the warp and woof of the daily life of the monk: the genuflections, the *crosfigell*, the compulsory reductions of food and sleep. It is informative that Columbanus did not include these in his Monks' Rule. But then this is not necessarily what the rules were meant to be. They were to be principles of ascetical living, not detailed practices.

There were, however, in the monastic enclosure, places attached to, but apart from, the main monastery for penances, which Ryan speaks of as being a part of most sixth-century monasteries. These were the places where people, sometimes those who were publicly excommunicated, went to 'expiate their crimes under monastic supervision before absolution and their re-admission to the community of the faithful'.[228] If this was the case, we can assume that the bulk of the Christian community were not normally given to doing penance to the same degree as those who had committed themselves to monastic living. Herein could lie the totality of commitment to the Christian lifestyle evident in the life of the monks. They not only professed to live more completely the gospel call to follow Christ, but their lifestyle gave concrete proof of this distinctiveness and radicality. The Christian symbolism of the cross in art and

---

227. The expression is used in preference to the New Testament. 'Hebrew Scriptures' is a way of noting that the Old Testament was written for the people before the time of Christ.
228. Ryan, *Irish Monasticism*, p. 321.

ritual[229] while focusing on the person of Christ and his suffering, was the means of helping those committed to him to integrate suffering, denial, penance and pain into their lives. Just as the horizontal and vertical bars of the conventional cross met, so the seemingly incongruous life of self-discipline could be transformed in the same spirit to achieve new life for the penitents and those with whom they came into contact. The transforming effects of the asceticism and *praxis* of the Irish monks of the sixth to the eighth century rippled out in ever-widening circles.

Food is taken, in this rule, in order that the monks will be able to watch, pray and work. The monk is content with what is given him to eat. The writer insists that 'life must be moderated just as toil must be moderated, since this is true discretion that the possibility of spiritual progress may be kept with a temperance that punished the flesh'.[230]

What is actually being guarded against here is the vice of pride. In spite of the heroic life, there is always the possibility that the monk can be tempted to judge himself better than those who do not perform such feats and so undo the virtuous work by the sin of pride. The writer of this rule suggests that 'virtues are placed in the mean between each extreme',[231] meaning that he is aware of the need for moderation and balance even in the austere life he lives so fully himself. He goes on to recommend, 'Keep yourselves from the right and from the left, we must ever proceed straight forward by discretion, that is, by the light of God.'[232]

All life begins with God and has its end with the same God. This is the Mirror of Perfection of which Kenney speaks. He also acknowledges, with admiration, that Columbanus accepted unflinchingly the logic of the precepts of the Christian Scriptures. Columbanus imposed penances on himself and others that would appear to require superhuman strength of mind and body (mainly found in the second section of the rules). What Kenney failed to comment on was Columbanus' great treatise on discretion.[233] The wisdom of this section permeated a good deal of what Columbanus recommended in the first section of his rule and therefore tended to balance the austerities that undoubtedly were in his overall lifestyle, only recommendations.

Columbanus' rule, the only one of Irish origin written in Latin still extant, principally contains the great treatment on discretion marking it out as different from all other rules treated in this chapter. If it was gestated in Bangor, under the guidance of Comgall, it was addressing followers on the continent amid

---

229. The *crosfigell* mentioned earlier and the multiple genuflections, signs of the cross, and the centrality of the cross in liturgy worship had an impact on everything in the monastery. The ever-present Scripture crosses (used as teaching aids for some of the illiterate population) studded throughout Ireland even today, particularly those at Clonmacnoise, Monasterboice, Glendalough, Kells, Donegal (the monastery of the Four Masters) and countless others are tangible evidence of the centrality of the cross in Irish monasticism.
230. Rule III iv (ed. and trans. Walker, p. 27).
231. Rule V iii, 34 (ed. and trans. Walker, p. 136).
232. Rule V iii, 35 (ed. and trans. Walker, p. 137).
233. Rule V iii (ed. and trans. Walker, pp. 135-39).

the internecine warfare of the times. These facts may explain the harshness of its many precepts. Its concentration on greed, moderation, humility and pride could be seen as foils for the continental context. The only virtue approximating the later vows treated was chastity. Scriptures and the Canonical Hours are also addressed.

Rule of Carthage[234]

Both O'Curry and de Bhaldraithe include Carthage's lengthy rule but Ó Maidín does not refer to it.[235] Most authors agree, with a precision unknown in the case of other Irish saints, that Carthage died on 14 May 636 CE. His rule, or that written at either Lismore or in nearby Darinis,[236] apart from being lengthy, addressed itself to the duties of many different members of the monastic community. These include bishops, abbots, priests, *anamchara*, monks, clerics of the enclosure and the king. It also gives guidelines for different activities such as the order of eating in the refectory,[237] and preaching the commandments to every person.[238] Though it gives wonderful insights into the monastic practice of the period, the rule of Carthage deviates significantly in that it moved from giving ascetical principles and emphasized detailed legislation.

The lengthy rule of Carthage also tends to reinforce the basic tenets of Irish ascetical theology. The abbot is reminded that he is to shepherd the brethren and to exhibit with cheerfulness the virtues of 'patience, humility, steadfastness, modesty, calmness',[239] together with fasting and abstinence. Bishops, who may be part of the monastic settlement, have primarily a liturgical function and, like the abbot, represent Christ only if they are learned in the Scriptures and are themselves obedient to Christ.

> You should know the holy Scriptures
> at the time that you take orders,
> because you are a stepson[240] of the church
> if you are deficient and ignorant[241]

---

234. According to Ó Maidín, *The Celtic*, p. 60 there are a number of manuscripts of this rule: (i) the British Museum, Additional 30512; (ii) the Library of Trinity College, Dublin, H.11f; (iii) a copy in *Lebor Brec*; (iv) the Library of The Royal Irish Academy, 23 N 10; (v) *The Yellow Book of Lecan* – a collection of items in the Library of Trinity College, Dublin, H.2 16; (vi) Volume 48 of the Murphy Collection of Saint Patrick's College, Maynooth (a copy of RIA 23 N 10).
235. This comment refers to the earlier copy I was using before the publication of his 1996 book. In this he does refer to it, pp. 59–73.
236. De Bhaldraithe, 'Two Rules', p. 65.
237. De Bhaldraithe, 'Two Rules', p. 74.
238. De Bhaldraithe, 'Two Rules', p. 65.
239. Rule V 28 (ed. and trans. de Bhaldraithe, p. 68).
240. To be a stepson would be anathema to the clan-conscious Celts.
241. Rule V 13 (ed. and trans. de Bhaldraithe, p. 66).

> For every unwise man is ignorant –
> this is the truth and the right –
> he is not the representative of the Lord
> if he does not read the Law.[242]

Moreover, if a bishop is ignorant he does not deserve obedience from the monks: 'people should not rise at your approach, nor should you be obeyed'.[243] This is a very different attitude from the hierarchically conscious Roman Church in the period under discussion.

The priest is admonished about his primary task of celebrating the Eucharist[244] and the soul-friend, *anamchara*, is reminded of the important ascetical practice of detachment from goods: 'If you receive their offerings, do not set your heart on them.'[245] The early Christian admonition about sufficiency and superfluous goods is here put forward and reiterates what many previously treated rules stress. The monk is warned about giving scandal by his life. He is reminded that his monastic vocation includes attending the Canonical Hours in order to contemplate with 'the men of the earth in all faith'.[246] What other rules stress, namely 'Let there be penitence of heart, shedding of tears and raising up of the hands',[247] is also to be foremost in the *praxis* of the soul-friend, 'pay for them the price of fasting and praying'.[248] This commutation,[249] specifically Irish, occurs when one gets somebody else, especially one's confessor, to do part of one's penance. With this reminder the *anamchara* is to put into operation his care for the persons who come to him for counsel, confession and/or penance.

> Two hundred genuflections at the *Beata*
> every day perpetually;
> to sing the three times fifty
> is an indispensable practice,[250]

This Culdee insistence above speaks clearly about the monastic's lifestyle and its concomitant penitential habits as an important injunction for the sinner, even if commutations are not sought.

---

242. Rule V 14 (ed. and trans. de Bhaldraithe, p. 66).
243. Rule V 16 (ed. and trans. de Bhaldraithe, p. 66).
244. There is no place to discuss the differences implied in the expression in the rule of being a 'chief of a church', V 18, p. 67, but what is intended is that the abbot is not just ordained for saying private masses as is the case with those in the order of monk-priest. It seems that in this period, some monks' sole function was to say masses, seven a day and sometimes up to twenty on a feast day. The monastic tradition and the rules clearly state that monk-priests can say masses from Terce to None.
245. Rule V 47 (ed. and trans. de Bhaldraithe, p. 69).
246. Rule V 55 (ed. and trans. de Bhaldraithe, p. 70).
247. Rule V 60 (ed. and trans. de Bhaldraithe, p. 70).
248. Rule V 48 (ed. and trans. de Bhaldraithe, p. 69).
249. The reader is directed to chapter 2 where these and the element of balance that they imply are discussed. While aware of the strictness of penance in this era there was always the consciousness of the ability of the penitent to perform the tasks.
250. Rule V 63 (ed. and trans. de Bhaldraithe, p. 71).

In suggesting conduct for the monk, the writer of the rule of Carthage uses the Irish poetic form of 'without', as do other rules. His seven verses of negatives are followed by seven verses of virtues, in penitential fashion reminding the monks of the wisdom of *contraries* and the virtues they are encouraged to cultivate. De Bhaldraithe holds that this section of Carthage's rule 'is a highly traditional piece, very closely resembling the rule of Ailbe'.[251] It seems that the number seven, being a sacred number in the Christian tradition, is used intentionally.

What sets this rule apart from the others already discussed is the great detail and legislation about 'the order of eating and of the refectory', which implies that it is of later date and more influenced by the Culdees than are the earlier rules. The individuality of each is preserved while it is the role of the abbot 'to decide for each according to his rank'.[252] In the case of fasting, it is to be practised 'by him who has the strength',[253] a reminder of what Columbanus said in reference to capacity, disposition and intellectual ability. True to the Celtic tradition, it is the seasons of the natural cycle and the seasons of the church year that dictate the differing food rites and rituals. Such details as:

Then they go into the house
and shed tears with fervour.
They repeat a *Pater* for rest in God;
they bow down three times.
Then they sit at the table,
They bless the meal.
Alleluia is sung, the bell is rung,
Benediction is pronounced,[253]

would never have occurred in the earlier rules, reinforcing the point that while many of the fundamental ascetical principles are contained in this rule, the attention to detail possibly places it after the Culdee reform. A further point concerning this rule can be made. From the text of the rule it appears that the monks were not priests and did not seem to be bound by the rule of reciting the Canonical Hours. De Bhaldraithe sees in this observance 'an anticipation of the choir and lay brother system which would prevail in the middle ages'.[255]

Conclusion

Kierkegaard, in the comment quoted at the beginning of this chapter, stresses the importance of the individual fighting 'decisive battles'[256] in themselves in order to lay permanent foundations for a life in community. This is said in the

251. De Bhaldraithe, 'A Review' p. 207.
252. Rule V 98 (ed. and trans. de Bhaldraithe, p. 74).
253. Rule V 110 (ed. and trans. de Bhaldraithe, p. 75).
254. Rule V 119–20 (ed. and trans. de Bhaldraithe, p. 76).
255. De Bhaldraithe, 'A Review' p. 77.
256. Connel and Evans, *Foundations*, p. 193.

context of the individual letting go of the ego and self-focus in order to be transformed into a person whose unselfishness makes community happen. He points to the 'chaotic nature of unquenchable personal striving'[257] where the person becomes their own objective reality resulting ultimately in loneliness. These are strong words but most self-conscious (in the good sense) people can affirm from personal experience that, while not using such emphatic words, the reality of what Kierkegaard is saying is true of human nature. Self-absorption is alienating of others, disruptive in groups and ultimately not satisfying for the person. All of these comments are by way of saying that we know from experience that the rules that were committed to writing in the early days of Irish monasticism were not necessarily oppressive, but were the ideals for which most people strive if they wish to be in relationship with others and the Other. However, many people may not strive with the same intensity, as did the monks of the Irish monasteries of the sixth to the eighth century.

The specific rules discussed in this chapter were metrical in form, acknowledging the powerful role of memorization in Celtic consciousness. They were attributed to Ailbe, Ciarán, Comgall, ColumCille, Columbanus and Carthage. They follow a semi-chronological order and show similarities, especially those of Comgall and Columbanus; the former was the founder of Bangor where Columbanus spent some years before he departed for the continent of Europe. The rule of ColumCille is the only one formulated for a single individual while the others are all for communities of monks. They varied in length and specificity. The later the rule the more detailed were the injunctions. Though names of prominent saints are given to each rule, they may not have been 'written' by that person. Indeed they may have been given the name as an honour to the person or to add dignity to the rule itself. However, it is agreed by most commentators (including Kenney, de Bhaldraithe, Ó Maidín and O'Curry) and editors of these rules that they embody the 'spirit' of the person in whose name they are put forward and no doubt had an integral association with the monastery or *paruchia* he founded.

Those who became members of monastic establishments were not all monks in the strict sense of the word. The enclosures included ascetics, probably those in Orders who most likely became the *anamchara*, soul-friend, to the group. Others were the *monachus*, committed to religious life, and *monach*, married laymen who supported the monastery by their labour and whose children benefited by the monastic school. The abbot was assisted by the vice-abbot or *seniors* as the rules call them. Because many of these monasteries became quite large they also required cooks and stewards. Simple wattle-and-daub structures were the original buildings but since these were insubstantial, the only structures that archaeology reveals today are the solidly built beehive hut like those on Hinba and Skellig Michael. The three cashels of Nendrum indicate some archaeological formation but further excavation would be required if more detailed issues of lifestyle and occupants were to be ascertained. Dates for the change-over of these buildings styles is not known. There

---

257. Connel and Evans, *Foundations*, p. 193.

was a church for the chanting of the Divine Office and individual cells that could house up to two persons. The framework of the monastic day was the Canonical Hours that, as some rules indicate, were prayed either alone or with the community, either in the monastery church or in the open.

While Máel-Rúain and Dublitir, the abbots of Tallaght and Finglas who initiated the reform movement of the late eighth century, discuss whether their monks can drink for the feast and whether this activity requires the purgation of Doomsday, earlier rules were inculcating ascetical principles. If these rules are to be seen as 'Mirrors of Perfection',[258] their advice of constant prayer, silence to enable meaningful communication with God, and not straying from the monastery except for pastoral reasons should be heeded. The exhortation to hard work befitting each person's strength, ability and disposition is not unlike the requirements for monasticism in general. Availability for service to the wider community, self-abasement and charity in speech likewise are injunctions of most monastic enclosures. Submission to another person or *anamchara* for direction in life's choices, which in principle is part of the lifestyle of those who choose a more radical way of living, is distinctive to Irish monasticism as it was the forerunner to the Irish monastic tradition's most important contribution to the penitential system ultimately adopted by the universal Church. This form of private confession vis-à-vis public confession was to mark a turning point in the mode of confession but it also was the lightning rod for much conflict among the Irish monks on the continent and the incumbent princes of Church and state.

Some of the rules indicate that part of their concern was for the pastoral care of both the members and those of the wider community outside the enclosure. The evangelical virtues of obedience, poverty and chastity that later became the vows of committed religious were not so evident in most of the rules discussed. Obedience was the exception. One reference to a practice that had implications for chastity, namely *syneisaktism*, is still a matter of contention with some Irish researchers. However, the fact that many Councils condemned it indicates that something of that nature must have been occurring; otherwise it would not have been mentioned.

Bodily penances, while not the same as those imposed by the penitentials, are undertaken by choice to enable the monk to be aware of the selfishness inherent in the human person. However, unlike some other attitudes to bodily restraint, the Irish monks and their whole culture saw it not as subduing a recalcitrant member but as the locus for penance and the path to future glory. Food in moderation, sleep in moderation, enjoyment in moderation were hallmarks of this monastic tradition of the sixth to the eighth century. Another specifically Irish bodily manifestation of this willingness to hasten on the path to glory was the *crofigell* or *figill*. This discipline for the body while praying was a way of disciplining the mind, in imitation of the men of the Hebrew Scriptures but ultimately in imitation of Christ.

---

258. Kenney, *The Sources*, p. 198.

Since ColumCille and Columbanus form the focus of the next two chapters of this work and appear to have more distinctive precepts in their rules, these will be analysed. Moreover, only ColumCille has formulated a rule for an individual.[259] Though de Bhaldraithe thinks that he is not too happy about the life of the hermit, he seems to leave such a choice to the individual. Moreover, this rule of ColumCille is the only one to highlight martyrdom and pilgrimage, those classic Irish forms of penance where regardless of clan and country the penitent leaves, sometimes for an unknown destination, obedient to 'the call' to participate in a form of mortification that almost denies cultural identification with homeland. Only a higher good could motivate such behaviour. ColumCille also stresses the role of the *anamchara* in the spiritual journey. The affectivity of the gift of tears and the pain of dryness in the spiritual life, ColumCille treats as though he had personal experience of them. Both ColumCille and Columbanus treat work, prayer and Scripture in common. Scripture, the basis for the Canonical Hours, had to be performed with fervour, according to ColumCille, and ever-conscious of the ancestors in whose name and presence they were being prayed.

Columbanus' precepts include discussion of greed, moderation, humility and the danger of pride in undermining the whole edifice of the spiritual life built on the ascetical practices. Though all rules clearly claim that wholehearted focus on God and things eternal constitute a major concentration of the monks life, Columbanus' rule specified how this is achieved: nakedness and a disdain for riches comes first, purging of vices second and third, 'the most perfect and perpetual love of God, which follows the forgetfulness of earthly things.'[260] He counsels silence when one has suffered wrong. His greatest contribution, though, is his chapter on discretion. It reveals the Irish great reverence for the Spirit, whose presence permeates the whole created world. The Spirit guides discernment, from which discretion gets its name. His treatment of this virtue emphasizes the Irish relationship with the Trinity (threeness) for which culturally the Irish had an abiding fondness.

Not only do these monastic rules inculcate a radical lifestyle, they undoubtedly arise from the idiosyncratic Irish social and spiritual perception of the *evangelium* to which they were being called. They emphasize that the primacy of prayer is a form of asceticism. In the understanding of asceticism that is used throughout this work, they are the exercises undertaken to bring about a transformation in the person. Not that the monk has to be forced to pray. It is the constant calling to prayer at seven times in the day and night that constitute the asceticism. Certain practices, in some instances the *crosfigell*, indeed would be experienced as penance. Rising from bed in the middle of the night in the midst of blizzards could not be undertaken unless the motivation was for a closer relationship with the God to whom these monks had committed their whole lives. Given the emphasis on the individuality of the Irish

---

259. Ó Maidín, *The Celtic*, p. 37, says that 'John Colgan, writing in or about 1630', claimed that ColumCille wrote another rule which has since been lost. All that is available to the student of monasticism is the rule for those who choose to live alone.

260. Rule V iv (ed. and trans. Walker, p. 127).

the mere coming together in community for prayer could have been mortification enough. The uniqueness of the individual is carefully safeguarded by most writers of rules in that the health, disposition and work regime is what dictates the practices to be performed. If the brother is too old, infirm, incapable in other ways, then the strictures of the rules apply to him in a 'commuted' form. Even those who cannot read are carefully protected from harm by being given a specific schedule. So the asceticism was not intended to break the spirit of those committed to it. It was to be willingly embraced in imitation of Christ.

As an example of this same imitation, work was treated by both Ailbe and ColumCille. Work is hard and tiring, it is a reminder of the injunction to Adam and Eve that they would have to toil for their livelihood when they exercised their freedom in the garden of paradise. Work, both physical and intellectual, was an intrinsic part of the life of the monastery. It was seen as a serious duty and part of the obedience one owed to one's abbot. The monk went to work not only as part of his contribution to the well-being of the monastery, but also as an exercise in imitation of Christ who, pious tradition tells us, worked as a tradesman with his foster-father Joseph.

Distrust of the world is also recommended by both Ailbe and ColumCille. Here the asceticism lies in the monk's preference for the things of heaven. What is needed will be given, and if it is not then one could remind oneself that what is needed and wanted are not the same thing. Elsewhere the virtue of moderation is counselled. If one exercises control by eating in moderation, sleeping in moderation and recreating in moderation one is more likely to be able to focus on what is necessary. Comgall refers to this aspect of the ascetical awareness of the monk as being wary of superfluities.

Distrust of the world and withdrawal from it constituted an important element of the monk's striving for communing with God. Silence also had the effect of creating the space for this, the major task of the monk. Monks were instructed to be sparing with conversation, even edifying conversation, because this distracted from their time for and their openness to communing with God. ColumCille warns the monk to guard against 'tattlers' who not only speak ill of others but also occupy the time given to communing with God. While this practice of silence was a source of puzzlement for outsiders, it was nonetheless that which encouraged them to use the monks as intermediaries with God on their behalf. Blessings, and asking for one, are sometimes the way people manifest their belief in the monk's closeness to God. In the rule of ColumCille he recommends that monks withhold giving a blessing in certain circumstances, not as a misuse of power but as part of the exercise of the virtue of charity.

There is no doubt that the call to radical living of the monastic lifestyle in the period under discussion was powerful. These rules and penitentials set out for the monks indeed encouraged a strict way of life. However it has been demonstrated that there was obvious balance in these two sets of monastic writings both in their interpretation and *praxis* in the sixth to eighth century in Ireland and on the continent.

One of the foundational tenets of this period was that holy people were held up as models of living. During their lives, and more especially after their deaths, what they said and did, how they acted in the community was to be emulated. Their 'voices' were heard through the *Vitae* written by contemporaries. Their 'voices' were also heard through their own writings in the form of prayers, poems and personal communications. The monastic ideal embodied in the foregoing rules and penitentials would not have exerted the wide influence it did if such ideals had not been evident in the lifestyles of the leaders of the monastic *paruchia*. Two such leaders are treated in the following chapters – ColumCille, founder of Iona, and Columbanus, the quintessential Irish *Peregrinus* on the continent in the latter part of the sixth century.

4 COLUMCILLE – FOUNDER OF IONA[1]

We begin to see the saint for what he really was: successor to the local pagan divinity, some of whose attributes he might inherit. If anywhere, there is continuity here.[2]

Introduction

Elsewhere in this work, it is has been said that ColumCille,[3] together with Columbanus[4] the two *'doves'* of the Irish Church, are the quintessential

---

1. There are, to my knowledge, seven editions of Adomnán's Life of ColumCille: M. O'Donnell (ed.), *Betha Colaim Chille*, compiled in 1532; W. Reeves (ed.), *Life of Saint Columba: Founder of Hy*, 1874; W. F. Skene (ed.), *Adomnán's Life of Columba*, published 1874; J. T. Fowler (ed.), *Adomnani Vita S.Columbae*, published 1894; W. Huyshe, (ed.), *The Life of Saint Columba by Adamnán*, published 1900s; A. O. Anderson and M. O. Anderson (eds), *Adomnán's Life of Columba*, published 1961, and R. Sharpe (ed.), *Adomnán's Life of St Columba*, published 1995. The MS of the O'Donnell Life is in the library of Schaffhausen in Switzerland known as 'A' and a second MS, partly a variant called 'B' is in the British Library. Sharpe (ed.), *Adomnan's*, p. 3, refers to a Life of ColumCille by Cummene, seventh Abbot of Iona, 657–69 CE (see Appendix 1 E for a chart of the abbots of Iona who were of the ColumCille clan). However, he goes on to say that the book is not referred to as a *Life* but as 'the book which he wrote on the miraculous powers of St Columba'; Fowler (ed.), *Adomnani*, Preface, p. x, states that Dr Reeves gives a list of seven Lives of St Columba. In 1994 a Celtic cleric made a comment about the Irish Church which reinforces the opening comment and highlights an underlying aspect of this work: that there is continuity between the pre- and post-Christian beliefs and *praxis* of the Celtic religions. Colm Kilcoyn from Cong is reported as having said, 'I love the Irish Catholic Church – when it is left alone... It is at its most honest when it is part pagan [*sic*], part Christian, part Celtic beliefs, whatever you are having yourself... It is too free, too contradictory, too tolerant, too wild a spirit to be a political power.' *National Catholic Reporter*, 30, no. 35 (29 July, 1994), p. 9.
2. J. M. Wallace-Hadrill, *Early Medieval History* (Oxford: Oxford University Press, 1975), p. 3.
3. 'Colum', 'Columba', 'Colman' and 'Columban' are all versions of the same name, with the latter two being diminutives; in Latin the name means *'dove'*. In the *Book of Leinster* there are 228 Colmans and 19 Colums. Sherley-Price (ed.), *Bede*, p. 279, refers to Columba, 'first teacher of the Christian faith to the Picts', and explains 'For this reason [the reason is not clear from the foregoing comments] Columba is now known by some people as Columbkill, a name compounded from Columba and cell. Sharpe (ed.), *Adomnán*, p. 243, says, 'Adomnán is at pains to show that the name meaning *'dove'* was given to Columba "from the days of his infancy" by divine providence'. Irish writers of later date thought that this was a name he acquired at a later stage, and give his original name as *Crimthann*, which means 'fox'. There is a story recorded in a later medieval commentary on the *Feliere Oengsso Celi De*, of how the saint was given the Irish name ColumCille *'dove* of the church'. This story is incorporated into Manus O'Donnell's life of the saint A. O' Kelleher and G. Schoepperle (eds.), *Betha Colaim Chille: Life of Columcille*, compiled by Manus O'Donnell in 1532 (Illinois: Graduate School Urbana, 1st edn, 1918).
4. Treated in chapter 5 of this work.

representatives of the sixth- to eighth-century Irish monastic movement.[5] The radicality of their monastic rules and penitentials, treated earlier in this work, bears this out. Their lives and extant writings will be discussed in the next two chapters with a view to understanding the ascetical theology and *praxis*, together with those elements of Celtic consciousness that underpin them. An examination will show that deeply embedded in their lives and *Vitae* aspects of clan or ancestor awareness, love of Scripture, complete familiarity with nature and all its manifestations are apparent. In addition the role of the individual in Irish society and the distinctiveness of the warring image will be evident. Finally fidelity to the *evangelium* lived out by an asceticism in theory and *praxis* that was distinctive will be evaluated.

Ancestry and Personal Characteristics of ColumCille

Before addressing the primary source being used in this chapter it would be important to set the scene by briefly looking at the larger context and examining ColumCille's ancestry, the notion of sanctity and his influence in his era and beyond. ColumCille, tradition tells us, was born approximately 520–22 CE in the county of Donegal at the village of Gartan,[6] into a royal family. However, the *AU*'s record for 518 includes the statement, 'the birth of ColumCille [occurred] on the same day in which Buite, son of Bronach slept'.[7] The *AT* gives the date as 519.[8] On his father's side he was the son of Feidhlimidh, great grandson of Niall Naoighiallach, 'Niall of the Nine Hostages', High King of Ireland, 'so called because he had taken five hostages from the provinces of Ireland, four from Scotland'.[9] According to Campbell, 'he is the traditional forebear of the O'Neills in Ireland and the MacNeils or MacNeills in Scotland'.[10] In the tradition of fosterage common in Ireland, ColumCille was fostered by Cruithnechan whose name suggests he was one of

---

5. This is not to deny the powerful formative influence of many other holy men such as Ninian, Comgall, Vinnian/Finnian, Kevin, Ciarán, to name a few, on the spiritual heritage of Ireland in the centuries under discussion.

6. Lehane, *Early Celtic*, chronological table Appendix, would concur that ColumCille's birth was 521 CE. Sharpe (ed.), *Adomnán's*, p. 9, would say that we do not know when ColumCille was born but he calculates his birth from the date of his death and his age at the time of his death in 597 CE given by the Irish *Annals*. Bede's dating is different by a year. Sharpe would also doubt the veracity of Gartan as the place of his birth as it depends on a tradition as 'recent' as the twelfth century. The story he says must be doubted as Gartan 'lies outside the territory ruled directly by Cenel Conaill. It probably reflects an interest of the author of the homiletic Life, who lived at Derry.'

7. MacAirt and MacNiocaill (ed.), *Annals*, p. 65.

8. Stokes (ed.), *Annals*, Vol. 1, p. 85.

9. J. Campbell, *Canna: The Story of a Hebridean Island* (Oxford: Oxford University Press, 1st edn, 1984), p. 2.

10. Campbell, *Canna*, p. 2.

ColumCille – Founder of Iona

the *Cruithne*, the Picts of Ireland. This could account for his familiarity with the Picts when he eventually arrived in Pictland in north-west Scotland.

From his mother, Eithne, he could also claim royal lineage, since she was daughter of Dioma, son of Naoi, of the race of Cairbre Nia Fear, King of Leinster.[11] With this family history he was eligible for election to the High Kingship of Ireland. *The Betha Colaim Chille*, the Old Irish life, records his birth as, 'in Gartan, in sooth, in Cenel Gulban, ColumCille was born'.[12] In the same ancient document all the saints of Ireland, including Patrick, Brigit, Brendan and others, foretold the birth of ColumCille.[13] Even 'druids of Connall Gulban, son of Niall of the Nine Hostages', foretold his birth.

> A child shall be born of thy kin in this place where thou now are, and he shall be of the third generation from thee; and Columcille shall be his name, and filled shall he be of the graces of the one God of All Power and Creator of the Elements. And he shall bless this place and be safeguard and sanctuary to everyone that shall need to come hither till Doom.[14]

His ordination was mentioned in the *MO*, 'Bishop Etchen is venerated in Clonard in the south of Meath, and it is to him ColumCille went to have the order conferred upon him.'[15] This account identifies the bishop, cousin of ColumCille, who conferred the priesthood on him, presumably when he was at Finnian's monastery in Clonard. There are many tales revolving around why ColumCille never became a bishop but the fact is that he established a tradition of the presbyter-abbot in his *paruchia* and not till later at Lindisfarne did a Celtic abbot, Aidan, become bishop in 635 CE.

His choice of the way of the monk did not altogether mean an abandonment of his political influence. This he used to effect in his missionary work in north-western Scotland,[16] as well as at the Conference of Druim Cette, where his considerable influence saved the poets as a class from extinction in Ireland. The motivation for his appearance at the Conference at Druim Cette can only be guessed at. His defence of the poets, however, reveals his concern for this group and his valuing of their contribution to society. These were the keepers of the story of the clan, the source of imagination and vision, and as such they had to retain their honoured place if the society was to flourish. His immersion in

11. Campbell, *Canna*, p. 2.
12. O'Donnell, *Betha*, p. 39.
13. O'Donnell, *Betha*, pp. 15–31.
14. O'Donnell, *Betha*, p. 31.
15. Marsden, *The Illustrated*, p.25.
16. Adomnán mentions that he went to, and possibly set up monastic establishments on, Iona, Islay, Mull, Coll, Eigg, Skye and possibly Hinba. Sharpe (ed.), *Adomnán's*, p. 18, holds that a different version of ColumCille's early life is given by Dr Smyth thus: 'Early Irish traditions (and the Old Irish Life of St Columba in particular) have reinforced the popular assumption that Columba founded Iona as soon as he reached Scotland in 563 CE . . . A close reading of Adomnán suggests that Columba's earliest base in Scotland was on the unidentified island of Hinba.' Sharpe himself does not agree with Dr Smyth's reading of the sources. He holds that Hinba was a dependency of Iona by 574 CE (p. 21).

poetry, including his use and writing of it, must have had a 'softening' influence on this man of iron.

In the Old Irish Life, *Betha Colaim Chille*, we are told that God helped ColumCille with grinding the corn, '[and] this honour did God show him above the others (monks of Clonard) for his gentle ways and his gentle birth and his gentle breeding'.[17] However, elsewhere in accounts of his life ColumCille is portrayed as a less gentle character, with an air of arrogance and the concomitant failing of pride and hot temper. These characteristics are mercifully balanced by the all-pervading quality of his asceticism, love of his homeland and his brethren.[18] From the *Life*, as written by Adomnán, it is clear that ColumCille had the 'gift', which, according to Campbell, 'some would call the burden'[19] of second-sight. This, together with the ease with which he integrated his pre-Christian heritage,[20] could have been evidence of his belonging to the druid class. In regard to this 'gift' Campbell gives a timely reminder that such a gift did not necessarily gain for its owner financial advantage, nor social prestige. Indeed it often resulted, in later centuries, in prosecution for witchcraft. Readers of the *Lives* of any of the saints of this period can take to heart Campbell's admonition, '[we] must remember that we are dealing with a very different age and different level of human consciousness and time dimension and one in which oral tradition... played a very important part.'[21]

One personal characteristic of ColumCille was evident when Adomnán and his monks were attempting to return to Iona for the celebrations honouring the anniversary of ColumCille's death. Adomnán admits that he complained to the deceased abbot,

17. O'Donnell, *Betha*, p. 57.
18. Expressions of affectivity, notably the kiss of peace, abound in Adomnán's *Life*. First of these is his conversation with Diarmait, his servant whom he calls 'my dear child', I 29; others include I 2, 3, 9, 30, 31, 32, 44, 45; III 3, 22. These references are to the Sharpe edition. Reeves' edition has different figures, usually only one figure difference: Sharpe, (ed.), *Adomnán's*, III 7 is in Reeves III viii.
19. Campbell, *Canna*, p. 2.
20. J. J. O'Riordain, *The Music of What Happens* (Dublin: The Columba Press, 1st edn, 1996), chapter 3 exemplifies this capacity of the Irish to integrate their primal past with their Christian present and to live comfortably within both. See also Edel (ed.), *Cultural*, Part 11, where there are the following references: Green, pp. 129–43; O'Riain, pp. 144–56; Schneiders, pp. 157–69. In these references there is discussion of the primal past and Christian present in Ireland of the period under discussion. See Appendix IV A for photos of stones in Elgin Cathedral, Scotland that carry pre-Christian drawings on one side and Christian on the reverse side, evidence of the easy cohabiting of these two traditions. Other stones that have similar dual-purpose markings include: *Aberlemno Stone*, purported to be a representation of the Battle of Nehtanssmere 685 AD where the Picts were depicted as defeating the Northumbrians. *Rossie Priory Stone* has similar markings with both the Christian cross and Pictish battle scenes. Appendix 1V B is from Westport, Ireland and has both Christian and pagan markings.
21. Campbell, *Canna*, p. 3; M. Smyth, *Understanding The Universe in Sixth-Century Ireland* (Indiana: The Medieval Institute, 1984), p. 6, drawing on Hubert's *Revue des Etudes Latines*, XXXVII (1960), p. 416, mildly criticizes people who judge the early monks by later scholarly criteria. She claims that early texts 'must be viewed against the learning of their own time in order to gauge their contribution'.

> Is it your wish, O saint, that I should stay here among the lay people till tomorrow, and not spend the day of your feast in your own church? It is such an easy thing for you on a day like this to change an adverse wind into a favourable one, so that I might partake of the solemn masses of your feast day in your own church.[22]

On reading of such an event one could feel ambivalence regarding the man of pride and princely dignity who is, nonetheless, able to be approached by his followers with a degree of familiarity and affection. That this is evidence of a gentleness and simplicity is attested to by the persistent 'devotion' towards him. What it might also highlight is the persistence in the Celtic tradition of a lack of a sense of hierarchy in the spiritual order. The brethren were equal in the eyes of God. The abbot simply had the responsibility to facilitate their growth in self-transformation in response to the living of the *evangelium*.

Adomnán's *Life of ColumCille* has a timeless element which removes it from the merely historical and anecdotal genre. Marsden claims that Adomnán's *Life* 'is a rich and reliable seam of history and biography to be found only a little way below the hagiographical surface'.[23] Reeves describes it as 'an inestimable literary relic of the Irish Church'.[24] Adomnán seems concerned to present his hero as just that: in the mould of Irish heroes of the stature of Cú Chulainn.[25] A more important concern of his is to present ColumCille as a man of God who is firmly established in the biblical tradition and with a universality that defies local boundaries. Likewise Adomnán, while keeping the tripartite structure, reminiscent of the Greek Lives, inserts his own threesome. Instead of the notion of *acta*, *virtutes* and *conversatio*, which Picard calls both a progression in time and sanctity, Adomnán opts for a different triad, which reveals a progression that represents a manifestation of divine power[26] and its natural concomitant, closeness to God, and in human terms, sanctity.

Sanctity

Since the period under discussion is so removed from our own age, a few words on the understanding of sanctity prevalent in the period would not be out of place. Auden once said, 'health is a state about which medicine has nothing to say; sanctity is the state about which theology has nothing to say'.[27] This, at

22. *Life*, II 45, (ed. and trans. Sharpe, p. 200).
23. Marsden, *The Illustrated*, p. 20.
24. Marsden, *The Illustrated*, p. 20.
25. The incident of the sorcerer who drew milk from a bull is an incident that could occur equally in the life of a saint or a druid. *Life*, II XV (ed. and trans. Reeves, p. 81). *Life*, I 13 (ed. and trans. Sharpe, p. 60), cites the account of ColumCille with the king of the Picts as further proof of his hero's status as presented by Adomnán. I. Finlay, *Columba* (London: Victor Gollancz, 1979), p. 73, makes the point that the cult of the saints did not drive out the cult of the hero, they became indistinguishable from each other in the later *Vitae*, as evident in the opening quotation from Wallace-Hadrill.
26. Picard, 'Structural Patterns', p. 76.
27. J. Fiennes, *On Pilgrimage: A Time to Seek* (London: Sinclair-Stevenson Ltd, 1991), p. 1.

first, seems like an absurd statement. If theology, in terms of the notion being used in this work, is about one's relationship with God[28] (faith seeking understanding referred to in chapter 1) and sanctity is that state which is universally acknowledged as one which implies an extraordinary intimacy and closeness of the person so described with the deity, then surely theology would have something to say about sanctity. Maybe Auden is recalling that, like love, sanctity is not merely philosophizing or theorizing about one's relationship with God. Nor is it solely an intellectual pursuit. In the lives of many mystics, it cannot even be verbalized. It is usually spoken about by observers, hagiographers or other 'outsiders'. Rarely, with some notable exceptions, do saints speak about their own sanctity. It is, then, that amalgam of all the faculties of the human person totally given over to what that person perceives as the most important, all-consuming, wholly other-focused life pursuit.

In this sense, sanctity, the living out, to an heroic degree, in daily life of a love relationship that is initially gift and only later a deliberate choice to respond to that gift, is not the lifestyle of every person.[29] It is not even the way of life of the majority of humanity. It is not the preserve of any one sex, religious affiliation, socio-cultural group, intellectual elite or adherents of any particular world religion. In the Irish tradition there were a plethora of 'saints' who seemed to justify the title *Insula Sanctorum*,[30] though most serious students of Irish ecclesiastical history would know that some of these people, honoured as saints, may have been apocryphal. On the sixth of November each year the Irish Church pays liturgical tribute to all the Irish Saints.[31] Whether apocryphal or not their number can be attributed to the *vox populi* or, more correctly, the

---

28. Sharpe (ed.), *Adomnán's*, preface, uses this 'definition' when referring to theology. It can almost be said to be a shorthand definition of this complex phenomenon. He also makes the point (p. 9) that theology is timeless in the sense that, in speaking about ColumCille's decision to opt for the life of the monastic rather than that of the princely politician in keeping with his family status, he was living out the time-honoured 'vocation' of Rom. 27–30.

29. D. Pochin-Mould, *The Celtic Saints: Our Heritage* (Dublin: Clonmore and Reynolds, 1st edn, 1956) in chapter 13 deals with the society of the period and makes the point that the saints are not different from the rest of society in the challenges they confront, only in the way they hear the call and respond to it. She discusses this in relation to a treatise called *De Duodecim abusivis seculi*, written not before 600 CE and not later than 725 CE, where twelve categories of bad people are listed and discussed. The point being made is that while everyone was exposed to the same society, only few rose to the heights of sanctity, i.e. acted in such a way that their lives were remembered as holy. This is not to deny the strongly 'political' element in who is proclaimed as holy in every era.

30. Pochin-Mould, *The Celtic*, chapter 13 treats the other individual islands that have been given the title of holy, but here the reference is to the whole of the island.

31. J. Ussher, *Incipit Catalogus Sanctorum Hiberniae secundum diversa tempora*, Vol. vi of his complete works, p. 477, details what is called the Three Orders of Irish saints: the first Order was most holy [*sanctissimus*]; the second Order very holy [*sanctior*]; the third Order holy [*sanctus*]. The first burns [*ardescit*] like the sun, the second like the moon, the third like the stars. De Paor, *St Patrick's*, pp. 225–6 gives a translation of the *Three Orders of Saints*; Chadwick, *The Age*, pp. 71–88 also discusses the *Three Orders of Saints*.

sensus fidelium, which was, no doubt, the initial 'canonizing' source. In the MO the poet prays:

> O lord of men, O king righteous,
> truly-good, let every profit be mine
> for (my) praise of thy kingfold.
> Thy kingfold whom I praise,
> for 'tis Thou art my sovran,
> I have borne in mind constancy in beseeching them.
> I pray a prayer to them:
> may what I have taken protect me –
> the fair people with beauty,
> the king-folk I have commemorated.[32]

The period of Irish history known as the *Age of the Saints* coincides with the dates for the life of ColumCille. Nora Chadwick in her classic work of the same title commences with the affirmation:

> The Age of the Saints is not only a period of especial beauty . . . but it also lies at the foundation of all our studies of Celtic history, since we owe to it most of our earliest written records . . . The contemplation of their austerity, their unworldliness, and their spiritual happiness is an inspiration to our present age.[33]

Her admiration for the saints of Ireland is unabated throughout this work. However, not all historians agree with Chadwick. Some have been critical of the catalogues of saints in the ancient texts. Binchy, when discussing the primal elements in Irish hagiography, maintains that while he did not intend to disparage the saints he nonetheless claims that Kenney has succinctly summarized the tendency of hagiography thus: 'Primarily the *acta sanctorum* are sources for the times in which they were written and revised, not for those in which their heroes flourished . . . But the amount of trustworthy information they give regarding the saints of whom they treat is, comparatively, slight.'

Further, Kenney says:

> Saintship itself was, to the popular mind, a concept of the magical order. Its essential characteristic was not moral goodness but the possession of that mysterious power which works miracles. The sanctifying grace of the legendary saint neither arose from habitual virtue nor resulted primarily in holiness: it was the Christianised counterpart of the magic potency of the Druid.[34]

This comment of Kenney echoes the point made by Wallace-Hadrill at the beginning of this chapter and reiterates those made in the previous chapter on

---

32. W. Stokes (ed.), *Filire Oengusso Celi De: The Martyrology of Oengus* (Dublin: Institute for Advanced Studies, 1984). Prologue, p. 17. K. Hughes, in D. Baker (ed.), *Sanctity and Secularity: The Church and the World* (Oxford:Basil Blackwell, 1973), p. 25, says of this ancient text, *Filire Oengusso*, that it is full of clichés, but the prologue and epilogue tell us very clearly what the Irish thought about their own saints.
33. Chadwick, *The Age*, Preface.
34. Kenney, *The Sources*, p. 297, p. 303, p. 304.

the penitentials. The close association with nature of both the druids and the great monastic foundresses[35] and founders could be seen as a prolongation of the activity of the former in the *Vitae* of the latter. Moreover, the power of prophecy and miracles was also attributed to druids in early Celtic societies.[36] This co-relation of some practices of druids and holy persons does not detract from the regard with which one honours the saint. It reiterates the vital point that fidelity, mostly subconscious, to one's cultural make-up manifests itself in countless ways throughout one's life.

In Book One of the *Life* Adomnán presents ColumCille, the contemplative, as a man whose life and vision is not limited by time and space. His closeness to the Spirit who can 'see'[37] the whole 'universe in its entirety'[38] enables him to 'see' events like the eruption in Italy, happening in far away countries.[39] Since prophecy and miracles, too, are the gifts of the Spirit, Adomnán, in putting so many such phenomena before the reader in Book Two, is strongly making a plea for ColumCille to be ranked among the saints,[40] even while he lived. Some of these miracles clearly parallel those of Christ in the New Testament, and by implication closely identify ColumCille with Christ. One such miracle is that at Cana.[41] This and the other ten or so miracles will be treated in more detail later in this discussion.[42]

---

35. Brigit in particular is recorded by Cogitosus as having a special relationship with animals and all creation. Who else, even in hagiography, has hung a cloak on a sunbeam?

36. Picard, 'Structural Patterns', p. 5; Reeves (ed.), *Adomnán's*, p. 92, Book Two, XXXIV, has the druid Broichan controlling the wind and storms. Green, in Edel (ed.), *Cultural*, p. 142, discusses the association of animals with the deity and especially the goddess; Smyth, in Edel (ed.), *Cultural*, p. 36 discusses birds in nature and in the cosmology of the Celts; she also (37) treats the druids and their claim that their ancestors could transform themselves into birds.

37. Among the Celts this is often called 'second sight' and to some people it is felt more as a curse than a blessing.

38. Picard, 'Structural Patterns', p. 76.

39. *Life*, 1 28 (ed. and trans. Sharpe, p. 132).

40. Sharpe (ed.), *Adomnán's*, p. 57. He further makes the point that his use of Sulpicius, Evagrius, Gregory's *Dialogues* and possibly (said with some hesitation, as both were being written contemporaneously) the *Life of Cuthbert* by an anonymous monk at Lindisfarne shows that he was attempting to present ColumCille as the equal of the saints whose lives he had read.

41. *Life* II 1 (ed. and trans. Sharpe, p. 154).

42. What cannot be attempted in this discussion are the many and varied approaches to biblical exegesis. Miracles at this point in time are seen as wonders worked through the power of God acting in the lives of the holy persons so used. Some of the miracles are too fanciful by today's standards, e.g., Brigit's hanging her cloak on a sunbeam. The Irish Church, however, was recognized for its scholars, most notably Pelagius and John Scotus Eriugena, whose Homily on the Prologue to the Gospel of John (C. Bamford (ed.), *The Voice of the Eagle: The Heart of Celtic Christianity* (New York: Lindisfarne Press, 1990)) clearly reveals a profound philosopher, theologian and Scripture scholar. He was born in Ireland early in the ninth century and was educated either in Ireland or in the Celtic tradition elsewhere, as the breadth of his learning reveals. Initially Augustine praised Pelagius, particularly for his commentaries on Scripture. This praise seems to have occurred before the politics of power overtook Augustine and the times.

Adomnán's interpretation of his hero's sanctity is informed by his own reading of the lives of other saints, particularly Martin of Tours. Adomnán's emphasis on Scripture, in the aspects of ColumCille's life he records, highlights the integral role of Scripture and especially the psalms in the lives of the Irish monks. His sanctity is poignantly portrayed in ColumCille's living among, and his relationship with, his monks. Maybe because he is abbot himself at the time of writing this *Life*, Adomnán is able to give an insight into the life of ColumCille. Book Three, as expressed by Reeves in the second preface, is about 'the apparitions of angels and some manifestation of the brightness of heaven upon the man of God'.[43] Probably of greater significance, though, is that in Book Three, Adomnán gives the reader a detailed account of the death of his hero. This takes up one-third of the contents of the book. The function of this book is, according to Picard, twofold: it confirms the divine origin of ColumCille's supernatural powers and shows by means of 'these visitations and the bright halo surrounding him – called by Adomnán *angelicae lucis claritudo* –[44] while still a man of flesh, Columba, was already part of the heavenly world'.[45]

The heroic virtue manifested in the lives of early saints and in the life of ColumCille, cannot be attributed to any other factor than the sheer doggedness of persistent practices by which, contrary to the human tendency to take the easy way out, they took seriously their new-found adoption of Christianity. Central to the belief system that underpinned the *praxis* was the person of Jesus, portrayed as selfless even to the point of giving up his life. This incarnational theology, as has been said earlier in this work, took its inspiration from Jesus, God among us, whose life and actions were constantly faithful to the Father's will. It did not indulge in an asceticism that denied the body as something to be punished, but saw the body rather as a part of God's creation to be the focus of penance but also the vehicle to glory and eternal salvation. In a word, the asceticism, the individual attempt at inner transformation, was a radical response to how the Irish, in this context, heard the message of the *evangelium* and their personal response of conversion to the ideals of that message. Underlying all these practices was the vitally important factor of the culture and Celtic consciousness, out of which the monastic founders and their followers operated.

The Influence of ColumCille

Before we look at the text of the *Vita*, it is important to address the scope of action and the influence of this, the first '*dove*' of the Irish Church. By way of general introduction to ColumCille's influence we can begin with the fact that he was well known. Though the monasteries he founded were scattered he was

---

43. Reeves (ed.), *Adomnán's*, p. 35.
44. *Life*, III XVIII (ed. and trans. Reeves, p. 123).
45. Picard, 'Structural Patterns', p. 77.

at the centre of a network of communications that included travel by land and sea. Sharpe[46] claims that he was in contact with his own churches in Dalriada, with those in Ireland and people in many places. He was familiar with the king of Strathclyde to the extent that he called him his friend. There was an extensive cult coalescing around him during his lifetime and more so at the time of his death. His influence was extensive and long-lasting. His biographer was well informed. Adomnán was portraying his subject as abbot in the monastic setting, as a holy man with a pervasive influence and as a revered father in a milieu that accepted supernatural powers as a natural attribute of special people.[47] In such a milieu that was alive with the supernatural, exemplified in Ireland in the druidic tradition, this *dove* of Irish monasticism stood tall as an example of the radical asceticism already explored in the chapters on monasticism and the Irish penitentials.

In terms of influence it is significant to note that Adomnán probably wrote the *Life* to commemorate the one hundredth anniversary of ColumCille's death in 697 CE.[48] This would, no doubt, dictate the contents, as such a commemoration would principally be about lauding the man who founded Iona. It would honour the man whose life, monastic rule, penitential and cultural consciousness permeated the whole island. William Reeves, in his *Life* of ColumCille, gives 'a list of nearly forty churches in Ireland belonging to the community',[49] but this is not necessarily a guide to how many churches were founded by ColumCille. It seems that his influence in Ireland did not become apparent till after the foundation of Iona. Tradition suggests that he was significant in the battle of Cúl Drebene and the subsequent events; in fact, that he was the 'cause' of the battle according to some authors. There is considerable doubt about this according to the latest edition of the *Life*.[50] Again, tradition tells us that ColumCille left Ireland in 565 CE,[51] an event which Sharpe calls a great turning point in his career,[52] and with twelve companions, reminiscent of the disciples of Jesus of the Gospels, landed on Iona, founded

---

46. Sharpe (ed.), *Adomnán's*, p. 23.
47. O'Riordain, *A Pilgrim*, p. 32 maintains that paranormal phenomena are part of the Hebridean life experience not only in the sixth century but in the twentieth century as well.
48. Sharpe (ed.), *Adomnán's*, p. 55. Reeves (ed.), *Adomnán's*, p. 17, seems to agree with this time and occasion. That the anniversary of ColumCille's death was an important feast in the life of Iona and its monks is shown in Book Two, v. 45, p. 200 when Adomnán and his monks are returning to Iona and find themselves confronted by contrary winds and they seek their dead hero's assistance. When it appears not to be forthcoming he chides ColumCille for not facilitating their presence at the anniversary mass.
49. Sharpe (ed.), *Adomnán's*, p. 29. This is more accurately called the Columban *paruchia*.
50. Sharpe (ed.), *Adomnán's*, p. 26 would not be too keen to lay the blame on ColumCille. In fact he maintains that ColumCille played no part in Irish history until after he left Ireland.
51. Lehane, *Early Celtic*, chronological table, appendix. This date is also the source of some debate. Sharpe questions if ColumCille actually made his first foundation on Iona. This has been an assumption that the evidence does not support. Reeves (ed.) *Adomnán's*, p. 23 gives the date as 563 CE.
52. Sharpe (ed.), *Adomnán's*, p. 12.

a monastic settlement and evangelized a great deal of north-western Scotland. However, the *Life* itself simply states that he 'sailed away from Ireland to Britain choosing to be a pilgrim for Christ',[53] and it gives the impression that the voyage was of the nature of a faith-journey where the way and destination were totally unknown. Such a fact cannot be substantiated, for the Hebrides were familiar to the Irish of the north and it is highly probable that ColumCille, being related to the reigning king, was already acquainted with Conall mac Comgaill, king of *Dal Riata* in Ireland and Scotland from about 559 CE.[54]

ColumCille may or may not have been a constant traveller around the region of his pilgrimage. Certainly, in the *Life*, he is recorded as having visited Hinba[55] at least six times and Ardnamurchan more than once. He also visited Skye at least once. It would be reasonable to assume that he did visit his monasteries in Scotland, at least till he became too old to travel the vast distances between them. Daughter monasteries were established in the Hebrides, with that at Mag Luinge on Tiree being the most important. Its significance is no doubt due to its fertility and the fact that, like Hinba, it had a prior appointed by ColumCille and hence was an integral part of the Columban *paruchia*.[56] A point of major significance in relation to the influence of ColumCille in Scottish Dalriada is recorded about 574 CE when, following the death of King Conall, the King's cousin and successor, Áedán mac Gabrain, is said to have come to ColumCille on Iona to be consecrated as king of Dalriada. According to Sharpe, it is '[probably] unsafe to presume that [the consecration] took place as described [in Adomnán's version in the Life]. Locally it suggests that a special relationship existed between ColumCille and the ruling dynasty of Cenél nGabráin.'[57]

What has constantly to be remembered when reading and analysing the work of Adomnán is that he was writing hagiography, and not biography or history. While this may be disappointing to the reader who wishes to get to know details of the man and his historical period, it nevertheless assumes its

---

53. *Life* (ed. and trans. Sharpe, p. 14) has some detailed discussion in the introduction of the motive for this pilgrimage of ColumCille. Using the sometimes conflicting evidence of the *AU* and *AT* and various editions of the *Life*, Sharpe personally concurs with the conclusions of Dr Marie Herbert, who says that ColumCille's decision to enter pilgrimage stemmed from the fact that he 'could not dissociate himself from the political and military concerns of his kin, and he prayed for their success presumably in a public manner'. She concludes that 'wearied by these events . . . he may have chosen to leave Ireland in the hope of releasing his religious commitment from the entanglements of Irish dynastic politics'.

54. Sharpe,(ed.), *Adomnán's*, p.16.

55. Two of his original twelve companions were priors of Hinba, his cousin Baithene [1 21] and his uncle Ernan [1 45].

56. *Life* (ed. and trans. Sharpe). It is mentioned in all Books: I 30, 41; II 15, 39, 189, 193; III p. 8; Sharpe (ed.), *Adomnán's*, p. 21 makes this point also about Durrow in Ireland.

57. *Life* (ed. and trans. Sharpe, p. 26). Áedán mac Gabrain features a number of times signifying his importance, not only to Scottish Dalriada, but also to the saint: I 8, 9, 49; III 5. Elsewhere Sharpe makes the point that 'whether anointing actually figured in the king-making rituals of Adomnán's time we cannot know. I think it unlikely, and it is still less likely that Columba even anointed a king of Dalriada', p. 62.

own style, aided by the genre of hagiography with which the 'writer' was familiar. It draws the reader to grasp the beauty of the inner person of ColumCille and to glimpse the motivation for such heroic deeds. Above all, it enables the serious reader to glimpse the motivation for such gentle *ascesis* within the context of a decidedly Celtic appropriation and articulation of early Irish monasticism.

Sharpe, in editing the latest edition in English of *Adomnán's Life of Columba*, says that the work is 'a source of the first importance for the early history of Ireland and Scotland',[58] with its influence extending over quite a few centuries. Further, he calls it 'the most engaging of the Lives of the Celtic saints'.[59] After a thorough, detailed, scholarly and sometimes iconoclastic introduction to the *Life*, he concludes that ColumCille still has the power to excite the imagination of those who visit Iona[60] and, as a result, there is still a burgeoning literature on this Hiberno-Scottish saint. Given the limitations of historical information about the life of ColumCille and the haphazard structure[61] of the *Life*, still 'nothing can detract from Adomnán's vivid depiction of the abbot among his own monks, written on the spot by the saint's successor'.[62]

The stories contained in this *Life*, though lacking in strictly historical veracity, have a strong ring of devotional truth. And this is in keeping with one of the rationales for the *Vitae* of any era: edification of the followers with the intention of eliciting emulation.[63] This is not to deny the often political component in the Irish *Vitae*.[64] Hence, in order to avoid the pitfalls of Kenney's earlier comments, all Irish *Vitae* should be validated in reference to the *Annals* if one is looking for an historical or social ambience. However, if that is not

58. Preface (ed. and trans. Sharpe).
59. Preface (ed. and trans. Sharpe).
60. Sharpe (ed.), *Adomnán's*, p. 99.
61. Picard, 'Structural Patterns', p. 75 treats the structure of these *Vitae* in the context of earlier continental *Lives* and makes the point that Adomnán's borrowings from Sulpicius, Evagrius and Jerome explain some of the misunderstood aspects of the *Life* that were evident in the Andersons' edition. He concludes that 'the surviving seventh-century *Vitae* belong to a new stratum of Irish hagiography, which corresponds to the time of development of the *paruchiae*'. T. M. Charles-Edwards, 'The New Edition of Adomnán's Life of Columba', *CMCS* 26 (Winter, 1993), pp. 65-73 (66) reiterates, in reference to the Anderson edition, the point made about the 1991 edition that it 'offers no consideration of the literary form of the text and its place in the development of Latin hagiography [which] is less forgivable in 1991 than it was in 1961'.
62. Sharpe (ed.), *Adomnán's*, p. 99.
63. Editors of Manus O'Donnell's compilation, p. xliv, in citing the texts of Gregory, Augustine, Bernard, Bonaventure, the Psalmist and St Paul are claiming that ColumCille is the exemplar of the ideals put forward by these men; it is clear that the moral edification that can be drawn from the stories of the lives of the saints was an important consideration to the authors of these *Vitae*.
64. Sharpe (ed.), *Adomnán's*, p. 56, would say that the *Life* may be used to serve purposes quite unknown or irrelevant to the saint himself; an example of this is the *Life of Patrick* which was used to lay claim to Armagh as the centre of Irish Christianity.

the purpose of one's reading of these *Vitae*, then the reader can let the story enthral, edify, or simply touch the heart.

Adomnán's concern for declaring his sources is noteworthy, as this is not usually a preoccupation among hagiographers.[65] He tries to assure his readers about the authenticity of his sources from the outset in his second preface:

> Let no one think of me as either stating what is not true regarding so great a man, or recording anything doubtful or uncertain. Let him know that I will tell with all candour, and without any ambiguity, what I have learned from the consistent narrative of my predecessors, trustworthy and discerning men, and that my narrative is founded either on written authorities anterior to my own times, or on what I have myself heard from some learned and faithful ancients.[66]

In his careful self-effacement, Adomnán acknowledges that he is writing the *Life* 'in compliance with the urgent requests of my brethren'.[67] It seems from both prefaces[68] that it was customary at Iona to record events of founders' lives both orally and in writing. Cummene's book on St ColumCille's miracles was the only written source that evidence records,[69] but Adomnán never mentions it in his work when he actually cites his sources.

The 'Voice' of ColumCille: Book One

The notion of 'voice' conjures up the direct vocal communication between two persons. It also includes written words that purport to be conveying the ideas, ideals, exhortations of a person to a group. Included in the concept of 'voice' are the poetic expressions either in written or oral form. An assumption in this context is that it is the voice of a significant person in the life or lives of its hearers. Generally the 'voice' varies in timbre from affection to strident exhortation. It may also be the somewhat second-hand 'voice' used by another person who wishes to continue the 'counsels' of the originating 'voice' or to

---

65. Chapter 5 of this work treats Columbanus' Sermons; a similar concern will be heard in Jonas as he states who his sources are and how close they were to Columbanus. Of course Jonas is closer to Columbanus in terms of time than is Adomnán to ColumCille.

66. Reeves, (ed.), *Adomnán's*, p.35; Sharpe, (ed.), *Adomnán's*, p.56 also makes the point that 'Irish law favoured eyewitness testimony (see 1 1, 112 Sharpe edition) over documents, so that Adomnán's use of the Latin language of testimony and his naming of informants may be seen as repeatedly underlining the credibility of what he writes'. In doing so he is being more credible than quoting from an earlier book on ColumCille written by Cummene.

67. *Life* (ed. and trans. Reeves, p. 33).

68. See Sharpe (ed.), *Adomnán's*, p. 242, fn 6, for a lengthy comment on *Lives* that have two prefaces. Picard, 'Structural Patterns', p. 75, commenting on the previously quoted 1961 edition of the Life of Columba by the Andersons, makes the point that the use of the second preface 'reflects the erudition of the author rather then a possible afterthought'.

69. Sharpe (ed.), *Adomnán's*, p. 56 fn 360, claims that a copy of the Life of ColumCille is the only evidence that Adomnán used this source. A later copyist, Dorbbene, inserted a section of this earlier *Life* in Book Three 5.

honour the memory of the owner of the 'voice' by way of commemoration. Some or all of these notions are included in the use of 'voice' when analysing the *Life of ColumCille* in this chapter.

In Book One the predominant notion of prophecy, variously called 'insights', 'inward revelations',[70] 'happy foreknowledge', or as Sharpe, the modern commentator, says, 'clairvoyance'[71] seems to be uppermost. The writer of the *Life* explains that prophecy which ColumCille 'began as a young man to enjoy [is] also the spirit to predict the future and to tell those with him about things happening elsewhere. He could see what was done afar off, because he was there in the spirit though not in the body.'[72]

What is prophesied? For whom? To what purpose? What does ColumCille wish the recipients of such 'happy foreknowledge'[73] to do with it? On a number of occasions he insists that the recipients do not speak about what has been revealed. Adomnán himself explains this and the reason for it in the final paragraph thus:

> For saints and apostles, seeking to avoid the world's empty praise, hurry to hide as far as they can the inner mysteries revealed to them inwardly by God. But willy nilly, God publishes some of them and brings them out into the open one way or another. For he desires to glorify his saints who glorify him, the Lord himself, to whom be glory for ever and ever.[74]

This is the asceticism of hiddenness. It includes the underlying dependence on God which so strongly came through the provisions of the Irish monastic rules treated earlier. This hiddenness is the ideal encouraged by the saint, in spite of his tendency, on occasions, to enter the political arena. It is captured in a quaint expression that occurs throughout Book One when Adomnán says, 'why say more?'[75] Given the nature of the man about whom this is being written, such insights are only to be expected. There is no need for further proof of the holiness of this man. This does not, however, stop Adomnán from saying more!

The 'more' will help to answer the first two questions posed. In the *Life* prophecies are made about people successfully negotiating storms;[76] about the battle with the Miathi;[77] and people coming to seek ColumCille's

---

70. *Life*, I 50 (ed. and trans. Sharpe, p. 152).
71. *Life*, I 17, 26, 35 (ed. and trans. Sharpe, p. 124, p. 131, p. 138). I find this word out of character with the historical period and the sentiments of Adomnán's life of ColumCille. The word has a too modern ring about it. Moreover it also has connotations of magic and/or deception which do not fit with the tone of the *Life*.
72. *Life*, I 1 (ed. and trans. Sharpe, p. 112).
73. *Life*, I 2, 48, 49 (ed. and trans. Sharpe, p. 112, p. 150, p. 151).
74. *Life*, I 50 (ed. and trans. Sharpe, p. 152).
75. *Life*, I 17, 18, 32, 37; 11 4, 34, 37, 39 (ed. and trans. Sharpe, p. 124, p. 125, p. 135, p. 139; p. 156, p. 183, p. 185, p. 188).
76. *Life*, I 4 (ed and trans., Sharpe, p. 117).
77. *Life*, I 8 (ed and trans., Sharpe, p. 119).

foreknowledge about their children.⁷⁸ He recognizes a bishop in their midst who, like ColumCille himself, wishes to be taken for a humble monk.⁷⁹ He prophesies about a layman's family and a marauding group.⁸⁰ On two occasions he is asked about his powers: once by Luigbe and another time by his monks. In the case of Luigbe there is an interesting encounter where Luigbe asks, 'Tell me I beg you, about your prophetic revelations such as this. How are they revealed to you? By sight, or hearing, or in some way men know not?'⁸¹

ColumCille replies at length with a requirement, reiterated on other occasions and understandable in the light of Adomnán's purpose of presenting his hero as a humble, saintly abbot: 'You are asking me now about a very delicate subject. I may tell you nothing, not the least word, unless you first kneel and promise me firmly in the name of God on high that you will tell no one of this most secret mystery as long as I am living.'⁸²

After Luigbe made the required promise, ColumCille goes on to an explanation of 'the power to see brightly and most clearly, with a mental grasp miraculously enlarged'.⁸³ Adomnán comments that ColumCille is speaking thus only out of humility and in imitation of St Paul before him. In the same spirit of humility he insists that his hearer, in this case Luigbe, not speak of the event as long as his abbot shall live.⁸⁴ Whether these monks kept their promise to ColumCille is not known but the fact that eventually they did reveal these incidents is why Adomnán can claim that his sources are impeccable.

The notion of obedience, immediate response to the voice of God heard through the abbot or one's *anamchara*, given such prominence in the monastic rules and monasticism on the whole, is treated in Book One with a slight difference: it is in relation to fasting. As Adomnán expresses it:

> Once the saint came to the island of Hinba, and the same day granted a relaxation of the rules about diet even for those living in penance. Among these penitents was a man called Neman mac Cathir, who disobeyed the saint and refused the little indulgence offered him.⁸⁵

ColumCille berated him. Obedience, if enjoined by the abbot, is better than personal sacrifice. In this case it was enjoined by both ColumCille, a visiting abbot of enormous spiritual stature, and the abbot of Hinba, Baithene. It was this kind of personal self-denial, this dying to self as an exercise of inner transformation, that constituted a real challenge to the uniquely individual

---

78. *Life*, I 16 (ed. and trans. Sharpe, p. 123).
79. *Life*, I 44 (ed. and trans. Sharpe, p. 146).
80. *Life*, I 46 (ed. and trans. Sharpe, p. 148).
81. *Life*, I 43 (ed. and trans. Sharpe, p. 145).
82. *Life*, I 43 (ed. and trans. Sharpe, p. 145).
83. *Life*, I 43 (ed. and trans. Sharpe, p. 145).
84. Sharpe (ed.), *Adomnán's*, p. 305, makes the point that this very example 'must cast doubt on the impression he tries to give that his statements depend on sworn witness', because this explanation comes from St Benedict's words to Germanus, as told in Gregory the Great's *Dialogues*.
85. *Life*, I 21 (ed and trans. Sharpe, p.127).

characters who were the monastic Irish. This constituted a truly radical lifestyle. It throws light on the asceticism or *ascesis* of ColumCille that could easily be ameliorated when the occasion arose. Sometimes it was a feast commemorating ancestors, other times it was a festival honouring some particular season like Easter or Pentecost. So while he is seen as a hard man, arrogant at times, his gentler side emerges in the affectivity that Adomnán reveals throughout this work. Such *ascesis* echoes the gentle breeze of the Hebrew Scriptures regarding God's presence. It is also evident in instances where he shows that radical living is not radical (that which is freely chosen and gets to the roots of a situation) if it does not take into account the humanness of those trying to live the monastic life. This point was often made in relation to stipulations in both the monastic rules and the penitentials.

Image of the Soldier of Christ

An image that resounded loudly with the warring Irish is that of the soldier of Christ used in Book One and also to be found in the writings of the other '*dove*', Columbanus.[86] The Celtic warriors knew the thrill of battle,[87] knew the hardship and terrors of warfare and so using this image accorded well with their Celtic consciousness and temperament. It also vividly spelled out what was expected in the life of the monk. In using the soldier of Christ image so consistently throughout his *Life*, Adomnán was, no doubt, reinforcing the notion of the monastic life as a battle to the death which only the brave – those who, by choice, took seriously the challenge of a life of asceticism and those who trusted in a higher power – should undertake.

Reeves reminds the reader that, primitive Irish ecclesiastics, and especially the superior class, commonly known as saints, were very impatient of contradiction and very resentful of injury.'[88] He is also reminding his readers of the close relationship of some ecclesiastics with royalty and as such their leadership role in society and warfare meant that they could be intolerant of others. His reminder reinforces the contention, mentioned elsewhere in this work, that the title saint does not necessarily mean one lacking in humanity. It does mean, however, someone who is striving to overcome human selfish tendencies, not one who has already overcome. In the case of ColumCille, Adomnán records the event when his hero pursued a plunderer with curses, to add emphasis to his speech, following him into the sea till the water was up to his knees. Other instances of ColumCille's cursing people would give credence to the conviction that he was in his lifetime as well as in memory treated with a degree

---

86. *Life*, I 36, 40, 43, 49; II 4, 10, 27, 31, 42; III 7, 23 (ed. and trans. Sharpe, p. 138, p. 142, p. 151; p. 156, p. 161, p. 179, p. 196; p. 210, p. 225).
87. B. Tierney, 'The Celtic Ethnography of Posidonius: Translation of the Texts of Athenaeus, Diodorus, Strabo, Caesar', *Pro RIA*, 60 (1960), p. 267, has Diodorus giving an interesting insight into Celtic battle customs.
88. Reeves (ed.), *Adomnán's*, p. 25.

of respect mingled with awe. The strident voice of the curse, from the lips and not the heart,[89] could indicate a burst of temper, a piece of theatricality or more likely the intensity of the care for the soul of the person being cursed.

ColumCille Speaks through his Miracles

Book Two is steeped in the tradition of Scripture, where the miracles attributed to ColumCille are often replicas of those performed by Jesus of Nazareth. Not only is ColumCille in the tradition of the great heroes of the sagas, he is also performing miracles at times echoing those of the Gospel stories. Readers have to keep reminding themselves that this work is hagiographic and, if it is being written to commemorate the hundredth anniversary of ColumCille's death, then these miracles are cited for edification, and the faith that underpins them, for emulation. Some of these miracles were performed while ColumCille was alive and others after his death. The former include changing water into wine, the preservation of manuscripts written by the saint even after their immersion in water for months, and miracles concerning fire and water. There are miracles of healing and raising from the dead, even in the case of a wizard, one of the druid class with whom the saint was sometimes in conflict, particularly in Scotland. Even the natural elements of sky and sea are altered in their natural course at the instigation of ColumCille. After his death he is seen as responsible for rain that breaks drought, favourable winds and alleviation of the effects of two plagues.

First to be treated are the miracles that echo those of the Hebrew and Christian Scriptures. In Book Two there occurs only one miracle that is reminiscent of the Hebrew Scriptures: during a journey a child was brought to the saint for baptism and there was no water in the place. Adomnán records, 'so the saint turned aside to the nearest rock, where he knelt and prayed a little while. When he stood up, he blessed the face of the rock, and at once water bubbled out from it in great quantity. Thereupon he baptised the child.'[90]

In keeping with the Irish consciousness of their ancestors and the prominent role they played in the lives of the people, it is no mental leap for the hearers of Adomnán's stories of ColumCille to cast their hero in such a thaumaturgic role. This Irish equivalent of Moses had not only shown his power over inanimate objects but also, as often happens in Adomnán's *Life*, a miracle is accompanied by a prophecy. In this case the child, called Ligu Cenncalad, is said to be a slave to desires of the flesh but will overcome them, become a

---

89. O'Riordain, *A Pilgrim*, p. 17 refers to a modern-day Celt, Peig Sayers, who lived on the Great Blasket, and he records this interchange: 'The people of the island have a fine gift of cursing,' said I. 'We have,' she answered, 'but there is no sin in it. If the curse came from the heart, it would be sin. But it is from the lips they come, and we use them only to give force to our speech, and they are a great relief for the heart.' The centrality of the heart, discussed in both chapters on the penitentials and monastic rules, seems to be a significant emphasis up to the present time, highlighting the pervasiveness of culture.

90. *Life*, II 10 (ed. and trans. Sharpe, p. 161).

soldier of Christ and end his days in extreme old age.[91] Whether the specialness of the child, indicated in this miracle soon after his birth, means that he is chosen by God for a great work, as was ColumCille, and therefore the entry into a monastic state was the natural lifestyle choice, the reader is not in any position to judge, as this is the only such miracle recorded.

Another incident which again highlights the abbot's 'sight' occurs in Book One. It also has overtones of the Hebrew Scripture story of the anointing of David as king. ColumCille was questioning King Áedán about his successor and when the king mentioned his three sons as possible successors ColumCille said, 'None of these three will be king. They will all be slaughtered by enemies and fall in battle. But if you have other, younger sons, let them now come to me. The one whom the Lord has chosen will run directly to my arms.'[92]

It is instructive that this sign of recognition, running into the abbot's arms, was used by Adomnán. ColumCille, the abbot who could be so hard on himself and others when the *evangelium* demanded it, could also be an affectionate and warm person. That a significant part of the *Life* is told through quasi-scriptural happenings should be expected given that, in the cultural consciousness of all Celtic peoples (particularly the Irish), Scripture was the basis for their living, praying and emulation.

Other miracles, those in the genre of the Christian Scriptures, are more plentiful. The first is the turning of water into wine. Jesus' miracle at the marriage feast of Cana was his first miracle and so was the equivalent miracle of ColumCille recorded by Adomnán. The saint is only a deacon under the tutelage of St Uinniau[93] when he discovers that there is no wine for the Mass. Though the miracle is attributed to ColumCille, he attributes it to St Uinniau. Adomnán comments, 'Let it shine like a lantern at the entrance of this book, this miracle of God manifested through our own Columba, so that we may pass forward to other miracles of power shown through him.'[94]

This attribution of 'through him' presages a very sound theology that only becomes more explicit as the miracles accumulate. The saint does not himself work the miracles. They are constantly attributed to God working through him. Even when the saint is dead, 'we should ask St Columba to obtain for us from the Lord that we should have favourable winds'.[95] Elsewhere similar sentiments are expressed thus: 'In this way God gave us a fast and fair voyage without the labour of rowing for St Columba's sake'.[96]

Ambivalence would be justified in a reader today about the theology surrounding Adomnán's rendition of the story of a plague. It seems that this is the only time in the *Life* when an 'Old Testament theology' is evident. The

---

91. *Life*, II 10 (ed. and trans. Sharpe, p. 162).
92. *Life*, I 9 (ed. and trans. Sharpe, p. 120).
93. *Life*, (ed. and trans. Sharpe, p. 317) has a lengthy comment on this person. He explains that he uses this spelling to dissociate the person from Finnbarr or one of the many Finnians.
94. *Life*, II 1 (ed. and trans. Sharpe, p. 154).
95. *Life*, II 45 (ed. and trans. Sharpe, p. 200).

peoples so afflicted were not without great sin, 'by which the eternal judge is moved to anger'.[97] Nonetheless he seems to have spared them when he was destroying other peoples. 'Surely this grace from God can only be attributed to St Columba? For he founded among both peoples [of Ireland and Britain] the monasteries where today he is still honoured.'[98]

Other miracles worked by ColumCille that seem to echo those in the Gospels include the bitter tree which was transformed with these words of the saint: 'In the name of almighty God, all your bitterness shall leave you, O bitter tree, and your fruit until now most bitter shall become most sweet.'[99] On the occasion of the Conference at Druim Cett, ColumCille was supposed to have healed many people who 'put their trust in him and received full healing, some from his outstretched hand, some from being sprinkled with water he had blessed, others by the mere touching of the edge of his cloak'.[100]

Only the attributing of these miracles to God who worked through ColumCille, and the genre of hagiography that informed most writers of Irish *Vitae*, could save this version of the *Life* from the accusation of blasphemy when the saint is equated with Jesus as recorded in the Gospel stories. Twice the winds are tamed by ColumCille's prayers when the people in the boat pleaded with him to pray for their safety and not to worry about helping with the mundane task of bailing out the water.[101] In the words of Adomnán: 'Once when the praiseworthy man was in the company of hardy fishermen'[102] he instructed them to 'cast the net in the river, and you will quickly find a great fish which the Lord has provided for me'.[103] If during his life ColumCille is credited with being the instrument through which God worked miracles for those beloved by the saint, after his death he was still working miracles on behalf of his beloved brethren and any person who asked his intercession.

Reeves makes the point that 'writing was an employment to which he was much devoted'.[104] We know that ColumCille's tendency to copy other persons' manuscripts led to conflict and Reeves believes that most of his work was copying. His 'voice' is heard through alleged Irish compositions[105] and these are mainly poems. This reiterates the point that along with being a leader of men in writing monastic rules and penitentials, he was also a poet at heart. Adomnán records that two works of his own hand met with a similar fate: being accidentally submerged in water. In each case, though the parts not

96. *Life*, II 45 (ed. and trans. Sharpe, p. 200).
97. *Life*, II 46 (ed. and trans. Sharpe, p. 203); this theology obviously comes out of a different cosmology and anthropology.
98. *Life*, II 46 (ed. and trans. Sharpe, p. 203).
99. *Life*, II 2 (ed. and trans. Sharpe, p. 155).
100. *Life*, II 6 (ed. and trans. Sharpe, p. 159).
101. *Life*, II 13 (ed. and trans. Sharpe, p. 163).
102. *Life*, II 9 (ed. and trans. Sharpe, p. 160).
103. *Life*, II 19 (ed. and trans. Sharpe, p. 168).
104. Reeves (ed.), *Adomnán's*, p. 26.
105. Reeves (ed.), *Adomnán's*, p. 26, makes the point that 'three Latin Hymns of considerable beauty are attributed to him, and in the ancient *Liber Hymnorum*, where they are preserved, each is accompanied by a preface describing the occasion on which it was written'.

written in the saint's hand were destroyed, his work was miraculously preserved,[106] as if the 'voice' of the saint in his writings could not be silenced even by the natural elements. On another occasion his garments and books were used to call down the power of the saint to come to the aid of his followers. There had been severe drought and at the intercession of ColumCille 'the thirsty ground was quenched in time, the seed germinated and in due course there was a particularly good harvest'.[107] What was particularly significant about this record of the 'voice' of ColumCille in miraculous events is that Adomnán contends that the miracle 'took place in our own time and we witnessed it with our own eyes'.[108]

As if to reinforce the affectivity present in Adomnán's *Life*, and to remind the readers that, in spite of the awe with which some people held this powerful '*dove*' of the Irish Church, he could be chided[109] by his followers when he appears not to be listening to their pleas. If this were Columbanus, there is every chance that his followers would not be saying 'Is this troublesome delay in our efforts what you wanted St Columba?'[110] After all, we have prayed to you for a favourable wind and you do not seem to be heeding us, 'Hardly a minute had passed when the west wind dropped and strange to say a wind immediately blew from the North-east.'[111]

ColumCille speaks in Revelations

In the first paragraph of the final book, Book Three, Adomnán recalls for his readers what he had treated in the other two and admits that '[the] third book is concerned with angelic apparitions that were revealed to others about the saint, and to him about others, and also those that were visible to both though in different measures'.[112] What is omitted in this statement is that nearly one-third of this last book gives a detailed account of the saint's death. Why Adomnán did not include this is a puzzle. He who is purported to be celebrating a significant anniversary by this *Life*, yet does not mention the death in his summary, leaves the reader with many questions. Huyshe reiterates what other commentators on the *Life* have said: that it is 'hagiography rather than biography, except in the very last chapter, which is pure biography of the most beautiful kind'.[113] It is this biography that will be treated in this last section. Book Three will be analysed for its ascetical theology in relation to three aspects: the angelic appearances, the importance of light and the death account.

---

106. *Life*, II 8, 9 (ed. and trans. Sharpe, p. 160).
107. *Life*, II 44 (ed. and trans. Sharpe, p. 199).
108. *Life*, II 44 (ed. and trans. Sharpe, p. 199).
109. *Life*, II 45 (ed. and trans. Sharpe, p. 200).
110. *Life*, II 45 (ed. and trans. Sharpe, p. 200).
111. *Life*, II 45 (ed. and trans. Sharpe, p. 200).
112. Prologue, Book III, *Life* (ed. and trans. Sharpe, p. 205).
113. Huyshe (ed.), *The Life*, p. xii.

Angelic appearances are noted prior to ColumCille's birth, in his childhood and in his youth. Like all great personages, angelic or other-worldly figures usually prepare those close to the person for the birth. In ColumCille's case his mother is visited by an angel in a dream. She is given a robe of marvellous beauty and then deprived of it. Her dismay is partly assuaged when the angel tells her, 'do not be distressed, for you shall bear to the man to whom you are joined in marriage a son of such flower that he shall be reckoned as one of the prophets'.[114]

In childhood, his foster-father, Cruithnechan, returning home saw his whole house 'bathed in a bright light, and poised over the face of the sleeping child was a fiery ball of light'.[115] As a youth, ColumCille was seen by the ageing Vinnian to be accompanied by an angel.[116] Since these occurrences were not the ordinary experiences of most people, those to whom they happened were seen to be in a closer relationship with God, and this, in his later years, was thought to be a result of ColumCille's more radically spiritual lifestyle.

Another group of angelic visitations accompany people to the next world.[117] In all these cases, ColumCille is enabled to 'see' the souls being accompanied by angels. The people seen by ColumCille include some of his friends like Brendan and the monks from St Comgall's monastery at Bangor and other simple lay people. Adomnán makes a significant point when he states that ColumCille did not want these events to come to public notice. 'This was for two reasons . . . First, he wanted to avoid boasting, and, second, so that widespread reports of these revelations should not attract unmanageable crowds of people wanting to put their questions to him.'[118]

Given what was a basic tenet of monasticism, namely communing with God, the fear of vast numbers of people coming to interrupt the contemplation of the monks could be legitimate. This warning about 'publicity' is so consistent in Adomnán's *Life* that one cannot but see it as part of the humility of ColumCille, despite what Reeves says about the arrogance of princely ecclesiastics. Humility does not necessarily preclude awareness of one's dignity stemming from being of royal blood. Indeed true humility demands that one acknowledge such attributes. This is simply one of the instances where the very humanness of ColumCille speaks loudly to readers of the limitations even of those called saints.

Unusual lights, always significant in depicting people with special characteristics, were recounted with regularity in this *Life*.[119] Angels also confer with the saints, but again these events were not to be witnessed by others. However, on one occasion, a monk disobeyed ColumCille and observed him, but was reprimanded for this. Adomnán then says: 'One should take notice of this story

114. *Life*, III 1 (ed. and trans. Sharpe, p. 205).
115. *Life*, III 2 (ed. and trans. Sharpe, p. 206).
116. *Life*, III 4 (ed. and trans. Sharpe, p. 208).
117. *Life*, III 6, 7, 9, 10, 11, 12, 13, 14, (ed. and trans. Sharpe, p. 210, p. 212, p. 213, p. 214, p. 215, p. 216).
118. *Life*, III 7 (ed. and trans. Sharpe, p. 211).
119. *Life*, III 17, 18, 19, 20, 21, (ed. and trans. Sharpe, p. 210, p. 220, p. 222).

and carefully think about the extent and nature of the sweet visits by angels that no one could know about but which, without doubt, were very frequent, for they generally came to him as he prayed in isolated places.'[120]

ColumCille looked forward to death, acknowledging as he was dying that 'the Lord granted what I desired with all my strength'.[121] Why would he not desire death when in true Celtic spirit he saw it as a reunion with his ancestors, his God and the reward of an asceticism that led to glory? Yet his dying is not without its sadness. The churches had prayed for him to remain, 'even though I do not want it, four years longer must I remain in this flesh. This sorrowful delay is the reason for my great distress today.'[122]

Even in death, he is, as he constantly exhorted his monks, obedient. He is faithful always to the *evangelium* which he accepted and lived, not only as a deeply held belief but as the leader of his monks and the faithful exemplar of the asceticism that underpinned his monasticism. When the four years had been endured, his affection for his monks and the Scriptures is evident in his comment, 'Scripture calls this day the Sabbath . . . today is truly my Sabbath for it is my last day in this wearisome life when I shall keep the Sabbath.'[123]

He goes on to remind the brethren of a specific Scripture passage, reminiscent of his love for his ancestors: 'I shall go the way of my fathers',[124] and when his faithful attendant, Diarmait, begins to grieve, ColumCille tries to console him. The consolation he gives is in the form of blessings: for the Island and its people,[125] for the crops, for the barns full of hay. In blessing the barns the departing abbot is assured that his monks will not face hardship when he leaves them. His blessing on the monastery, with hindsight, seems to have become a reality.

> This place, however small and mean, will have bestowed on it no small but great honour by the kings and peoples of Ireland and also by the rulers of even barbarous and foreign nations with their subject tribes, and the saints of other churches too will give it great reverence.[126]

Finally, his love for all creatures is enacted in a scene with the white horse who approached the saint and 'it began to mourn like a person, pouring out its tears in the saint's bosom and weeping aloud with foaming lips'.[127] When Diarmait, out of consideration for the illness and weariness of his abbot, tried to remove the horse, ColumCille, revealing his consistent love for all creatures and gently chiding his assistance, stopped him saying,

---

120. *Life*, III 16 (ed. and trans. Sharpe, p. 218).
121. *Life*, III 22 (ed. and trans. Sharpe, p. 224).
122. *Life*, III 22 (ed. and trans. Sharpe, p. 224).
123. *Life*, III 23 (ed. and trans. Sharpe, p. 227).
124. *Life*, III 23 (ed. and trans. Sharpe, p. 227).
125. *Life*, III 23 (ed. and trans. Sharpe, p. 225).
126. *Life*, III 23 (ed. and trans. Sharpe, p. 228).
127. *Life*, III 23 (ed. and trans. Sharpe, p. 227).

let him be! Let him that loves me pour out the tears of bitterest mourning here at my breast. Look how you, though you have a man's rational soul, could not know of my going if I had not myself just told you. But according to his will the creator has clearly revealed to this brute and reasonless animal that his master is going away.[128]

This is the kind of behaviour one came to expect from the man who told a monk one day that he was to expect an important visitor to Iona who turned out to be a heron or crane. The instruction to the monk was exactly as it would be for a person – 'look after it and feed it as a guest for three days'[129] – till it was able to return to Northern Ireland.

ColumCille's 'crossing over from this weary pilgrimage to the heavenly home'[130] seemed simple. It was preceded by writing out a copy of psalm 34, giving instructions 'to the brethren [with only his faithful servant Diarmait] to hear'[131] and, ever faithfully, answering the call to prayer. Since he had arrived for the midnight office before the other monks, Diarmait found him lying before the altar. Displaying tenderness to the end, ColumCille was found by the community in the arms of his faithful companion, who 'held up the saint's right hand to bless the choir monks'.[132] Finally, angels come to take ColumCille, as he had foretold: 'when [God's] holy angels will meet me at the time and I shall be glad to depart to the Lord'.[133] The reader is reminded that there seems not to be any reference to a transition place for the holy abbot after his departure. There appears not to be any fear of a nether world in his rejoicing. Nor is there any sense that his life merits any ever-so-small time of purgation. Maybe it would not be politic for Adomnán to hint at this. Such an eventuality would not accord with the whole Celtic consciousness that not only had no word for original sin, but had such a positive approach to its living of the *evangelium* that the God they loved would not countenance any further separation from his creatures.

True to form, ColumCille arranges the weather so that his beloved community will not be overcome by outsiders intruding on their grieving. A fierce storm rages for the three days and nights of mourning,' befitting one of his honour and status',[134] so that no people could approach the island. When the saint is buried, 'in the chosen grave with all due reverence, from where he will arise in bright everlasting light',[135] Adomnán continues to laud him with recollections of his great deeds.

By way of summary Adomnán's conclusion in his *Life of ColumCille* could be used as a final statement about this the first *dove* of the Irish Church:

128. *Life*, III 23 (ed. and trans. Sharpe, p. 227).
129. *Life*, I 48 (ed. and trans. Sharpe, p. 150).
130. *Life*, III 23 (ed. and trans. Sharpe, p. 229).
131. *Life*, III 23 (ed. and trans. Sharpe, p. 228).
132. *Life*, III 23 (ed. and trans. Sharpe, p. 229).
133. *Life*, III 22 (ed. and trans. Sharpe, p. 224).
134. *Life*, III 23 (ed. and trans. Sharpe, p. 231).
135. *Life*, III 23 (ed. and trans. Sharpe, p. 231).

Every conscientious reader who has finished reading this ... should mark well how great and special is the merit of our reverend abbot ... his honour in God's sight ... his experiences of angelic visits and heavenly light ... the grace of prophecy in him ... the brilliant light of heaven which shone on him as he dwelt in mortal flesh and which, after his most gentle soul had left the tabernacle of the body, does not cease even today.[136]

Conclusion

This chapter set out to examine the *Life of ColumCille* written by the tenth abbot of Iona in commemoration of the anniversary of the saint's death. Its aim was to examine the *Life* for the ascetical theology that underpinned it. We saw that his birth from two royal families meant that he was intended for political life. Many of the early founders of monastic establishments were from the nobility. His renunciation of the possibility of political leadership was thought to be a deliberate choice on his part and furthermore his departure from Ireland was seen by Herbert and Sharpe as an attempt to escape from the inevitable political involvement in his families' decisions and judgements.[137] His choice of the ascetical life of the monk and subsequent founding of many monasteries says something about the character of ColumCille who could forsake the prestige of leadership in society for that of the humble monk who though ordained to priesthood never became, by his own choice, a bishop. Ever conscious of his Celtic ancestry he inspired his followers through his monastic rule with a love of homeland, and a deep regard for the druidic tradition so intrinsic to the Celts. It may be too strong a contention to say, like Wallace-Hadrill in the quotation at the beginning of this chapter, that he was successor to the local pagan (*sic*) divinity, but part of the purpose of the *Vita* was to highlight those actions and attributes of the person which seemed to establish him firmly in the company, if not the category, of the local pagan (*sic*) divinity. He was deeply contemplative as befits those called to monastic austerity in the Irish tradition.

His movement to Scotland may not have been such a wrench, for the Kingdom of Dal Raita was actually ruled by a king of his own clan. However, as his missionary endeavours took him over wider territories than Iona he confronted druids and other hostile groups who challenged him. In the challenge was also revealed his strong belief in an incarnate God in whose mission he was convinced he participated. Conversions seemed miraculous and copious according to the way Adomnán told the story. He was blessed with the gift of insight, with the power to see people and events that were happening at a distance from Iona. This gift was thought to be a sign of a person's closeness to God and the result of a more radical asceticism. In ColumCille's case it gave people confidence in his intercessory power with God, and Adomnán includes many such instances in his *Life*.

---

136. *Life*, III 23 (ed. and trans. Sharpe, p. 233).
137. Sharpe (ed.), *Adomnán's*, p. 14.

The 'voice' of ColumCille is evident in three manifestation in the *Vita*: in Book One it is heard in prophecy, insights and imagery. In Book Two it is heard in the miraculous events that occurred, before and during his life and after his death. The final voice of Book Three is the most poignant as it is that which is heard just prior to his death and in the event of his passing.

While ColumCille had the power of prophecy he assiduously tried to prevent others from revealing this to outsiders. Many instances throughout his *Vita* point to this humility and his living of the asceticism of hiddenness. On occasions he insisted that monks swore not to reveal something before he would communicate with them. His humility and hiddenness were epitomized for his monks when finally their mourning for him was not interrupted by outsiders because ColumCille caused it to rain for the three days of their grieving, thus preventing visitors from approaching the island of Iona.

ColumCille's influence was evident in the number of daughter foundations, both in Ireland and Scotland, attributed to him. His *paruchia* was extensive and his 'spirit' pervaded each establishment. His valuing of the role of the poet led, according to some historians, to his presence at the Conference to decide the fate of these 'keepers of the stories of the clans'. Not only did his Celtic consciousness not allow him to contemplate the demotion of the poets but also his spirituality knew only too well the contribution of the creative imagination to the Irish use of the psalms and Scripture as a whole. These ancient prayers resonated with the Irish love of verse and the use of creation as a way of communicating with the 'lord of the elements'. This same love of poetry can be seen in his use of imagery and particularly that of the solider of Christ. Not only did this image resonate with the warring Irish, more importantly it captured their imagination and made sense of the life of asceticism put forward by ColumCille, for they were following the obedient Christ, the incarnate God to whom they had committed their lives and to whose presence they were confident the ascetical life would lead.

The comments above by Adomnán, the author of the *Life of ColumCille*, are within the genre of hagiography that persisted for many centuries in the fledgling Church in Ireland. This was a specific way of recording the lives of people thought to be saints. Sainthood and sanctity have a special place in the Christian community in every age. People so named are thought to be closer to God than the ordinary person. Sometimes miraculous happenings are attributed to them. In some cases their lives are thought to be very ascetical and their penances are told for the emulation of the whole community. These were the perception of sanctity in the period under discussion.

As emulation was an important component of any *Vitae*, the influence that ColumCille exerted both in Ireland and north-west Scotland was extensive. His enthusiasm for the pilgrimage that every Irish Christian saw as a form of martyrdom was taken up by his twelve companions. His care for his monks shone through his monastic rule and the instances cited in the *Life*. He could also be a tough leader of men and women, if the designation of the island of Hinba, the island of women, is accurate.[138] His leadership, tough or compassionate, was

---

138. See Appendix III G for a photo of Hinba and the remains of the monastery. On this island is a burial stone purporting to be the resting place of ColumCille's mother, Princess Eithne.

inspired by the basic monastic principle enunciated throughout this work: prayer, work, penance in their varied forms, all in the name of a closer relationship with God and the other members of the monastic enclosure.

One other Columba makes a unique contribution to the monastic scene on the European continent where the penitential system, developed by the Irish of the sixth to the eighth century, has lasting effects. His name is Columbanus and it is his Sermons that are discussed in the next chapter. They, like the injunctions of the penitentials, monastic rules and the words of ColumCille, highlight the asceticism of the lifestyle of these monks of early Irish monasticism.

5 Columbanus – Quintessential Irish *Peregrinus*

Behold how the Ocean, previously raging, has now paved the way for the feet of holy men; its barbarian heavings, which earthly rulers were unable to tame by the sword, the mouths of priests bind with simple words by virtue of the fear inspired by God; and the one who, when an unbeliever, never had the least fear of bands of warriors, now, as a believer, already fears the tongues of humble men.[1]

Introduction

In the history of the Irish Church of the sixth to the eighth century, the other 'Colum' whose name is indelibly etched on Western consciousness and whose life embodied aspects of Celtic consciousness is Columban[2] or Columbanus as he is sometimes called. Kenney claims that Columbanus, together with ColumCille, had the greatest influence on the course of development of civilization in Western Europe.[3] Both these men embody the sentiments of the reference above about the impact 'holy men' had on the unbelievers. Columbanus, in the company of his twelve disciples, truly [bound] with simple words by virtue of the fear inspired by God' his many hearers, whether they were kings, bishops or simple peasants. It will be seen in the discussion that follows that his words were not always simple, but the fear he inspired was real. A fear not so much of the physical kind but one which had the eternal salvation of his hearers at heart.

The map of the monasteries he personally founded and the travels he undertook to make the foundations[4] indicate that his life on the continent was

---

1. Dumville (ed.), *St Patrick*, p. 12. These words were referring to Augustine, sent to evangelize the British, and were part of Gregory the Great's reflections on verses from Job. They can also be applied to the transformation effected by Columbanus when he went on pilgrimage to the continent in the late sixth and early seventh century.

2. In his prose letters the saint always calls himself Columba. In his letter to Pope Boniface IV, Columbanus makes a play on words with his name thus: 'the last to the first, the foreigner to the native, a poor creature to a powerful lord, (strange to tell, a monstrosity, a rare bird) the Dove dares to write to Pope Boniface'; Walker (ed.), *Sancti Columbani*, p. 37 (Letters VI, I). 'Columbanus' is used in the poem to Hunaldus. Both forms occur in Jonas, *Vita Columbani*; Columbanus in I 5,14; II 15,16, 21, 22, 43; III 12. In this work 'Columbanus', the Latinised form, will be used.

3. Kenney, *The Sources*, p. 187.

4. See Appendix V.

one of constant activity. Even by today's standards the distance travelled by these monks, by the most primitive forms of transport (often on foot) is monumental. Only a single-minded man impelled by his Celtic consciousness and acting out of a radical response to the *evangelium*, with the charism of Columbanus, could conceive of such an enterprise (bringing the message of the gospel to the people of Gaul and environs), inspire such devotion in his many followers and accomplish the task. This is not to say that he did not encounter opposition. He did.

In this chapter we will look at aspects of Columbanus' ancestry and character that might reveal the person behind the literary works to be analysed. Since pilgrimage and holiness are inextricably linked in the Irish psyche of the period these will also be treated before looking specifically at the Sermons of Columbanus. The influence he exerted on the continent in the seventh century, particularly among the people of Frankish Gaul will add more insights about the person and his impact on the continent. The ultimate aim of this analysis of Columbanus' sermons is to discover the ascetical theology, and its underlying cultural consciousness, for these are the particular focus of this chapter.

Ancestry and Personal Characteristics of Columbanus

But who was this magnetic character who could justifiably be called the archetype of the Irish *peregrinus*? He does not figure in early Irish genealogies. Very little is known of the details of the early life[5] of Columbanus[6] from the *Life*, written by Ionas of Susa[7] (most often called Jonas) published in 643 CE. Jonas puts it simply:

> Columban, who was also known as Columba, was born in Ireland, which the Irish race inhabits. They do not observe the same laws as other people, but they are strong in the truth, and surpass their neighbors in their Christian faith. Columban was born in the early days of the faith in Ireland. The seeds of the faith had not yet all fructified.[8]

Most writers, including Jonas, would attest to the miraculous events surrounding his mother's experiences during her pregnancy: 'While he was still

---

5. Walker (ed.), *Sancti Columbani*, Introduction p. x, makes the point that of the salient dates in the chronology of Columban's life: his birth, arrival in France, exile from that country, and death are a source of differences of opinion among hagiographers. The evidence for the first is inconclusive; for the second it is contradictory; for the third and fourth it is certain.

6. A metrical life by Flodoard, published in Mabillon AA.SS.o.s.B.11 30–40; Migne PL CXXXV pp. 869–82, does not add anything to the knowledge of the career of Columbanus that is not contained in Jonas' Life.

7. Watkins, *A History*, p. 612, calls him Jonas of Elno but there seems not to be any reason given for this.

8. J. Wilson (ed.), *St Columban by Jonas*, translated from the Latin and for private circulation only, possibly 1950s, p. 13. See also Bullough in Lapidge (ed.), *Columbanus*, pp. 1–28, where using more up-to-date information he still comes to similar conclusions as earlier writers.

in the womb, his mother one night dreamt that she saw a great dazzling sun shine forth from her womb and fill the world with its light'.⁹ What is puzzling is that she is recorded as consulting a seer, or as Jonas puts it 'her more learned friends'¹⁰ about how to interpret this event. Were these friends druids? Is it possible that Columbanus' parents were not as yet Christian? As with his famous namesake is it possible that biographers, in the hagiographic genre, were writing only positively about their heroes? ColumCille, his contemporary, actually addressed Christ as druid,¹¹ and Columbanus converted pre-Christian temples and shrines into monasteries. In keeping with the belief that syncretism was operating in the Ireland of the period under discussion, there did not seem to be such a strongly held aversion, in the lives of these two great monastic founders, to the pre-Christian religions as is often thought.¹²

Ó Fiaich says Columbanus was 'born about 543 CE on the borders of the modern counties of Carlow and Wexford.'¹³ It seems that he was put to study early, apparently without leaving home. This implies that he was not of humble origin but it could also suggest that he was not of the social class, unlike ColumCille, where fosterage was an accepted practice.¹⁴ It appears that his teachers were probably indigenous. Jonas records that he studied rhetoric, grammar, geometry and the Sacred Scriptures, all of which would have been part of the study schedule of Irish monastic schools then proliferating throughout Ireland. Kenney, however, is not so sure about the details of the early days of this continental monastic founder. He refers to the poetic epistle of Fidolius as the source of the date of Columbanus' birth. The dilemma is compounded by the dates Jonas gives for the career of King Sigebert showing, according to Kenney, that his notions of Frankish history are vague and consequently not to be relied upon.¹⁵

9. *Life* (ed. and trans. Wilson, p. 14).
10. *Life* (ed. and trans. Wilson, p. 14).
11. Sharpe (ed.), *Adomnán*, p. 11 in his introduction conjectures that ColumCille was born of pre-Christian parents.
12. It must also be noted that the fact of using primal shrines for Christian purposes was a way of Christianizing these places. It could also be seen as obliterating primal practices or superimposing on the primitive the 'superior' Christian beliefs and worship. In the early stages of religious identification it was a general practice for differing traditions to use each other's places of worship. Schneiders and Ó Riann, in Edel (ed.), *Cultural*, pp. 157-69, pp. 144-56, both discuss this 'Pagan Example and Christian Practice' and 'Pagan Past and Christian Present' in Ireland of this time.
13. T. Ó Fiaich, *Columbanus in His Own Words* (Dublin: Veritas, 1st edn, 1974), p. 19. In his Introduction he claims that 'well over a hundred copies of [the *Life*] survive in manuscript in continental libraries', p. 8. However, I was only able to find the Wilson edition, and this was an edition for personal use only. M. Lapidge (ed.), *Columbanus: Studies on the Latin Writings* (Suffolk: The Boydell Press, 1st edn, 1997) has a very lengthy fn in chapter 1, by Bullough, regarding the many sources for the *Vita S. Columbani*.
14. See Lapidge (ed.), *Columbanus*, fn 12, regarding the relationship of fosterage and status, *Cáin Iar-raith*. See Kelly, *A Guide*, pp. 86-90 for detailed study of fosterage in ancient laws.
15. Kenney, *The Sources*, p. 187, fn 100.

Pious tradition says that early in his life he felt the sting of the flesh and to offset the solicitations of a young woman he sought counsel from an anchoress, 'a holy woman who had dedicated her life to God'.[16] The specific details of the answer he received are more in the genre of a literary device 'as a much later Gaelic writer might take off on an alliterative run in a dramatic situation'.[17] His subsequent action, according to Jonas, leaves the reader in no doubt that this was an extraordinary man who would stop at nothing to follow this evangelical call, even to walking over the prostrate body of his grieving mother. His reply to her sounds cruel: 'Have you not heard: "He that loveth father or mother more than Me is not worthy of Me?"'[18] Ó Fiaich claims that Jonas put even harsher words into the mouth of Columbanus on this occasion: 'the enemy holds the sword over me to strike me down; so what should I care for a mother's tears . . . The true piety here is to be cruel.'[19] The kind of single-mindedness, represented by this comment, sets the tone for the later life of Columbanus as interpreted by those whom Jonas consulted and whose stories are, at times, those of eye-witnesses.[20] His time at Cleenish, under the guidance of the abbot Sinell, seems to have laid the foundation for his future learning and spirituality. His commentary on the psalms and some of his earlier poetry may have been written at Cleenish, if they were actually written by him. Bullock points to the ninth-century manuscripts of both Sankt Gallen and Bobbio as evidence that these works were attributed to Columbanus.[21] Prior to his heroic journey throughout Europe, and it seems while he was in the monastery of *Bennchor* (Bangor, Co. Down), with Comgall as abbot, 'he began to desire the pilgrimage'.[22] It is generally accepted that his ordination took place at Bangor as did his acceptance of the future influential concept and practice of private confession and tariffed penance treated in chapter 2. The date of his departure from Ireland is the subject of varying interpretations.[23] Some writers put it at

---

16. *Life* (ed. and trans. Wilson, p. 15).
17. Ó Fiaich, *Columbanus*, p. 20.
18. *Life* (ed. and trans. Wilson, p. 16).
19. Ó Fiaich, *Columbanus*, p. 21. He claims that these are the words of St Jerome, put into the mouth of Columbanus by Jonas, but he does not give the reference, or the editor of the version of the *Life* he is using. These words are not in the Wilson edition of the work I used.
20. Jonas entered the monastery of Bobbio in 618 CE just three years after the death of Columbanus. Most people would have known the founder of Bobbio and had their stories to tell. Walker (ed.), *Sancti Columbani*, p. ix fn 2, says 'Attala and Eustasius in particular provided a mine of information; Theudegesilus (Jonas, I 15 17), Sonicharius and Gall (I 11) and Chagnoald (I 17) supplied details from their own experience; Potentinus, who accompanied Columban into exile, Donatus, and other of his immediate disciples were still alive when Jonas wrote.
21. Bullock, in Lapidge (ed.), *Columbanus*, p. 4.
22. *Life* (ed. and trans. Wilson, p. 187, p. 14).
23. Bangor, from which Columbanus departed, is purported to have been one of the most populated of the early Irish monasteries and also one of the most austere; see Appendix II A for copy of the Rule of the monastery of Bangor. It was here at Bangor that Columbanus spent his formative years. The austerity of his later monastic rule and his penitential is said to have been learned from the spirit and person of St Comgall.

590 CE, or a little earlier,[24] others 591 CE, still others easily 15 years earlier.[25] He departed, reluctantly blessed by Comgall, with 12 companions for the coast of Brittany, where after a short delay they entered Frankish Gaul, and began to preach and live the gospel.

Sanctity and Pilgrimage

Sanctity in the period of the sixth to the eighth century in Ireland was identified with persons who performed heroic deeds and manifested miraculous events in their lives. Chadwick, in relation to the Age of the Saints, claims that 'the contemplation of their austerity, their unworldliness, and their spiritual happiness is an inspiration to our present age'.[26] In these few words she summarizes the characteristics that people associate with saints and sanctity in every age. In the case of the Irish, though, in this period there is a distinctive activity associated with those who strive for sanctity and it is the notion of pilgrimage and its relationship with martyrdom. Earlier in this work this association has been discussed. Briefly, then, it implies that those who want to imitate the great figures of the Christian tradition go on pilgrimage. Because of the heroic connotations of such a movement away from clan and country it is likened to martyrdom. Colours represent the different form it may take: red, giving one's life in death, green a life of penance, and white the abandonment of one's clan and country to travel to foreign lands in search of communion with God and as a more total form of mortification. This, then, is part of the asceticism that identified those monks who made a more radical response to the call to holiness.

Before attempting to analyse the Sermons of Columbanus we could ask why the Irish embraced *peregrinatio pro Christo* with such alacrity. Pilgrimage arose in the fourth century and was a popular activity in the fifth. The literature regarding it is prolific, including log-books like that of Egeria in the fourth century which is of extraordinary detail, particularly describing the Easter ceremonies in Jerusalem which she attended. Within this societal groundswell, the Irish monks sought specifically the 'place of one's resurrection' in their wanderings, in a withdrawal from home and kindred to pass their lives, or a specified period, in solitude and a peculiarly Irish form of asceticism. The *Old Irish Life of Columba* in a sermon clearly gives the rationale for pilgrimage thus:

> God counselled Abraham to leave his own country and go in pilgrimage into the land which God had shown him, to wit, the 'Land of Promise' . . . Now the good counsel which God enjoined here on the father of the faithful is incumbent on all the faithful; that is to

---

24. Kenney, *The Sources*, p. 187.
25. Ó Fiaich says that modern biographers place Columbanus' arrival in Gaul shortly after 570 CE when Sigebert was still reigning, p. 28. Walker (ed.), *Sancti Columbani*, p. xi, gives the date of arrival in France as 591 CE.
26. Chadwick, *The Age*, Preface.

leave their country and their land, their wealth and their worldly delights for the sake of the Lord of the Elements, and go in perfect pilgrimage in imitation of Him . . .[27]

Moreover, the Irish knew the importance of motivation, and to stem wholesale movement for inappropriate reasons had the saying:

To go to Rome
Is much trouble, little profit;
The King [of Heaven] whom thou seekest there,
Unless thou bring Him with thee, thou wilt not find.[28]

The answer to the question 'why *peregrinatio* for the Irish?' is not so simple. It could be a manifestation of the wanderlust of the Irish. Maybe it is a part of that ever-restless journeying of the creative and imaginative soul.[29] It could equally be attributed to the Irish subconscious need to reclaim the territory from which their ancestors, the Celts, were driven in the period before the coming of Christianity. They were the 'People who came out of the Darkness'[30] and their collective memories tell of those days when their ancestors were forced from central Europe to retreat west to the ends of the world. However, according to Watkins, the motivation was decidedly mortification.[31] It had little to do with evangelization as we know it today, or indeed as what motivated the later Irish who became the great missionaries.

In fact the conversion of the heathen seems hardly to have entered the purview of the Irish monks who at this period began to overrun the Christian communities of continental Europe . . . They were monks, and the going forth into an unknown land seemed to them desirable in the first instance as being a further grade of mortification.[32]

This mortification was one manifestation of the asceticism that was intrinsic to the lifestyle promoted by Columbanus and other monastic founders. It

27. W. F. Skene, *Celtic Scotland* (Edinburgh: David Douglass, 2nd edn, 1887), p. 467, for a translation of the *Old Irish Life*. Further on in the *Life,* pilgrimage is classified into three types: (a) when a man leaves his country in body only, but with spirit still uncleansed; (b) when a man leaves his fatherland in zeal of heart, though not in body, being detained under authority in his own land, though dedicated in spirit to God; (c) when a man leaves his country altogether in body and soul, as the apostles and people of perfect pilgrimage left it. Chadwick, *The Age,* p. 83, says that this excerpt is actually a text of *c.* 1000, a commemorative sermon on the saint's festival.
28. Stokes and Strachan (eds.), *Thesaurus,* p. 84.
29. This creativity is referred to in chapter 1 of this work. It has been commented on in relation to their art, poetry, stone crosses and present-day jewellery. Those who could not go on a literal pilgrimage did so in their mind's eye.
30. G. Herm, *The Celts: The People Who Came Out of the Darkness* (London: Weidenfeld & Nicolson, 1975). Herm, *The Celts,* p. 251 claimed that the first Celtic-speaking tribes were in Ireland in the Hallstatt period (700–450 BCE). After the beginning of the La Tène era these were followed by other wandering hordes who spoke a Brythonic, that is a P-Celtic dialect.
31. Watkins, *A History,* p. 612.
32. Watkins, *A History,* p. 613.

seems that after their conversion to Christianity the Irish, those Christians on the edge of the world, were captivated by the beauty of the Christian *evangel*. As *peregrini* they sought to emulate their ancestors in the faith like Abraham and to search for their Promised Land even though it took them far from their homeland and clan.[33]

In comparison with ColumCille, Columbanus seems to have a more abrasive personality and consequently exhibited a more rugged asceticism. His presence among foreigners in Gaul and the whole of Europe, unlike that of ColumCille among the expatriate Irish in north-western Scotland, may be partly the reason why he is seen as more pugnacious, more the fighting monk. He seemed ever ready to take up the sword of the tongue and pen. His asceticism is more extreme and this can be seen in the vivid language[34] of disease and bodily fluids of Sermon VII. In an attempt to add impact to his words he castigates 'wretched mankind,[35] inwardly rotten, full of bile, rheum, blood and phlegm . . . outwardly with skin washed but never clean . . . Why do you not see what your ulcerated skin discharges through its pores?'[36] Though he confesses, 'I know not what to say', which is no doubt a rhetorical device, nevertheless he continues to enunciate different facets of his ascetic doctrine: 'one thing which I know I shall say: the man who here battens, here sates himself, here makes merry, here smiles, here is drunken, and here plays, shall hereafter hunger, thirst, mourn, wail, lament'.[37] The final exhortation of this sermon echoes the sentiments of his monastic rule: 'let us eat in part . . . what is needful, not what panders'.[38] Again he is insisting on the rejection of the superfluous.

The introduction of the poor as in the following excerpt, 'let us share with the poor, that even so we may deserve to share with the poor in that place where they shall be satisfied who here for Christ's sake hunger and thirst after righteousness. For to whom belongs the kingdom of heaven save to the poor',[39] reiterates one of the fundamental tenets of monasticism and an intrinsic component of his mortified life: sharing with the less fortunate as one would

---

33. They were not intent primarily on converting others. If this occurred as a result of their monastic living, it was incidental. That the Irish became the great missionaries later in their history is more a result of their contact with the Roman Church and a particular theological interpretation in the later Middle Ages. Pilgrimage is better understood in the Irish early culture as a form of martyrdom.
34. Walker (ed.), *Sancti Columbani*, p. lxx holds that Columbanus' style is intimately wedded to his personality and to the purpose of the particular type of writing: the letters have a different style from the penitential. He claims that the words are charged with a nervous energy and power. This is undeniably the case with this particular Sermon or group of Sermons.
35. Walker (ed.), *Sancti Columbani*, p. xviii refers to a poem *De Mundi Transitu*, which he claims was written by Columbanus. It is echoing the sentiments of this sermon: dwelling on the universality of corruption and decay but concluding on the joys of the future life.
36. Sermon VII (ed. and trans. Walker, p. 91).
37. Sermon VII (ed. and trans. Walker, p. 93).
38. Sermon VII (ed. and trans. Walker, p. 93).
39. Sermon VII (ed. and trans. Walker, p. 93).

with Christ in their person. This exhortation is strongly based on aphorisms derived from Scripture, which permeate Celtic monastic writing.

If Columbanus' listeners heed his words, then those

> who are on the way, hasten home: for our whole life is like the journey of a single day. Our first duty is to love nothing here; but let us place our affection above, our desires above, our wisdom above and above let us seek our home; for the fatherland is where our Father is.[40]

He enunciates the distinctively Celtic stance of these *peregrini* and he calls it the principle that should abide in those to whom these sermons are addressed, 'that on the road we so live as travellers, as pilgrims, as guests of the world, entangled by no lusts, longing with no earthly desires, but let us fill our minds with heavenly and spiritual impressions'.[41]

His Irish compatriots would certainly understand the import of the images of pilgrim and travellers: that definitive choice of Christ over Clan (*Túatha*); that kind of detachment most of them had experienced for many years on the continent, freedom from encumbrances of material possessions and a total reliance on the provident and omnipresent God. After all they were on *peregrinatio pro Dei amore*. Given that all around the monastic settlements kings were warring for more land, greater power and more material wealth, this principle of pilgrimage involving deeply personal privation could be seen as radical and an intrinsic part of the life of the ascetic and the sanctity to which they felt called.

The Influence of Columbanus – Monastic Foundations on the Continent

Most historians would agree that, despite the dilemma about which specific part of Gaul Columbanus and his band of twelve disciples[42] first reached, their first monastery was founded at Annegray with sister establishments quickly being founded at Luxeuil, which soon became the principal monastery on the continent, and Fontaine. Initially the surrounding population was impressed with the lifestyle and 'sanctity' of the monks and many disciples flocked to them. However, the political situation in Merovingian Gaul was always on a knife-edge. Profligate kings and the warring Queen Brunhilde of Burgundy taking sides and negotiating treaties in order to shore up her own or her sons'

---

40. Sermon VIII (ed. and trans. Walker, p. 95). It has been suggested that this could be a form of dualism. However, it is one of the claims of this work that the Irish Celts were not dualistic, but given that Columbanus' asceticism is harsher than that of his contemporaries, maybe his enthusiasm for the *evangelium* is 'heard' as dualistic.

41. Sermon VIII (ed. and trans. Walker, p. 97).

42. Ó Fiaich, *Columbanus*, p. 25 claims that the names he gives are those found in the letters of Jonas and Columbanus. These are: Gall, Domoal, Comininus, Eunocus, Equonanus, Columban óg, Libranum, Aedh (the bishop of the group), Deicola, Lua, Leobard and Caldwals: the last two named were Anglo-Saxons.

powers did not endear themselves to the single-minded Columbanus. His proclivity to speak his mind often challenged both royal and ecclesiastical authorities with the result that King Theoderich sent his soldiers to escort the troublesome monks to the coast to be shipped back to Ireland. As Jonas tells the story, God was on their side and they never left the country.[43] Columbanus and his monks found themselves passing from Nantes to the court of two Frankish Kings, Clothaire of Neustria and Theodebert of Austrasia. He next proceeded along the Rhine to present-day Switzerland and, failing to convert the inhabitants, crossed the Alps and finally was received in Milan by Agilulf and Theodelinda, king and queen of the Lombards. These two Christians granted him land in the valley of the Apennines where he established the now-famous monastery of Bobbio.[44] This always remained an Italian monastery, but was the one in which Columbanus found his final resting place (the place of his resurrection).

Not only the above monasteries but many others were founded on the Irish model on the continent in the seventh century, taking as their rule of life that of Columbanus. Luxeuil, however, was called the 'monastic capital of the Gauls'[45] and in comparison with it all other monastic houses were thought to be 'relaxed and decayed'.[46] Columbanus' influence can be attested to by briefly recalling the holy people and establishments taking shape from his inspiration and recounted by Watkins.[47] St Eligius, who founded Solignac, insisted that all future abbots follow the path of the most holy men of Luxeuil monastery, and firmly maintain the rule of the most blessed father Columbanus. The houses of Paul and Joussamoutier, founded under the guidance of Donatus, a companion of Columbanus, in the diocese of Besançon are other examples of his influence. Adon, brother of Ouen, founded the monastery at Jouarre and prescribed for it the rule of Columbanus. Ouen himself founded Rebais, and made Agilus, who had been brought up at Luxeuil, the first abbot. Burgundofara, who during Columbanus' exile had been blessed by him, founded, with the help of Eustasius of Luxeuil, the monastery at Faremoutier, where she was abbess for forty years according to the rule of Columbanus. No less that ten other monasteries are cited by Watkins as taking their inspiration from this imposing '*dove*' of the Irish monastic movement. With knowledge of his monastic rule, previously treated in chapter 3, one can only imagine the impact of the asceticism of this group of Celtic monasteries on the continent in the seventh century.

Besides these people and places influenced by the spirit of Columbanus, some prominent bishops of the period also came under the spell of Luxeuil.[48] From

---

43. *Life*, section on Banishment from Luxeuil (ed. and trans. Wilson, p. 40).
44. Kenney, *The Sources*, p. 188, says that there are the texts of two charters (Migne PL LXXX pp. 321–23), the first of which purports to be the grant of Bobbio to Columbanus, made by King Agilulf in 598 CE, and the second a grant of the monastery made by Columbanus to the Pope. Neither charter is regarded as authentic.
45. Watkins, *A History*, p. 623.
46. Watkins, *A History*, p. 623.
47. Watkins, *A History*, p. 623.
48. Watkins, *A History*, p. 625.

Luxeuil alone came 21 saints honoured by the Church.[49] Such enthusiasm for living the *evangelium* had to be inspired by God but, in this case, mediated through a person whose commitment, convictions and living of the gospel captivated others. Of Columbanus, Lapidge writes: 'his fiery personality led him into conflict with Gallic bishops and Roman popes, and he defended his position on such matters as monastic discipline in a substantial corpus of Latin writings marked by burning conviction and rhetorical skill'.[50]

Just what other areas of influence did Columbanus exert on the continent? There are three spheres worth considering. The most important is the impetus he gave to the growth of monasticism (noted above). In Gaul, Luxeuil seemed to be the focus to which all eyes looked for inspiration. The monastic rule attributed to Columbanus was wide in its influence and persisted even with the introduction of the less austere rule of Benedict. The staunchly Irish cultural influence that pervaded Columbanus' monasteries, where the bishop was subject to the abbot, according to Kenney 'began that movement for monastic exemptions which played so large a part in medieval Church history'.[51]

In the early Church, particularly in the Roman sphere of influence, public penance was said to be the common practice. Actual confession of sins, apart from the penance and reconciliation with the community, was still public. It was the widespread and reiterated practice of private penance that was introduced in Ireland with monasticism and simultaneously introduced on the continent with the movement there of Irish monks that 'worked a revolution in the penance-discipline of continental Europe'[52] and marked the second major sphere of influence of Columbanus.

A third significant and important Columban influence came as a result of the establishment of his monastic 'chain' throughout Europe. These monasteries became centres of learning, as they were in Ireland, and in the midst of the brutality and internecine warfare of Gaul and its surrounding kingdoms, these monastic schools preserved, encouraged and furthered the art of learning, not only in the sacred but also in the secular sciences. How could a man of Columbanus' learning not encourage it? His foundation in Bobbio became, in later centuries, the repository of ancient literature. One only has to look at the references for so much of the manuscript material of Irish and continental history to find it traceable to Bobbio.

An aspect of his influence noted by Kenney makes the point that Columbanus 'inaugurated that long struggle between the Celtic and the Roman ecclesiastical system in which the Synod of Whitby and the 'Bull' of Adrian VI were but episodes'.[53]

49. These were: Chagnoald of Laon (c. AD 619); Acharius of Vermnd, Noyon and Tournai; Ragnacharius of Basel; Audomarus of Boulogne and Therouane; Faro of Meaux; Andoenus, or Ouen, of Rouen; Remaclus of Maastricht; Hildebert also later bishop of Meaux; and Deodatus of Nevers. This list is taken from Montalembert, *Moines d'Occident* (1860), 11, p. 494 and given in full in Watkins, *A History*, p. 626.
50. Lapidge (ed.),*Columbanus*, preamble.
51. Kenney, *The Sources*, p. 188.
52. Kenney, *The Sources*, p. 188.
53. Kenney, *The Sources*, p. 188.

If by 'inaugurated' he means that Columbanus was the initiator, then the historical facts do not support this contention. The Easter controversy was well and truly a point of contention[54] before Columbanus' correspondence with the Pope. Maybe his presence on the continent brought the differences to the notice of a wider group of people. Hitherto the contesting parties seemed to be those in Northumbria, Ireland and Iona. That much of the south of Ireland had conformed to Roman ways before the Whitby Synod, 664 CE, indicates that when the politics of the issue took centre stage the liturgical and supposedly unorthodox theological tenets receded. Columbanus can be said to have championed the cause of the Irish devotion to the ancestral practices. In his third Letter, probably written about 604 CE, he pleads with the bishop of Rome:

> that you would grant to us pilgrims in our travail the godly consolation of your judgement, thus confirming, if it is not contrary to the faith, the tradition of our predecessors, so that by your approval we may in our pilgrimage maintain the rite of Easter as we have received it from generations gone before.[55]

So it can be seen that Columbanus forthrightly wrote about the point of contention, but he is hardly the only or original champion. ColumCille, Colman, Aidan, and Hilda all fought for the retention of the ancient Celtic practices that eventually submitted to Peter's power under the sophisticated onslaughts of Wilfrid. The letter to the bishop of Rome, Boniface, referred to is only a part of the extant literature left to the student of history by this prolific writer of the seventh century of Irish monasticism.

What has to be reiterated here is that 'the long struggle' noted above was not necessarily because the Irish had no regard for the Roman Church and its bishop. On the contrary the struggle stemmed more from Columbanus' deep conviction that what had been handed down from the ancestors was the authentic (for the Irish) way of celebrating Easter. Other points of disagreement between the Roman faction and the Irish monks under the leadership of Columbanus could be seen as their desire for a more faithful living of the *evangelium* as it had been heard by these converts and the enthusiasm they displayed in living out this message. Since his penitential has been analysed in the chapter on this topic and his rule has been discussed in the chapter on monastic rules, the remainder of this chapter will be given over to discussing the ascetical theology that underpins his sermons.

The 'Voice' of Columbanus in General

The understanding of 'voice' being used here is similar to that used in the chapter on ColumCille. It is the means by which a reader comes into contact with the ideas, ideals and inspiration of significant persons. Herbert claims that

---

54. During the reign of Pope Victor (c.189–c.199) the date for celebrating Easter was being discussed.
55. Walker (ed.), *Sancti Columbani*, p. 25.

'each Irish life is implicitly a source for its own time. It speaks from within the monastic community for which its subject was patron, conveying the attitudes and interests of that community.'[56]

She concludes, 'the hagiographical text thus bears an encoded message from the milieu in which it was compiled and received'.[57] Implicit in this understanding of the 'encoded message' is the assumption that so often the attitudes of the community are decidedly those of the founder of the said *paruchia*. When such *Vita* are the work of one person, written for a particular purpose, it can tend nonetheless to incorporate an amalgam of attitudes. In the case under consideration, that is the Sermons of Columbanus, it is more likely that we are hearing a single 'voice', coloured by the context and awareness of the *evangelium*, but nevertheless it is a single personal 'voice'.

The 'voice' of Columbanus heard in this chapter can be compared to a megaphone, for at times it is stentorian and strident. It is the tone used by powerful leaders, rousing their hearers to action in the interest of a cause. The 'voice' of ColumCille, on the other hand, is less strident and more in the timbre of the father of the community living among his confrères and aware of the needs and personal characteristics of each. Both these men were fundamentally part of a front of evangelization. In the case of Columbanus its ambit spread throughout the length and breadth of what is today called central and western Europe. The motivation for the evangelizing, epitomized by ColumCille and Columbanus, had its origins in Ireland and its driving force was a distinctively Irish and practical response to the gospel.

Just as his origins and the man himself are enigmatic, so there is debate about the authenticity of the works attributed to Columbanus. No less than 17 sermons or homilies have been attributed to him, most of which according to Kenney, do not belong to him.[58] However, Walker, in his *magnum opus* on Columbanus, while acknowledging the debates of previous historians and linguists and giving due weight to their arguments, would attribute 13 of these sermons to Columbanus.[59] The more recent work edited by Lapidge seems to be the most authoritative on the issue of authenticity of the Columban corpus. Stancliffe's thorough scholarly work concludes:

> Columbanus himself was the author of all the thirteen sermons that we have been considering: and that he composed them as a series, for his monks in northern Italy towards the end of his life, between his arrival in Lombardy in 612 and his death in 615.[60]

56. M. Herbert, *Iona, Kells and Derry: The History and Hagiography of the Monastic Familia of Columba* (Oxford: Clarendon, 1st edn, 1988), p. 2.
57. Herbert, *Iona*, p. 2.
58. Kenney, *The Sources*, p. 196.
59. Walker (ed.), *Sancti Columbani*, for a detailed discussion on xli–xliv. J. W. Smit, *Studies on the Language and Style of Columba the Younger (Columbanus)* (Amsterdam: A. M. Hakkert, 1st edn, 1971), doubts that Columbanus authored any of the Sermons. Preference will be given here to Stancliffe's and Walker's conclusions about the authenticity of the Sermons.
60. Stancliffe in Lapidge (ed.), *Columbanus*, p. 199. In the course of her article, pp. 93–199, she appraised the works of Smit, Hauck, Seebass and Fleming and still came to the conclusion given above.

She would also reiterate the point being made in this chapter about Columbanus' writings:

> once correctly attributed, these sermons take their place as the only coherent exposition of Irish ascetic spirituality to have come down to us from the formative period of early Irish monasticism. They also provide us with an insight into the religious inspiration of one of Ireland's greatest and most forceful *peregrini*.[61]

In dismissing the dilemma of the authenticity of his Sermons so summarily, it is not intended to devalue the discussion. However, the purpose here is to read the Sermons for the ascetical and theological content and in the light of the possibility of their Celtic cultural context. This will give further insights into the asceticism of the Irish Church of the sixth to the eighth century, asceticism seen as a radical response to how the Irish monks of the period heard the message of the *evangelium* and how they responded to it within their particular cultural context. The very fact that their living the Irish monastic ideal on the continent aroused so much opposition, and not only because of the personality of Columbanus, speaks for its radicality and its challenge to the profligate and half-hearted living of the Christians of the day. Though the bishops of Gaul protested against Columbanus' lifestyle and presence, it was primarily the Christian kings and laity that rejected and ostracized him and his followers. Royalty and lay people alike, as no doubt in Ireland itself, had only partly assimilated church belief and practice.

In the 13 Sermons translated by Walker a few preaching styles are prominent: these include the didactic (typical of the skilful teacher), exhortation and reflective praying. Columbanus, the preacher, begins with a profession of faith and meditation on the mystery of the Godhead who created the visible universe. This creator should be sought through faith, righteous living and prayer. All of these are Christian qualities intimating that his 'audience' was not confined to monks only. Life is transient, the inspirational teacher suggests, so our sights should be clearly focused on our true homeland, heaven. It is important to note that in Irish 'theology' of this period, there is no negativity or threats of damnation regarding the afterlife. Columbanus is simply employing his skills as a leader of men to encourage his followers and the whole of Gaul to take seriously the call of the gospel while using every device possible to effect his evangelizing aim.

Common themes, some of which have parallels in discussion in previous chapters, can be heard in the sermons in general: Sermons II and X have forceful arguments about fighting here so as to receive rewards in eternity.[62] Sermons I and III both put forward the belief that we should try to understand those things we cannot see by comparison with those we can see.[63] Sermons III

---

61. Stancliffe in Lapidge (ed.), *Columbanus*, p. 199.
62. Sermons II. 3 and X. 3 (ed. and trans. Walker, p. 67, p. 101).
63. Sermons I. 4 and III. 2 (ed. and trans. Walker, p. 61, p. 3).
64. Sermons III. 4 and VI. 1 (ed. and trans. Walker, p. 73, p. 87).

and VI warn about being foreigners in this material world.[64] They also treat another important facet of monastic *praxis*: that is, the necessity of dying daily to selfishness.[65] Sermons II and XI reiterate the fact that it is no advantage knowing how to live the Christian life if one does not put theory into practice.[66] While these elements of life and living are forcefully voiced by Columbanus, they are a long way from the moralizing of earlier leaders such as Cesarius of Arles.

In keeping with the approach of the poetic Irish, Columbanus' sermons often make use of imagery and other poetic devices. The same image is continued throughout quite a number of sermons. It is the *roadway* that appears in various forms in Sermons V, VI, VIII, IX, and X. Consistent with the instincts of the warring Celto-Irish, the spiritualized notion of being a *soldier of Christ* appears in Sermons II and X. As if reiterating the strong emphasis of his penitential, in Sermon II Columbanus deals at some length with the place of *contraries* in the warfare of the Christian soldier. *Dying to the world*, that classic exhortation of monasticism, is treated in Sermon III, which is probably the strongest evidence for Columbanus, the great exhorter to ascetic living, as the author.

As if moving his exhortations from the merely cognitive level, he speaks about the heart's role in a mortified life. Intrinsic to these Sermons, as with the penitential and monastic rules of Columbanus and other founders of Irish monasticism, is the indispensable 'heart's belief' which he explicates as 'the basis of all men's salvation', the' foundation of our talk', the 'point whence all that is arises and that has not been begins'.[67] It is the capacity of the 'heart' to hear and see beyond the tangible. The Celtic awareness of another world, which is separated from this world by the thinnest of veils, is here brought into focus. Sheldrake, reflecting on the island of Iona and remembering the comments of the founder of the modern Iona Community, Dr George Macleod, refers to this awareness as 'a thin place' where the membrane between this world and the other world, between the material and the spiritual, between the here and the hereafter, is very permeable.[68] This Otherworld is the focus and goal of all the ascetical activity that Columbanus is recommending, reinforcing the earlier comment about his single-mindedness being perceived as a form of dualism.

The 'Voice' of Faith Heard on the Roadway

The first Sermon begins with a discussion of faith as 'the basis of all men's salvation . . . belief first in God the first and last, one and three, one in substance, three in character; one in power three in person; one in nature, three

65. Sermons III. 3 and VI. 2 (ed. and trans. Walker, p. 73, p. 87).
66. Sermons II. 3 and XI. 1 (ed. and trans. Walker, p. 67, p. 61).
67. Sermon 1 (ed. and trans. Walker, p. 61).
68. Sheldrake, *Living*, p. 7.
69. Sermon I (ed. and trans. Walker, p. 63).

in name'.[69] Then Columbanus spends the whole Sermon unfolding the elements of this belief in the Trinity, as one would expect from a Celtic exponent.[70] Equally Celtic is the linking of the heart[71] with the confession of belief. Columbanus puts it this way: 'we have spoken of what we believe, and the heart's faith has drawn forth the confession of the mouth'.[72] As if conscious of the underlying activity that facilitates inner transformation, Columbanus stresses that the mystery of the Trinity is 'more for pondering than preaching'.[73] It is the doctrine, whose wisdom and fruit emanate 'not [from] verbal debate, but by the perfection of a good life, not with the tongue but with faith which issues from singleness of heart'.[74]

Could anyone fail to hear in this that the fundamental work of the monk is contemplation of God, steeped in a faith that underpins all activity and ultimately is the source of inner transformation? Asceticism like this must have faith as its basis. This same faith is what leads the monk to know the Creator through an understanding of creation, 'for those who wish to know the great deep must first review the natural world'.[75] Created things contain within themselves a revelation of the one who made them.[76] In theology this is called the principle of sacramentality. It is also faith that reminds the aspirant to perfection of the great communion of saints, so beloved by the Irish of this era, whose intercession can throw 'light upon . . . our dullness and ignorance on the dark roadway of this world'.[77]

Sermon V, which addresses human life and the human condition, could be said to be the core of Columbanus' 13 sermons. Using the image of the roadway he details the path, the dangers and supports for human life on this way and clearly maps the end of this roadway. This image of the roadway, used so frequently in these sermons, consciously or not may emphasize the wanderlust[78] or tendency to pilgrimage so prevalent among the Irish monks. Turning from primal religions and taking up the Christian calling is no task

---

70. Bullock, in Lapidge (ed.),*Columbanus*, p. 23, claims that Columbanus' belief in traditional Trinitarianism as the basis of all true Christian faith found expression, according to Jonas (1.30), in a 'treatise of burgeoning learning', written while he was resident in Milan. In its original form it is called *De Fide*, but the original document appears to be lost. Its existence is known by references in his later sermons. Given that the Arian heresy regarding the divinity of Christ made an impact on the continent, Columbanus' detailed treatment is understandable.

71. Heart and tears that double combination used in his monastic rule and penitential is also evident in Letter IV (ed. and trans. Walker, pp. 27–28).

72. Sermon I (ed. and trans. Walker, p. 63).

73. Sermon I (ed. and trans. Walker, p. 67).

74. Sermon I (ed. and trans. Walker, p. 65).

75. Sermon I (ed. and trans. Walker, p. 5).

76. Since pantheism was seen to be a form of idolatry, the word 'Panentheism' is used to refer to this doctrine of transcendent immanence.

77. Sermon I (ed. and trans. Walker, p. 67).

78. Walker (ed.), *Sancti Columbani*, p. xviii fn 2. Compare with *Vita S.Galli* auctore Walahfrido, ii.46, where it is stated that the habit of travelling had become 'almost second nature to the Irish'.

for weaklings; it can be embraced only by the radically courageous. Columbanus insists, 'we must thus make our journey through you [the roadway] so anxiously, so carefully, so hastily, that all men of understanding should hurry like pilgrims to their true homeland, confident of the past, troubled for that which remains'.[79]

While the roadway may be solid, the life one encounters on it can be equated with a mirage or a shadow full of vanity and deception. Since this implies a lack of vision, then those who walk the road are susceptible to 'specious entanglements'.[80] The ever-vigilant teacher cautions, 'therefore let us flee you before you flee from us',[81] before death overtakes us. He continues with the eternal challenge to human nature: 'and since you are mortal, brief, tottering, unsure, inconstant, transient, fickle, changeful, let us hold ourselves as lovers and merchants of God and eternal life rather than of you, and let us flee you as you flow and fly, lest you claim us with your lovers'.[82]

Sermons V to X can be regarded as one poetic exhortation to an asceticism that is faithful and involves following the road used by those who have been the inspiration for a life of asceticism. Only Sermon III is specifically addressed to monks. With the lack of any specified audience, these six sermons appear to be addressed to the laity as well as to those within the monastic enclosure, unless, of course, they were specifically given in the monastic church at the Canonical Hours. Sermon V is a powerful address about human life, experienced as mortal, with its many enticements to follow another path. Without a constant asceticism on the road of life any deviation carries with it the threat of ultimate ruin. The brevity and poetic form give this work an impact not experienced in Columbanus' other writings:

> Oh human life, feeble and mortal, how many have you deceived, beguiled and blinded! ... while you arise, you are but smoke ... sweet to the stupid, bitter to the wise. Those who love you do not know you, and those who scorn you really scan you. Thus you are not true but false; you show yourself as true, render yourself in falsehood.[83]

To what end this accumulation of negatives? Surely they stem from the enthusiasm of Columbanus for the totality of commitment that he expects of all who choose to follow Christ. Maybe he is warning the monastic aspirants and newly converted Christians of fratricidal Gaul that life is only a gift to be used as a means to an end, that we have not here a lasting city; that the fulfilment at the end of the road, the life of glory, is reserved for those who walk the road full of faith and listen for the voice of the ascetic master who leads in response to the call of the *evangelium*.

---

79. Sermon V (ed. and trans. Walker, p. 87).
80. Sermon VI (ed. and trans. Walker, p. 89).
81. Sermon VI (ed. and trans. Walker, p. 89).
82. Sermon VI (ed. and trans. Walker, p. 89).
83. Sermon V (ed. and trans. Walker, p. 85).

A Warning 'Voice': Sermons IX and X

A note of warning is introduced into Sermons IX and X: it is the sound of pain and death for those who seek to walk the road in defiance of Columbanus' instruction. Each walks an identical road, but it is the attitude and intentionality one adopts that avoids the misery and trouble caused by the travail of a tortuous track.[84] Daily examining of ourselves with the guide of the Scriptures,[85] and in the company of an *anamchara* or soul-friend (though Columbanus does not specify this here as he does in both his monastic rule and penitential), is imperative as we 'ponder without ceasing this aforesaid end of that roadway'.[86]

In commenting that his hearers should be free and living, 'instead of bond and crucified'[87] he is naturally speaking metaphorically, for later he refers to Christians as being 'slaves of Christ'[88] meaning, of course, that the Christian is bound in bonds of love and devotion to one who has shown the way of loving and living in total conformity to the will of his Father. It is love alone that saves. It is being loved by God and responding to this love that is the life task of those who seek entry to monasteries and are guided by such founders as Columbanus. Ultimately it is only through this freedom that the life of asceticism and mortification leads to a radical response to divine love.

Image of the Soldier of Christ

Understanding the ascetic life in terms of a freely chosen commitment leads one to the image of the soldier of Christ, who is put before the new Christian as the model for their imitation. Celts, and especially the Irish, knew what exhilaration came from the life on the battlefield. They, so historians tell us, and the first-century Greek geographer Strabo reinforces this,[89] engaged the enemy with gusto, childlike playfulness and a certain daredevil flamboyance. Vercingetorix was the last Celtic hero on the continent and O'Donoghue has even likened him to the suffering Christ in his defeat and humiliation by the Romans after Caesar's rampage through Gaul.[90] Columbanus, while challenging his hearers, has a warning: 'when you hear of battle, trust that wounds and pursuit are there . . . We must therefore strive first, then stand and apply

---

84. Sermon IX (ed. and trans. Walker, p. 99).
85. Sermon X (ed. and trans. Walker, p. 101).
86. Sermon IX (ed. and trans. Walker, p. 101).
87. Sermon X (ed. and trans. Walker, p. 105).
88. Sermon X (ed. and trans. Walker, p. 105).
89. Tierney, 'The Celtic Ethnography', p. 267 'The whole race . . . is madly fond of war, high-spirited and quick to battle . . . whatever pretext you stir them up, you will have them ready to face danger, even if they have nothing on their side but their own strength and courage.'
90. O'Donoghue, *The Mountain*, p. 9. He says that the statue commemorating this hero is still to be seen in a place called Gergovie near Clermont-Ferrand in central France. Recent archaeological debate regarding monuments at Gergovie is in progress.

ourselves in warfare',[91] otherwise we will not deserve the crown. Before the crown, however, comes the dying to ourselves and the paradoxical notion of 'let us die to ourselves that we may live to Christ. For we cannot live to Him unless first we die to ourselves.'[92] Deeply embedded in the Irish psyche, and being acted out in the monastic theory and *praxis* of the period under discussion, was the whole notion of martyrdom and, as Columbanus exhorts, 'if the opportunity of such blessedness [actual martyrdom] is lacking, yet we shall not lack the mortification of our wills, so that he who lives, let him not live for himself'.[93]

How alien this must have sounded in the Gaul of the seventh century. Yet this was not only the thinking of Columbanus and his followers. Every monastic establishment in Ireland, Iona and Northumbria was inspired by the same notion of *ascesis*: total dedication to God in imitation of Christ who sacrificed himself even to an ignominious death. Why would not the members of monastic communities strive to live this radical doctrine? Such asceticism was a foundational aspect of the Christian monastic choice, both of the hermit and the coenobite. This monastic ideal found a ready response among the Irish and was stamped by them with a particular and distinctive articulation.

The 'Voice' and the 'Fountain of Life': Sermon XIII

Sermon XIII gives an insight into the motivation for these literary compositions. Columbanus says, using the plural of formal address, 'we are not trying to arouse others' inertia so much as our own'.[94] He acknowledges that he has used his own experience, which he calls 'the wretchedness of human life', together with 'divine prophecies' to make the 'previous discourses'.[95] He is not attempting merely to arouse his hearers from their human weakness but, in keeping with the notion of ascetical theology as inner transformation, he is putting before them the radical ideals of perfection using the image of the divine fountain of living water that he sustains throughout this Sermon. A strong and insistent timbre of exhortation is heard as he pleads, 'So still, my dearest brethren, give ear to our words, in the belief that you will hear something needful, and refresh the thirst of your mind from the streams of the divine fountain of which we now wish to speak.'[96]

The Fountain of life 'calls us to himself' so that we can slake our thirst in the 'fullness of our longing, and be gladdened by some pleasure of His loveliness'.[97] No doubt his familiarity with the Scriptures, particularly with the image in John's Gospel of the fountain of living water, would be the inspiration for Columbanus'

91. Sermon II (ed. and trans. Walker, p. 73).
92. Sermon X (ed. and trans. Walker, p. 103).
93. Sermon X (ed. and trans. Walker, p. 103).
94. Sermon XIII (ed. and trans. Walker, p. 115).
95. Sermon XIII (ed. and trans. Walker, p. 115).
96. Sermon XIII (ed. and trans. Walker, p. 117).
97. Sermon XIII (ed. and trans. Walker, p. 117).

use of this image. With a 'voice' almost echoing that of ColumCille, Columbanus, uncharacteristically, continues with the love of a father for very dear children: 'Justly, my brethren, the Fountain of wisdom, the Word of God on high, is to be desired by us, sought after and ever loved, in Whom are hid . . . all the treasures of wisdom and knowledge, which He calls them that thirst to quaff.'[98]

With greater urgency and the power of the poet blending pleading with inspiration he insists, 'For that is lovely to excess which is ever eaten and drunk, and ever hungered and thirsted after, ever tasted and ever desired.'[99]

In words reminiscent of the Song of Songs in the Hebrew Scriptures, Columbanus concludes this Sermon with a mystical prayer that further sets before his companions the ideals of the ascetic life. Maybe the urgency is due to the fact that, if historical evidence is correct, these sermons were written in Milan, and therefore towards the end of his life.[100] The sentiments expressed are evidence of that end of the road, to use his own image, to which each is called and for which they left mother and motherland so long ago. It does seem that the inner transformation, as Columbanus puts it of 'the inner parts of our soul',[101] sought by monastic asceticism, was well on the way to being achieved when he could pray, for himself and his followers:

> Inspire our hearts . . . with the breath of Thy Spirit, and wound our soul with Thy love, that the soul of each one of us may be able to say in truth, Show me Him Whom my soul has loved, for by love am I wounded . . . Blessed is such a soul, which is thus wounded by love; such seeks the Fountain, such drinks though it ever thirsts in drinking, ever quaffs in longing, and it ever drinks in thirsting.[102]

This is the prayer of the true mystic, both experiencing and yet continually longing for the mystical union that is the desired culmination of all genuine Christian *ascesis*.

At the outset of his Sermons, Columbanus claims that he bears 'the responsibility for very needful teaching'.[103] This appears to be part of the motivation for the strength and forcefulness of all of his writings: 'Necessity rather than vainglory compels me to write', he explains to Pope Boniface,[104] and he goes on to say:

> Watch, therefore, I beg you, Pope, watch, and again I say, watch; since perhaps Virgilius was not very vigilant, whom our friends, who lay blame on you, describe as the main stumbling block. Watch first for the Faith, then for bidding works of faith and for spurning vices, since your watchfulness will be the salvation of many, just as on the other side your carelessness will be the destruction of many.[105]

---

98. Sermon XIII (ed. and trans. Walker, p. 119).
99. Sermon XIII (ed. and trans. Walker, p. 119).
100. This is the case according to the latest research with which I am familiar.
101. Sermon XIII (ed. and trans. Walker, p. 121).
102. Sermon XIII (ed. and trans. Walker, p. 121).
103. Sermon I (ed. and trans. Walker, p. 61).
104. Letter 1 (ed. and trans. Walker, p. 55).
105. Letter 1 (ed. and trans. Walker, p. 41). The 'Virgilius' referred to was Pope from 537–55 CE and his vacillation led to the 'Three Chapters' schism.

Who would dare address the bishop of Rome in these challenging words? What would motivate a person to confront queens and kings with the fearlessness evident in Columbanus' writings? It seems that he saw himself as a teacher whose duty it was to put before his followers and, indeed all people, the ideals of a Christian life and point out the pitfalls that were part of what it is to be human. The dilemma about such a conviction is always: when does the purity of the ideal give way to the vanity of the self-important reformer?

Conclusion

Columbanus and ColumCille, the two *'doves'* of the Irish Church, near contemporaries, were inspired by the same monastic ideal: prayer, work and penance in its many forms. They wrote monastic rules and set out penances in the style of the day to encourage their companions to live faithfully the ideals of their newfound Christianity. The sources reveal two different but similar approaches to the life-long task of communing with God in the monastic tradition. Both fervently expected eternal glory as the reward of the asceticism they had enthusiastically embraced.

Columbanus' early life, though written by a near contemporary, was not as detailed as some other hagiographies. Some aspects of his life are clear, but his birth and monastic experience prior to Bangor are vague. However, his activity on the continent is attested to partly by the opposition he aroused from the Merovingian and Gaulish powers and partly by the Roman churchmen on the continent. His monastic establishments at Annegray, Luxeuil and Bobbio saw the ordinary people flocking to be part of the life of the community.

In the life of Columbanus we saw how deeply engraved on the psyche of the Irish was the notion of pilgrimage or *peregrinatio*. It was undertaken as a form of martyrdom in the absence of the ultimate giving of one's life for the faith. Since the clan was the primary unit of identity for the Irish then to choose to leave this group required a powerful motivation indeed. In many cases the motivation was the call to pilgrimage or white martyrdom. In terms of the notion of radicality used throughout this work, this form of mortification could only be truly beneficial if it was deliberately chosen. Chosen, not in the sense of an intention to journey to a place, but in the sense of 'hearing' the call of God to go on pilgrimage: truly an act of faith and undertaken in a spirit of faith, with no notion of the destination. This pilgrimage could also be imposed as a form of penance sometimes by one's *anamchara*. Its rationale has to be seen in the wholehearted response to the *evangelium* that took precedence over all other considerations. This single-minded asceticism demanded the totality of one's commitment.

The influence of Columbanus is attested to by the monastic foundation he established and the places that still bear his name. It is also evident in the scores of monastic foundations inspired by his life or following his monastic rule. The pre-eminence of Luxeuil is attested to by the number of canonized saints that claim the place as their monastic home and the asceticism of Columbanus as the inspiration for their lifestyle. His copious writings include letters to two popes and one pope elect. Some thirteen Sermons have been authenticated as coming from him. Prayers, poems and other literary works give testimony to his prolific output and the way he used many literary devices to enhance his teaching potential. His own motivation is evident in many statements throughout his writing.

Hagiography in that era would not permit any undermining of people honoured as saints. Hence the *Vitae* of history could be seen as fanciful accounts of the lives of the saints. However, as the purpose of such writings was for edification of the readers and a call to emulation, there needs to be some suspension of disbelief on the part of the reader. Sanctity, understood today as the preserve of all those called to holiness, was in the period under discussion attributed to those persons who performed extraordinary feats of penance or miraculous deeds. Such people were thought to be very close to God and in the Irish tradition; they were often called by the word used for a madman.

As an orator of considerable skill Columbanus utilized vivid imagery to drive home his message. Like ColumCille his image of the ideal monk as a *soldier of Christ* had a powerful appeal to the warring Irish. It was heroic but in their cultural experience it was often futile. Proneness to value the individual over the group meant that they were enthusiastic for the battle but had no strategic plan for its prolongation. However, the image of the *roadway* was more sustainable. The road had a beginning, a middle and an end. It was solid even if life on it was less predictable. The *fountain of life* used as an image, borrowing no doubt from the Gospel of John, was not so much a challenge as a reward for those who walked the roadway, fought the good fight and thus were enabled to slake their thirst at the *fountain of life*. Truly this was a reward for the life of ascetic denial.

His asceticism has been seen as extremely harsh and the 'voice' he employed to call others to penance was at times strident and stentorian. Given that he spent some time at Bangor with Comgall as abbot he had to be affected by the harshness of Comgall's rule. His apparent obsession with the Otherworld and eternity has led readers of his Sermons in particular to think him dualistic. His passion for the totality of commitment seems to put him outside the very humanly immediate and incarnational theology of his compatriots, especially ColumCille, the other '*dove*' of the Irish monastic movement. Maybe he was dualistic, but his passion for the *evangelium* could also be the result of his being so captivated by Christ that he wished to share this 'good news' with everyone and so could not disguise his enthusiasm under the cloak of mediocrity.

This same insistence on totality of adherence to his monastic calling led him to challenge the bishops of Rome to reform. Both his letters to prelates and princes, which are extant, reveal a man whose conviction about the *evangelium* urged him not to be fearful. In these letters he calls on the power of his ancestors to support his challenge and in the light of this body of witnesses he feels courageous in speaking. Since both prelate and prince were in positions of leadership they owed it to their subjects to give a good example. The former were responsible for calling other Christians to perfection, and if they were seen to be failing in their duty, Columbanus took it on himself to remind them of their duty. This was in a spirit of brotherly concern and, in the light of the rules analysed in chapter 3, carrying out fraternal correction was seen as a personal responsibility. The opposition he encountered revealed that those being challenged did not seem to share his exalted ideas of leadership. However, this did not deter him. Nor did the fact that they seem not to have replied to his copious correspondence. Maybe a clear conscience is its own reward.

In the life of this other '*dove*' of the Irish Church of the seventh century, the facts remain that Columbanus has continued to be an inspiration for many believers. His extant writings do give insights into the character of the man. His total commitment to the *evangelium*, as understood by him and his contemporaries, took him away from country and clan, and his death in Bobbio meant that, like ColumCille, he never saw his homeland again. His spirit is alive and permeates the present-day missionaries of the Society of St Columban who, like their founder, forsake homeland to bring the Word to foreign parts of the world.[106] This has, in our own day, involved two of the significant components of Irish monastic living, namely pilgrimage for all and martyrdom for some.

---

106. Two diocesan priests, Fathers Galvin and Blowick, founded the Society of St Columban in Ireland in 1918. Originally the group was known as the Maynooth Missionaries. The missionary activity and spirit of Columbanus was integral to the formation of priests called colloquially, the Columbans.

6 Conclusions

> The most characteristic belief of modern man is that history is consciously and voluntarily made by human beings ... This assumption ... distinguishes us from the peoples of ancient cultures ... They saw human life ... and events as the pale shadow of divine realities ... They therefore did not see themselves as making events but as living out divinely established patterns.[1]

In coming to conclusions about the ascetical theology and *praxis* of sixth- to eighth-century Irish monasticism in its cultural context, it seems that the above quotation makes a pertinent point. It holds true that the period under discussion, while not actually classed as an ancient culture, was significantly different from our own time and culture, particularly in its understanding of how its newly-found Christianity was to be lived. The gaps in perception and appreciation between then and now in relation to the foundational issues of monastic rules, penitential practices and lives of the saints, needed highlighting and reappraisal. If the Irish Christians of the sixth to the eighth century did believe that events were manifestations of divine realities (and the lives of the two founders, ColumCille and Columbanus are proof of this conviction) then it could be said that they were steeped in the sacred in all its manifestations. The monastic rules enabled those who intentionally obeyed them to participate in an act of 'living out divinely established patterns'. Herein lay the strong connection of these newly Christian people with their primal past. That humankind in this modern era still sees itself as the centre, focus and maker of history is a tragic misreading of fundamental cultural evolution. While Grant elsewhere holds that in earlier eras 'it was the religious element that conferred reality',[2] this is not the case in our post-Christian age. Therefore to initiate discussion of an epoch that does have the deity as the centre of its emerging self-consciousness makes the task more demanding, but not futile. This study has shown that it was the specific Celtic consciousness of the Irish Christians of the sixth to the eighth century that underpinned their adoption of Christianity and later its articulation in monastic rules, lives of saints and penitentials. The most idiosyncratic aspect of this adoption and articulation was found in their *praxis*. Intrinsic to this consciousness was their strong, if subconscious, identification with their primal past, including an awareness of the omnipresence of the deity in the whole of creation: trees, rivers, waterholes,

---

1.   G. P. Grant, *Philosophy in the Mass Age* (Toronto: Copp Clark, 1959), p. 15.
2.   Grant, *Philosophy*, p. 17.

forest glens, animals and the underworld. Their dependence upon, and respectful attitude to, the spirits who pervaded all creation was easily transferred to the Holy Spirit of the Christian tradition when they began to embrace it some time before the ministry of Patrick. An important part of their indebtedness to their ancestors lay in the druidic tradition and its distinctive form of education. This was so strong in memorization of the stories of the clan, of a belief in conversion and an afterlife that it became the pattern for the beliefs in cosmology and theology that pervaded education in the monastic schools. It seems that the prominence given to the *filid* in Irish culture was a double-edged sword: they held the secrets of the tribe and, at the same time, were able to keep even the kings and other leaders in check by their persuasion and sometimes ridicule. Later 'democratic' Irish church and monastic structures could be seen as a prolongation of this willingness to call even those responsible for the leadership of the group to account.

Another aspect of the Irish consciousness operating in monasticism was the influence of the sagas of heroic deeds, and the imaginative, creative, poetic and paradoxically pragmatic and individualistic approach they brought to tasks, particularly their adoption of Christianity, and its idiosyncratic manifestation in monasticism, that marked this period as the Age of Saints. The genre of story pervasive at the time borrowed heavily from the sagas of Cú Chulainn and the accounts of the war exploits of Vercingetorix and other heroes and heroines of the Irish/Celtic (both Maeve and Boudicca are recalled here) and helped the Irish monk identify with the image of 'soldiers of Christ' that later writers of penitentials and monastic rules utilized. The strongly individualistic proclivity, of vital importance to an understanding of the Irish cultural context, was always balanced in monasticism with the monk's immersion in a community. Withdrawal from the group was justified in terms of pastoral care, penance and its extreme manifestation in martyrdom, but re-membering with the community was one of the strongest reasons for many of the stipulations of both the monastic rules and the earlier penitentials. So the monastic practices of reciting the Canonical Hours throughout the day and night not only kept before the monk the awareness of God and the praise and honour due to the deity, but it brought the brothers together in communion and solidarity. This very coming together in community for prayer was penance for the individualistic Irish monks.

In chapter 1 of this work the foundational aspects of Celtic/Irish consciousness were delineated. The aim of this delineation was to set before the reader those aspects of Irish cultural life in the pre-Christian era that were thought to be basic to an understanding of the later Christian Irish monastic lifestyle. These aspects of Irish culture were mainly deduced from the sagas, Brehon law and structure of society as evidenced in the primary sources. Archaeology, history, anthropology, literature and to a lesser extent linguistics all played a part in revealing what was distinctive about the Irish in the sixth to the eighth century of monasticism. Since Scripture was a foundational component of monasticism, examining how it was understood pointed to the Irish approach that was an historical-literal one, again highlighting the cultural difference from the pervading spiritual-allegorical methodology.

Conclusions

From this survey of some of the aspects of Celtic/Irish consciousness it was concluded that though not all elements of consciousness were treated in chapter 1 there were sufficient to use as a guide for analysing the primary sources of monastic rules, penitentials, *Vitae* and other writings of two prominent founders of Irish monasticism. Archaeology revealed that themes of water and remoteness resonated with the Irish desire for ascetic living. The sagas taught that the individual was of great importance, even in a tightly knit clan society. This emphasis on the individual was an intrinsic part of how the Irish understood history. The impact of being a warring nation meant that later in the penitentials and monastic rules the image of the soldier of Christ would be sufficient to rouse them to deeds of heroism in the spiritual life.

Chapter 2 aimed at using the primary sources of the penitentials of three monastic founders, Vinnian, Columbanus, Cummean, as well as the ecclesiastical *Canones Hibernenses* to reveal the ascetical theology and *praxis* of the monks of the period. It also employed the evidence of distinctively Irish practice of commutation of penances to the same end. An examination of asceticism thought to be a form of madness, particularly as some of the early Irish sagas had stories of similar behaviours as madness, helped to clarify the notion of ascetical theology being used in this work and highlighted its radicality in the monastic context. By an explanation of the texts of the penitentials (exegesis) the distinctively Irish form of asceticism was revealed. The fundamental principle – that of *contraries* by John Cassian – previously elaborated on was ultimately borrowed from the Pythagoreans and was based upon a medical model. This gave rise to the basic purpose, in the Irish Christian context, of the penitentials as healing the sinner and his rehabilitation both personal and eventually communal.

From this exegesis one conclusion about the penitentials was that personal growth and inner transformation were primary outcomes of penitential practices. Human well-being was reiterated in many of the suggested injunctions emphasizing the oft-repeated principle that the individual and his/her inner conversion was paramount. It is a contention of this study that the different effects of conversion and the varying degrees of radicality were due to the different expectations of the two groups, viz., monks and laity. Again, the calling to account referred to earlier, understood as an important component of the relationship between the *anamchara* and the soul-friend, is here intrinsic not only to Irish monasticism but to the whole private penitential system begun and promulgated by the Irish.

A further conclusion deduced from an analysis of the penitentials as primary sources was that the emphasis was clearly on love of God and neighbour with one's whole heart. Distinctive to the Celts of Ireland was the practice of commuting penances, evidence of the intention of healing rather than punishment. Lengthy penances were commuted to a shorter time with more intensity. That they existed at all could also indicate that, again, the individual person and his rehabilitation and restoration to the community were of prime importance, and that the sooner the penance was executed the sooner the sinner could be restored to the community and to worship with the group. In an era when most people were struggling with the twin demands of ancient loyalties to primal religious beliefs and the new call of Christianity, persons who took up the challenge of the latter wholeheartedly, manifested in the ascetical practices of penance, were thought, even by their peers, to be living radically. While an intuitive sense of theology and asceticism is universal in religious experience, their articulation and *praxis* in Irish monasticism revealed an orthodox theology but an idiosyncratic *praxis*.

In chapter 3 the monastic rules of Ailbe, Ciarán, Comgall, ColumCille, Columbanus and Carthage were treated in their historical and chronological sequence with the aim of distilling the ascetical theology therein. Another aim was to see if they conformed to the assumptions in chapter 1 that the monastic *praxis* of the period manifested a distinctively Irish cultural consciousness. Each rule was analysed historically, linguistically (briefly) and according to the ascetical theology and *praxis* evident in its regulations, and the exegetical exercise revealed that there was a great deal of dependence by later formulators of rules on earlier ones. It was seen that these rules initially were merely principles for living according to the *evangelium*. The rules, like the Gospels, gave only a guiding principle, succinctly expressed as love of God and neighbour as oneself. Since the penitentials, treated in chapter 2, also were based on ascetical theology, some comparison was made with the images used in both these primary sources (the image of the soldier of Christ). Aspects of asceticism were common in both chapters (the central place of the heart and tears). The heart played a major role in many of the stipulations in monastic regulations.

One had to conclude after analysing these rules that obedience was the virtue *par excellence*: they enjoined obeying the abbot in the same spirit as one would obey Christ. Obedience was also due to one's *anamchara* or soul-friend, without whom no personal decisions were taken. As the primary focus of the monastic life is communion with God, then the Canonical Hours, drawing the monks to prayer seven times by day and night, were also part of the virtue of obedience. ColumCille, though his rule was for the use of a single monk, laid great stress on one of the most important aspects of Irish monasticism: that is, the interlinked concepts of martyrdom and pilgrimage, twin foundations of the distinctiveness of monasticism in Ireland. To go on pilgrimage, in obedience to the call of God, was a prime form of asceticism, for it took one away from one's connection with *Túatha* or clan and ensured that one rely solely on God. Pilgrimage took the pilgrim to the place of God's choosing: the pilgrim often set off in a curragh with nothing but the wind and the will of God to determine the destination. What mattered most was not a destination but that the movement away from homeland was *peregrinatio pro Christo*. So while the fact of pilgrimage as martyrdom was deeply engrained in the Irish psyche, its practice led to the spreading of Irish monasticism to the continent in a response to the *evangelium*.

Chapter 3 also concluded that living according to the monastic rules was transformative: the inner person was transformed in an atmosphere of faith and as a result of faith. No one could be part of the monastic institution by accident, or by the will of another, though in later centuries this did occur. The demands of this ascetical lifestyle, spelt out both in the monastic rules and penitentials, were such that the person adopting it intended to live this commitment. Irish monasticism of this period was not a matter of cognitive assent to sterile principles, but a deliberate personal response to an incarnated God who, in the person of Jesus, walked the way of obedience and mortification even to death.

In chapters 4 and 5 the lives and writings of ColumCille and Columbanus were submitted to the exegetical process. Again the aim in looking at these lives was to see how the Irish culture and ascetical principles were manifested. Since hagiography, not history is the genre of these lives then an initial historico-cultural setting was used. A further aim of using these particular primary sources was, as in the chapters on the monastic rules and penitentials, to ascertain if the work was evidence for a radical living of the *evangelium* by the Irish monks of the sixth to the eighth century. ColumCille's biographer, Adomnán, would have us believe that it was only religion that motivated him but the evidence of the *Life* confirms that he was motivated by both religion and the traditions coming from his nobility, and experienced equal success in responding to both of them.

A reader of ColumCille's life had to conclude that the affectivity with which he treated his monks and the many visitors who went to Iona sets him apart from his near namesake, Columbanus. Only in the recounting of his dying does Jonas' *Life of Columbanus* give any hint of the affection Columbanus might have had for his monks. This bond of affection between ColumCille and his followers does not, however, detract from the radical clarion call of his choice to leave country and clan. For ColumCille this pilgrimage was more significant than for Columbanus, as the former was of royal lineage and was eligible for the High Kingship of Ireland. Though he challenged kings, druids and ordinary people with persuasion, his *ascesis* and lifestyle were more gentle and balanced than those of his near contemporary on the continent. This is not to say it was less radical. It was simply more human in its radicality. Finally ColumCille's voice, heard in the tripartite structure of Adomnán's *Life*, includes many miracles reminiscent of those performed by Christ in the Christian Scriptures. This aspect of his life alone reinforced the belief that this man, their abbot, was close to God and, though gone from them in person, was somehow among them and could still perform miracles in response to their prayer.

Columbanus' 'voice' was also heard clearly and unadulterated in his extant writings, including, letters, sermons, monastic rules, penitential and poems. In using only the sermons it was intended to concentrate on one of his writings and so distil more clearly the ascetical theology. The accumulation of evidence from previous primary sources obtained through analysis and contextual discussion, confirmed that the exegesis of this last resource led the reader to the conclusion that the abbot Columbanus was a fiery reformer who saw his task as teaching all people – popes, kings, courtiers, country folk and first and foremost himself and his monks – about how the *evangelium* was to be lived in accordance with a consciousness that was specifically Irish. True to the Celtic spirit that underpinned this age, his exhortations were vivid in language and imagery, most particularly in the images of warfare and the roadway. It was clear that he was uncompromising in his insistence on radical living, deliberately chosen and faithful to the end, for his monks and himself.

Of his 13 sermons, few would be called soothing: inspirational yes, but also challenging and confrontational. The *anvil*, the image used by Ailbe, could equally be the source of Columbanus' insistence on the strength needed for fidelity to one's commitment. The *Fountain of Life* was that reward for a life of fidelity on the *Roadway*. Both these images were constantly used by Columbanus. What gave added weight to his writing was the fact that Columbanus firmly believed that he was challenging himself as well as his hearers.

The energy and focus evident in these sermons spoke about a person of great strength and single-mindedness. The dispersed nature of his monastic foundations on the continent, some of which include Luxeuil, Fontaine, Annegray and Bobbio, would put to shame later missionaries who did not have to endure the inconvenience of travel on foot. The *Life* is evidence of how he antagonized rulers of Church and empires and finally sought refuge in Bobbio, where he eventually died and was buried. Like ColumCille his choice of *peregrinatio pro Christo* meant that his identity with clan and motherland was to be severed early in his monastic life and revealed that the radical call was possible if one had one's focus clear.

This study presupposed that change in people's outlook on the world and investigation of that change are integral aspects of an historical study. The movement from primal religion to Christianity within the lives of the sixth- to eighth-century Irish, on the edge of the known world, may be traced by the plethora of literature that is extant. Developing perceptions of cosmology, philosophy and theology, the compost from which change draws its nourishment and subsequent growth, can itself manifest change. There was gradual evolution in the Irish attitude to cosmology. The philosophical amalgam of Christian and primal religion that emerged and became articulated in a distinct, while orthodox, theology gave rise to a distinctive monastic *praxis*.

Therefore, the early medieval Irish response to the *evangelium* was definitely lived within the ambit of their culture. It was radical in that the monasticism of the Age of the Saints was attractive to both cleric and lay person but was lived by the former in a way that transformed them into beacons for others. The ascetical practices laid down for all sinners contained different expectations for clerical and lay members of the monastic enclosures. Some of them whose lives were written for the edification of the Church may not have been all that different from the vast mass of those who inhabited the monastic settlements. Politics may have played a part in who was chosen to be remembered. However, this does not detract from the motivation of the many to live the gospel fully and who embarked on the *peregrinatio pro Christo*. In the words of Nouwen, this lifestyle of monks, apart from enabling the individual to be personally transformed, ideally spoke of the God who could fill the emptiness felt by many. Those committed to monastic living 'did not fill their lives with events, people and actions for which they [would] be remembered' . . . but in this [seeming emptiness] believed that God [would] be recognized as the source of all human thoughts and actions'.[3] The monastic lifestyle, with its prominent persons, rules, penitentials and asceticism that this work has discussed have the perennial value of witnessing to ideals that challenge a world of ambiguities.

Radical living of the *evangelium* is possible in every age. It requires that one's vision of the road be focused. There needs to be a clarity about the omega point of one's life and one needs to believe that one never travels alone. Rules are sometimes important. Self-denial and other ascetical practices, however one understands them, are imperative. Tolstoy may have said 'The meaningless absurdity of life is the only incontestable knowledge accessible to man',[4] but it is the contention of this work that humankind is not merely a victim of surrounding forces. Each person can and indeed must make choices within the limitations of intellectual capacity, cultural environment and beliefs. People who go before us in history and live by their convictions, regardless of how these differ from our own, do influence future generations regardless of their specific intention to do so. This study, therefore, contended and demonstrated that the Irish monastic tradition of the sixth to the eighth century was indeed radical in how it articulated and lived its asceticism.

Go m-baḋ buan beaṗla ṗaoi aguṡ naoim.

"May the tongue of Sage and Saint be lasting." [5]

---

3. H. J. Nouwen, *Clowning in Rome: Reflections on Solitude, Celibacy, Prayer and Contemplation* (New York: Image Books, 1972), p. 48.
4. Dodds, *Pagan*, p. 1.
5. Healy, *Ireland' Ancients*, p. vii.

APPENDICES

Appendix I

A

Crinog of melodious song,
No longer young, but bashful-eyed,
As when we roved Niall's Northern Land,
Hand in hand, or side by side.

Peerless maid, whose looks ran o'er
With the lovely lore of Heaven,
By when I slept in dreamless joy
A gentle boy of summers seven.

We dwelt in Banva's broad domain,
Without one stain of soul or sense;
While still mine eye flashed forth on thee
Affection free of all offence.

To meet thy counsel quick and just,
Our faithful trust responsive springs;
Better they wisdom's searching force
Than any smooth discourse with kings.

In sinless sisterhood with men,
Four times since then, hast thou been bound,
Yet not one rumour of ill-fame
Against thy name has travelled round.

At last, their weary wonderings o'er,
To me once more thy footsteps tend;
The gloom of age makes dark thy face,
Thy life of grace draws near its end.

O, faultless one and very dear,
Unstinted welcome here is thine.
Hell's haunting dread I ne'er shall feel,
So thou be kneeling at my side.

Thy blessed fame shall ever bide,
For far and wide thy feet have trod.
Could we their saintly track pursue,
We yet should view the Living God.

You leave a pattern and bequest
To all who rest upon the earth –
A life-long lesson to declare
Of earnest prayer the precious worth.

God grant us peace and joyful love!
And may the countenance of Heaven's King
Beam on us when we leave behind
Our bodies blind and withering.

Source: K. Meyer (ed.), *Selections From Ancient Poetry* (London: Constable and Company Ltd, 1913, 2nd edn), pp. 37–88.

Appendices

B

The letters of the Ogham alphabet are divided into four groups of five letters each, twenty in all. Taking the angular edge of the upright pillar to be represented by a straight line the following is the score:

Besides these we find a few diphthongal symbols, but apparently of a later date.[1]

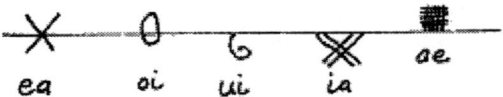

The following is the name of ColumCille written in Ogham; reading from the bottom of the page to the top, with the Ogham script along the fold (represented by a thin line) on the page.

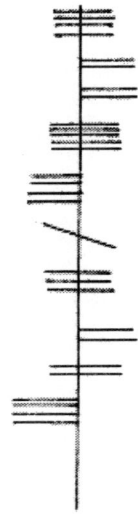

---

1. J. Healy, *Ireland's Ancient Schools and Scholars* (Dublin: Sealy, Bryers and Walker, 1890), p. 15.

C

The Bishops Licinius, Melanius and Eustochius to the Priest Lovocatus and Catihenus, Their Most Blessed Lords and Brothers in Christ.

We have learned through the report of that venerable man the priest Spertatus that, bearing certain altars [portable altars], you do not cease from making a circuit of the dwellings in the territories of different cities, and that you presume to celebrate masses there with women, whom you call *conhospitae* [joint hostesses] and whom you admit to the divine sacrifice to such an extent that while you distribute the eucharist they hold the chalices in your presence and presume to administer the blood of Christ to the people.

The novelty and unheard-of superstition of this action grieves us to no small extent because such a horrible sect, which demonstrably never has existed in Gaul, seems to be emerging in our times. The oriental fathers called it Pepodianism on account of the fact that Pepodius was the originator of this schism. Because these people presume to have women as their associates in the divine sacrifice, the fathers prescribed that whoever wished to cling to this error was to be rendered separated from ecclesiastical communion.[2]

2. L. Duchesne, 'Lovocat et Catihern, prêtres Bretons de temps de Melaine', *Revue de Bretagne et de Vendée* 7 (1885), pp. 5–18.

D Book of Kells[3]

3.   P. Brown (ed.), *The Book of Kells*, selected by P. Brown, librarian of Trinity College, Dublin (London: Thames and Hudson, 1981), p. 19.

E Abbots of Iona[4]

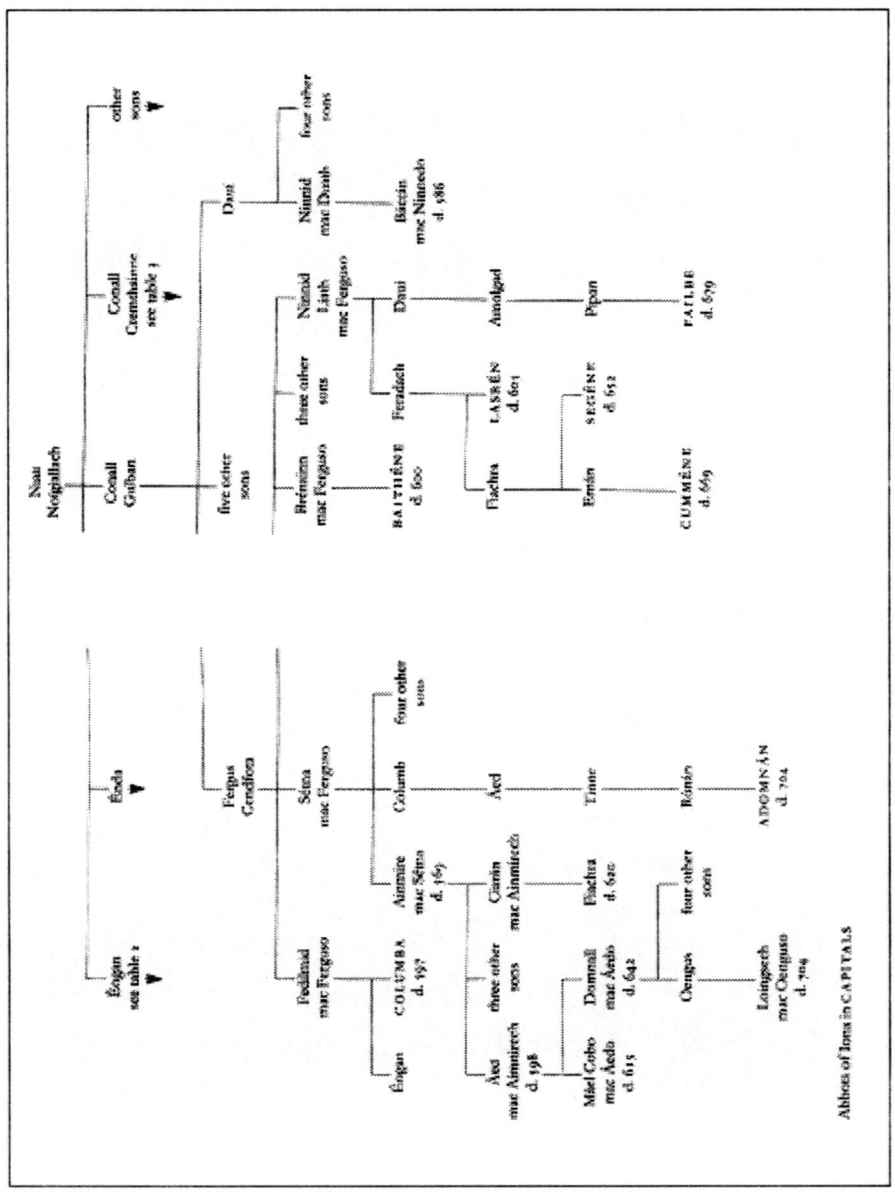

4. Sharpe, *Adomnán's*, Preface.

Appendix II

A Rule from Bangor – Antiphony of Bangor.[5]

VERSICULI FAMILIÆ BENCHUIR.

multitudinem magnitudinis tuæ te laudamus, Domine, gratia laudationis ostensæ [Fol. 28v.] immolatione per psalterium, mortificatione per tympanum, congregatione per chorum, exultatione per organum, jubilatione per cymbalum, ut semper misericordiam tuam habere mereamur, Christe, Salvator mundi, Qui cum æterno Patre vivis, &c.

[94.] ✠ SUPER CANTEMUS DOMINO.

Domine, qui Cinchrim fugientes tueris bis senas per invisa tribus æmulum itinera, prius fluctibus in binis montium utrimque redactis celsorum, ceu, jugis abrupte arentibus talis æquore murum, quasi et de petra lymphas producens; mergatur ergo ut olim piorum supplicium hostis æterni, quæsumus, statores curruum, quod est cujus affatus, [Fol. 29r.] actusque cum cogitatu celeri nequam sit Pharaoni; rex Israelem verum, quæ unda salvat, ut Christo carmina canat per sæcula, Qui cum Patre vivit, &c.

[Fol. 30r.]
[95.] VERSICULI FAMILIÆ BENCHUIR.

   i. Benchuir bona regula,
      Recta, atque divina,
      Stricta, sancta, sedula,
      Summa, justa, ac mira.

   ii. Munther Benchuir beata,
      Fide fundata certa,
      Spe salutis ornata,
      Caritate perfecta.

   iii. Navis numquam turbata,
      Quamvis fluctibus tonsa,
      Nuptiis quoque parata
      Regi Domino sponsa.

   iv. Domus deliciis plena,
      Super petram constructa,
      Necnon vinea vera
      Ex Ægypto transducta.

   v. Certe civitas firma,
      Fortis, atque unita,
      Gloriosa, ac digna,
      Supra montem posita.

   vi. Arca Cherubin tecta,
      Omni parte aurata,
      Sacro-sanctis reperta,
      Viris quatuor portata.

   vii. Christo regina apta,
      Solis luce amicta,
      Simplex, simulque docta,
      Undecumque invicta.

   viii. Vere regalis aula,
      Variis gemmis ornata,
      Gregisque Christi caula
      Patre summo servata.

   ix. Virgo valde fecunda
      Hæc, et mater intacta,
      Læta ac tremebunda,
      Verbo Dei subacta.

[Fol. 30v.]
   x. Cui vita beata
      Cum perfectis futura,
      Deo Patre parata
      Sine fide mansura.

      Benchuir bona regula.

[96.] COLLECTIO SUPER HOMINEM QUI HABET DIABOLUM.

Domine, sancte Pater, omnipotens æterne Deus, expelle diabolum et gentilitatem ab homine isto, de capite, de capillis, de cerbero, de vertice, de fronte, de oculis, de auribus, de naribus, de labiis, de ore, de lingua, de sublingua, de faucibus, de gutture, de collo, de corde, de corpore toto, de omnibus compaginibus membrorum suorum, intus et deforis, de ossibus, de venis, de nervis, de sanguine, de sensu, de cogitationibus, de verbis, de omnibus operibus suis, de virtute, [Fol. 31r.] de omni conversatione ejus, hic;

---

5.   F. E. Warren (ed.), *Antiphony of Bangor: An Irish Manuscript in the Ambrosian Library of Milan, Parts 1 and 11* (London: Harrison and Sons, 1895).

Appendix III

III A

The Rule of Ailbe
The Rule of Colmcille
The Rule of Comgal

The Rule of Ciarán
Riagail na Manach Liat
Riagail Chormaic
The Rule of the Celi De
Prose Rule of the Celi De, The Monastery of Tallaght

III B

Rule of Brigit	+532
Rule of St Mochta	+543
Rule of Brendan of Clonfert	+577
Rule of Lua (Molua)	+600
Rule of St Coemgenus	+618
Rule of St Laisren (Molaisse)	+639
Rule of St Adamnán	+704
Rule of St Coman	+747[6]

III C[7]

Rule of Ciarán	Clonmacnois	680	16	verses
Rule of Grey Monks	Glendalough?	680	10	verses
Rule of Comgall	Bangor	750	28	verses
Rule of Ailbe	Emly	750	56	verses
Rule of ColmCille	Kells	820	29	paragraphs
Rule of Carthage	Lismore	850	140	verses
Rule of Cormac	Castledermot	900	14	verses
Rule of Celi De	Tallaght	900	65	verses

6. Ó Maidín, *The Monastic*, p. 24.
7. De Bhaldraithe, 'Irish Monastic Rules', p. 83.

III D[8]

St Ailbe	+541	Imliuch(Emly)	276 line poem
St Ciaran	+548	Clonmacnois?	64 lines
St Comhghall	+552	Beannchuir (Bangor)	144 lines
St ColumCille	+592	Iona	3 pages
St Carthach	+636	Raithin/Lis Mor	580 lines
St Maelruain	+787	Tamhlacht (Tallaght)	9 small quarto pages
Celidhe De (Culdees)			
Grey Monks			
Cormac Mac Cuilennain	+903	Cashel	56 lines

III E

Now two maidens with pointed breasts used to lie with him every night that the battle with the devil might be the greater for him. And it was proposed to accuse him on that account. So Brenainn came to test him, and Scothin said, 'Let the cleric lie in my bed tonight.' Saith he. So when he reached the hour of resting the girls came in to the house wherein Brenainn, with their lapfuls of glowing embers in their chasubles: and the fire burnt them not, and they spill (the embers) in front of Brenainn and go into the bed to him.
'What is this?', asks Brenainn.
'Thus it is that we do every night,' say the girls. They lie down with Brenainn, and no wise could he sleep with longing.
'That is imperfect, O cleric,' say the girls. 'He who is here every night feels nothing at all. Why goest thou not, O cleric, into the tub (of cold water) if it is be easier for thee? 'Tis often that the cleric, even Scothin, visits it.'
'Well,' says Brenainn, 'it is wrong for us to make this test, for he is better than we are.'
Thereafter they make their union and their covenant, and they part *feliciter*.[9]

---

8. O'Curry, *Lectures*, p. 374.
9. W. Stokes (ed.), *Filire Oengusso Celi De: The Martyrology of Oengus the Culdee* (Dublin: Institute for Advanced Studies, 1984), p. 41. There is a copy of this in R. E. Reynolds, *Virgines Subintroductae* in Celtic Christianity', *HTR* 61 (1968), pp. 547–66 (229).

III F
I have pondered on victorious Fionnbarr
whose mind was lofty,
who denied the raging princess,
the daughter of Dangail d'Uib Ennaig.

I have thought on Ciaran of Cluan,
much have I heard of his piety,
who denied Aillind the daughter of Bran,
and slept beneath . . .
(the Irish reads 'of cigibh' O'Faolian speculates
that among other meanings this may
read, 'beneath a woman's breasts').

I thought also of the great piety
of Scuitin Maircce Moir
who used to lie, God will it in his love,
between the white paps of women.

And I thought of Columcille
who for the love of the King of Truth
denied for all her great fame
(the pleasure of) Aidan's fair daughter.

I recalled Patrick and his austerities
the chief apostle of Erin
who rejected the blazing brightness
of the maiden of the valiant Milchu.[10]

---

10. S. O'Faoláin, 'Éirigh, a ingen an righ', *RC* 47 (1926), pp. 197–200. There is a reference to this same poem in Reynolds, '*Virgines Subintroductae*', fn 73.

Appendices 191

III G Island of Hinba with ruins of a beehive cell

III H
View from the top of the stairs leading up to the beehive cells on Skellig Michael

192   *Early Irish Monasticism*

Appendix IV

A

Stone found in Elgin's ancient churchyard. On the one side is a Pictish battle scene and on the reverse is a Christian cross

B
'Monument' in Westport, Ireland, with similar pagan and Christian markings

194   Early Irish Monasticism

Appendix V

Map showing the journeys of Columbanus on the continent and the many places called after him[11]

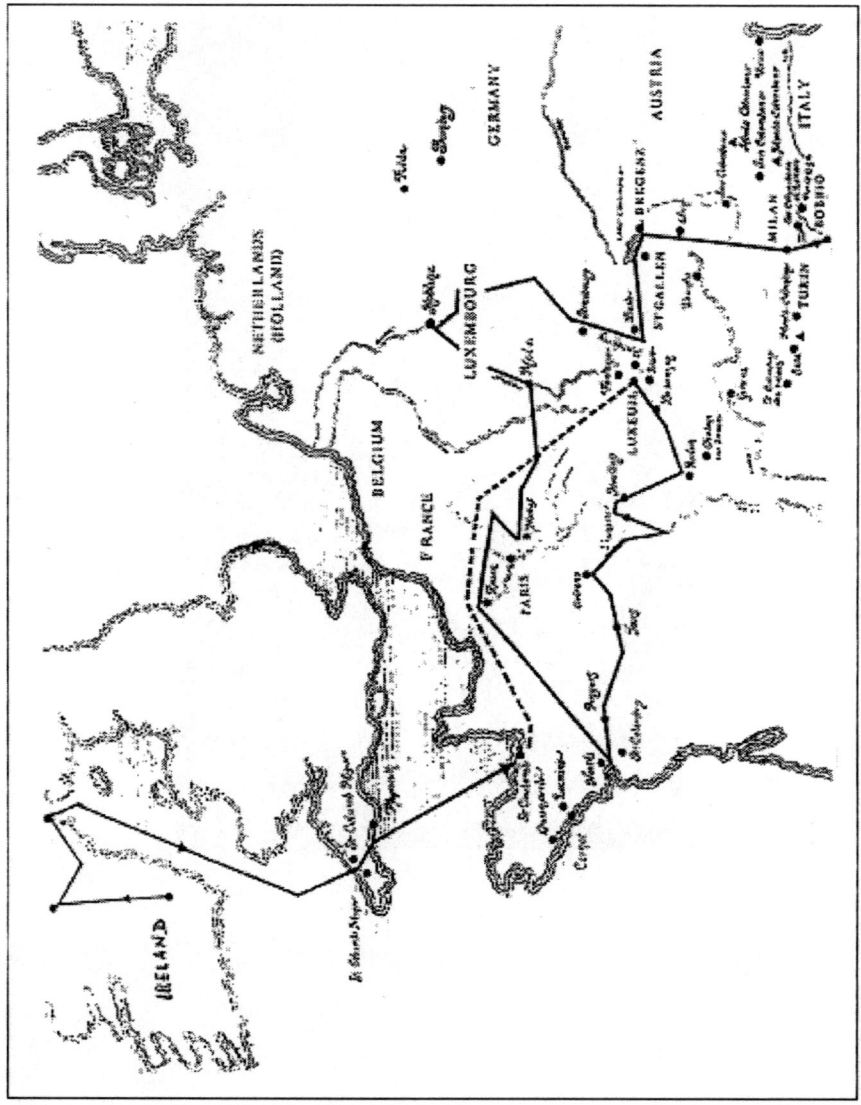

11. T. O'Fiaich, *Columbanus in His Own Words* (Dublin: Veritas, 1974), p. 49. Maps and diagrams were executed by Steven Hope.

BIBLIOGRAPHY

Primary Sources

Anderson, A. O., *Early Sources of Scottish History A.D. 500 to 1286* (Vol. 1; London: Oliver and Boyd, 1st edn,1922).
Anderson, A. O. and M. O. Anderson, *Adomnán's Life of Columba* (London: Thomas Nelson and Sons, 1st edn, 1961).
Bastable, P., *The Letters of St Patrick-Daniel Connelly* (Maynooth: An Sagart, 1st edn, 1993).
Best, R. and H. Lawler, *The Martyrology of Tallaght* (London: Harrison and Sons Ltd, 1931).
Bieler, L. (ed.), *The Irish Penitentials* (Vol. 5; Dublin: Institute for Advanced Studies, 1963).
Bright, W., *The Canons of the First Four Councils: Nicea, Constantinople, Ephesus, Chalcedon (*Oxford: Clarendon Press, 2nd edn, 1892).
Cusack, M. E., *The Trias Thaumaturgia, or Three Wonder-Working Saints of Ireland* (London: J. G. Murdock, 1890s).
Duchesne, L., 'Lovocat et Catihern, prêtres Bretons de temps de Melaine', *Revue de Bretagne et de Vendée* 7 (1885), pp. 5–18.
Fowler, J. T. (ed.), *Adamnani Vita S. Columba* (Oxford: Clarendon Press, 1st edn, 1894).
Gwynn, E. J. (ed.), *Liber Ardmachanus – The Book of Armagh* (Dublin: Hodges Figgis and Co. Ltd, 1913).
Haddan, A. and W. Stubbs (eds), *Councils and Ecclesiastical Documents Relating to Great Britain and Ireland* (Vol. 1; Oxford: Clarendon, 1869).
Hennessy, W. M. (ed.), *Annals of Ulster* (Vol. I; Dublin: A. Thom and Co., 1887).
Huyshe, W. (ed.), *The Life of St Columba (Columb-kille) A.D. 52–597* (trans. from the Latin; London: Routledge & Sons Ltd, 1905).
Lapidge, M. and R. Sharpe, *A Bibliography of Celtic-Latin Literature 400–1200* (Dublin: Royal Irish Academy, 1985).
Lawler, R. (ed.), *The Book of Mulling* (Edinburgh: David Douglass, 1897).
MacAirt, S. and G. MacNiocaill (eds), *The Annals of Ulster* (Part I, 7 vols; Dublin: Dublin Institute for Advanced Studies, 1st edn, 1983).
MacEclaise (ed.), 'Rule of Carthage', *IER*, 4th ser., 27 (1910), pp. 495–517.
McNamara, M., *Glossa in Psalmos: The Hiberno-latin Gloss on the Psalms of Codex Palatinus Latinus 68* (Vatican City: Biblioteca Apostolica Vaticana, 1st edn, 1986).

McNeill, J. T., 'The Celtic Penitentials – Part I', *RC* 39 (1923), pp. 256–300.
—— 'The Celtic Penitentials – Part II', *RC* 39 (1923), pp. 51–103.
—— 'The Celtic Penitentials – Part III', *RC* 40 (1923), pp. 132–319.
—— 'The Celtic Penitentials – Part IV', *RC* 40 (1923), pp. 320–41.
Meyer, K. (ed.), *Cain Adamnáin: An Old-Irish Treatise on The Law of Adomnan* (Oxford: Clarendon Press, 1st edn, 1905).
Meyer, K. (ed.), *Selections from Ancient Irish Poetry* (London: Constable & Co., 1913), p. 37.
Moran, P. F. (ed.), *Acta Sancti Brendani: Original Latin Documents Connected with the Life of Saint Brendan* (Dublin: W. B. Kelly, 1st edn, 1872).
Murphy, D. (ed.), *The Annals of Clonmacnoise: Being the Annals of Ireland from the Earliest Period to AD 1408* (Felinfach: Llanerch, 1993).
O'Keeffe, J. G., 'The Rule of Patrick', *Eriu* 1/2 (1904/5), pp. 216–24.
—— '*Cain Domnaig*: The Epistle Concerning Sunday', *Eriu* 1/2 (1904/5), p. 101.
O'Kelleher, A. and G. Schoepperle (eds), *Betha Colaim Chille – Life of ColumCille* (Illinois: University of Illinois, 1st edn, 1918).
Ó Maidín, U. (ed.), *The Celtic Monk: Rules and Writings of Early Irish Monks* (Massachusetts: Cistercian Publications, 1st edn, 1996).
O'Meara, J. J. and B. Naumann (eds), *Latin Scripts and Letters AD 400–900* (Leiden: E. J. Brill, 1st edn, 1976).
O'Muraile, N., 'The Autograph Manuscripts of The Annals of the Four Masters', *Celtica* XIX (1987), pp. 75–95.
O'Neill, J., 'The Rule of Ailbe of Emly', *Eriu* 3/4 (1907/10), pp. 92–115.
OhAodha, D. (ed.), *Bethu Brigte* (Dublin: Institute for Advanced Studies, 1st edn, 1978).
Plummer, C. (ed.), *Vitae Sanctorum Hiberniae* (2 vols, London: Oxford University Press, 1st edn, 1910).
Reeves, W. (ed.), *Adomnán's Life of Columba* (Lampeter: Llanerch, 1st edn, 1988).
Sharpe, R. (ed.), *Adomnán's Life of St Columba* (Middlesex: Penguin, 1st edn, 1995).
Sheehy, M. (ed.), *Pontifica Hibernica: Medieval Papal Chancery Documents Concerning Ireland 640–1261* (Vol. I; Dublin: M. H. Gill and Son Ltd, 1962).
Stevenson, J. (ed.), *Creeds, Councils and Controversies: Documents Illustrating the History of the Church AD 337–461* (London: SPCK, 2nd edn, 1989).
Stokes, W. (ed.), The Transactions of the Royal Irish Academy: The Calendar of Oengus (Dublin: The Royal Irish Academy, 1st edn, 1880).
—— (ed.), *Anecdota Oxoniensia: Lives of the Saints from the Book of Lismore* (Oxford: Clarendon, 1st edn, 1890).
—— (ed.), *Martyrology of Gorman* (London: Harrison and Sons Ltd, 1st edn, 1895).
—— 'The Bodleian Amra Choluimb Chille', *RC* 20 (1899), pp. 30–55.
—— (ed.), *Filire Oengusso Celi De: The Martyrology of Oengus the Culdee* (Dublin: Institute for Advanced Studies, 1984).

—— (ed.), *The Annals of Tigernach* (Vol. 1, Felinfach: Llanerch, 1993).
—— (ed.), *The Annals of Tigernach* (Vol. 2, Felinfach: Llanerch, 1993).
Stokes, W. and J. Strachan (eds), *Thesaurus Palaeohibernicus: A Collection of Old-Irish Glosses Scholia Prose and Verse* (Vol. 1, Cambridge: The University Press, 1st edn, 1901).
—— (eds), *Thesaurus Paleohibernicus: A Collection of Old-Irish Glosses Scholia Prose and Verse (*Vol. 2. Cambridge: University Press, 1st edn, 1903).
Strachan, J., 'Cormac's Rule', *Eriu* 1/2 (1904/5), pp. 62–68.
—— 'Two Monastic Rules: Riagul Chiarai Annso; Riagul Na Manach Liaath Annso', *Eriu* 1/2 (1904/5), pp. 227–9.
—— 'An Old-Irish Metrical Rule', *Eriu* 1/2 (1904/5), pp. 191–208.
Tirechan. 'Memoirs of St Patrick', *EHR* 17 (1902), pp. 235–46.
Walker, G. S. M. (ed.), *Scriptores Latine Hiberniae: Sancti Columbani Opera* (Dublin: Institute of Advanced Studies, 1957).
Warner, G. F. (ed.), *The Stowe Missal* (2 vols; Dublin: The Royal Irish Academy, 1st edn, 1915).
Warren, F. E. (ed.), *The Antiphony of Bangor: An Irish Manuscript in the Ambrosian Library of Milan – Part I* (London: Harrison and Sons, 1893).
—— (ed.), *The Antiphony of Bangor: An Irish Manuscript in the Ambrosian Library of Milan – Part II (*London: Harrison and Sons, 1895).
Wiles, M. and M. Santer (eds), *Documents in Early Christian Thought* (Notre Dame: University Press, 1975).
Wilson, J. (ed.), *St Columban by Jonas* (private collection), 1950s.

Secondary Sources

Books

Ireland in Past Times: An Historical Retrospect, Ecclesiastical and Civil (2 vols; Dublin: Dugdale. B and Tims. R, 1st edn, 1826).
Achelis, H. *'Agapetae' Encyclopedia of Religion and Ethics*, Vol. 1 (Edinburgh: T&T Clark, 1st edn, 1908).
Addleshaw, G. W., *The Pastoral Structure of the Celtic Church in Northern Britain* (York: St Anthony's Press, 1st edn, 1973).
Alexander, L., *The Ancient British Church and Iona* (London:The Religious Tract Society, 1860s).
Allen, J. R., *The High Crosses of Ireland* (Felinfach: Llanerch, 2nd edn, 1992).
—— *The Romano-British Period and Celtic Monuments* (facsimile repr. Felinfach: Llanerch, 2nd edn, 1992).
Allison, T., *English Religious Life in the Eighth Century* (New York: AMS, 2nd edn, 1971).
Baker, D., *Sanctity and Secularity: The Church and the World* (Oxford: Basil Blackwell, 1973).
Baldick, R. and B. Jones (eds), *Lives of the Saints* (Middlesex: Penguin, 1st edn, 1981).

Bamford, C. *The Voice of the Eagle: The Heart of Celtic Christianity* (New York: Lindisfarne Press, 1990).
Barley, M. and R. Hanson (eds), *Christianity in Britain 300–700* (Vol. 1; University of Nottingham: Leicester University Press, 1967).
Baur, F. C., *The Church History of the First Three Centuries* (2 vols; London: Williams and Norgate, 3rd edn, 1879).
Benko, S., *Pagan Rome and The Early Christians* (Indiana: Indiana University Press, 1986).
Beresford-Ellis, P., *Celt and Saxon: The Struggle for Britain AD 410–937* (London: Constable, 1993).
—— *Celtic Inheritance* (London: Muller, Bond and White, 1st edn, 1985).
—— *Dictionary of Celtic Mythology* (London: Constable, 1992).
Berger, P., *The Social Reality of Religion* (Norwich: Fletcher and Son, 2nd edn, 1973).
Berry, T., *The Great Work: Our Way into the Future* (New York: Bell and Tower, 1999).
Bettenson, H., *The Later Christian Fathers* (London: Oxford University Press, 2nd edn, 1977).
Bieler, L., *Ireland Harbinger of the Middle Ages* (Switzerland: Walter-Verlag Ag Olten, 1966).
—— *The Life and Legend of St Patrick* (Dublin: Clonmore and Reynolds Ltd, 1st edn, 1949).
—— *St Patrick and the Coming of Christianity, A History of Irish Catholicism* (Dublin: M. H. Gill and Son, 1st edn, 1967).
Bevans, S., *Models of Contextual Theology* (New York: Orbis Books, 1995).
Binchy, D. A., *Studies in Early Irish Law* (Dublin: Hodges, Figgis and Co., 1st edn, 1936).
Bitel, L. M., *The Isle of Saints: Monastic Settlement and Christianity in Early Ireland* (Ithaca: Cornell University Press, 1st edn, 1990).
Blair, J., and J. Sharpe (eds), *Pastoral Care Before the Parish* (Leicester: Leicester University Press, 1992).
Blamires, S., *The Irish Celtic Magical Tradition* (London: Aquarian Press, 1st edn, 1992).
Bonner, G. (ed.), *Famulus Christi: Essays in Commemoration of the Thirteenth Centenary of the Birth of the Venerable Bede* (London: SPCK, 1976).
—— 'Ireland's Contribution to Northumbrian Culture', in *Famulus Christi* (London: SPCK, 1976).
Boswell, C. S., *An Irish Precursor of Dante* (London: Sign of the Phoenix, 1st edn, 1908).
Bradley, I., *The Celtic Way* (London: Darton, Longman and Todd, 1st edn, 1993).
—— *Columba: Pilgrim and Penitent* (Glasgow: Wild Goose, 1st edn, 1997).
—— *God is Green: Christianity and the Environment* (London: Darton, Longman and Todd, 1st edn, 1990).
Bromiley, G., *Historical Theology: An Introduction* (Edinburgh: T&T Clark, 1978).

Broun, D. and T. O. Clancy, *Spes Scotorum Hope of Scots: St Columba Iona and Scotland* (Edinburgh: T&T Clark, 1999).
Brown, P., *Augustine of Hippo* (London: Faber, 3rd edn, 1967).
—— *Authority and the Sacred* (Cambridge: Cambridge University Press, 1st edn, 1995).
—— *The Body and Society: Men, Women and Sexual Renunciation in Early Christianity* (United Kingdom: Clays Ltd, 4th edn, 1991).
—— *The Cult of the Saints* (London: SCM, 1st edn, 1981).
—— *Religion and Society in the Age of Saint Augustine* (London: Faber and Faber, 2nd edn, 1973).
—— *The Rise of Western Christendom: Triumph and Diversity AD 200–1000, The Making of Europe* (Oxford: Blackwell, 1st edn, 1996).
—— *Society and the Holy in Late Antiquity* (Berkeley: University of California Press, 1st edn, 1982).
—— *The World of Late Antiquity: AD 150–750* (London: Thames and Hudson, 1st edn, 1971).
Brown. P. (ed.), *The Book of Kells*, Selected and edited by P. Brown, librarian of Trinity College, Dublin (London: Thames and Hudson, 1981).
Browne, G., *The Christian Churches in these Islands Before the Coming of Augustine* (Brighton: SPCK, 1st edn, 1894).
Brunner, E., *Christianity and Civilisation* (London: Nisbet and Co., 1st edn, 1948).
Bryant, S., *Celtic Ireland* (London: Kegan Paul, Trench and Co, 1st edn, 1889).
Bulloch, J., *The Life of the Celtic Church* (Edinburgh: The Saint Andrew Press, 1st edn, 1963).
Burke, C., *Patrick: The Archeology of a Saint* (Belfast: HMSO, 1993).
Burke, P., *New Perspectives in Historical Writing* (Pennsylvania: Pennsylvania University Press, 1991).
Burtchaell, J. T., *From Synagogue to Church* (Cambridge: Cambridge University Press, 1st edn, 1992).
Butterfield, H., *Christianity and History* (London: Collins, 1st edn, 1949).
Campbell, J. L., *Canna: The Story of a Hebridean Island* (Oxford: Oxford University Press, 1st edn, 1984).
Carmichael, A. (ed.), *Carmina Gadelica: Hymns and Incantations* (Edinburgh: Floris Books, 2nd edn, 1994).
Carney, J. (ed.), *Medieval Irish Lyrics* (Dublin: Dolmen Press, 1967).
—— *New Moon of the Seasons: Prayers from the Highlands and Islands* (Trowbridge: Floris, 2nd edn, 1986).
Chadwick, H., *Early Scotland: The Picts, The Scots and the Welsh of Southern Scotland* (Cambridge: Cambridge University Press, 1st edn, 1949).
—— *The Early Church* (Vol. I; London: Penguin, 2nd edn, 1990).
Chadwick, N., *The Age of the Saints in the Early Celtic Church* (London: Oxford University Press, 1st edn, 1963).
—— *The Celts* (London: Penguin, 2nd edn, 1991).
—— *Studies in the Early British Church* (Connecticut: The Shoe String Press, 2nd edn, 1973).

Chadwick, O. (ed.), *Western Asceticism* (London: SCM, 1st edn, 1958).
Chamberlain, G. A., *St Patrick: His Life and Work* (Dublin: SPCK, 1st edn, 1959).
Cherici, P., *Celtic Sexuality: Power, Paradigms and Passion* (London: Duckworth, 1st edn, 1994).
Clark, H. B. and M. Brennan (eds), *Columbanus and Merovingian Monasticism* (Vol. 113; Oxford: B.A.R., 1st edn, 1981).
Colet, J., *An Exposition of St Paul's First Epistle to the Corinthians* (London: G. Bell and Sons, 1st edn, 1874).
Colgrave, B. and R. Mynors (eds), *Bede's Ecclesiastical History of the English People* (Oxford: Clarendon Press, 1969).
Connel, G. and C. S. Evans, *Foundations of Kierkegaard's Vision of Community: Religion, Ethics and Politics in Kierkegaard* (New Jersey: Humanities Press, 1993).
Collinge, W., *St Augustine: Four Anti-Pelagian Writings, The Fathers of the Church – A New Translation* (Washington, DC: Catholic University of America, 1992).
Connolly, H., *The Irish Penitentials and Their Significance for the Sacrament of Penance Today* (Dublin: Four Courts Press, 1st edn, 1995).
Constable, N., *Ancient Ireland* (London: Promotional Reprint Co., 1966).
Corish, P. (ed.), *The Christian Mission* (Vol. 1; Dublin: Gill and Macmillan, 1st edn, 1972).
—— *The Irish Catholic Experience: A Historical Survey* (Dublin: Gill and Macmillan, 1st edn, 1985).
Costley, S. and C. Kightly, *A Celtic Book of Days* (London: Thames and Hudson, 1998).
Cote, R. G., *Revisioning Mission: The Catholic Church and Culture in Postmodern America* (New York: Paulist Press, 1st edn, 1996).
Daniel-Rops, H., *The Miracle of Ireland* (Dublin: Cahill and Co., 1959).
D'Arcy, M. R., *The Saints of Ireland* (Dublin: The Mercier Press, 3rd edn, 1985).
Davies, O. and F. Bowie, *Celtic Christian Spirituality: An Anthology of Medieval and Modern Sources* (London: SPCK, 1st edn, 1995).
Davies, O. and T. O'Loughlin, *Celtic Spirituality* (New York: Paulist Press, 1999).
Dawson, C., *The Formation of Christendom* (New York: Sheed and Ward, 1st edn, 1967).
Deanesly, M., *The Pre-Conquest Church in England* (London: Adam and Charles Black, 2nd edn, 1961).
Delaney, F., *The Celts* (London: HarperCollins, 1st edn, 1986).
—— *Legends of the Celts* (London: Hodder & Stoughton, 1989).
Delehaye, H., *The Legend of the Saints: An Introduction to Hagiography* (London: Geoffrey Chapman, 1st edn, 1962).
De Paor, L., *St Patrick's World: The Culture of Ireland's Apostolic Age* (Dublin: Four Courts Press, 1st edn, 1993).
De Paor, M. and L. de Paor, *Early Christian Ireland* (London: Thames and Hudson, 1961).

Dodds, E. R., *Pagan and Christian in an Age of Anxiety* (New York: W. W. Norton and Co., 1st edn, 1965).

Doran, R., *A Birth of a Worldview: Early Christianity and Its Jewish and Pagan Context* (Oxford: Westview Press, 1995).

Dubois, M. M., *Saint Columban: A Pioneer of Western Civilization* (Dublin: M. H. Gill and Son Ltd, 1st edn, 1961).

Duckett, E., *The Wandering Saints* (London: Collins, 1st edn, 1959).

Dufour, L. X., Dictionary of the New Testament (London: G. Chapman, 1980).

Dumville, D. (ed.), *Celtic Britain in the Early Middle Ages: Studies in Scottish and Welsh Sources* (Suffolk: The Boydell Press, 1980).

—— *Liturgy and the Ecclesiastical History of Late Anglo-Saxon England* (Studies in Anglo-Saxon History, Vol. 5; Suffolk: The Boydell Press, 1st edn, 1992).

—— (ed.), *St Patrick A.D. 493–1993* (Vol. XVIII, Woodbridge, Suffolk: The Boydell Press, 1st edn, 1993).

—— (ed.), *Church and Society in Ireland A.D. 400–1200* (London: Variorum, 1987).

Dunleavy, G., *Colum's Other Island: The Irish at Lindisfarne* (Madison: The University of Wisconsin, 1st edn, 1960).

Eade, J. and M. J. Sallnow (eds), *Contesting the Sacred: An Anthropology of Christian Pilgrimage* (London: Routledge, 1991).

Edel, D. (ed.), *Cultural Identity and Cultural Integration: Ireland and Europe in the Early Middle Ages* (Dublin: Four Courts Press, 1st edn, 1995).

Edwards, D., *Human Experience of God* (New York.: Paulist, 1983).

—— *Jesus and the Cosmos* (New York: Paulist, 1991).

—— *The God of Evolution* (New York: Paulist, 1999).

Elliott, D., *Spiritual Marriage: Sexual Abstinence in Medieval Wedlock* (New Jersey: Princeton University Press, 1st edn, 1993).

Eluere, C., *The Celts: First Masters of Europe, New Horizons* (London: Thames and Hudson, 1st edn, 1992).

Eriugena, J. S., *The Voice of the Eagle: The Heart of Celtic Christianity. Homily on the Prologue to the Gospel of St John* (New York: Lindisfarne Press, 1st edn, 1990).

Evans, G. R., *Augustine on Evil* (Cambridge: Cambridge University Press, 1982).

—— (ed.), *The Science of Theology* (Vol. I; Hants: M. Morgan and Scott Ltd, 1st edn, 1986).

Evans, R., *Four Letters of Pelagius* (New York: Seabury Press, 1968).

Evans Wentz, W., *The Fairy-Faith in Celtic Countries* (England: Gerrards Cross, 1977).

Fairbairn, A. M. (ed.), The Influence of Greek Ideas and Usage upon the Christian Church (London: William and Norgate, 1907).

Ferguson, J., *Pelagius: A Historical and Theological Study* (Cambridge: W. Heffer and Sons, 1st edn, 1956).

Fiennes. J., *On Pilgrimage: A Time to Seek* (London: Sinclair-Stevenson Ltd, 1991).

Finlay, I., *Columba* (London: Victor Gollancz Ltd, 1st edn, 1979).
Fox, M., *Creation Spirituality: Liberating Gifts for the Peoples of the Earth* (San Francisco: Harper, 1st edn, 1991).
—— *Original Blessing: A Primer in Creation Spirituality* (Santa Fé: Bear and Co., 1983).
—— (ed.), *Western Spirituality: Historical Roots, Ecumenical Routes* (Indiana: Fides/Claretian, 1979).
Fox, R. L., *Pagans and Christians* (San Francisco: Harper and Row, 1988).
Garmonsway, G. (ed.), *The Anglo-Saxon Chronicle* (London: Dent, 1953).
Gibson, E. C. S., 'The Works John Cassian', in *Nicean and Post-Nicean Fathers* (2nd ser., Vol. 2, repr. W. B. Eerdmans, 1964: Oxford: James Parker and Co., 1894).
Glover, J. R., *The Story of Scotland* (London: Faber, 1st edn, 1960).
Goldstein, J. (ed.), *Foucault and the Writing of History* (Massachusetts: Blackwell, 1st edn, 1994).
Gougaud, L., *Christianity in Celtic Lands* (London: Sheed and Ward, 1932).
—— *Devotional and Ascetic Practices in the Middle Ages* (London: Burns Oates and Washbourne Ltd, 1st edn, 1927).
—— *Gaelic Pioneers of Christianity* (Dublin: M. H. Gill and Son Ltd, 1st edn, 1923).
Grant, G. P., *Philosophy in the Mass Age* (Toronto: Copp Clark, 1959).
Grant, R., *Second Century Christianity: A Collection of Fragments* (London: SPCK, 1890s).
Green, M., *The Gods of the Celts* (Avon: The Bath Press, 1993).
Gregory, L., *A Book of Saints and Wonders* (Dundrum: The Dun Emer Press, 2nd edn, 1906).
Gwynn, A. and R. N. Hadcock, *Medieval Religious Houses: Ireland* (London: Longman, 1st edn, 1970).
Gwynn, A., *The Writings of Bishop Patrick 1074–1084* (Dublin: The Institute for Advanced Studies, 1st edn, 1955).
Gwynn, S., *The History of Ireland* (Dublin: Talbot Press, 1924).
Hanks, P. (ed.), *Hamlyn Encyclopaedic World Dictionary* (Middlesex: Hamlyn, 1971).
Harbison, P., *Pilgrimage in Ireland: The Monuments and the People* (London: Barrie and Jenkins, 1st edn, 1991).
—— *Pre-Christian Ireland* (Ancient Peoples and Places, Vol. 104; London: Thames and Hudson Ltd, 1988).
Hardinge, L., *The Celtic Church in Britain* (London: SPCK, 1st edn, 1972).
Hatch, C., *The Influence of Greek Ideas and Usages upon the Christian Church* (London: Williams and Norgate, 1907).
Haventy, M., *The History of Ireland* (New York: Kelly, 1st edn, 1881).
Hazlett, I. (ed.), *Early Christianity: Origins and Evolution to A.D 600* (London: SPCK, 1991).
Healy, J., *Insula Sanctorum et Doctorum: Ireland's Ancient Schools and Scholars* (Dublin: Sealy, Bryers and Walker, 1890).
—— *The Life and Writings of St Patrick* (Dublin: M. H. Gill, 1905).

—— *Papers and Addresses: Theological, Philosophical, Biographical, Archaeological* (Dublin: Catholic Truth Society, 1909).
Heine, S., *Women and Early Christianity: Are the Feminist Scholars Right?* (London: SCM Press, 1986).
Hennessy, W. M. (ed.), *Chronicum Scotorum: From the Earliest Times to A.D 1135* (London: Longmans, Green, Reader and Dyer, 1866).
Herbert, M., *Iona, Kells and Derry: The History and Hagiography of the Monastic Familia of Columba* (Oxford: Clarendon Press, 1st edn, 1988).
Herm, G., *The Celts: The People Who Came Out of the Darkness* (London: Weidenfeld & Nicolson, 1975).
Herrin, J., *The Formation of Christendom* (London: Fontana Press, 1st edn, 1987).
Hodgson, P. C. (ed.), *Ferdinand Christian Baur on The Writing of Church History* (New York: Oxford University Press, 1st edn, 1968).
Hollis, S., *Anglo-Saxon Women and the Church* (Suffolk: The Boydell Press, 1992).
Howard, M., *Angels and Goddesses: Celtic Christianity and Paganism in Ancient Britain* (Chieveley: Capall Bann, 1st edn, 1994).
Howlett, D. R. (ed.), *The Book of Letters of Saint Patrick the Bishop* (Dublin: Four Courts Press, 1st edn, 1994).
Hubert, H., *The History of the Celtic People* (London: Bracken Books, 1993).
Hughes, K., *Church and Society in Ireland A.D. 400–1200* (London: Variorum Reprints, 1st edn, 1987).
—— *The Church in Early Irish Society* (London: Methuen and Co., 1st edn, 1966).
—— *The Modern Traveller to the Early Irish Church* (London: SPCK, 1977).
—— *Early Christian Ireland: Introduction to the Sources* (London: Camelot Press, 1st edn, 1972).
Hull, E., *A History of Ireland and Her People to the Close of the Tudor Period* (Dublin: Maunsel and Roberts, 1st edn, 1926).
Hunter-Blair, P., *The World of Bede* (Cambridge: University Press, 2nd edn, 1990).
Jackson, K. H. (ed.), *Celt and Saxon* (Cambridge: Cambridge University Press, 1st edn, 1963).
—— *A Celtic Miscellany* (London: Penguin, 2nd edn, 1971).
James, S., *Exploring the World of the Celts* (London: Thames and Hudson, 1993).
James, W., *The Varieties of Religious Experience* (London: Collins, 1982).
Jamieson, J., *A Historical Account of the Ancient Culdees of Iona* (London: Simpkin, Marshall, Hamilton and Co., 1890).
Jeanrond, W., *Theological Hermeneutics: Development and Significance* (New York: Crossroads, 1991).
Joyce, P. W., *The Story of Ancient Irish Civilization* (Dublin: M. H. Gill and Son Ltd, 1st edn, 1907).
Kelly, F., *A Guide to Early Irish Law* (Vol. 3; Dublin: Mount Salus, 1st edn, 1988).

Kelly, J., *Early Christian Centuries* (London: Adam and Charles Black, 4th edn, 1968).

Kennedy, E., *Tomorrow's Catholics Yesterday's Church: The Two Cultures of American Catholics* (Missouri: Ligouri, 1995).

Kenney, J. F., *The Sources for the Early History of Ireland: Ecclesiastical* (Shannon: Irish University Press, 3rd edn, 1968).

Kerr, W. S., *The Independence of the Celtic Church in Ireland* (London: SPCK, 1st edn, 1931).

Kilgallen, J. J., *First Corinthians: An Introduction and Study Guide* (New Jersey: Paulist Press, 1987).

Killen, W., *The Ecclesiastical History of Ireland* (London: Macmillan and Co., 1875).

Küng, H., *Christianity: Its Essence and History* (Munich: R. P. GmbH and Co., 1995).

Kutter, S., *Studies in the History of Medieval Canon Law* (Hampshire: Variorum, 1st edn, 1990).

Laing, L., *The Archaeology of Late Celtic Britain and Ireland 400-1200 A.D.* (London: Methuen and Co. Ltd, 1st edn, 1975).

—— *Celtic Britain: Britain before the Conquest* (London: Routledge and Kegan Paul, 1st edn, 1979).

—— (ed.), *Studies in Celtic Survival* (Vol. 37; Gt Britain: British Archaeological Reports, 1977).

Lapidge, M. (ed.), *Columbanus: Studies on the Latin Writings* (Suffolk: The Boydell Press, 1st edn, 1997).

Latourette, K. S., *A History of The Expansion of Christianity: The First Five Centuries* (Vol. I; Devon: The Paternoster Press, 1970).

Le Goff, J., *Medieval Civilization* (Oxford: Blackwell, 1997).

Leclercq, J., *The Love of Leaning and the Desire for God: A Study of Monastic Culture* (London: SPCK, 1st edn, 1961).

Lehane, B., *Early Celtic Christianity* (London: Constable and Co., 1994).

Lindsay, T. M., *The Church and the Ministry in the Early Centuries* (London: Hodder & Stoughton, 2nd edn, 1903).

Loades, J. (ed.), *Monastic Studies: The Continuity of Tradition* (Bangor: Copycat, 1990).

Lonigan, P. R., *The Early Irish Church* (New York: Celtic Heritage Press, 2nd edn, 1986).

Low, M., *Celtic Christianity and Nature: Early Irish and Hebridean Traditions* (Edinburgh: Edinburgh University Press, 1996).

Macalister, R., *Ireland in Pre-Celtic Times* (Dublin: Maunsel and Roberts, 1921).

—— *Tara: A Pagan Sanctuary of Ancient Ireland* (London: C. Scribner's Sons, 1st edn, 1931).

MacCulloch, J., *The Religion of the Ancient Celts* (Suffolk: St Edmundsbury Press Ltd, 1st edn, 1992).

MacHaffie, B. J. (ed.), *Readings in Her Story: Women in Christian Traditions* (Minneapolis: Fortress Press, 1st edn, 1992).

Mackey, J. (ed.), *An Introduction to Celtic Christianity* (Edinburgh: T&T Clark Ltd, 1989).
Macmanus, F., *Saint Columban* (Dublin: Clonmore and Reynolds Ltd, 1st edn, 1963).
MacManus, S., *The Story of the Irish Race* (New York: The Devin-Adair Co., 1944).
MacMullen, R., *Christianizing the Roman Empire AD 100–400* (London: Yale University Press, 1984).
MacMullen, R. and E. Lane (eds), *Paganism and Christianity 100-425 C.E; A Sourcebook*. (Minneapolis: Augsburg Fortress, 1992).
MacNaught, J. C., *The Celtic Church and the See of Peter* (Oxford: Basil Blackwell, 1st edn, 1927).
MacNeill, E., *Early Irish Laws and Institutions* (Dublin: Burns Oates and Washborne Ltd, 1935).
MacNiocaill, G., *The Medieval Irish Annals* (Dublin: Historical Association, Medieval Irish History Series, Vol. 3; 1st edn, 1975).
Maher, M. (ed.), *Irish Spirituality* (Dublin: Veritas Publications, 1981).
Markale, J., *Celtic Civilization* (London: Gordon and Cremonesi, 1st edn, 1976).
—— *The Celts: Uncovering the Mythic and Historic Origins of Western Culture* (Vermont: Inner Traditions International, 1st edn, 1978).
—— *Women of the Celts* (Vermont: Inner Traditions International Ltd, 1st edn, 1975).
Marsden, J., *The Illustrated Columcille* (London: Macmillan, 1st edn, 1991).
Marsh, A., *Saint Patrick and His Writings* (Dundalk: Dundalgan Press, 1st edn, 1966).
Mathisen, R., *Ecclesiastical Factionalism and Religious Controversy in Fifth-Century Gaul* (Washington, DC: The Catholic University of America Press, 1st edn, 1989).
Mayr-Harting, H., *The Coming of Christianity to Anglo-Saxon England* (USA: Pennsylvania State University Press, 2nd edn, 1991).
McBrien, R., *Catholicism* (San Francisco: Harper and Row, 1st edn, 1981).
McCarthy, D. (ed.), *Dissertations Chiefly on Irish Church History* (Dublin: James Duffy, 1st edn, 1864).
McDonogh, S., *'To Care for the Earth' A Call to a New Theology* (London: Cassell, 1986).
McIntire, C. (ed.), *God, History and Historians* (London: Oxford University Press, 1977).
McMullen, R., *Christianising the Roman Empire (A.D. 100–400)* (Massachusetts: Yale Univesity Press, 1984).
McNamara, J. A., *A New Song: Celibate Woman in the First Three Christian Centuries* (New York: The Haworth Press, 1st edn, 1983).
McNamara, M., *The Apocrypha in the Irish Church* (Dublin: Institute for Advanced Studies, 1975).
McNeill, J. T., *The Celtic Churches: A History A.D. 200 to 1200* (Chicago: University of Chicago Press, 1974).

McNeill, J. T. and H. Gamer, *Medieval Handbooks of Penance: Records of Civilisation* (New York: Octagon, 2nd edn, 1965).
—— *Medieval Handbooks of Penance: A Translation of the Principal libri poenitentiales and Selections from Related Documents* (Records of Civilization, Vol. 29; New York: Octagon Books, 1st edn, 1965).
Meissner, J. L., *The Celtic Church in England After the Synod of Whitby* (London: Martin Hopkinson, 1st edn, 1929).
Menzies, L., *Saint Columba: A Study of His Life, His Times and His Influence* (Felinfach: J. M. F. Books, 1992).
Michalson, G. E., *Lessing's 'Ugly Ditch': A Study of Theology and History* (USA: Pennsylvania State University, 1985).
Minahane, J., *The Christian Druids: On the Filid or Philosopher-Poets of Ireland* (Dublin: Sanas Press, 1993).
Momigliano, A. (ed.), *The Conflict between Pagans and Christianity in the Fourth Century* (Oxford: Clarendon Press, 1963).
Montague, H. P., *The Saints and Martyrs of Ireland* (Dublin: Colin Smythe, 1st edn, 1981).
Moody, T. and F. X. Martin, *The Course of Irish History* (New York: Weybright and Tally, 1968).
Moore, C. J. (ed.), *Carmina Gadelica: Hymns and Incantations Compiled by A. Carmichael* (Edinburgh: Floris Books, 1994).
Moore, G., *Celibate Lives* (London: W. Heinemann Ltd, 1st edn, 1927).
—— *A Story-Teller's Holiday*, Vols I and II (New York: Horace Liveright, 1st edn, 1928).
Morris, J., *Nennius: British History and the Welsh Annals* (History from the Sources. Vol. 8; London: Phillimore, 1980).
—— *A History of the British Isles from 350–650: Roman Britain the Empire of Arthur* (History From the Sources, Vol. 2; London: Phillimore, 2nd edn, 1977).
Murray, A., *St Columba – Corrievreckan* (Edinburgh: T&T Clark, 1st edn, 1920s).
Mytum, H., *The Origins of Early Christian Ireland* (London: Routledge, 1st edn, 1992).
NiChathain, P. and M. Richter (eds), *Ireland and Europe: The Early Church* (Stuttgart: Klett-Cotter, 1st edn, 1982).
—— (eds), Ireland and Europe in the Middle Ages (Stuttgart: Klett-Cotter, 1996).
Nock, A. D., *Conversion: The Old and the New in Religion from Alexander the Great to Augustine of Hippo* (Oxford: Clarendon Press, 1st edn, 1933).
Nouwen, H. J., *Clowning in Rome: Reflections on Solitude, Celibacy, Prayer and Contemplation* (New York: Image Books, 1972).
Oakley, T. P., *English Penitential Discipline and Anglo-Saxon Law in their Joint Influence* (New York: Columbia University, 1st edn, 1923).
O'Cathain, S., *The Festival of Brigit: Celtic Goddess and Holy Woman* (Dublin: DBA, 1st edn, 1995).
O'Clerigh, A., *The History of Ireland to the Coming of Henry II* (Dublin: Sealy, Bryers and Walker, 1st edn, 1961).

O'Corrain, D., L. Breatnach and K. McCone, *Sages, Saints and Storytellers: Celtic Studies in Honour of Professor James Carney* (Maynooth: An Sagart, 1st edn, 1989).
O'Curry, E., *Lectures on the Manuscript Material of Ancient Irish History* (Dublin: W. A. Hinch, 1878).
—— *Manners and Customs of the Ancient Irish* (Dublin: W. B. Kelly, 1st edn, 1873).
O'Donnell, M. (ed.), *Betha Coluim Chille, from Mms Rawl. B. 514 in Bodleian Library* (Dublin: Franciscan Convent, 1532).
O'Donoghue, N. D., *The Angels Keep Their Ancient Places: Reflections on Celtic Spirituality* (Edinburgh: T&T Clark, 2001).
—— *Aristocracy of Soul: Patrick of Ireland* (The Way of Christian Mystics, Vol. 1; Delaware: M. Glazier, 1987).
—— *The Mountain Behind the Mountain* (Edinburgh: T&T Clark, 1993).
O'Donohue, J., *Anam Cara: Spiritual Wisdom from the Celtic World* (London: Transworld, 1997).
O'Driscoll, R. (ed.), *Celtic Consciousness* (Edinburgh: Canongate, 1981).
Ó'Duinn, S., *Where Three Streams Meet: Celtic Spirituality* (Dublin: Columba Press, 2000).
O'Dwyer, P., *Celi De: Spiritual Reform in Ireland 750–900* (Edinburgh: Clark Constable Ltd, 1981).
O'Fiaich, T., *Columbanus in His Own Words* (Dublin: Veritas, 1st edn, 1974).
O'Hanlon, J., *St Brigit* (Dublin: J. Dollard, 1st edn, 1877).
O'Kelly, S., *Illustrated Guide to New Grange* (Wexford: J. English, 1967).
O'Meara, J., *The Voyage of St Brendan: Journey to the Promised Land* (Portlaoise: Dolmen Press, 1985).
O'Rahilly, T., *Early Irish History and Mythology* (Dublin: Cahill and Co. Ltd, 1946).
O'Rahilly, T. F., *The Two Patricks: A Lecture on the History of Christianity in Fifth-Century Ireland* (Dublin: Institute for Advanced Studies, 1st edn, 1981).
O'Riordain, J., *The Music of What Happens* (Dublin: The Columba Press, 1st edn, 1996).
—— *A Pilgrim in Celtic Scotland* (Dublin: The Columba Press, 1st edn, 1997).
O'Riordan, S. and S. Danie., *New Grange and the Bend of the Boyne* (London: Thames and Hudson, 1964).
Oskamp, H. P., *The Voyage of Mael Duin* (Groningen: Wolters-Noordhoff, 1st edn, 1970).
Owen, T. M., *Welsh Folk Customs* (Llandysul: Gomer Press, 3rd edn, 1987).
Painter, J., *Theology as Hermeneutics: Rudolf Bultmann's Interpretation of the History of Jesus* (Sheffield: Sheffield Academic Press, 1987).
Palmer, R. E., *Hermeneutics: Interpretation Theory in Schleiermacher, Dilthey, Heidegger and Gadame* (Evanston: Northwestern University Press, 1969).
Patterson, N., *Cattle-Lords and Clansmen: The Social Structure of Early Ireland* (London: University of Notre Dame Press, 1st edn, 1994).
Pennick, N., *The Celtic Cross* (Sussex: The Bath Press, 1st edn, 1997).

—— *Celtic Sacred Landscapes* (London: Thames and Hudson, 1st edn, 1996).
—— *Leylines: Mysteries of the Ancient World* (London: Weidenfeld & Nicolson, 1st edn, 1997).
—— *The Pagan Source Book: A Guide to the Festivals, Traditions and Symbols of the Year* (London: Rider, 1992).
Phillips, W. A. (ed.), *The History of the Church of Ireland from the Earliest Times to the Present Day* (Vol. I; London: Humphrey Milford, 1933).
Piggott, S., *The Druids* (repr. 1968, London: Thames and Hudson, 1991).
—— *The Prehistoric Peoples of Scotland* (London: Routledge and Kegan Paul).
Plummer, C. (ed.), *Irish Litanies* (London: Harrison and Sons, 1st edn, 1925).
Pochin-Mould, D., *The Celtic Saints: Our Heritage* (Dublin: Clonmore and Reynolds Ltd, 1st edn, 1956).
—— *The Irish Saints* (Dublin: Clonmore and Reynolds Ltd, 1964).
—— *The Monasteries of Ireland: An Introduction* (London: Batsford Ltd, 1976).
—— *Scotland of the Saints* (London: B. T. Batsford Ltd, 1st edn, 1952).
Powell, T., *The Celts, Ancient Peoples and Places* (London: Thames and Hudson, 1991).
Power, P. C., *Sex and Marriage in Ancient Ireland* (Dublin: Mercier, 1st edn, 1976).
Quast, K., *Reading the Corinthian Correspondence: An Introduction* (New Jersey: Paulist Press, 1994).
Rahner, K., *Foundations of Christian Faith: An Introduction to the Idea of Christianity* (London: Darton, Longman and Todd, 1978).
Ramsey. B., *Beginning to Read the Fathers* (London: SCM, 1993).
Ramsey, I., *Religious Language* (London: SCM Press, 1982).
Rees, A., *Celtic Heritage* (USA: Thames and Hudson, 2nd edn, 1989).
Rees, B., *Pelagius: A Reluctant Heretic* (Suffolk: St Edmundsbury Press, 1988).
Reeves, W., *Culdees of the British Islands, as They Appear in History* (Dublin: M. H. Gill, 1864).
Reeves, W. (ed.), *Life of Saint Columba, Founder of Hy* (Edinburgh: Edmonston and Douglas, 1874: facsimile repr. 1988).
Richter, M. (ed.), *Medieval Ireland, Saints and Martyrologies* (Northampton: Variorum Reprints, 1st edn, 1989).
—— *Medieval Ireland: The Enduring Tradition* (London: Macmillan Education, 2nd edn, 1988).
Robinson, M., *Sacred Places, Pilgrim Paths: An Anthology of Pilgrimage* (London: HarperCollins, 1997).
Rollason, D. (ed.), *Cuthbert: Saint and Patron* (Durham: Dean and Chapter of Durham, 1st edn, 1987).
Rolleston, T. W., *Myths and Legends of the Celtic Race* (London: Constable, 1986).
Rosenthal, J. T. (ed.), *Medieval Women and the Sources of Medieval History* (Georgia: The University of Georgia Press, 1st edn, 1990).
Ross, A., *Pagan Celtic Britain: Studies in Iconography and Tradition..*(London: Routledge and Kegan Paul, 1st edn, 1967).

Rousseau, P., *Ascetics, Authority and the Church in the Age of Jerome and Cassian* (Oxford Historical Monographs, Oxford: Oxford University Press, 1st edn, 1978).
Ryan, J. (ed.), *Irish Monks in the Golden Age* (Dublin: Clonmore and Reynolds Ltd, 1st edn, 1963).
—— *Irish Monasticism: Origins and Early Development* (London: Longmans, Green and Co., 1931).
—— (ed.), *The Monastic Institute* (Dublin: Gill and Macmillan, 1st edn, 1972).
Sadler, A. W. (ed.), *The Journey of Western Spirituality: The Annual Publication of the College Theology Society* (Chicago: Scholar Press, 1981).
Salmon, J., *The Ancient Irish Church as a Witness to Catholic Doctrine* (Dublin: Gill and Son, 1st edn, 1897).
Schökel, L. A., *A Manual of Hermeneutics* (Sheffield: Sheffield Academic Press, 1998).
Sellner, E. C., *Wisdom of the Celtic Saints* (Indiana: Ave Maria Press, 1993).
—— *The Celtic Soul Friend: A Trusted Guide for Today* (Indiana: Ave Maria Press, 2002).
Severin, T. *The Brendan Voyage: An Epic Crossing of the Atlantic By Leather Boat* (Australia: Hutchinson, 1978).
Sharpe, R. (ed.), *Ireland and the Culture of Early Medieval Europe* (London: Variorum Reprints, 1st edn, 1987).
—— *Medieval Irish Saints' Lives: An Introduction to Vitae Sanctorum Hiberniae* (Oxford: Clarendon Press, 1st edn, 1991).
Sheils, W. J. (ed.), *Monks, Hermits and the Ascetic Tradition* (Padstow: T. J. Press, 1985).
Sheils, W. J. and D. Wood (eds), *The Churches, Ireland and the Irish* (Oxford: Basil Blackwell, 1989).
Sheldrake, P., *Living Between Worlds: Place and Journey in Celtic Spirituality* (Massachusetts: Cowley, 1996).
—— *Spirituality and History* (London: SPCK, 1st edn, 1991).
Sherley-Price, L. (ed.), *Ecclesiastical History of the English People* (London: Penguin, rev. edn., 1990).
Skene, W. F. (ed.), *Adomnan's Life of Columba* (Edinburgh: Edmonston and Douglas, 1874).
Skene, W. F., *Celtic Scotland: A History of Ancient Alban* (2, 3 vols; Edinburgh: David Douglass, 2nd edn, 1887).
Smit, J. W., *Studies on the Language and Style of Columba the Younger (Columbanus)* (Amsterdam: A. M. Hakkert, 1st edn, 1971).
Smyth, M., *Understanding the Universe in Seventh Century Ireland* (Indiana: The Medieval Institute, 1984).
Stevenson, J., *The Liturgy and Ritual of the Celtic Church, Studies in Celtic History* (Suffolk: Boydell Press, 2nd edn, 1987).
Stokes, G. and C. Wright, *The Writings of St Patrick, The Apostle of Ireland* (London: James Nisbet and Co., 2nd edn, 1888).
Stokes, G. T., *Ireland and the Celtic Church* (London: Hodder & Stoughton, 1886).

Stone, M., *Ancient Mirrors of Womanhood* (Boston: Beacon Press, 1990).
Streib, H., *Hermeneutics of Metaphor, Symbol and Narrative and Faith Development Theory* (Frankfurt: Peter Lang, 1989).
Tanner, K., *Theories of Culture: A New Agenda for Theology* (Minneapolis: Fortress Press, 1997).
Thiselton, A. C., *New Horizons in Hermeneutics* (London: HarperCollins, 1993).
Thomas, C., *Christianity in Roman Britain to AD 500* (London: B. T. Batsford Ltd, 1st edn, 1993).
—— *The Early Christian Archaeology of North Britain* (London: Oxford University Press, 1971).
Todd, J. H., *St Patrick Apostle of Ireland: A Memoir of His Life and Mission* (Dublin: Hodges, Smith and Co., 1864).
Toulson, S., *The Celtic Alternative: The Christianity We Lost* (London: Random Century, 1987).
—— *The Celtic Year* (Dorset: Element, 1st edn, 1993).
Turner, V., *Image and Pilgrimage in Christian Culture: Anthropological Perspectives* (New York: Columbia University Press, 1st edn, 1978).
Wallace-Hadrill, J. M., *The Long-Haired Kings* (London: Methuen and Co, 1962).
—— *Early Medieval History* (Oxford: Oxford University Press, 1975).
Walsh, J. R. and T. Bradley, *A History of the Irish Church 400–700 AD* (Dublin: The Columba Press, 1991).
Walsh, P., *The Four Masters and Their Work* (Dublin: The Sign of the Three Candles, 1944).
Warin, A., *Wilfrid* (York: William Sessions, 1st edn, 1992).
Warren, F. E., *The Liturgy and Ritual of the Celtic Church* (Oxford: Clarendon Press, 1881).
Watkins, O. D., *A History of Penance: Being a Study of the Authorities; Vol. II The Western Church from 650A.D.–950A.D.* (Vol. 16; New York: Burt Franklin, 1st edn, 1920).
—— *A History of Penance: Being a Study of the Authorities; Vol. I The Whole Church to A.D. 450* (Vol. 16; New York: Burt Franklin, 1st edn, 1920).
Watt, J. and F. X. Martin (eds), *Medieval Studies Presented to Aubrey Gwynn* (Dublin: Institute for Advanced Studies, 1961).
White, C., *Christian Friendship in the Fourth Century* (Cambridge: Cambridge University Press, 1st edn, 1992).
Whitlock, D., R. McKitterick and D. Dumville (eds), *Ireland in Early Medieval Europe* (Cambridge: Cambridge University Press, 1st edn, 1982).
Wood-Martin, W. G., *Traces of the Elder Faiths of Ireland: A Handbook of Irish Pre-Christian Tradition* (Vol. 2; London: Longmans, Green and Co., 1902).
Zimmer, H., *The Celtic Church in Britain and Ireland* (London: David Nutt, 1902).

Journals, Papers, Theses

Anderson, M. O., 'Columba and Other Irish Saints in Scotland', *HS* 5 (1965), pp. 26–58.
Barry, J., 'The Erenagh in the Monastic Irish Church', *IER* 89 (March, 1958), pp. 424–32.
Bethell, D. L. T., 'The Originality of the Early Irish Church', *JRSA* 13 (1981), pp. 36–49.
Bieler, L., 'The Problem of *Silua Focluti*', *IHS* 3, no. 12 (1942/3), pp. 351–64.
—— 'Recent Research on Irish Hagiography – Part II', *Studies* (1946), pp. 536–44.
—— 'An Austrian Fragment of the Life of St Patrick', *IER* 35 (1961), pp. 176–81.
—— 'Interpretationes Patricianae', *IER* 107 (January, 1967), pp. 1–13.
—— 'Recent Research on Irish Hagiography – Part I', *Studies* (June, 1946), pp. 230–8.
—— 'The Christianization of the Insular Celts', *Celtica* 8 (1968), pp. 118–29.
Binchy, D. A., 'The Old-Irish Table of Penitential Commutations', *Eriu* 19–20 (1962/6), pp. 47–72.
—— 'St Patrick's "First Synod"', *SH* (1968), pp. 49–54.
Bolton, B. M., 'Via Ascetica: A Papal Quandary', *SCH* 22 (1985), pp. 57–89.
Bourgeault, C., 'The Monastic Archetype in the Navigatio of St Brendan', *JMS* 14 (Advent, 1983), pp. 104–22.
Bradshaw, B., 'The Wild and Woolly West: Early Irish Christianity and Latin Orthodoxy', *SCH* 25 (1987/8), pp. 123–34.
Bray, D. A., 'The Making of a Hero: The Legend of St Patrick and the Claims of Armagh', *MS* 14 (Advent, 1983), pp. 145–59.
Brown, P., 'The Patrons of Pelagius: The Roman Aristocracy between East and West', *JTS* 21, Part I (April, 1970), pp. 56–72.
Bury, J. B., 'The Itinerary of Patrick in Connaught, According to Tirechan', *Pro R.I.A.* 24 (1903), pp. 153–68.
—— 'Sources of Early Patrician Documents', *EHR* 19 (1904), pp. 493–503.
—— 'Tierchan's Memoirs of St Patrick', *EHR* 17 (April, 1902), pp. 235–63.
Byrne, F. J. and P. Francis., 'Two Lives of St Patrick: Vita Secunda and Vita Quarta', *JRSAI* 124 (1994), pp. 5–16.
Byrne, M. E., 'Feilire Adamnain', *Eriu* 1/2 (1904/5), p. 255.
Carville, G., 'The Road from Camus to Moone – Advance a Step Each Day: An Expression of Celtic Monasticism', *JMS* 14 (Advent, 1983), pp. 161–78.
Chadwick, H., 'All Things to All Men, *NTS* 1/2 (1954/6), pp. 261–75.
—— 'The Ascetic Ideal in the History of the Church', *SCH* 22 (1984/5), pp. 1–23.
Charles-Edwards, T. M., 'Book Review', *SH* 15/16 (1975/6), pp. 194–6.
—— 'The Social Background to Irish Peregrinatio', *Celtica* 11 (1976), pp. 43–59.
—— 'Bede, The Irish and the Britons', *Celtica* 15 (1983), pp. 44–52.
—— 'The New Edition of Adomnán's Life of Columba', *CMCS* 26 (Winter, 1993), pp. 65–73.

Coates, S., 'Dwellings of the Saints: Monasteries in the Scottish Borders in the Early Middle Ages', *DR* Vol. 114, no. 396 (July, 1996), pp. 166–84.

Colgrave, B., 'The History of British Museum Additional MS.39943', *EHR* 54 (1939), pp. 673–7.

Congar, Y., 'Church History as a Branch of Theology', *Concilium* 7 (1971), pp. 85–96.

Connolly, S. and J. Picard, 'Cogitosus: Life of Saint Brigit', *JRSAI* 117 (1987), pp. 11–27.

Corish, P., 'St Patrick and Ireland', *IER* 35 (Jan–June, 1961), pp. 223–8.

Crawford, O. G. S., 'Iona', *Antiquity* 7 (1933), pp. 453–6.

Cremin, A., 'Review of R. Megaw's Book on Celtic Art', *ACJ* III (1990), p. 62.

Dark, K. R., 'Celtic Monastic Archeology: Fifth to Eighth Centuries', *MS* 14 (Advent, 1983), pp. 17–29.

Deanesly, M. and P. Grosjean, 'The Canterbury Edition of the Answers of Pope Gregory I to St Augustine', *JEH* 10 (1959), pp. 1–49.

De Bhaldraithe, E., 'Obedience: The Doctrine of the Irish Monastic Rules', *MS* 14 (Advent, 1983), pp. 63–84.

—— 'A Review of Monastic Spirituality and Liturgy', *Hallel* 14 (1987), pp. 47–92.

—— 'Two Rules of Ailbe and Interpolated Verses', paper presented at the Celtic Studies Conference, Maynooth, 1995.

Doherty, C., 'Some Aspects of Hagiography as a Source for Irish Economic History', *Peritia* 1 (1982), pp. 300–328.

—— 'The Basilica in Early Ireland', *Peritia* 3 (1984), pp. 303–15.

Edwards, N., 'Two Sculptural Fragments from Clonmacnois', *JRSAI* 114 (1984), pp. 57–62.

Enright, M. J., 'Royal Succession and Abbatial Prerogative in Adomnan's Vita Columbae', *Peritia* 4 (1985), pp. 83–103.

Espin, O. O., 'Latino/a Theology', Paper presented at the CTSA, University of San Diego, California, 2001.

Esposito, M., 'The Patrician Problem and a Possible Solution', *IHS* 10 no. 38 (September, 1956/7), pp. 131–55.

Etchingham, C., 'The Early Irish Church: Some Observations on Pastoral Care and Dues', *Eriu* 42 (1991), pp. 99–118.

—— 'The Implications of Paruchia', *Eriu* 44 (1993), pp. 139–62.

Finnane, R., 'Late Medieval Irish Law Manuscripts: A Reappraisal of Methodology and Context', Masters Thesis, Sydney, 1991.

Firey, A., 'Cross-Examining the Witness: Recent Research in Celtic Monastic History', *JMS* 14 (Advent, 1983), pp. 31–49.

Fitzpatrick, L., 'Raiding and Warring in Monastic Ireland', *HI* (Autumn, 1993), pp. 13–18.

Forte, B., 'Memory and Reconciliation: The Church and the Faults of the Past', *ITC*, December, 1999.

Frend, W. H., 'The Divjak Letters: New Light on St Augustine's Problems, 416–428', *JEH* 34, no. 4 (October, 1983), pp. 16–17.

Frye, D., 'Bishops as Pawns in Early Fifth-Century Gaul', *JEH* 42, no. 3 (1991), pp. 349–61.

Garstin, J. R., 'The Ancient Irish Church from Unwritten Sources', Paper presented at the Church Conference, Armagh, 1892.
Gerriets, M., 'Theft, Penitentials and the Compilation of the Early Irish Laws', *Celtica* 22 (1991), pp. 18–32.
Goosen, G., 'Syncretism and the Development of Doctrine', *Colloquium* (2000), pp. 137–50.
Gougaud, L., 'Mulierum Consortia: Etude sur le Syneisaktisme chez les Ascètes Celtiques', *Eriu* 9/10 (1921/8), pp. 147–56.
—— 'The Isle of the Saints', *Studies* 13 (September, 1924), pp. 363–80.
Graham, T., 'A Man with a Mission', *HI* (Spring, 1993), pp. 52–5.
Gwynn, A., 'St Patrick and Rome', *IER* 35 (Jan–June, 1961), pp. 217–22.
Gwynn, E. J., 'An Irish Penitential', *Eriu* 7/8 (1913/16), pp. 121–95.
Halliden, W. H., 'The Irish Believing in Christ', *IER* 35 (Jan–June, 1961), pp. 160–6.
Harper, J., 'John Cassian and Sulpicius Severus', *CH* (December, 1965), pp. 371–80.
Harrison, K., 'A Letter from Rome to the Irish Clergy, AD 640', *Peritia* 3 (1984), pp. 222–9.
Hay, M. V., 'Columbanus and Rome', *RC* 38 (1920/1), pp. 315–18.
Healy, J., 'The Ancient Irish Church', Paper presented at the Church Conference, Armagh, 1892.
Hennessy, W. M. and M. O'Looney, 'Notes on the Life of Brendan', *IER* 8 (1871), pp. 179–90.
Hennig, J., 'Ireland's Place in the Tradition of the Martyrologium Romanum', *IER* (December, 1967), pp. 385–401.
—— 'Ireland's Place in the Tradition of the Cistercian Menology', *IER* 35 (Jan–June, 1961), pp. 306–17.
Herity, M., 'The Buildings and Layout of Early Irish Monasteries before the Year 1000', *MS* 14 (Advent, 1983), pp. 247–84.
Herity, M., 'Two Island Hermitages in the Atlantic', *JRSAI* 125 (1995), pp. 85–128.
Howe, J., 'Hagiographical Handbooks – A Review', *CHR* 80, no. 4 (1994), pp. 757–61.
Hughes, K., 'The Changing Theory and Practice of Irish Pilgrimages', *JEH* 11 (1960), pp. 143–51.
—— 'The Historical Value of the Lives of St Finnian of Clonnard', *EHR* 272 (July, 1954), pp. 353–72.
—— 'Early Christianity in Pictland', Paper presented at the Jarrow Lecture 1970.
—— 'The Early Celtic Idea of History and the Modern Historian', Paper presented at the Inaugural Lecture, Cambridge, 1977.
Ireland, C. A., 'Boisil: An Irishman Hidden in the Works of Bede', *Peritia* 5 (1986), pp. 400–403.
James, E., 'Bede and the Tonsure Question', *Peritia* 3 (1984), pp. 85–98.
James, M. R., 'Irish Apocrypha', *JTS* 20 (1918), pp. 9–11.
Jenkins, C., 'A Newly Discovered Reference to the Heavenly Witnesses in a Manuscript of Bede', *JTS* 43 (1942), pp. 42–5.

Kelly, J. F. T., 'The Irish Monks and the See of Peter', *MS* 14 (Advent, 1983), pp. 207–23.

Kinsella, N., 'St Patrick's Way to Sanctity: The Witness of the Confession', *IER* 35 (Jan–June, 1961), pp. 146–59.

Laing, L., 'The Romanization of Ireland in the Fifth Century', *Peritia* 4 (1985), pp. 261–78.

Lapidge, M., 'Columbanus and the Antiphony of Bangor', *Peritia* 4 (1985), pp. 104–16.

Law, D. R., 'Kierkegaard on Monasteries', *DR* Vol. 114, no. 396 (July, 1996), pp. 185–91.

Le-Tissier, L., 'The Pastoral Relationship between Church and Co-habitees', *Theology* 96 (1993), pp. 468–76.

Lucas, A. T., 'The Social Role of Reliquaries in Ancient Ireland', *JRSAI* 116 (1986), pp. 5–37.

Macdonald, A. D., 'Aspects of the Monastery and Monastic Life in Adomnan's Life of Columba', *Peritia* 3 (1984), pp. 271–302.

—— 'Iona's Style of Government among the Picts and Scots: The Toponymic Evidence of Adomnan's Life of Columba', *Peritia* 4 (1985), pp. 174–86.

MacEoin, G. S., 'Invocation of the Forces of Nature in the Loricae', *SH* 2 (1962), pp. 212–17.

MacGinty, G., 'The Influence of the Desert Fathers on Early Irish Monasticism', *MS* 14 (Advent, 1983), pp. 85–91.

Mackey, J., 'Was There (Is There) a Celtic Christianity?' *SCHS* 25, Part I (1993), pp. 68–88.

MacNeill, E., 'The Earliest Lives of St Patrick', *JRSAI* 58 (1928), pp. 1–21.

Markus, G., 'Do Macc Maire – For the Son of Mary: Exploring the Sources of Early Celtic Christianity', *Spirituality* 1 (March/April, 1996), pp. 124–7.

—— 'Mary's Tears and Our Salvation', *Spirituality* 2 (May/June, 1996), pp. 165–70.

Markus, R. A., 'The Chronology of the Gregorian Mission to England: Bede's Narrative and Gregory's Correspondence', *JEH* 14 (1965), pp. 16–30.

—— 'Pelagianism: Britain and the Continent', *JEH* 37, no. 2 (April, 1986), p. 14.

Martindale, C. C., 'The Problem of the Saints', *Studies* 15 no. 58 (1926), pp. 241–54.

McCarthy, D., 'The Chronological Apparatus of the Annals of Ulster AD 431–1131', *Peritia* 8 (1994), pp. 47–79.

McCone, K., 'Brigit in the Seventh Century: A Saint with Three Lives', *Peritia* 1 (1982), pp. 107–45.

—— 'An Introduction to Early Irish Saints' Lives', *MR* 8–11 (1983/4), pp. 26–59.

McNamara, K., 'The Study of Theology', *MR* 1 (1975), pp. 24–44.

McNamara, M., 'Psalter Text and Psalter Study in the Early Irish Church (AD 600–1200)', *Pro R.I.A.* 73, no. 1–8 (1973), pp. 201–98.

—— 'The Psalter in Early Irish Monastic Spirituality', *MS* 14 (Advent, 1983), pp. 179–205.

McNeill, J. T., 'Medicine for Sin as Prescribed in the Penitentials', *CH* 1 (1932), pp. 14–26.
—— 'Note on Cummean the Long and His Penitential', *RC* 50 (1933), pp. 289–91.
Meyer, K., 'An Old Irish Treatise, *De arreis*', *RC* 15 (1894), pp. 485–98.
Moore, N., 'Vitae Sanctorum Hiberniae Review', *EHR* 26 (1911), pp. 562–65.
Morris, J., 'The Dates of the Celtic Saints', *JTS* 17, n.s. (1966), pp. 342–91.
—— 'Pelagian Literature', *JTS* 16 n.s. (April, 1965), pp. 26–60.
Murphy, G., 'Scotti Peregrini: Parts I and II', *Studies* (1928), pp. 39–49; 229–44.
Murphy, G. V., 'The Place of John Eriugena in the Irish Learning Tradition', *JMS* 14 (Advent, 1983), pp. 93–107.
Newlands, T., 'The Changing Position of Women in Early Christian Ireland', *ACJ* III (1990–91), pp. 38–55.
NiChathain, P., 'The Liturgical Background of the Derrynavlan Altar Service', *JRSAI* 110 (1980), pp. 127–48.
NiDhonnchadha, M., 'The Guarantor List of Cain Adomnain, 697', *Peritia* 1 (1982), pp. 178–215.
O Riain, P., 'Towards a Methodology in Early Irish Hagiography', *Peritia* 1 (1982), pp. 146–59.
O'Briain, F., 'Miracles in the Lives of the Irish Saints', *IER* 2 (1945), pp. 331–42.
—— 'The Expansion of Irish Christianity to 1200 Part I', *IHS* 3, no. 11 (March, 1942/3), pp. 241–66.
—— 'The Expansion of Irish Christianity to 1200 Part II', *IHS* 4, no. 14 (September, 1944), pp. 131–63.
O'Coileain, S., 'Some Problems of Story and History', *Eriu* 32 (1981), pp. 115–36.
O'Corrain, D., L. Breatnach and A. Brean, 'The Laws of the Irish', *Perita* III (1984), pp. 382–438.
O'Croinin, D., 'New Heresy for Old: Pelagianism in Ireland and the Papal Letter of 640', *Speculum*, Vol. 60, no. 3 (1985), pp. 605–16.
—— 'New Light on Palladius', *Peritia* 5 (1986), pp. 276–83.
O'Donoghue, N., 'The Spirituality of Patrick', *Studies* 50 (Spring, 1961), pp. 152–64.
—— 'Newman's "Idea" and the Irish Reality', *TF* (July–August, 1991), pp. 435–43.
—— 'Celtic Spirituality', *PP* 9 (March, 1995), pp. 117–20.
O'Dwyer, P., 'The Trinity in the Early Irish Church', *MS* 17 (1986), pp. 121–42.
O'Faolain, S., 'Éirigh, a ingen an righ', *RC* 47 (1926), pp. 197–200.
O'Fiaich, T., 'Book Reviews', *SH* 5/6, Part 3 (1965/66), p. 195.
—— 'St Patrick and Armagh', *IER* 35 (Jan–June, 1961), pp. 229–35.
—— 'St Patrick and Armagh', *IER* 89 (March, 1958), pp. 153–70.
O'Keeffe, D., 'The Via Media of Monastic Theology: The Debate on Grace and Free Will in Fifth-Century Southern Gaul', *DR* 389 (October, 1994), pp. 264–83.

O'Keefe, J., 'The Law of Sunday', *Eriu* (1904/5), p. 191.
—— 'The Rule of Patrick', *Eriu* 1-2 (1904/5), pp. 216-24.
O'Laoghaire, D., 'The Celtic Monk at Prayer', *MS* 14 (Advent, 1983), pp. 123-43.
Olden, T., 'The Ancient Irish Church: Its Organisation, Worship and Missionary Spirit, and How Best that Spirit may be Revived', paper presented at the Church Conference, Armagh, 1892.
O'Lochlainn, C., 'An Irish Version of the Prayers of St Nierses of Clai', *IER* 35 (Jan-June, 1961), pp. 361-71.
O'Loughlin, T., 'Medieval Papal Letters: A Source for Local History', *HI* (Autumn, 1993), pp. 56-8.
—— 'Theologians and Their Use of Historical Evidence: Some Common Pitfalls', *TM* (Jan, 2001), pp. 30-5.
O'Maidín, U., 'The Monastic Rules of Ireland', *CS* 15 (1980), pp. 24-38.
O'Rahilly, T. F., 'The History of The Stowe Missal', *Eriu* 9/10 (1921/8), pp. 95-109.
O'Raifeartaigh, T., 'Misplacings in the Text of Saint Patrick's Confession', *MR* 8-11 (1983/4), pp. 67-71.
O'Riain, P., 'Towards a Methodology in Early Irish Hagiography', *Peritia* 1 (1982), pp. 146-59.
Orth, C. R., 'The Approbation of Religious Institutes', unpublished doctoral thesis, Catholic University of America, 1931.
Oulton, J. E. L., 'On a Synod Referred to in the De Controversia Paschali of Cummian', *Hermathena* 24 (1935), pp. 88-93.
—— 'Ussher's Work as a Patristic Scholar and Church Historian', *Hermathena* 88 (November, 1956), pp. 3-11.
Picard, J. M., 'The Purpose of Adomnan's Vita Columbae', *Peritia* 1 (1982), pp. 160-77.
—— 'Structural Patterns in Early Hiberno-Latin Hagiography', *Peritia* 4 (1985), pp. 67-82.
Poole, R. L., 'The Chronology of Bede's Historia Ecclesiastica and the Councils of 679-680', *JTS* 20 (1918), pp. 24-40.
Reynolds, R. E., '*Virgines Subintroductae* in Celtic Christianity', *HTR* 61 (1968), pp. 547-66.
Richter, M., 'The European Dimension of Irish History in the Eleventh and Twelfth Centuries', *Peritia* 4 (1985), pp. 328-45.
Ryan, J., 'Origins and Ideals of Irish Monasticism', *Studies* 19 (1930), pp. 637-48.
—— 'The Early Irish Church and the Holy See', *Studies* 49 (Spring, 1960), pp. 1-16.
—— 'The Mass in the Early Irish Church', *Studies* 50 (Winter, 1960), pp. 371-84.
—— 'St Patrick, Apostle of Ireland', *Studies* (Summer, 1961), pp. 113-51.
—— 'Ireland and the Holy See: Carolingian Renaissance to the Gregorian Reform', *Studies* (Summer, 1961), pp. 165-74.
—— 'The Sacraments in the Early Irish Church', *Studies* 51 (Winter, 1962), pp. 508-20.

Sellner, E. C., 'A Common Dwelling: Soul-Friendship in Early Celtic Monasticism', *CS* 29 (1994), pp. 1–21.
Sharpe, R., 'Some Problems Concerning the Organisation of the Church in Early Medieval Ireland', *Peritia* 3 (1984), pp. 230–70.
—— 'The Patrician Documents', *Peritia* (1982–83), pp. 363–9).
—— 'Vitae S. Brigidae: The Oldest Text', *Peritia* (1982–83), pp. 81–106.
Shaw, F., 'The Myth of the Second Patrick', *Studies* 50 (Spring, 1961), pp. 5–27.
Sheehy, M. P., 'The Relics of the Apostles and Early Martyrs in the Mission of St Patrick', *IER* 35 (Jan–June, 1961), pp. 372–6.
Smith, J. M., 'Celtic Asceticism and Carolingian Authority in Early Medieval Brittany', *SCHS* 22 (1984/5), pp. 53–63.
Stevens, C., 'St Cuthbert: The Lindisfarne Years', *CS* 26 (1991), pp. 25–39.
Stokes, W., 'The Eulogy of Saint Columba', *RC* 20 (1899), pp. 132–83.
Tierney, B., 'The Celtic Ethnography of Posidonius: Translations of the Texts of Athenaeus, Diodorus, Strabo, Caesar', *Pro R.I.A.*, 60 (1960), pp. 189–275.
Thurston, H., 'Fact and Legend in Hagiography', *Studies* Vol. 14, no. 55 (1925), pp. 389–402.
Walsh, P., 'The Dating of the Irish Annals', *IHS* Vol. 2, no. 8 (September 1941), pp. 355–75.
Wood, I., 'The Vitae Columbani and Merovingian Hagiography', *Peritia* 1 (1982), pp. 63–80.

INDEX

abbot *see erenagh*   57, 63–4, 79, 82, 84–6, 91–5, 117, 119–20, 123, 127–9, 133–6, 139, 142, 146–8, 154, 159–60, 171, 176–7
Abbot Sinell   154
abstinence   117
Achelis, H.   91n
Acta Sanctorum   16, 131
Adomnán   9, 128–9, 132–5, 137–45, 147–9, 177
adopted sisters see syneisaktism   36n
agapetae see syneisaktism   63n, 141
Aidan   127, 161
Ailbe   81, 83, 86–9, 94, 120, 123, 176–8
âin didem 'last fast'   3
anamchara see soul-friend   31, 34, 40, 64, 66, 71–5, 81, 95–6, 99, 102–3, 107–10, 112, 117–18, 120–2, 140, 175–6
ancestry   33, 126, 148, 152
Ancient Laws *see* Brehon laws   42
anger   32, 34, 60, 62, 88, 115, 143
Annals   136
Annegray   158, 170
anthropology   20, 64, 174
archaeology   32, 120
arrum   69
ascesis see Asceticism   2, 27, 46, 136, 168–9, 177
Asceticism   2, 26–8, 31, 33–4, 39, 44–5, 53, 60, 72, 78–80, 84–5, 87–8, 93, 100, 103, 105–9, 115–16, 122–3, 126, 128, 133–4, 138, 140, 146, 149–50, 155–7, 160, 163, 166–71, 175–6, 179
askesis see Asceticism   27
Augustine, St   52
avarice   61

Bangor *see* Bennchor   97, 116, 120, 145, 154, 170–1
Banshenchas   10
Beati Immaculati   99n
Beatific Vision   78
Bede, Ven   125
benediction *see* blessings   105
Bennchor see Bangor   154
Beresford-Ellis, P.   23n
Betha Colaim Chille   125, 127–8
Betha Máedoc Ferna   31
Bevans, S.   18n
biblical exegesis   3
biblical exegesis literal-historical   3
biblical exegesis spiritual-allegorical   3
Bieler, L.   21, 48
Binchy, D. A.   43, 67–8, 131
Bishop Etchen   127
Bishops   23–4, 117, 151, 159–60, 171, 183
blasphemy   63, 143
blessings *see* benediction   105, 123, 146
boasting   78, 145
Bobbio   154, 159–60, 170, 172, 178
body   27–8, 31, 34, 40, 46, 58, 66, 70, 88, 90, 95, 103, 107, 112–13, 116, 121, 133, 137, 148, 171
Boniface Pope   24n, 160, 169

Bonosiacu heretics 59
Book of David 46
Book of Kells 15–16
Boudicca 10n, 174
Bradshaw, B. 3
Brehon law *see* Ancient Laws 9, 36, 42–3, 66–7, 174
Bretha Crolige 11
Bretha Nemed déidenach 9
Brides of Christ see syneisaktism 92n
Brigit, St 10, 32, 127, 132
Brown, P. 15, 27, 52
Brown, P. Trinity Librarian 16n
Burke, P. 19
Bury, J. 5n

Cahir Island 17n
Cáin Adamnáin 9, 43
Cáin Domnaig 37, 43
calmness 117
Campbell, J. 126, 128
Canones Hibernenses 36, 48, 67, 69, 75, 175
Canonical Hours 83, 88, 90, 96, 102, 114, 117–19, 121–2, 166, 174, 176
Canons 43, 58, 63, 65, 67
Carmichael, A. 72n
Carmina Gaedelica 72
Carthage 117, 119–20, 176
Carville, G. 78n
Cassian 34, 45, 74, 100, 175
Celestine Pope 5
Celtic Church 2, 3, 21–3, 33, 82
cétáin 'first fast' 31
Chadwick, H. 27, 85
Chadwick, N. 22, 27, 37, 41, 72, 82, 85, 131, 155
change 42, 55, 115, 120, 129, 178
charism 85, 152
charity 93, 95, 105, 107, 121, 123
Charles-Edwards, T. 5n, 38, 54
chastity 63, 91, 109, 111–13, 117, 121
Cherici, P. 9

Christianity 1, 5–6, 9–11, 18, 21–2, 24–6, 29–30, 32–3, 39, 41, 45–6, 52, 59, 66, 73, 91, 103, 105–6, 113, 133, 156–7, 170, 173–4, 176
Ciarán 80, 94, 96–7, 111
Cleenish 154
Clonard 49, 127–8
Clonmacnoise 94, 96
coenobitic 6, 49, 102
Cogitosus 10n, 132n
Collectio Canonum Hibernensis 36, 67
Colman 125n, 161
Colum 125n, 151
Columba *see* ColumCille 8, 125n, 133, 136, 142–4, 150, 153, 155
Columban *see* Columbanus 23, 60, 135, 153, 160–2, 172
Columbanus *see* Columban 2, 3, 15, 17–8, 21, 31, 35–7, 40–1, 46, 54–7, 59, 61, 65, 74, 81, 83–8, 97, 101, 109–11, 113–16, 119–20, 122, 124, 140, 144, 150–78
ColumCille *see* Columba 2–3, 10, 15, 17–18, 23, 35, 41, 71, 90, 97, 99–108, 120–2, 125–50, 153, 157, 161–2, 170–2, 176–9
Comgall 98, 116, 120, 123, 154–5, 171, 176
commitment 3, 13, 35, 37, 42, 46, 48, 56, 61–4, 77, 82, 98–9, 103, 108, 115, 160, 166–7, 170–2, 177–8
Communion 60–1
communion of saints 165
community living 94, 101, 162
commutation 69–71, 75, 118, 175
compassion 64
compensation 43, 47n, 75
conarb 22, 82n
confession 31, 39, 44, 55, 61, 71, 73, 95, 118, 121, 154, 160, 165
Cong 125n
conhospistae see syneisaktism 11, 92n

Connolly, H.   40, 54, 60–1, 66
Continent   21, 31, 35, 37–9, 54, 59, 99, 109–10, 116, 120–1, 124, 151–2, 158–9, 161, 163, 167, 177–8
continuity   125, 125n
contraria contrariis curare see contraries   45
contraries   34, 45–9, 53–4, 63, 74–5, 100, 111, 119, 164
Corpus Juris Hibernici   56
Cosmology   174, 178
Cote, R. G.   13
crannogs   17n
Creation   14, 66, 74, 93, 100, 113, 133, 149, 165, 173–4
Creator   7, 14, 25, 35, 42, 53, 76, 96, 127, 147, 163–5, 173
Cremin, A.   15n
Críth Gablach   43
crosfigell see fighill   70, 90, 115, 122
cross   70–1, 85, 90, 115–16
Cruithnechan   102, 126, 145
Cú Chulainn   129, 174
Cúl Drebene   134
culdee   118–19
culture   1–3, 7–8, 11, 13, 15–16, 18, 20, 25, 29–30, 32, 34, 39–40, 42, 66, 84, 96, 112–13, 121, 133, 173–4, 177–8
Cummean *see* Cumminianus   36, 46, 55, 60, 66, 74, 175
Cumminianus *see* Cummean   66
curse/cursing   62, 140–1n
Cusack, M. E.   10n

Dalriada   134–5
Darerca *see* Monnena   6n
darts of the world   89
De Arreis   68n, 75
de Bhaldraithe, E.   80–1, 86–8, 90–1, 93, 99, 101, 117, 119–20, 122
de Paor, L.   5n
dejection   46, 60, 62–3

desire   38, 45, 63, 66, 74, 93, 98, 105, 146, 154, 161, 175
Diarmait   146–7
Diodorus   65
discernment   113, 122
discretion   109, 113, 116, 122
disobedience   63
distinctiveness (of Irish Christianity)   3, 11, 21, 24, 115, 126, 176
distrust of the world   89, 123
Dodds, E. R.   27
Dodwell, H.   91n
'Doing the rounds'   96
Donegal   126
Doomsday   78, 121
'dove'   93, 133–4, 140, 144, 147, 159, 171–2
'down-to-earthness'   26
dreams   17, 33
druidism   36, 41, 69
Druim Cette   15n, 127
duality   15, 32, 113
Dublitir   78, 93, 121
Dumville, D.   3n, 5n
dying daily   164

Edel, D.   2
Egeria   155
Eithne   102n, 127, 149n
Eluere, C.   38n
entrenched behaviours   64
envy   46, 52, 63–4
equilibrium   39, 56, 100
erenagh see Abbot   91, 93n
Evangelium   7, 15, 26–7, 30–1, 34–5, 40, 42, 48, 52, 71, 74, 79–80, 84, 92, 96, 100, 106, 114–15, 122, 126, 129, 133, 142, 146–7, 152, 160–3, 166, 170, 171–2, 176–9
Exegesis   4, 20, 175, 177
exhortation   121, 137, 157–8, 163–4, 166, 168

faith   1–2, 25–6, 29–30, 55, 73, 81, 85, 93, 118, 130, 135, 141, 152,

157, 161, 163–6, 169–70, 176
fasting   31–2, 45, 55, 62, 117–19, 139
Feidhlimidh   126
Feliere Oengusso Celi De   125n
Fiennes, J.   129n
fighill see crosfigell   90
filid   8, 20, 33, 74, 96, 104, 112, 174
Finlay, I.   129n
Finnian *see* Vinnian   49
First Synod of Patrick   36, 41, 47–8, 63
Fontaine   158, 178
fornication   50, 53, 60, 64–5
Fountain of life   168, 171
Fowler, J. T.   125n
Fox, M.   13n
Frankish Gaul   152, 155

Gallic bishops   160
Gartan   126–7
geilt   72, 75
'gift'   108, 128, 139, 148, 166
Glendalough   17n
gluttony   61–2
Gougaud, L.   19
grace   30, 52, 79, 85, 131, 143, 148
Grant, G. P.   173
Grove of Victory   46

hagiography   131, 135–6, 143–4, 149, 177
Hardinge, L.   23
Hatch, C.   11, 12n
heart   12, 15, 46, 48–9, 51–3, 62–4, 71, 74–5, 85, 88, 95, 100, 103, 105, 111, 115, 118, 128, 137, 141, 143, 151, 164–5, 176
Hebrides   73, 135
Herbert, M.   135n, 148, 161
heresy   59, 63–4, 69
hermit   6, 101–2, 108, 111–12, 122, 168
Hinba   102n, 120, 135, 139, 149

'history from below'   19
History, Irish   131, 136
Hollis, S.   32
Holy Spirit   14, 66, 79, 174
Hughes, K.   2, 18, 23, 38, 43, 82, 111
Huyshe, W.   125n, 144

imagination   12, 14, 15–17, 19–20, 36, 112, 127, 136, 149
imitation of Christ   63, 103, 112, 121, 123, 168
Incarnation   33, 113
incarnation   33, 113
inculturation   25
inis   17
inner transformation   29, 45, 48, 60, 66, 70, 85, 88, 100, 109, 133, 139, 165, 168–9, 175
Innisboffin   17n
innocence   8n, 113
instability   63
Insula Sanctorum   130
insular   5
intentionality   32, 44, 63, 69, 167
invisible world   12
Iona   23, 124, 128, 134–5, 137, 147–9, 161, 164, 168, 177
Ionas of Susa *see* Jonas   152
Irish Church   21–2, 24, 31, 36, 45–6, 48–9, 52, 68, 72, 97, 106, 110, 125, 129–30, 133, 144, 147, 151, 163, 170, 172, 174
Ita   40n

Jonas *see* Ionas of Susa   152–4, 159, 177
justice   54, 56–7, 61, 113, 115

Kelly, F. A.   8–9
Kenney, J. F.   54, 67, 80, 84, 86–9, 109–10, 116, 120, 131, 151, 153, 160, 162
Kierkegaard, S.   77, 119–20
King Conall   135
King Sigebert   153

labour 47, 82, 108, 120, 142
Laing, L. 5n
laity *see* layman 46, 48, 50, 53, 55–6, 58, 62, 75, 89, 163, 166, 175
Lapidge, M. 162
law 8–9, 13–14, 32, 36–7, 42–4, 51, 56–7, 66–7, 69, 73, 79, 81, 118
layman *see* laity 53, 59, 65
Le Goff, J. 19
leannawn shee 14
Lectio Divina 79, 94
Lehane, B. 91
Lindisfarne 127
Lonergan, B. 25
Loves of Taliesin 28
Low, M. 12n
lowliness 111
lust 111
Luxeuil 158–60, 170, 178

Mackey, J. 3, 24, 33, 84
Máel Rúain 78, 93, 98, 121
Maeve 174
manach see monk 82
Manichean 28n
marginal world 18
Markale, J. 38n
Martin of Tours 16, 34, 133
martyrdom general 96, 98, 101, 105–9, 122, 149, 155, 168, 170–6
martyrdom *glas*/blue 107n
martyrdom green 107
martyrdom red 106
martyrdom white 106, 170
Mbiti, Professor 1
McBrien, R. 84–5
McNamara, M. 4
McNeill, J. T. and H. Gamer 40, 50, 60, 67
Medb Queen 9
meekness 111
Meissner, J. L. 22
mentoring 102

methodology historico-cultural 7
methodology poly-focal 7, 18
Meyer, K. 37n
Minahane, J. 40n
miracles 33, 96, 131–2, 139, 141–3, 177
'Mirrors of perfection' 84, 110, 116, 121
missionaries 156, 172, 178
moderation 62, 86, 92–3, 98, 100, 116–17, 121–23
Monastic rules 8, 13, 30–1, 34, 44, 49, 55, 57, 61, 63, 65, 70, 76–7, 79–82, 84–5, 98, 102, 109, 112, 114, 122, 126, 138–40, 143, 150, 161, 164, 170, 173–7
monks 3, 12, 15, 21, 25, 28, 30, 39, 42–4, 49–50, 53–6, 59, 62, 64, 74–5, 78–9, 81, 83–6, 88–90, 91–6, 98–107, 109–24, 128, 133, 136, 139, 145–50, 152, 155–66, 175–9
Monnena *see* Darcea 6n
mortification 24, 27, 70, 95, 109, 122–3, 155–7, 167–8, 170, 177
mulieres see syneisaktism 91n
murmuring 63–4, 95, 97
mystics 6, 130
myths 13, 19, 42

naked/nakedness 103, 105, 111–12, 122
Nendrum 120
Newlands, T. 9n
Nouwen, H. J. 178

Ó Duinn, S. 79
Ó Fiaich, T. 153–4
Ó Maidín, U. 80–1, 83, 86, 94, 100–1, 120
O'Curry, E. 77, 80–1, 85–6, 94, 101, 117, 120
O'Donoghue, N. D. 14, 16, 21, 96, 167
O'Loughlin, T. 24, 26, 28, 31, 33–4, 73

Oakley, T. P. 43
obedience 48, 63–9, 88–93, 95, 109, 112, 118, 121, 123, 139, 176–7
octade *see* ogdade 46, 55
Oengus 131n
ogdade *see* octade 45n
Ogham 4n
Old Irish Treatise 4
Opus Dei 79, 90, 94
Original Sin 147
orthodoxy 23n

Paruchia 22–4, 33, 79, 82, 121, 124, 127, 135, 149, 162
patience 46, 98, 111, 117
Patrick, St 5, 10, 21–2, 36–7, 41, 47–8, 63, 81, 86, 107, 127, 174
Pelagius 52
Penitential Columbanus 54–60
Penitential Cummean 60–5
Penitential Vinnian 49–54
Penitential, Old Irish 44
Penitentials 36–76
Penitentials opinions about 37–9
peregrinatio pro Christo 15, 21, 30, 35, 55, 106, 156, 158, 170, 176, 178,
perfection 55, 62, 84–5, 109–10, 112, 116, 121, 165, 168, 172
perjury 57–8, 69
Picard, J. M. 129, 133
Picts 127
piety 89, 98, 100, 154
pilgrimage 23–4, 30–1, 47, 66, 96, 98, 102, 106–9, 122, 135, 147, 149, 152–8, 161, 165, 170–2, 176–7
Plummer, C. 37–9, 50, 72
praxis 2, 3, 7, 13, 18, 22–4, 26, 29, 36, 68, 71, 81, 92, 105, 114, 116, 118, 123, 126, 133, 164, 168, 173, 175–6, 178
pre-Christian 2, 7–8, 12, 32, 34, 68, 96, 112, 128, 153, 174
Preface of Gildas 46

pride 57, 60, 63–4, 99, 116–17, 122, 128–9
prophecy 132, 138, 141, 148–9
prophetic revelations 139
Prosper Chronicle 5n
public penance 39, 59, 160
punishment 28, 41, 44, 47, 51, 58, 62, 99, 175
purgation 78, 121, 147
Pythagoreans 34, 175

radicality 2, 13, 28–31, 34, 42, 45–6, 52–3, 56, 62, 91, 98, 105, 109, 115, 126, 163, 170, 175, 177
Rahner, K. 30
Rathlin O'Birne 17n
Rees, B. 52n
Reeves, W. 41, 125n, 128n, 129, 133–4, 140, 143, 145
Regula monachorum 109–11
renunciation 27, 148
Revelation/s 14, 26, 39, 138–9, 145, 165
Reynolds, R. 91n, 92
ri 8
Richter, M. 1n
righteousness 113, 157
roadway 165–7, 171, 178
romantic individualism 77
Rule Ailbe 81, 83, 86–94
Rule Carthage 117–20
Rule Ciarán 94–7
Rule Columbanus 109–17
Rule ColumCille 100–9
Rule Comgall 97–100
Ryan, J. 79, 92

Sacraments 86
sanctity 61–2, 126, 129–33, 149, 155, 158, 171
Sankt Gallen 154
Scotland 23, 101, 107, 126–7, 135, 141, 148–9, 157
Scriptures 15, 44–5, 90, 96,

103–4, 109, 114–7, 121, 140–6, 153, 167–9, 177
self-awareness *see* self-knowledge 2, 44
self-knowledge *see* self-awarenesss 95, 97, 111
Sellner, E. C.   40n
Senchas Már   19–20, 43
sensus fidelium   131
Sermons   35, 55, 110, 150, 152, 155, 158, 161–7, 169–71, 177–8
Sheldrake, P.   73, 83, 164
Sharpe, R.   23, 127n, 134–6, 138
silence   31, 62–3, 68, 86, 88–9, 94–5, 97, 101, 105, 109, 111–12, 121–3
sisters see syneisaktism   92n
Sitz im Leben   40
Skellig Michael   17n, 101, 120
Skene, W. F.   6n, 125n
Smyth, M.   4n, 22n
sodomy   57–8
Soldier of Christ   140, 142, 164, 167, 171, 175–6
soul-friend *see anamchara*   40, 71, 74–5, 95, 99, 102–3, 107, 118, 120, 175
spiritual marriage see syneisaktism 92n
steadfastness   117
Stevenson, J.   2, 7
Stokes, G.T.   21
Strabo   167
Strachan, J.   31n, 98, 100
syneisaktism   4, 63, 91n, 92, 121
syneisaktoi   91n
Synod of Arles   23
Synod of Whitby   22, 29, 160

Táin Bó Cúailnge   9
Tanner, K.   11
tears   71, 108–9, 118–19, 122, 146–7, 154
theology   1–3, 7, 14, 16, 18, 20, 24–6, 28–9, 33, 36, 42, 45, 52, 66, 84–5, 94, 103, 126, 130, 142, 152, 163–4, 168, 171, 178
theology ascetical   46, 78, 81, 101, 109, 117, 144, 148, 161, 173, 175–7
theology, various   25
Three Orders of Saints   130n
transformation   27–9, 34, 45, 48, 60, 66, 70, 85, 88, 95, 100, 103, 109, 122, 129, 133, 140, 165, 168–9, 175
Triads of Ireland   9, 39
Trias Thaumaturgia   10n
Trinity   7, 113, 122, 165
truth   26, 36, 84, 113, 118, 136, 152, 169
Túatha   7, 20, 33, 47, 74, 158
Túatha De Danann see Goddess Danu   14, 103n

uxor spiritualis see syneisaktism 92n

vainglory   60, 62, 169
vanity   109, 111, 166, 170
Vercingetorix   167, 174
vigil   63, 70–1, 83, 90
Vinnian *see* Finnian   36, 49–53, 56–7, 61, 64–5, 74–5, 145, 175
virgines subintroductae see syneisaktism   91n
virtues   37, 44, 46, 53, 63–4, 88, 94, 100–1, 111, 113, 116–17, 119
visible world   12
visions   72
Vitae   11, 16, 33, 42, 102, 124, 126, 132, 136–7, 149, 171, 175
'voice'   90, 137–9, 141, 162, 164, 166
'Voice' Columbanus   161–9
'Voice' ColumCille   137–44, 149
vows of sanctity   61
vox populi   130

Walker, G. S. M.   55–6, 90, 162–3
Wallace-Hadrill, J. M.   131, 148
Walters, D.   72

Watkins, O. D.   54, 156, 159
Welsh   24, 28, 46
Wilson, J.   152n
withdrawal from the world   89, 95, 109, 123, 156, 174

witness   53, 57–8, 68, 85, 94–5, 97, 105